# Research on Theory and Practice of Teaching

SPECIAL ISSUES

www.royalcollins.com

# Research on Theory and Practice of Teaching

## SPECIAL ISSUES

CHEN XIAODUAN

Translated by Dai Kun
School of International Studies,
Shaanxi Normal University

Books Beyond Boundaries
ROYAL COLLINS

Research on Theory and Practice of Teaching: Special Issues

Chen Xiaoduan

Translated by Dai Kun
School of International Studies, Shaanxi Normal University

First published in 2023 by Royal Collins Publishing Group Inc.
Groupe Publication Royal Collins Inc.
BKM Royalcollins Publishers Private Limited

Headquarters: 550-555 boul. René-Lévesque O Montréal (Québec) H2Z1B1 Canada
India office: 805 Hemkunt House, 8th Floor, Rajendra Place, New Delhi 110008

© Chen Xiaoduan, 2023

All rights reserved. Without limiting the rights under copyright reserved above, no part of this publication may be reproduced, stored in or introduced into a retrieval system, or transmitted in any form or by any means (electronic, mechanical, photocopying, recording or otherwise), without the prior written permission of both the copyright owner and the above publisher of this book.

ISBN: 978-1-4878-1200-3

To find out more about our publications, please visit www.royalcollins.com.

This project entitled "Research on Theory and Practice of Teaching: Special Issues" is sponsored by Shaanxi Normal University's Fund for the Translation of the Humanities and Social Sciences in China (《当代教学理论与实践问题研究》受到陕西师范大学中华学术外译项目基金资助). Project Number: 1301030548, Project Leader: Dai Kun (戴琨).

# Contents

# Preface

The substantive content of this book consists of two parts: the first part is the revised version of some research papers on the theory and practice of teaching published since the mid-1990s. The second part is the latest revision of some lecture notes from the course "Special Research on Contemporary Teaching Theory" for graduate students in recent years. Focusing on the development of the times and the deepening of educational reform, as well as the renewal of contemporary teaching ideas and the shift of teaching focus, and also focusing on my own reflection on some teaching theories and practical problems in recent years, as well as the improvement of my understanding and the change of my thoughts on this basis, I revised and enriched some published papers during the process of writing, so as to better reflect the new characteristics and development trends of contemporary teaching theory. It should be noted that because some papers are the research and discussion of specific teaching theory problems in specific time periods, there is no substantive change in the book. However, it should be affirmed that these papers still have certain theoretical value for our understanding of the characteristics of curriculum and teaching theory research in different stages. For example, the article "A Review of 20 Years' Teaching Theory Research in China—Statistical Analysis of Teaching Theory Research in China from 1979 to 1999" in Chapter 2 can be regarded as a typical example. I hope that this article can be published in 2000 and communicated with peers, but because I studied abroad, this article did not meet the readers in time. However, it seems that it still has certain reference value for people to understand the development of mathematical theory research.

Because this book is not a systematic and structured study of teaching theory, but an integration based on special research, it is difficult for the arrangement of chapters and contents in the book to have a complete system and a more meticulous logical expression structure from concept to practice as in previous teaching theory works. Because of this, it should be more appropriate for the author to name this book *Research on Theory and Practice of Teaching: Special Issues.* Of course, in the process of writing, considering the logical connection between the topics and the reading habits of Chinese readers, the author still tries his best to show the readers a certain mainline and level according to the contents of the chapters: that is, from the research on basic theoretical problems to the research on practical problems, from domestic research to foreign research, from the research on basic teaching strategies to the comparative research on schools of teaching thought.

The main content of the book is divided into seven chapters. Most of the content in the book is completed by myself, and a small part of it is completed by graduate students and me. These contents include: Section 3 of Chapter 2, Section 2 of Chapter 5, and Section 4 of Chapter 6. In addition, the fifth section of the fourth chapter is the subject paper I completed in cooperation with Ma Qimin. Here, I would like to express my heartfelt thanks for their work!

Here, I want to say that as a teacher engaged in the teaching and research of curriculum and teaching theory in the Department of Education, although I have little talent and limited ability, through many years of teaching practice and research experience, and the academic influence of my peers in China, especially in recent years, I have also significantly improved my understanding of some issues of teaching theory and practice through visits, exchanges and doctoral studies in British and American universities. In addition, the desire to communicate with peers is also increasing, and the publication of this book is precisely for this purpose. Since this book is a monograph, problems and defects are inevitable in terms of the arrangement of the structural system, the organization of the research content, and the depth of understanding of related topics. Hope every colleague is generous with your criticism!

In the process of writing, I have consulted and quoted many research results from relevant experts and scholars at home and abroad. Although I have listed them one by one in this book as far as possible, there may still be omissions. Thank you for your understanding!

Finally, I would like to take this opportunity to express my sincere gratitude to the leaders and teachers who care about and support the publication of this book. They are Professor You Xuqun, Professor Li Hongwu, and Professor Hao Wenwu of the School of Educational Sciences of Shaanxi Normal University; Gou Yafeng, deputy director of the Social Sciences Department of Shaanxi Normal University, Li Jikai and Jing Feng, directors of the Postgraduate Department.

**Chen Xiaoduan**

# Contemporary Teaching and Its Paradigms

With the arrival of the information era and learning society, the connotation of teaching is becoming increasingly abundant, with more diversified forms and more complex activities, which prompts us to re-recognize pedagogy and re-comprehend the pedagogic system and process, even contemporary paradigms by standing in the developing forefront of the times. In the first section of this chapter, the author puts forward a new conception of socialized teaching after analyzing the limitations of the definition of traditional pedagogy; the next section elaborates complexity of contemporary teaching paradigms beginning with the analysis of the five basic teaching paradigms to which Western scholars broadly pay attention: the paradigm of art, science, system, skill, and reflection. And the author advocates that educational researchers and participants should master complex teaching situations from various perspectives so as to systematically understand the interrelationship between factors of the teaching process on all sides, to experience affection and aesthetics infiltrated in the pedagogic activities from the view of art, to scrutinize the regular process of teaching activities from the view of science, to examine the application of teaching theory and the effects of teaching practice from the reflective aspect, to comprehend the foundation of smooth teaching activity implementation from the perspective of knowledge, and to understand the fundamental approach of specialized development of pedagogy from the view of ability, and thereby to lay a solid theoretical foundation to implement class teaching effectively and promote students' learning and development.

## 1.1 Conception of Contemporary Teaching: Focusing on the Thought of Information Era and Learning Society

As a teacher in the Department of Education who majors in curriculum teaching and research of pedagogy and didactics at university, I have read a lot of works and teaching materials about pedagogy and didactics in the past few years, and I find that nearly every book defines or explains the conception of teaching. While during my teaching, I mainly introduce some definitions of teaching that I think are acceptable for students and then analyze a certain one that I think is authoritative, but I rarely intend to think further and make my own definition about it. With the accumulation of teaching theories and practical experience, as well as the increasing interest in research on teaching issues, I begin to pay close attention to theoretical scientific and practical rationality of the definition of teaching and try to talk about my own understanding with students during my teaching. Recently, along with the impact of reflective teaching, I got involved in it subconsciously and began to think over the problems of teaching theory and practice, even the educational reformation deeply, one of which is to reflect the definition of pedagogy before. I have clearly realized that reflection can deepen our re-understanding and re-recognition of pedagogic theory and, more importantly, can enhance our specialized development of pedagogy. This is also the reason why I still want to discuss it here, even though it has nothing new to the explanation of teaching.

There are various explanations for the conception of teaching at all times and in all countries. In the documents about didactics I have read, almost every book has a review on the issue of what teaching is. If we sort out the conceptions of teaching in this kind of books published in the 1980s at home and abroad and make factor analysis, I believe at least they can be separated into dozens of different types. With regard to this point, there are two excellent examples. One is the conclusion about different kinds of the definition of teaching that B. O. Smith made in his *Handbook of Research on Teaching* (1986), and the other is the summary in *Research on Didactics for Twenty Years* edited by Chinese scholars Dingren Li and Jicun Xu (1999). In many years of teaching didactics, the author mainly concludes people's explanation of teaching into three basic angles: the first one is defined from the angle of teacher's teaching and regards teaching as an activity in which teachers transfer their knowledge and craft to students. The second one is defined from the angle of students' learning and regards teaching as a process in which students obtain certain experiences under the guidance of the teacher and further arouse their behavior change by means of learning. The third one is explained from the angle of interaction between teachers and students and regards teaching as a bilateral activity that is composed of the teacher's teaching and students' learning. Generally speaking, the third viewpoint brings to light the essential feature of teaching activity in the main. Accordingly, when I give lessons to students, I tend to define teaching as teaching is a centralized activity that takes course content as a medium and is composed of the teacher's teaching and students' learning under specific conditions. Exactly speaking, such activity is carried out like this: students get systematic cultural knowledge and basic ability, develop their intelligence and physical power, cultivate their morality and affection, and form good psychological qualities in a planned, purposeful, organized, and active way under the guidance of the teacher.

However, with the advent of the learning society and the new requirement for the development of teachers' professionalization, the definition of teaching, as said above, cannot satisfy me. From my point of view, it can't make known the whole connotation and essential features of contemporary teaching as a complicated professional activity. In recent years of teaching, I have reflected frequently on my view of teaching and discussed it with my students in class, and sometimes even had heated arguments with them. I get much inspiration therefrom, which can be called "teaching benefits teachers as well as students." Meanwhile, the influence of people from the same occupation in academic circles also urges my motivation to relearn teaching. At present, my comprehension of teaching connotation and its essential features has already got a fundamental outcome; that is, we should do such explanations to teaching when focusing on the transformation of the information era and roles between teachers and students in this learning society: teaching is a professional activity that facilitates students' learning and development through a purposeful, systematic exchange and interaction between teachers and students in a specific environment. It should be noted that this definition is not an original achievement but is indeed unique in the reflection and transcendence of previous research and self-awareness. At least, I personally think that this re-definition of teaching based on previous studies penetrates three latest educational ideas: lifelong learning idea, subject educational idea, and teaching specialized idea. Meanwhile, this definition makes a re-location of the respective position, effect, and interrelation of teachers, students, curricula, teaching, and learning in the teaching system. Next, I would give an elementary analysis of this.

Firstly, I hold the view that contemporary teaching as an activity of purposeful and planned exchange and interaction between teachers and students is carried out under the interaction of a number of factors. About this point, I still subscribe to the former basic partition of teaching elements. Put another way, teaching activity has to include the following four elements: teachers, students, curricula, and teaching means. Although the performance of the four factors has shifted now, for example, there are some "invisible teachers," and the form of activity has changed because of the emergence of computers, the teaching activity is still inseparable from the specialized trained formal teachers. We know that each profession has its own clients; thus, we can get that the relationship between teachers and students is to serve and be served since the object of professional service of teaching is students. In this professional service process, the beneficiaries should mainly be students, followed by teachers, and the last should be society. And students are the focus as well as the main body in the course of this professional activity. Teachers should clearly understand that students are the main body, and students should also establish their own subject consciousness. Of course, we must see that the early formation and development process of this subject consciousness of young students depends on the teacher's inspiration, or more importantly, depends on the teacher's organization and guidance of teaching activities. In other words, students' early subject consciousness is gradually formed and developed in a good environment and classroom atmosphere created by teachers as the main body of teaching activity, which can perform students' main initiatives. Undoubtedly, such an atmosphere should rely on a democratic teaching atmosphere and teaching strategies that encourage students to participate in activities.

Secondly, what should we do to promote students' learning and development? The answer undoubtedly is to realize this goal by appropriating course content and effective teaching methods and means, teaching organization, and teaching evaluation strategies. Here, the course is the vehicle for the achievement of students' development targets, and teaching methods and means are medium, while evaluation is the guarantee which supports the effective operation of teaching activities. What's more, the goal of evaluation is to facilitate students' learning and further development. At present, in the practice of education, more and more people agree that the ultimate goal of evaluation of teachers' teaching is to promote teaching reform, but people don't admit the view that the ultimate goal of evaluation of students' learning is to promote students' development. Exam-oriented education system still affects people in its way of evaluation and selection of students in testing. And we should have sufficient knowledge about this point.

Thirdly, what should students learn in the process of teaching? Traditional teaching puts its focus on the philosophy orientation of "knowledge is power" and puts its key point on learning only. Modern teaching theories clearly state that students should not only acquire knowledge but also conduct moral learning, behavior learning, attitude learning, and craft learning. Teachers should lay a good foundation for students' overall development through teaching rather than only paying attention to the acquiring and mastery of knowledge. Especially now with mankind entering into an information age and learning society and the speed of knowledge is accelerating, if teaching in schools only focuses on knowledge acquiring while ignoring the fostering of students' good learning habits and the mastery of effective learning methods, it would not provide a latent capacity of students in the future growth.

Fourthly, what should students develop through teaching activities? The traditional view is that teaching should mainly promote the development of students' craft, but the development teaching view argues that teaching should promote the development of both students' abilities and intelligence. In the information age and learning society, teaching should not only continue the development of the above-mentioned aspects, but also pay more attention to the development of students' emotions, morality, personalities, learning ability, potential and social awareness. Its ultimate goal is to promote students' overall development and personality formation through kinds of teaching activities. In brief, we should make students grow and mature by virtue of taking into teaching activities actively and forwardly. It should be stressed here that learning is students' task and the elementary target, and through it, students would get acquisition; development is the high-level target. Learning and development should be a process that goes around and begins again. This point has been fully demonstrated by the introduction of the concept of lifelong learning and by the arrival of a learning society. Unceasing development cannot continue without constant learning. And only constant learning can make sure of constant improvement. In accordance with the basic spirit of the *Outline of Elementary Education Course Reform* (pilot model), new course reform should focus on cultivating teenagers into a new generation with four virtues (lofty ideas, moral integrity, good education, and a strong sense of discipline). To this end, the goal and tasks of contemporary education not only include making students grasp knowledge and craft and form good moral characters and personality, but also should include cultivating students' active learning consciousness and creative consciousness, learning ability and creative ability. In this way, the goals and tasks of contemporary education are multiple rather than unitary, open to the outside world rather than isolated, are developing rather than monotonous. Seeing from the angle of quality-oriented educational thought and elementary course target, primary and middle schools should try hard to promote all students' harmonious development through effective teaching, and to make them a new generation of talent that develops in all sides while possessing personal characters.

Finally, we should be clear that teaching is a profession showing that teachers have to be cultivated and trained professionally, just as the profession of doctors and lawyers that cannot be qualified by anyone. Actually, normal schools and training organizations extending all over the world have demonstrated that only after systematic learning and training can teachers be qualified for their initial work.

## 1.2 Contemporary Teaching Paradigms: A Composite Perspective

### 1.2.1 Paradigms and Teaching Paradigms

The word *paradigm* is a verb that originated in Greek. Its original meaning is "to show one by one." This word is translated as "an example, a sample" or "a table of variation of language and verbs" in the modern English dictionary.[1] In Western research of social science, the concept of paradigm is usually used to refer to the system of people's basic views and perspectives towards things based on ontology, epistemology, and methodology. Specifically, the paradigm can also be taken as the fundamental principle applied to look upon and deal with a phenomenon or a series of questions in a specific field.[2] In the upper concept of contemporary educational research, the word *paradigm* is also used to describe the basic types of educational research methodologies and the ownership of research questions and methods, such as scientific research paradigms and humanities research paradigms, qualitative research paradigms and quantitative research paradigms, empirical research paradigms, and phenomenological paradigms.[3] In contemporary research on curriculum and teaching theory, the word *paradigm* is used widely, such as the so-called curriculum research paradigm, curriculum development paradigm, curriculum exploitation paradigm, teaching paradigm, and so on. The word *paradigm* not only means the method people use to summarize views, but also includes people's values, attitudes towards things, and the corresponding practical activities. In fact, most Western scholars believe that this word is very suitable to summarize complicated phenomena that mingle with theory and practice when only focusing on its connotation and denotation.[4] Some researches show that in the field of Western contemporary social science research, it is not in a dominant position that one kind of paradigm tries to replace another kind, and at the same time, it's also difficult to be the main trend of its theory development. On the contrary, it is always presented in controversy and co-existence of many kinds of paradigms. The change of teaching paradigms is presented in this way as a complicated phenomenon.

The teaching paradigm refers to people's basic comprehension and view of the special phenomena and complex teaching activities in the field of education. In brief, it refers to the basic definition and explanation of teaching.[5] There are five kinds of paradigms that focus on the basic definition of teaching that are paid close attention by scholars and make an extensive effect on teaching practical activities when considered from the main achievement of Western research of teaching paradigm even though there are kinds of explanations of teaching at all times and all over the world (in the first section of this chapter, the author has made exploration to the concept of teaching from the angle of developing features of the information age and learning society). These five paradigms are the artistic paradigm, scientific paradigm, systematic paradigm, ability-craft paradigm, and reflective paradigm.

### 1.2.2 The Evaluation of the Five Kinds of Popular Teaching Paradigms

As stated above, seeing from the angle of Western research on the teaching paradigm, there are five paradigms focusing on the definition of teaching to which scholars pay close attention. They are the artistic paradigm, scientific paradigm, systematic paradigm, ability-craft paradigm, and reflective paradigm. However, if we inspect and analyze these five paradigms attentively, we can find that even though each of these paradigms provides a specific angle of view for people to understand and master the essence and features of teaching activities, they cannot conclude all aspects of teaching as a complicated activity. Next, we try to give a rational analysis and evaluation of the above five paradigms following the contemporary research of teaching theories.

#### *The Artistic Paradigm of Teaching*

In the West, the view of teaching as an art has lasted for a long time and has presented obvious modern features. The representative in the embryo can be traced back to famous Czechic educator J. A. Comenius. He defined teaching as an art of knowledge teaching in the introduction part of his book *Great Didactic of Comenius*. But it is a pity that he didn't make a further discussion of questions like why teaching is an art and what is the pattern of the art of teaching. It is generally thought that Comenius's art mainly means teachers' ability to arrange time rationally, instruct course knowledge, and select teaching methods.

There was more and more discussion about teaching as an art in Western countries until the publication of Highet's *The Art of Teaching* (1951) in the 1950s. Then there arose a debate for a long time about whether teaching was an art or a science when the American psychologist Gagne proposed that teaching is a science. As the early representative of artistic paradigm, Highet, G. points out clearly in the introduction part of his book *The Art of Teaching*: "The reason why I name this book the art of teaching is that I do believe that teaching is an art rather than a science."[6] In this book, Highet solves the following questions about teaching: why teaching is an art rather than a science, the connotation of teaching, and what kind of teaching art teachers should master in order to improve the teaching effect continuously. He stresses that teaching is an art and opposes the idea that teaching is a science. He thinks that it's unsuitable to apply scientific methods mechanically for teachers even though they need to map their teaching work. He thinks that teaching has no fixed formula like conducting a chemical experiment, rather, it's just like drawing a picture with concentrated attention or playing a piece of music, or we can say it is like cultivating a garden or writing a letter to a friend. If a teacher doesn't recognize this point, then his/her teaching will not be successful. He also thinks that teaching is a kind of ability, so the selection of teachers and their cultivation is of equal importance. He states three essential conditions that a good teacher has to possess: firstly, a good teacher has to own solid professional knowledge; secondly, a good teacher should be enthusiastic about his/her teaching subject; thirdly, a good teacher has to love his/her students.[7] Although Highet's study is relatively feeble compared with contemporary works about the teaching art and stresses the artistry of teaching but repels its scientificity excessively, he is still the earliest scholar in the West to do systematic research of the teaching art and a prominent representative that advocates the idea of teaching zealously as an art. His thought lays the foundation for later study of the artistry of teaching.

E. W. Eisner considers the reason why teaching is regarded as an art is that it has four basic features: the first one is the teaching activity gives people an experience of beauty through its graceful performance along with its special craft; the second one is the implementation of teaching requires teachers to possess qualitative and essential judgment; the third one is the teaching activity has its own contingency and uncertainty since it is not always carried out conventionally; the fourth one is that teaching result is usually produced during the process of teaching, and is even unpredictable.[8] However, Rosie Turner Bisset (2001) considers that the salient problem of treating teaching as an art is it is liable to make people believe that teaching is an inborn ability or gift rather than learned. In this way, teachers should be selected rather than cultivated and trained.[9]

The potential problem of the artistic paradigm is it may lead teachers to stress more about the flexibility, creativity, and affection of teaching, particularly the personality and personal style of teaching but ignore the regularity, procedure, necessary discipline, and classroom rule of teaching, and then it may lead to the liberal tendency in teaching. In Western countries, especially the practice of contemporary teaching in Britain and America, there are still many and more people who regard the classroom as the paradise of teachers. This, to a large extent, relates to people's opposite views towards teaching artistry and scientificity.

Although the artistic paradigm of teaching is not perfect and dominant, research about it still can be widely found among the documents of teaching, especially more in the research about effective teaching by British and American scholars. It is obvious that teaching artistry has been accepted by growing individuals and even has been thought to reflect in all links of teaching, to name only a few, the art of teaching preparation, the art of organizing of teaching process, the art of communication with students, the art of interpersonal relations in teaching and the art of asking questions. Of course, this issue is not as easy as listed above. Can we explain and master the complicated teaching situation only from the angle of art? People can't and shouldn't simplify their vision towards teaching with the deep-going of teaching research day by day.

### *Scientific Paradigm of Teaching*

With the rise of scientism in the 20th century in the West, especially the emergence of research in modern psychology and behavioral science, many scholars began to emphasize the scientificity of teaching. Scholars who treat teaching as an applied science often emphasize that teachers' profession and teaching activity should regard scientific principles as their basic guidance. From a broader point of view, this paradigm firmly believes that teaching practice restricted and affected by disciplines of the basic courses like history, philosophy, sociology, and psychology should follow some basic principles and laws. Until now, the paradigm of teaching as an applied science still occupies an important position in the training of teachers in Western English-speaking countries.[10] This paradigm looks more dynamic when the public sharply criticizes teaching quality in schools. They would make sharp criticism of those who do not follow the routine of teaching and do not adhere to the basic principles of teaching and believe that the decline in the teaching quality is due to the excessive freedom of teachers. The scientific paradigm stresses that teachers should follow the rules in teaching rather than act willfully. People who engage in teaching activities that could train them to be more professional must follow the objective laws of teaching and adhere to the basic principles of teaching, and conduct teaching in accordance with certain procedures.

Such a paradigm illustrates teaching from the angle of regularity and principle of teaching. Just as P. Woods says: "Saying that teaching is a science is tantamount to saying that it is a disciplined rational activity ... it also means that teaching is a more systematic, more structured and more stable activity."[11] In addition, this paradigm emphasizes the theoretical basis of teaching, such as philosophy, sociology, and psychology. It believes that the basic principles of these disciplines, as the gist of teaching research and practice, provide a solid theoretical basis and effective practical guidance for teaching research. One of the advocates of the scientific paradigm Gagne insists that applied science adapted to medicine, engineering, and other social science is also adapted to education and teaching science. In addition, literature research also shows that many contemporary Western teaching models are based on psychology and sociology. For example, the four types of teaching models summed up by well-known American scholars Joyce and Weir are closely linked with modern psychology and learning theories, and they fully reflect the guidance of psychological principles to teaching. In particular, the active advocacy of general induction teaching and general deduction teaching by the information processing model firmly reflects that these scholars have infinite faith in the scientificity of teaching.[12]

The main characteristic of the scientific paradigm is to try to apply the basic principles of philosophy, sociology, and psychology, as well as educational psychology and learning theories, to classroom teaching activities. It emphasizes that teaching should not only have scientific theories as its basis, but also can be studied by applying scientific methods. The study of classroom teaching behaviors of teachers and students that prevailed in the West in the 1970s is another manifestation of the implementation of the scientific paradigm of teaching in classroom practice.

It should be noted that since the 1980s, there was a new trend of development seeing from a large number of teaching and research works in the West, which was the weakening of the opposition between artistic and scientific paradigms and, at the same time, the view of the unity of art and science replaced the former opposite view quickly. As R. F. Biehler and J. Snowman said in their book *Psychology Applied to Teaching*: "a good teacher always combines the artistic and scientific feature of teaching together; good teaching is inevitably the combination of artistic and scientific factors."[13] Parsons further pointed out: "Effective teaching is a real art based on science."[14] Therefore, teaching is not only an art but also a science. The view of teaching as a combination of art and science has been accepted by more and more scholars.

### *The Systematic Paradigm of Teaching*

In the mid-20th century, the emergence of system theory, information theory, and cybernetics provided a new theoretical basis for scholars to explore and study complex educational and teaching phenomena. And under the guidance of the "three theories," system theory, information theory, and cybernetics of teaching also emerged as the times required. The research of teaching by applying basic principles of system theory is the most prominent one among these theories, and teaching as a system paradigm is a typical representative.[15] In the eyes of some Western scholars, explaining teaching activities through the concept of system theory still belongs to the variant or the development of the scientific paradigm, and system theory is considered a special form of applied science. But most scholars believe that this paradigm emphasizes the systematic integrity of teaching, and it must be analyzed, understood, and operated from the perspective of systematic integrity. It has a wide impact on the theory and practice of teaching reflection in the late 20th century.

To examine teaching as a system in order to locate the elements of the system and their respective status and mutual relations and to avoid isolated or single analysis of teaching, which is beneficial to teaching decision and arrangement. The American scholar Kozma analyzed maturely the systematicness of teaching in his book *Teaching Methods in University* (1985). He not only stresses the positions and co-relation of teachers, students, teaching content, and teaching means in the teaching system, but also highlights the special function of environment and evaluation.[16] Kozma's thought prevailed in the West in the 1970s and in Chinese universities in the 1980s, and as a thinking methodology being raised highly by educators. The author has positively advocated for a long time systematic teaching in the course of teaching theory of Pedagogy Major of normal universities. We should admit that systematic thought has been accepted by most educators in the 1980s and until now in our country. The sentence "teaching is a system" has been seen in many articles, books about teaching, and some documents about education and teaching reform in our country. This firmly shows that people approve of systematic theory. The reason why it is approved is that this theory does provide a new angle in recognizing the complex teaching situation.

Nevertheless, with careful analysis of the emphasis of this paradigm, we can easily find that there are deficiencies. The first is that it is extensively concerned about the teaching system itself but ignores the flexibility and contingency of teaching and learning. The systematic paradigm seems to be substantial theoretically. Especially its systematic tree family in teaching has given a refreshing feeling to people. But the teaching situation is actually more complex than its paper and pencil composition. The catholicity that influences teaching and the abruptness of teaching events in classroom practice are often unpredictable. At this point, the artistic paradigm that emphasizes flexibility and creativity would be more promising. Secondly, the systematic paradigm is a purely process-oriented paradigm that pays little attention to the substantive factors—teaching content (curriculum). It emphasizes that teaching is a purposeful, planned, clearly directed, and compactly structured activity, but at the same time, ignores the educational function and particularity of teaching. In addition, this paradigm fails to reveal the essence of teaching. As Bisset points out in the evaluation of the systematic paradigm, this paradigm ignores the potentiality of the course content and the contingency of teaching events while emphasizing the co-relation of each element in the system.[17] Therefore, we must admit that teaching usually contains many unpredictable factors because it is carried out in a broad context. The factors affecting teaching are varied, so teachers must adjust their teaching according to varied circumstances and the types of students. It is difficult to manage and carry out teaching activities as operating a small commercial department or conducting teaching in accordance with the procedures that have been designed step by step.

### *The Ability-Craft Paradigm of Teaching*

The idea that teaching is an ability or skill is mainly advocated by American scholars. It was formed with the development of American ability-based vocational and normal education from the 1960s to 1970s and then consolidated the ability-based normal education in turn. The theoretical basis of this paradigm is the observability of behavioral psychology on the specificity of educational goals and teaching behavior. In Britain, the ability-based paradigm was gradually recognized by educators in the mid-1980s with the development of vocational and technical education. At the same time, some scholars put forward that the craft-based paradigm, whose meaning is teaching, can be improved by training and personal craft activities. From the author's viewpoint, although these two formulations are different in literal expression, they are essentially the same in revealing problems.

Of course, the connotation of the word *ability* is richer than *craft* and *skill* if analyzed only from the aspect of psychology and education. It not only includes the transfer of teaching craft and performance, but also includes the appropriate combination and effective application of teaching craft in the complex environment. It can not only refer to a specific, practical ability or skill, such as blackboard-writing, but also include observable teaching behaviors, such as the ability to manage and regulate the classroom teaching process. In addition, the skill-based paradigm is different from the ability-based paradigm, which has a more direct definition of teaching. Here we need to explain the difference between art and craft. Art has not only intuitive, personalized features, but also has a mysterious and genius composition. For instance, people always say that somebody is a gifted singer or painter. And craft is objective and can be explained and transmitted. Art is derived mainly from personal experience, while craft is derived from repeated reinforcement and practice. One can demonstrate a craft to another person and asks his/her to imitate, practice, and master it. It can be concluded that the artistic paradigm emphasizes the individuality of teaching, the selection of teachers, and the experience of practice, while the ability-craft paradigm emphasizes teachers' pre-service training and cultivation. If teaching is seen as a skill, then one can decompose it into basic elements and build a program to train teachers on this basis, so that teaching can be as neither mysterious nor messy as the operation of the machine. It should be noted that the craft-based paradigm is more persuasive in vocational education and technical education of teacher training. The Western employs micro-teaching technology in the university environment to train the teaching craft of normal school students by means of micro-laboratory, such as the craft of leading in, the craft of strengthening, and the craft of asking questions, which is obviously connected with the ability-craft paradigm in teaching.

After the 1980s, the development of the ability-craft paradigm was closely linked with moral education. Tom, A. R. argues that teaching is a complex social practice that is fraught with moral and value issues. Teachers, as the main body of teaching activity, must have good conduct. The center of instruction should be the improvement of students' morality and the formation of their correct values rather than just imparting ready-made knowledge to them. Therefore, we should think about the question of what teaching is from the perspective of moral education, and then reveal the nature of teaching. The elementary position of teaching given by Tom is: teaching is a skill of moral transmission.[18] Obviously, this view reveals the nature of teaching based on the idea of educational ethics. Its significance is to remind people to pay attention to the moral function of teaching. Its problem is the ignorance of students' cognitive and ability development at the time of highlighting the moral problems. This is clearly not consistent with the modern teaching philosophy that attaches great importance to the diversified teaching objectives—the collaborative development of cognition, ability, and morality.

The advantage of the ability-craft paradigm is it emphasizes that the ability and craft of teaching can be trained and improved continuously. This view makes great promotion in the change of educational patterns from traditional intellectual or academic standards to ability-based or practice-based standards. Obviously, its value lies in highlighting that the teaching profession needs a special craft rather than being qualified by anyone. But its limitations rest with overemphasizing teaching craft and neglecting knowledge and affective factors of teaching.

### *The Reflective Paradigm of Teaching*

There are three kinds of paradigms in the West that treat teaching as an activity: the first view is universal and treats teaching as a common practice activity. In the eyes of many people, teaching has nothing special compared with other activities in daily life. But this view is not dominant in the teaching theory research field; the second view regards teaching as a bilabial activity between teachers and students. This view holds that "teaching without learning" or "learning without teaching" cannot be called a real sense of school teaching. Teaching should be the unity of the teacher's teaching activity and students' learning activity; the third view treats teaching as a reflective practice. This is a new paradigm of teaching that appeared after the 1980s with the publication of

D. A. Schon's *The Reflective Practitioner* (1983).[19] A large amount of research literature shows that this paradigm can be regarded as the most influential teaching paradigm in current Western. Some people think that the reflective paradigm is also a process paradigm whose operational structure is similar to the above-mentioned systematic paradigm. However, the reflective practice paradigm has its own characteristics in terms of content. As Schon engaged in management research, architectural research, and later in teaching research, his reflective practice paradigm has not only influenced the field of education extensively but also influenced other areas of social science. Schon believes that the teaching process should actually be a process of continuous reflection of teaching practice to promote the development of the teaching profession, so teachers should be reflective practitioners. Only continuous reflection or reflective practice in teaching can improve teaching ability and teaching level, and thus make sure the improvement of teaching quality. It is worth mentioning that the reflective paradigm takes excellent teaching as a development concept and that the teacher's teaching can be improved through continuous practice. This view has been approved by scholars.

In fact, any professional activities of their own development are closely linked with reflection. The sustainable development of a profession is difficult to imagine without reflection on practical issues. However, there hasn't been any reflective habit and effective model of scientific reflection in the field of teaching practice. The vast majority of teachers just stay at the level of summing up experience rather than reflect effectively on their teaching thought and the effect of teaching practice with the result that the sustainable development of teaching professional level is affected. The contribution of the reflective paradigm is that it not only emphasizes the significance of reflective teaching to the professional development of teachers, but also constructs a complete reflective mode of practice.[20] It is indisputable that the introduction of reflective teaching is useful for the professional development and teaching practice of teachers. The research literature shows that the theory and practice of reflective teaching have been widely used in training teachers in North America and have achieved remarkable results.

However, the problem with this paradigm is that it regards reflection as the only factor in the development of teaching activities and teachers' profession, which leads to the neglect of substantive knowledge and the relative craft that teaching should transmit. In addition, the answer to the question about how to appraise reflective teaching seems not clear enough. Therefore, we believe that focusing on the communication theory of contemporary teaching, this paradigm cannot reveal the fundamental problem of what teaching is. It only points out the value of reflection on teaching practice and should be regarded as an important link or necessary road for teachers' teaching and professional development.

### 1.2.3 Understanding the Compound Feature and Meaning of Teaching Paradigms

We can find it isn't objective and scientific to orient and summarize teaching by a single and fixed thought after the observation, analysis, and assessment of the five basic teaching paradigms that attract the close attention of Western scholars. According to the thinking mode commonly used in the research of education and teaching theory, if we divide teaching paradigms into three basic types: unitary paradigm, binary paradigm, and multi-compound paradigm, then we regard contemporary teaching as neither unitary nor binary, but multi-compound paradigm activities.

At present, the complexity of teaching is generally acknowledged in both Western and Eastern countries. Doyle, W. discusses and analyzes the complexity of teaching from six aspects. He argues that why people regard teaching as a complex activity mainly because teachers' task in class is not only to transmit knowledge to students, but also to face other tasks such as multidimensional working tasks, concurrent classroom problems, problem feedback of great urgency, the unpredictability of incidents, the openness of activities, and the conditionality of teaching by social, historical and cultural tradition.[21] There are many different understanding paradigms because of the complexity of teaching. Scientific research shows that People's understanding of objective things and social phenomena is always through the process of wave progress and spiral rise, which is difficult to achieve in one move and reach the designated position at one time. Moreover, teaching itself is a process of development and change, and it needs people's constant exploration. In this way, any unitary view towards teaching cannot explain and grasp it on every side in terms of teaching as a complex social phenomenon and practice activity.

It is true that even though the above-mentioned teaching paradigms can neither uncover the complexity of teaching in essence nor provide people with a basic frame to have a whole knowledge of teaching, they do offer us some different viewpoint and thought in recognizing the complexity of teaching entirely. The implication of probing into teaching paradigms lies not only in their definition from the height of epistemology and methodology, but more in the great influence and guidance it makes to the teaching ideology, teaching idea, and teaching practice. As Bisset once said: "the function of teaching paradigm is like a series of teaching lenses and teaching beliefs that can be used to filter and control people's objective intention and practical action."[22] We can note that knowing various teaching paradigms is not only beneficial for us to understand the complex situation of teaching, but also helpful in our Meta-teaching research and conducting effective teaching practice. But at the same time, we should be clear that if we just treat teaching as a unitary paradigm, we may make derivations in teaching ideas and practices or extreme trends in teaching requirements. For example, some teachers stress the artistry of teaching but ignore its scientificity, and some may emphasize teaching skills but ignore the reflection on teaching practices and the attention in sustainable development of teaching profession. These derivations in cognition could always affect the effectiveness of teaching practice.

Therefore, focusing on the multi-integration development trend of the current curriculum and teaching theory, classroom teachers should set up new ideas of multi-paradigm of contemporary teaching and persist in grasping teaching with multiple viewpoint, so as to understand from a systematic and entire angle the correlation of all elements in the process of teaching, to practice the emotion and aesthetic permeating in teaching activities from the perspective of art, to see closely in a scientific view the disciplined teaching process, to examine the application of teaching theories and the effects of teaching practice from the view of reflection, to comprehend the foundation of successful teaching activity implementation from the angle of knowledge, and to understand the fundamental road of professional development of teacher from the angle of ability. In this way, teachers can properly master the complex teaching phenomenon from different aspects, so that they can achieve the win-win target of curriculum enactment and students' development through effective teaching practice conducted under the framework of the presupposed curriculum

# Developmental Characteristics of Contemporary Teaching Theory and Practice

This chapter is mainly about the developmental characteristics of contemporary teaching theories and practices. In the first section, the author puts focus on the new characteristics of the development of contemporary teaching theories and practices after generalizing their traditional features. In the next section, the author concludes eight hot topics as well as eight cold topics in this field and puts forward that the study of educational theories in our country needs strengthening further by reviewing the developmental condition of our national research on teaching theories from 1979 to 1999. The third section proposes the methodological turning of Chinese research on teaching theories in the 21st century from the perspective of its subject foundation, research paradigms, research contents, as well as research references and innovations. The last section of this chapter analyzes the native theory of "Inducing thinking and exploring," which is developed from China's own teaching theories and practices and characterized by "teachers as guides; students as main body; training as a main line; thinking as main attack." The author then makes a comment about the application value of this theory to achieve quality-oriented education in primary and middle schools in China under the existing classroom teaching conditions.

## 2.1 New Concepts and New Characteristics of Contemporary Teaching Theory and Practice

Compared with traditional teaching, contemporary teaching has undergone great changes at both theoretical and practical levels, showing new concepts and characteristics consistent with the information age and learning society. Understanding the new changes and new concepts of contemporary course teaching is of great significance for us to carry out teaching activities effectively according to the requirements of the times. Here, combined with the development trend of modern teaching theory and practice and the basic direction of the curriculum reform of basic education in China, the core concept of contemporary curriculum teaching will be briefly analyzed.

### 2.1.1 Goals Should Be Multiple

In contemporary society, people truly realize that people are the creators of history, that people are the most valuable resources, and that all material and spiritual civilizations depend on the creation of people. Therefore, social resources are no longer limited to tangible material resources, and all kinds of abilities and qualities acquired by individuals innately and later in life have become a kind of social resource. In this way, Human society enters the so-called people-oriented era, in which all abilities, qualities, and endowments of people have been recognized and respected by mainstream society. Moreover, modern society is a commercial society, and profit is the basic weight to measure people's success. People with different abilities and talents can obtain huge commercial profits through their unique ways in modern society. In this era, the social criteria for success are more multiple than ever. This change has had a significant impact on education, leading to a breakthrough in the traditional perception of student success, where success does not just mean success in academic activities by virtue of mathematical and logical abilities; any student who has attained success in a particular field can be called a successful student.

Therefore, the diversified development of human beings has become the basic pursuit of contemporary education. Accordingly, the goals of curriculum and teaching have also changed, which should provide space and reference standards for students' diversified development. The traditional teaching goals of mastering knowledge and students' learning achievement as the only pursuit have been gradually replaced by students' diversified development goals. In the process of basic education curriculum teaching reform in the new century, the pluralistic goals are as follows: through the course teaching, "the students should have the spirit of patriotism, collectivism, love socialism, inherit and carry forward the excellent traditions of the Chinese nation and revolutionary traditions; have a sense of socialist democracy and legal system, abide by national laws and social morality; gradually form a correct world view, outlook on life and values; have a sense of social responsibility and strive to serve the people; have a preliminary spirit of innovation, practical ability, scientific and humanistic literacy, and environmental awareness; have the basic knowledge, basic skills, and methods to adapt to lifelong learning; have a strong body and good psychological quality, develop a healthy aesthetic interest and lifestyle, and become a new generation with ideals, morals, culture, and discipline."[1]

### 2.1.2 Curriculum Should Be Integrated

The traditional curriculum is subjects based, and the contents of each subject are independent of each other. Few teachers consciously integrate the knowledge of each subject in their teaching activities, which causes the knowledge of each subject to be stored in students' minds in isolation, and even leads to the disconnection of students' knowledge structure. Most of the problems in real life are very complex and require students to use all kinds of knowledge they have learned. However, the fault of their knowledge structure makes what they have learned to be "dead knowledge" without any vitality that the original knowledge should possess. Students are often at a loss in applying their knowledge to the current situation and lack practical skills in front of the complex and changing practical problems in life.

In fact, "knowledge cannot exist in isolation."[2] Knowledge exists in the form of integrated experience before it is abstracted by induction. The integrated knowledge combines the knowledge contents of all the other courses together, and it requires students not only to apply multiple knowledge they get from various courses in the process of study but also to refine and process this knowledge in order to revive their original experienced form, so that to make students' study activities related with the reality of life and be glamour again.

At the same time, the integrated curriculum can not only integrate the subject curriculum in the traditional sense, but also incorporate the irrational factors of people ignored by traditional education into the curriculum content. It can not only develop students' abilities based on rational thinking, but also develop students' abilities based on irrational thinking, such as intuition and insight, so as to provide students with the complete education necessary to become a whole person. Therefore, curriculum from division to integration is the need to promote people's all-round development.

### 2.1.3 Knowledge Should Be Constructed

The process of acquiring knowledge can be an active constructive process or a purely receptive process. In modern teaching, the acquisition of knowledge should not be receptive but constructive, "discovered" by the students themselves in the process of interaction with the learning environment. In traditional teaching activities, students acquire knowledge in a receptive way. Although Ausubel believes that meaningful receptive learning is the most efficient way to learn knowledge, pure receptive learning can easily cause students' passivity and lead to machine learning.

During the process of accepting knowledge, students always get material knowledge instead of such knowledge that could help them settle down and get on with their pursuit in this knowledge explosion age and help them to acquire knowledge again. Thus, acquiring knowledge through acceptance always makes students submerge into a mass of materials rather than make efficient use of their rich information resources. On the contrary, the process of acquiring knowledge in a constructive way is a process in that knowledge and ability can grow in step with each other; that is to say, students not only master knowledge from materials but also obtain the ability to acquire knowledge by themselves.

In addition, the rapid change of knowledge makes our evaluation of what knowledge is the most valuable constantly change,[3] which requires us to cultivate students' ability to judge the value of knowledge. However, in the process of acquiring knowledge in an accepted way, because knowledge is selected by teachers, students omit the link of knowledge selection in the learning process, and students' ability to evaluate the value of knowledge cannot be well cultivated.

The process of construction itself is a filtering process of removing the false and retaining the true, and removing the crude and retaining the essence. The process of construction is unified with the process of judging and selecting the value of knowledge. The improvement of students' ability to judge the value of knowledge is related to the improvement of students' knowledge. The growth goes hand in hand, and the cognitive process of the students becomes the production process of knowledge.

### 2.1.4 Students Should Be Developing

Educators in our new age should regard students as developing individuality rather than containers. If they treat students as containers, it means that they think students are all the same without individual differences. Because no matter what shape a container is, it is essentially a vessel for holding something else. Put differently, the variety of its shape does not change the identical character of its function and nature. Actually, human beings are just the opposite of containers. Children that are all 12 years old may differ in thousands of ways from each other.

Since students come to school with their own unique characteristics and their study here is based on the level of socialization previously formed, their acquisition of knowledge at school is assimilated and absorbed by means of their already formed conceptions and views. Personalized teaching would be rational and legal only if it treats students as developing individuals and admits their differences exist in both innateness and acquisition.

The view that students are like containers means that their development level is fixed because the capacity of the container is determined after it is formed. If students are just containers, then it means that the maximum level and state of development of each individual has been determined after birth. Those who have "large capacity" and can hold more knowledge are "smart students," otherwise they are "stupid students," which is essentially the point of view of genetic determinism.

On the contrary, the view that students are different individuals doesn't stipulate their future development level and state. The best development of individuals doesn't mean their adherence to some external and fixed standard, but means their potential is maximized, and then they get their best development level. Students' future is infinite, and so is their development. Besides, the container's content can only be "poured or instilled into" from outside rather than "instilled" by itself, but we human beings are initiative and subjective; we can make further development by ourselves.

The traditional view essentially denies students' self-development level and makes the study an external and enforced process rather than a process that students wish to happen; thus, their studies may be suffering for them rather than enjoyment. Contemporary teaching theories regard students as constantly developing individuals, recognizing not only the development promoted by external forces, but also the development promoted by students' self-power. In this way, contemporary teaching should strive for individualization of teaching and actively seek students' personalized development.

### 2.1.5 Teachers Should Be Reflective

Modern teachers should be reflective. "If a teacher only knows how to teach but has no idea of why to do so, then his/her teaching must lack creativity and is easy to be defeated."[4] Self-reflection of teachers can give them internal authority. Jaspers said: "real authority is from the internal spirit power, and the external authority will fade away once such internal power disappears."[5]

Reflective teachers manage classes and promote teaching activities by relying on their own thoughtful understanding. Their teaching decisions are rational and full of wisdom. Traditional teachers rely on "administrative order" to push forward their teaching activities. Their teaching decisions are blind and only according to their own taste. Teachers don't possess the inner spiritual power that could support their actions, so their authority is always combined with power and domination.

Since authority is indispensable in the bureaucratic system, teachers, as directors of class, have to own certain power. Traditional teachers always break with freedom as their power is usually related to might. The presence of power means to tail behind, to abide by, and even to follow blindly, so the freedom of students as behavior individuals is permitted by might and based on tailing behind rather than real freedom.

The presence of reflective teachers indicates that students have supporters who can give hands to them and that students trust teachers, so their actions are their own willingness rather than forced by teachers. Freedom of students also gives teachers freedom. Because teachers can teach with skills and ease in teaching activities, they get approval and respect from their students. Teachers' handles of teaching events are positive, their actions are free, and their strong sense of equality gives them spiritual happiness and mental freedom.

Teachers who rely on might are not free, and it seems that they are compelled to take action by events happening in their duty without such freedom that is competent to teaching activities and such spiritual freedom taken by the sense of competence and spiritual pleasure. Thus, it can be seen that contemporary teachers should be reflective. Through reflection, teachers can not only renovate their professional knowledge but only extricate their authority from the shadow of might and become their inner, real authority.

### 2.1.6 Teaching Should Be Interactive

The easiest and simplest teaching for teachers is to transfer the already existing answers that are given by experts directly to students.[6] However, the current teachers are not controllers anymore, they are chiefs among equals.[7] The variation of teachers' roles requires people to rethink the function, effect, and formation of the whole teaching system. The effect on teaching activities embodies mainly in its form—from unilateral transfer to communication and interaction between students and teachers.

The change in teacher's role status in teaching activities is an inevitable requirement in the era of advocating individual development. Traditional unilateral teaching is based on the assumption that students' development levels and interests are the same, and that teaching activities are controlled by teachers. There is a single flow of information in teaching activities, and the role and value of students in teaching activities are to absorb as much information as possible from teachers. Students are all the same since such teaching ignores students' individual variation.

When teaching becomes equal communication and interaction between students and teachers, the flow of information in teaching activities becomes complicated. It includes not only bidirectional flow between teachers and students, but also bidirectional flow among students. In the process of multi-directional communication, each student interacts with others in his/her own unique way; thus, their individual characteristics get displayed and developed. Besides, the internet nowadays is permeating every corner of our society, including teaching, in an irresistible way. The important effect of the internet on teaching is that it disintegrates the administrative management system of traditional teaching, and makes the hierarchical arrangement between teachers and students yield to equal cooperation.

As education was the only way for students to acquire knowledge before, teachers could get the supremacy position in teaching activities because of their monopoly on knowledge. The emergence of the internet clears up teachers' position as knowledge monopolists. Teachers can't maintain their position as the only way to deliver intellect to students, and the correctness of their possessed knowledge suffers severe challenges from students.

Because students acquire much more knowledge than teachers by using resources such as the internet, students can use the knowledge acquired in other ways to raise critical doubts about the correctness of the knowledge taught by teachers. All this is bound to make teachers go down from the "altar," and only when teachers go into students can they eliminate questions and solve problems for students.

In interactive teaching, the acquisition of students' knowledge is created through the interaction between teachers and students. This knowledge is not only new to students, but also brand-new to teachers sometimes. Thus, contemporary teaching should be a process of interaction between teachers and students, and the exchange of information should be multi-direction. Henson, K. T. (1993) showed us in his book *Methods and Strategies for Teaching in Secondary and Middle Schools* that multiple classroom communication diagrams are valuable to use for reference.

### 2.1.7 Study Should Be Active

In modern education, real efficient learning should be conducted actively by students themselves. First of all, only initiative and independent learning can produce real interaction with teachers and can produce interactive teaching. The conditions of interaction are the independent consciousness and independent personality of teachers and students, and the two sides could reciprocate the exchange and communication and finally reach a consensus according to their own views and positions. Students are independent only in the process of learning by themselves, thus leading to a hinge in the exchange of teachers and students. Students who learn passively lack self-awareness of their own behavior. The so-called teacher-student interaction is only students' obedience to the order of teachers rather than the real interaction.

Second, the meaning teachers produce or disseminate during teaching activities can be students accepted meaning only when it is being absorbed actively. Psychology studies have shown that we can remember 20% of what we heard, 30% of what we saw, 50% of both heard and seen, 80% of what we said, and 90% of what we said and did.[8] Obviously, the more active the learning is, as well as the higher degree the participation in learning is, the better the effect of learning is, and the learning process is more likely to be the process of meaning production.

Third, the creative ability of students can only be released in the course of their active learning. Human beings have the potential for creative thinking; thus, their education should be the process of liberation and development process of their creative thinking. This is why the cultivation of students' creative ability has become a universal pursuit in the education field around the world.

In passive learning, students lose their impetus and space by losing their freedom of thought and action. In the process of active learning, students' thinking, imagination, and so on have been liberated, so that students' creative thinking would obtain a developing space in the process of free thinking and action. In addition, due to respect for students' will, active learning enables students to experience their own power, thus arousing their curiosity about themselves and exploring their own power, finally forming students' sense of responsibility for their own learning and developing their personality.

Students can experience joyously from active learning and exploration and thus transfer "harsh learning" to "happy learning." Currently, we have already known that human beings are a self-organizing system with the power of self-production. For a self-organizing system, growth relying on its internal power is the most harmonious. Therefore, striving for development by relying on autonomous learning should be a fundamental learning method for students.

### 2.1.8 Means Should Be Multimedia

In sharp contrast with traditional teaching using single media, the technology and means of contemporary teaching have been characterized by multimedia. Adopting multimedia means in teaching activities is not a fashion fostered by the advance of technology but a road the contemporary teaching must take due to its pursuit of individualized development. What contemporary instruction seeks is the optimal development of the student as an individual rather than the average development among students.

Different individuals have different optimal ways of learning. Some take hearing as the main channel to obtain information, some take vision as the main channel to obtain information, and some get a lot of information in movement and operation. The traditional way of teaching with language as the main media is only suitable for those students who take hearing as the main means of receiving information. The use of multimedia can meet the needs of students with different learning tendencies. Traditional teaching mode only adapts to those who take audition as their major channel to obtain information, for it treats language as its main media, while the use of multimedia can satisfy all needs of different students with different learning inclinations. "A teacher passes down at least 25 courses to 25 students with the help of information technology,"[9] and each course can be designed for a particular purpose according to students' unique learning methods, cultural background, learning interests, and learning targets and thus to make students' personality be reality.

Besides, teaching should be such activity that caters to the future and owns the ability of foresightedness rather than an activity of summarizing. The demand for talented people in the future must be reflected in teaching. At present, we are marching into an information society little by little, and what can be foreseen is that the development of information technology will provide unprecedented and infinite challenges to the development of students in the future, so we have to help students to acquire the basic knowledge and ability to face up to such opportunities and challenges in our nowadays curriculum and teaching activities. Multimedia teaching means is the application of information technology in teaching, and it can help students to acquire a tentative recognition of information technology and makes them freer and more relaxed in the future.

### 2.1.9 Evaluation Should Be Successive

Evaluation, or we call it criticism inquiry, should be an extensive and lasting effort used to obtain useful information, and its aim is to study surface phenomena to make a sensible judgment.[10] Seeing from the angle of teaching activities, evaluation should be successive progress which incarnates in the following two aspects: one is that the collection of data should be overall and run through the whole teaching process, and further to supply abundant materials to summary evaluation; the other is that evaluation is not one-off, rather, it should be gone on at any time in the process of teaching.

The purpose of teaching evaluation is to improve teaching and to make students learn better rather than to classify students by rank. Since successive evaluation obtains detailed information about the teaching process, it provides teaching feedback on teaching quality and the corresponding evidence to improve teaching for teachers. So, it is more helpful to improve teaching quality in comparison with summary evaluation.

Evaluation of a process can help the evaluators to find the intrinsic value of teaching activities, and compared with the evaluation that relies solely on the teaching effect, successive evaluation has high validity and reliability. Successive evaluations can also compensate for the drawbacks of summary evaluation. Summary evaluations are generally based on the results of a unified standardized test score. Although this is the fast and convenient way to collect the evaluation information, the information collected is not comprehensive because the score cannot truly reflect students' real learning situation and teachers' various effort states carried on in their day-to-day teaching activities as well as the real condition teachers' effect on their students.

To have a high degree of validity and reliability, summary evaluation has to get rid of the situation of relying solely on standardized tests to collect information, and to use the continuous evaluation of information in routine teaching, and this is the best solution. Because successive evaluations can record and analyze the real self of teachers in teaching activities, and the information obtained from it is true and natural, to make summary evaluation avoid mistake partial for overall. As successive evaluation penetrates the whole process of teaching activity and provides teachers with information about their teaching state, teachers can improve their teaching according to such information, and it makes the teaching activity keep opening on the whole.

In addition, teachers' obtainment of teaching feedback information and their improvement of teaching should base on the exploration and comprehension of teaching activities, and this is probably a process of exploring teaching. Seeing from this point, the successive evaluation combines teachers' teaching closely with the study of teaching, and it makes the teaching process a teachers' exploration and reflection process; what's more, it also makes the evaluation process of teaching a teachers' exploration process. In this way, the contemporary teaching evaluation should be successive.

### 2.1.10 Education Should Be Lifelong

Courses are the carriers to achieve education aims, and teaching is the basic way to put courses into effect. The lifelong development trend of contemporary education is bound to have an important influence on the orientation and way of curriculum teaching. From isolated to open, schools enroll students of all ages and offer suitable education to different ages; the course is rich in content, thus meeting people's personalized needs such as survival, leisure, or self-improvement.

Lifelong education is the inevitable result of the knowledge explosion, which not only means an increase in the total amount of knowledge but also means the acceleration of the renewing speed of knowledge. In order to keep pace with the speed of knowledge renewing, individuals have to take part in post-job education many times. Especially for a full-time teacher, it's necessary to be a member of a learning society for the sake of the development of the educational age because the traditional way of lifelong teaching after accepting one-off education and getting a bachelor's degree has gone over.[11]

In the era of advocating the liberation of individual characters, people engage in certain occupations that do not confine to making a living, but pursue the development and perfection of personality. People's career will change more frequently, and when individual career changes, re-education is a shortcut for individuals to adapt to new occupations. As a result, lifelong education is necessary for the future society.

Accompanied by lifelong education is the emergence of lifelong learning. Since traditional social education resources were centralized in schools, the only way for individuals to accept education was by going to school. In modern society, the penetration of information technology in education enriches forms of education such as long-distance education, correspondence, and self-study educational form rather than only school education as in the past time. With the popularization of the internet, teaching through computer networks goes directly into remote synchronization and remote asynchronous, and this provides a convenient condition for people other than school students to receive an education.

Moreover, we have found that the role of schools in the growth and development of learners is diminishing. The knowledge provided by schools is quickly replaced by the knowledge provided by other knowledge institutions and forms of education, especially the latest knowledge, and the most influential knowledge is usually obtained outside schools. It can be seen that lifelong education and lifelong learning have become the inevitable trend of educational development.

## 2.2 A Review of 20 Years' Teaching Theory Research in China—Statistical Analysis of Teaching Theory Research in China from 1979 to 1999*

In order to investigate the development of curriculum and teaching theory research since my country's reform and opening up, and to further analyze and reflect on the problems of curriculum and teaching theory research, in 1997, I conducted a review of the teaching theory published by some educational theory magazines in my country in the 1990s (90–96). Statistical analysis was carried out on theoretical research articles, and the article "Current Situation and Prospects of Teaching Theory Research—Statistical Analysis of Teaching Theory Research Articles in My Country in the 1990s" was written and submitted to the sixth academic annual meeting of the National Teaching Theory Professional Committee.

After the article was published, it soon received the attention of peers, and also caused certain social repercussions. This prompted me to have the idea of quantitative statistical analysis of China's curriculum and teaching theory research articles since the reform and opening up, and I soon got the approval of my peers and put it into practice. In fact, there has been a lot of research and discussion on the development and changes of curriculum and teaching theory research in different periods since China's reform and opening up. However, it is relatively rare to study and analyze through quantitative statistical methods. The purpose of this study is to more specifically explain the development and changes in China's curriculum and teaching theory research since the reform and opening up through the statistical analysis of China's curriculum and teaching theory research articles from 1979 to 1999, and then analyze and reflect on the problems existing in the curriculum and teaching theory research, with a view to putting forward reasonable suggestions for future research.

### 2.2.1 Basic Work Involved in Study

This study involves three basic issues, namely, the source of data, the time limit, and the classification standard of research projects.

Data sources: articles (refers to essays or thesis that have a certain theory basis) used to do statistical analysis in this study are from 12 educational journals, which are *Education Research*, *Education of the People*, *Course · Teaching Materials and Teaching Methods*, *Foreign Educational Research*, *Foreign Education Material* (now referred to as *Global Education Outlook*), ***Theory and Practice of Education***, *Education Research and*

* This part is a research paper completed by the author in 2000. It was intended to be published in relevant domestic educational magazines after careful revision, but it failed to achieve its original goal because of being invited to visit the United States. Now it is presented to readers as a part of this book, hoping to provide you with some references.

*Experiment*, *Studies of Comparative Education*, *Journal of East China Normal University* (EDUCATION EDITION), *Journal of Northwest Normal University* (SOCIAL EDITION), *Journal of Southwestern Normal University* (SOCIAL EDITION), and *Journal of South China Normal University* (SOCIAL EDITION).

These 12 kinds of publications were selected as the source of the data, mainly considering the objectivity and accuracy of the data through the universality, representativeness, and hierarchy of the data source. It should be noted that because this study is still an exploratory study by the author, there is inevitably a certain subjective intention in the selection of data sources.

Time limit: the duration of the selected publications in this study is from 1979 to 1999 (a total of 20 years). Statistics were also made on the articles published in some magazines in 1978, but only as a reference for research. Because the number of articles published that year was indeed too small. And 80% of the magazines used in this study were published after 1979. The reason for the statistical analysis of the research on curriculum and teaching theory in this period is that China began the unprecedented reform and opening up in the late 1970s, and the research on education and teaching theory has also entered a new period that is more active than ever before. After 20 years of development, in 1999, with the arrival of the new century, it is undoubtedly a task in front of us to review previous studies in order to sum up experience and further promote the development of China's curriculum and teaching theory research in a more in-depth and systematic direction, This is the original intention of the author to try to explain the development and changes of curriculum and teaching theory research in China since the reform and opening up through quantitative statistical analysis rather than traditional thinking.

Classification standard: that is, the standard for classifying teaching theory articles in this study. In order to carry out a specific, quantitative, and qualitative combination of statistics and analysis on the 20 years of research on curriculum and teaching theory (practice and experiment) by Chinese educators, this research refers to the main fields and fields involved in ten teaching theory textbooks. The author believes that it is currently an important issue and hotspot in curriculum and teaching theoretical research, and the theoretical research (including practical and experimental research) articles published in 12 educational journals are classified into 35 projects, and then a multi-angle statistical analysis is carried out (see Table 2-1 for specific classification). Due to the complexity of curriculum and teaching practice, the research topics on curriculum and teaching theory are also complicated, and there is no scientific standard for the classification of such research, so the classification of this research is also an attempt.

**Table 2-1** Classification Table of Research Item

| Number | Items | Number | Items | Number | Items |
|---|---|---|---|---|---|
| 1 | Teaching process | 13 | Curriculum theory | 25 | Teaching & moral education |
| 2 | Teaching rules | 14 | Curriculum reform | 26 | After-school activities |
| 3 | Teaching principles | 15 | Teaching design | 27 | Classroom teaching |
| 4 | Teaching methods | 16 | Teaching environment | 28 | Curriculum provision |
| 5 | Teaching forms | 17 | Double pedagogy | 29 | Potential curriculum |
| 6 | Teaching means | 18 | Subject teaching | 30 | Activity curriculum |
| 7 | Teaching art | 19 | Learning method | 31 | Spoken lesson of theory&practice |
| 8 | Teaching mode | 20 | Quality-oriented education & classroom teaching | 32 | Learning psychology |
| 9 | Teaching content | 21 | Didactics basic problem research | 33 | Teaching psychology |
| 10 | Teaching feeling | 22 | Teaching evaluation | 34 | Creative teaching |
| 11 | Teaching goal | 23 | Teaching theory and "three arguments" | 35 | Others |
| 12 | Objective teaching | 24 | Teaching reform and experiment | | |

**Table 2-2** The Overall Sequence of the Number of Articles about Research Items from Less to More

| Sequence Number | Items | Number of articles | Percentage (%) | Sequence number | Items | Number of articles | Percentage (%) |
|---|---|---|---|---|---|---|---|
| 1 | Learning psychology | 42 | 0.9 | 14 | Learning method | 96 | 2.1 |
| 2 | Target instruction | 45 | 1.0 | 15 | Teaching model | 104 | 2.3 |
| 3 | Instructional target | 47 | 1.0 | 16 | Quality education & classroom instruction | 118 | 2.6 |
| 4 | Teaching principle | 48 | 1.0 | 17 | Pedagogy and "Three Theories" | 149 | 3.2 |
| 5 | Teaching content | 59 | 1.3 | 18 | Classroom instruction | 168 | 3.7 |
| 6 | Creative teaching | 60 | 1.3 | 19 | Curriculum design | 215 | 4.7 |
| 7 | Teaching psychology | 67 | 1.5 | 20 | Curriculum reform | 249 | 5.4 |
| 8 | Teaching process | 68 | 1.5 | 21 | Study of essential issues about pedagogy | 299 | 6.5 |
| 9 | Teaching means | 73 | 1.6 | 22 | Teaching method | 313 | 6.8 |
| 10 | Teaching evaluation | 76 | 1.7 | 23 | Teaching reform and experiment | 317 | 6.9 |
| 11 | Teaching design | 76 | 1.7 | 24 | Curriculum theory | 342 | 7.4 |
| 12 | Teaching art | 87 | 1.9 | 25 | Others | 587 | 12.8 |
| 13 | Teaching & moral education | 91 | 2.0 | 26 | Subject teaching | 803 | 17.5 |

### 2.2.2 Statistic Analysis of Research Articles of Curriculum and Teaching Theory

Since the reform and opening up, China's teaching theory research has made gratifying progress and fruitful results. Only in terms of the number of research articles, the total number of articles published on 35 projects in 12 magazines selected by the Institute in 1979 was 67, which increased to 4955 in 1999, a full increase of nearly 80 times. Statistics show that although different research projects have different development trends, the overall development shows a wave forward and spiral upward trend.

From Figure 2-1, it can be seen that since the reform and opening up, the development of curriculum and teaching theory research in China has experienced six peaks: 1982, 1986, 1989, 1992, 1996, and 1999. In 1999, it reached its peak. In the 20 years of reform and opening up, the research on curriculum and teaching theory in China has shown a rising trend of development. The main reasons are as follows:

First, since the reform and opening up, people's enthusiasm for curriculum and teaching research has been rising.

Second, people have improved their understanding of the status of curriculum and teaching research in the whole educational research.

Third, there are more and more places to show people's research results, and there are more and more educational magazines.

Fourth, the promotion of educational reform experiments. The experimental research of teaching reform not only builds a bridge between theory and practice, and promotes the integration of theoretical workers and practical workers, but also cultivates a large number of scientific research teachers for primary and secondary schools. With the enhancement of their educational research awareness and the improvement of their research capabilities, they will naturally have new ideas and research interests,

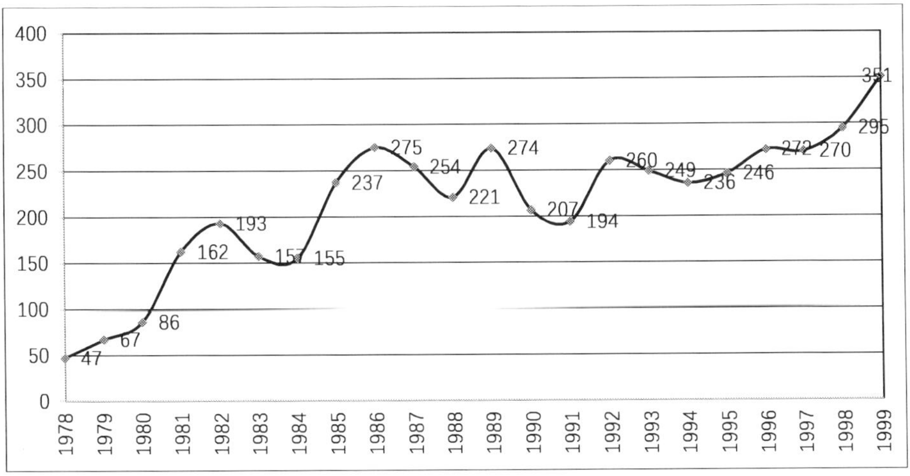


**Figure 2-1** Statistical Chart of Articles Published Between 1978–1999

and research articles will also increase. It can be said that a virtuous circle has been formed.

Fifth, the need for teachers' professional development promotes curriculum and teaching research. With the improvement of social requirements for teachers, not only the promotion of professional titles requires teachers to have scientific research papers, but also teachers' professional development itself requires teachers to improve their research ability. Being a research-oriented teacher has become the goal of teachers.

Sixth, a virtuous circle of research and teaching has been formed. Curriculum and teaching research, especially teaching research, has injected fresh vitality into the teaching practice of the majority of teachers. The teaching benefits obtained by teachers through research continue to stimulate their pursuit of research.

Seventh, the research field is constantly expanding, and new research topics and research fields are constantly emerging. From the statistics and classification of this article, in just a few years, from the late 1970s to the early 1980s, six new research fields have been added. At the same time, the emergence of new problems also provides more and more research options for researchers.

Eighth, the state attaches importance to education and scientific research and the investment of research funds. As we all know, there are many factors that affect people's education and teaching research, such as interest in research topics, the need to promote professional development, and the call to solve practical problems. Of course, for the research of some problems, funding plays a role in supporting and maintaining the in-depth development of research. Since the reform and opening up, the investment of education management departments in educational research has been on the rise, especially since the 9th Five-Year Plan, the national investment in educational research has doubled.

The above eight aspects should be said to be the basic reasons to promote the continuous prosperity and development of the research on curriculum and teaching theory and practice in our country.

### 2.2.3 Analysis of the Eight Hot Research Fields and the Reasons for Their Formation

Statistics show that in the past 20 years of reform and opening up, there have been eight hot research areas of the curriculum and teaching theory research in China, which have been concerned by people (see Table 2-3). The eight hot research areas listed in this paper are determined according to the number of published articles. Generally speaking, they are highly representative and can also reflect the researchers' accurate grasp of the selection of research topics.

One of the reasons why subject teaching can become the most researched project is the classification of projects in this study. Second, subject teaching is the main front to achieving educational goals, implementing curriculum and teaching, and itself is a

**Table 2-3** Eight Hot Research Items

| Sequence number | Items | Number of articles (pieces) | Sequencing by quantity | Number of annual publications |
|---|---|---|---|---|
| 1 | Subject teaching | 803 | 1 | 40.15 |
| 2 | Curriculum theory | 342 | 2 | 17.1 |
| 3 | Teaching reform and experiment | 317 | 3 | 14.85 |
| 4 | Teaching method | 313 | 4 | 15.65 |
| 5 | Research of essential issues about teaching theory | 299 | 5 | 14.95 |
| 6 | Curriculum reform | 249 | 6 | 12.45 |
| 7 | Curriculum design | 215 | 7 | 10.75 |
| 8 | Classroom teaching | 168 | 8 | 8.4 |

broad research field. Moreover, there are a large number of theoretical researchers and practical researchers, so the number of published articles is also expected before the statistics.

The reason why curriculum theory, curriculum reform, and curriculum setting can enter the eight hot research fields is that curriculum has always been the core of any educational reform and practice. As a breakthrough in educational reform, curriculum reform has always been concerned by people. After entering the 1990s, social life changed and developed rapidly, and high and new technologies emerged one after another. Social productivity has put forward higher requirements for the specification of talents. How to reform the curriculum system and cultivate cross-century high-quality talents will inevitably become a topic of concern to all countries. Others, such as the research of teaching art and subject teaching, are the specific manifestations of deepening education and teaching reform and improving education and teaching efficiency.

The reason why people pay attention to teaching methods is mainly that teaching methods are the intermediary and bridge between teachers, students, and textbooks. It has strong practical significance and has an important impact on teaching efficiency and teaching effect. As long as teaching activities are carried out, teachers must face the problem of choosing teaching methods. Whether they are used properly or not is directly related to the success or failure of teaching. Therefore, people's attention to the research of teaching methods is not only in line with the basic principles of modern teaching theory, but also of great practical significance.

### 2.2.4 Eight Cold Spot Research Areas

From the eight cold spots shown in the statistics of this study (see Table 2-4), the research on extracurricular activities is an area that people have not paid enough attention to in recent years. There are only ten articles published in 12 journals in the past 20 years, and the average annual number of articles published is only 0.5. It shows that the importance of extracurricular activities has not been recognized by people. The research on the theory and practice of lecture presentation started relatively late in China, and most of the research articles were published in local magazines. Among the 12 professional magazines counted in this paper, the number of research articles is also relatively small. In addition, statistics also show that there are relatively few research articles on teaching laws and teaching forms, which seems to be inconsistent with the tradition that China's educational circles have always attached importance to the study of laws. Of course, people may think that the study of laws is not easy. Although the voice about the impact of potential courses on student development is not low, the number of research articles is still insufficient.

### 2.2.5 Quantity Distribution of Research Projects

Through Table 2-2, we can know the number of research articles for each project selected in this paper. Tables 2-5 and 2-6 show us the top 8 projects with the largest number of research articles from 1979 to 1999 and the research projects with the largest number of published articles in 1999. The main reason why subject teaching research can become the project with the most research articles is that it involves a wide range of research articles on the curriculum and teaching of major subjects in

**Table 2-4** Eight Cold Research Projects

| Sequence number | Items | Number of articles (piece) (1979–1999) | Sequencing by quantity | Number of annual publications |
|---|---|---|---|---|
| 1 | After-class activity | 10 | 1 | 0.5 |
| 2 | Lesson presentation theory and practice | 16 | 2 | 0.8 |
| 3 | Teaching rules | 18 | 3 | 0.9 |
| 4 | Potential course | 21 | 4 | 1.05 |
| 5 | Teaching environment | 27 | 5 | 1.35 |
| 6 | Teaching emotion | 30 | 6 | 1.5 |
| 7 | Instruction form | 34 | 7 | 1.7 |
| 8 | Activity curriculum | 35 | 8 | 1.75 |

**Table 2-5** Projects with the Top 8 Research Articles from 1979 to 1999

| Year Ranking | 1 | 2 | 3 | 4 | 5 | 6 | 7 | 8 |
|---|---|---|---|---|---|---|---|---|
| 1979 | Subject teaching (15) | Learning method (6) | Teaching theory and three theories (6) | Teaching reform and experiment (6) | Research on basic problems of Pedagogy (5) | Teaching method (5) | Classroom teaching (4) | Instruction form Curriculum theory Curriculum reform (2) |
| 1980 | Subject teaching (20) | Teaching reform and experiment (17) | Curriculum reform (6) | Teaching method (5) | Teaching theory and three theories (5) | Research on basic problems of Pedagogy (4) | Teaching environment (3) | Teaching means teaching emotion Teaching objectives teaching evaluation (2) |
| 1981 | Subject teaching (45) | Teaching method (15) | Teaching reform and experiment (13) | Teaching content (9) | Teaching process (6) | Research on basic problems of Pedagogy(6) | Curriculum theory (5) | Learning method Curriculum design (4) |
| 1982 | Subject teaching (58) | Teaching and moral education (14) | Research on basic problems of Pedagogy (12) | Teaching method (11) | Didactics and three theories (10) | Teaching process (8) | Teaching reform and experiment (8) | Learning method Teaching content (7) |
| 1983 | Subject teaching (32) | Teaching method (14) | Teaching and moral education (12) | Teaching reform and experiment (10) | Curriculum theory (9) | Teaching content (7) | Research on basic problems of Pedagogy (7) | Quality-oriented education and classroom teaching (5) |

*(Continued)*

| Year Ranking | 1 | 2 | 3 | 4 | 5 | 6 | 7 | 8 |
|---|---|---|---|---|---|---|---|---|
| 1984 | Subject teaching (30) | Teaching method (16) | Research on basic problems of Pedagogy (12) | Teaching reform and experiment (9) | Potential course (7) | Teaching model (6) | Teaching and moral education (5) | Curriculum design (5) |
| 1985 | Subject teaching (59) | Research on basic problems of Pedagogy (26) | Teaching method (23) | Teaching reform and experiment (17) | Curriculum design (14) | Curriculum theory (9) | Curriculum reform (8) | Classroom teaching and creative teaching (6) |
| 1986 | Subject teaching (65) | Research on basic problems of Pedagogy (24) | Teaching method (23) | Teaching reform and experiment (17) | Curriculum reform (15) | Curriculum design (13) | Learning method (11) | Teaching theory and three theories classroom teaching (10) |
| 1987 | Subject teaching (53) | Research on basic problems of Pedagogy (21) | Teaching reform and experiment (16) | Teaching method (15) | Curriculum reform (15) | Classroom teaching (10) | Teaching content (9) | Curriculum theory (9) |
| 1988 | Subject teaching (31) | Teaching reform and experiment (23) | Curriculum reform (17) | Teaching method (17) | Curriculum theory (13) | Classroom teaching (11) | Curriculum design (11) | Teaching theory and three theories (11) |
| 1989 | Subject teaching (52) | Curriculum theory (29) | Teaching method (22) | Teaching reform and experiment (20) | Curriculum design (19) | Curriculum reform (16) | Teaching theory and three theories (12) | Teaching evaluation (10) |

*(Continued)*

| Year Ranking | 1 | 2 | 3 | 4 | 5 | 6 | 7 | 8 |
|---|---|---|---|---|---|---|---|---|
| 1990 | Subject teaching (23) | Teaching method (19) | Curriculum reform (16) | Curriculum design (15) | Research on basic problems of Pedagogy (14) | Curriculum theory (10) | Art of teaching (9) | Teaching reform and experimental teaching and moral education (9) |
| 1991 | Subject teaching (23) | Curriculum reform (14) | Teaching reform and experiment (14) | Research on basic problems of Pedagogy (12) | Curriculum theory (11) | Teaching theory and three theories (11) | Teaching method (10) | Curriculum teaching (10) |
| 1992 | Subject teaching (28) | Teaching reform and experiment (25) | Curriculum reform (22) | Curriculum theory (21) | Curriculum design (14) | Teaching method (13) | Research on basic problems of Pedagogy (11) | Teaching model (10) |
| 1993 | Subject teaching (33) | Curriculum reform (25) | Teaching method (21) | Curriculum design (16) | Teaching reform and experiment (16) | Research on basic problems of Pedagogy (13) | Teaching theory and three theories (11) | Teaching model and curriculum theory (10) |
| 1994 | Subject teaching (33) | Teaching method (19) | Teaching reform and experiment (18) | Curriculum reform (15) | Curriculum theory (15) | Curriculum design (14) | Classroom teaching (12) | Research on basic problems of Pedagogy (10) |
| 1995 | Curriculum theory (37) | Subject teaching (31) | Curriculum reform (26) | Curriculum design (18) | Classroom teaching (14) | Teaching method (12) | Research on basic problems of Pedagogy (10) | Teaching model (9) |

*(Continued)*

| Year Ranking | 1 | 2 | 3 | 4 | 5 | 6 | 7 | 8 |
|---|---|---|---|---|---|---|---|---|
| 1996 | Curriculum theory (40) | Subject teaching (36) | Curriculum reform (26) | Research on basic problems of Pedagogy (16) | Classroom teaching (14) | Teaching reform and experiment (13) | Quality education and classroom teaching (10) | Teaching method and art of teaching (10) |
| 1997 | Subject teaching (39) | Curriculum theory (36) | Curriculum reform (31) | Research on basic problems of Pedagogy (20) | Teaching reform and experiment (13) | Quality education and classroom teaching (12) | Classroom teaching (10) | Teaching design and teaching method (9) |
| 1998 | Subject teaching (40) | Curriculum theory (39) | Curriculum reform (29) | Research on basic problems of Pedagogy (26) | Teaching method (16) | Teaching method (16) | Quality education and classroom education (15) | Teaching reform and experiment (15) |
| 1999 | Subject teaching (61) | Curriculum theory (44) | Curriculum reform (36) | Research on basic problems of Pedagogy (23) | Curriculum design (20) | Teaching model (17) | Quality education and classroom education (16) | Teaching reform and experiment (14) |

Note: The number in the above brackets is the number of published articles.

**Table 2-6** Research Projects with the Most Published Articles in 1999

| Items | Number of all publications during 20 years | Number of annual publications | Number of publications in 1999 |
|---|---|---|---|
| Subject teaching | 803 | 3.05 | 61 |
| Curriculum theory | 342 | 17.1 | 44 |
| Curriculum reform | 249 | 12.45 | 36 |
| Research on basic problems of Pedagogy | 233 | 11.65 | 23 |
| design | 215 | 10.75 | 20 |
| Teaching model | 104 | 5.2 | 17 |
| Quality-oriented education and classroom teaching | 118 | 5.9 | 16 |

primary and secondary schools. The reason for the small number of articles on learning psychology is that although "learning" is one of the keywords in the statistics of this article, the journals for the statistics are all educational journals, which will inevitably affect its number. Judging from the top eight projects in terms of the number of research articles, in addition to subject teaching has always been a hot topic, in the mid-to-late 1980s, the basic issues of teaching theory were paid attention to by researchers. Research on issues such as scientization and modernization development once became a hot spot in academic circles. In fact, at the same time, a lot of teaching theories have also been published

In the 1990s, experimental research on teaching methods and teaching reform became a field of attention, and the number of published articles also increased significantly. In the late 1990s, the focus of research began to turn to curriculum theory and curriculum reform. In addition, in the research projects with the most published articles in 1999, the course category accounted for 50% and ranked 2nd, 3rd, and 4th, respectively. It can be seen that the research on curriculum issues at the turn of the century has received more attention.

### 2.2.6 The Focus of Attention at the Turn of the Century: Research on Curriculum Theory and Curriculum Reform

Statistics show that since the late 1980s, people have done more and more research on curriculum theory and curriculum reform, and maintained a stable upward trend. By 1999, the number of articles in the two studies had increased to the highest point since the reform and opening up, with annual publications of 44 and 36, respectively. In terms of the total ranking of the number of papers published, it is second only to the research on subject teaching.[12] In terms of the content of the research projects divided in this paper, the scope of subject teaching should be said to be the most extensive research project. Therefore, the number of articles belonging to this research project is undoubtedly the largest. Statistics show that, except for 1995 and 1996, the number of articles on subject teaching research has always been in the first place. However, from the overall development trend, since 1995, the research on curriculum theory and curriculum reform has gradually become a research hotspot. As can be seen from Figure 2-2, in fact, in terms of the development trend, the upward trend of the number of articles in curriculum theory and curriculum reform research is more significant.

As can be seen from Figure 2-3, subject teaching research has been a key research field of concern in the 1980s. Although its trend is wavy, the total number of articles is still considerable. After the 1990s, its development showed a steady upward state. It is not difficult to find that curriculum theory and curriculum reform are the focus of attention at the turn of the century. In addition, statistics also show that the projects that published the most research articles in 1999 include: curriculum, teaching mode, quality education, and classroom teaching.

### 2.2.7 Research Fields that Should be Strengthened in New Century

The statistics of this study show that the research on curriculum theory and curriculum reform was the focus of attention in the late 20th century, and the number of research articles is increasing. Now it seems that this development trend has become more obvious at the beginning of the new century. As the core of China's basic education reform in the early 21st century, curriculum reform has established its dominant position. Future research will focus more on the combination of theoretical and practical programs of the curriculum. In other words, in the first decade of the new century, people will focus on how to effectively implement the new curriculum plan and curriculum standards.

Here, it should be noted that through the statistics of this study, we can easily find that although some research projects are classified into eight cold spot research fields, they still need more attention from the theoretical and practical circles in terms of their impact on teaching effect and teaching quality. These projects include research on teaching evaluation, research on teaching environment, research on potential courses, research on activity courses, and research on teaching forms. Here are some views.

Taylor, the father of modern curriculum theory, pointed out in his book *Basic Principles of Curriculum and Teaching*, published in 1949, that the theory and practice of studying curriculum and teaching should mainly explore four basic problems: first, why design the curriculum; second, how to organize the curriculum contents that should be taught to students; third, how to teach students to learn these contents; fourth, how to evaluate the effect of curriculum implementation and teaching activities.

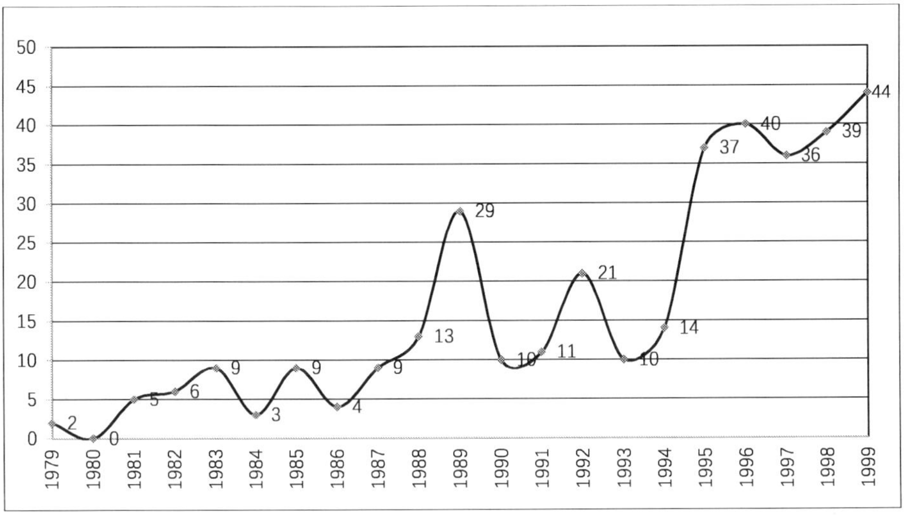


**Figure 2-2** Graph of Changes in the Number of Articles Published in the Course Theory Research from 1979 to 1999

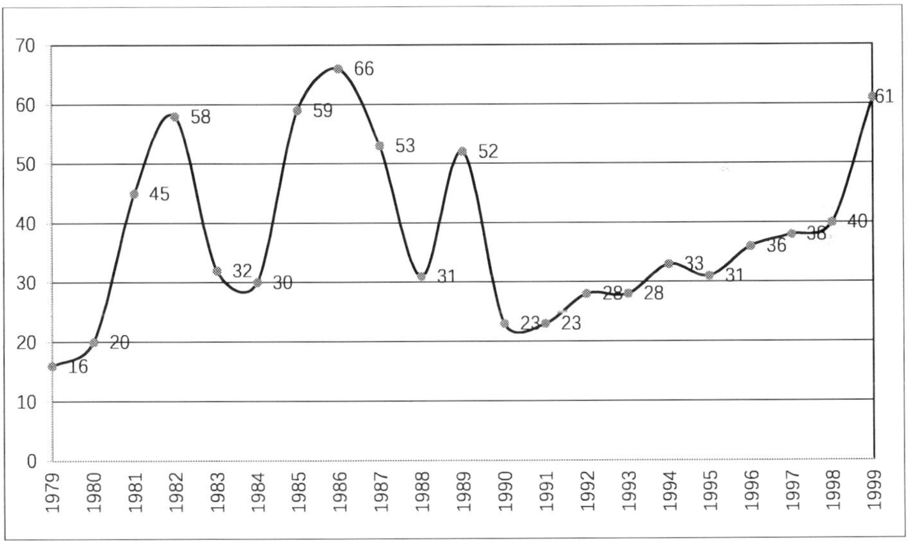


**Figure 2-3** Variation Curve of the Number of Articles Published in the Subject Teaching Research from 1979 to 1999

In Taylor's view, the objectives, contents, methods, and evaluation of curriculum and teaching should be the main issues of our research. It should be affirmed that since the early 1980s, the understanding of educational evaluation in China has become clearer and clearer, and many research results have been published. However, statistics show that there are still few research articles on teaching evaluation. Compared with its position and role in the whole teaching activities, there is still a big gap. According to the statistics of the number of articles published by various studies from 1979 to 1999, the research on teaching evaluation only entered the 8th place in the overall ranking in 1980 and 1989. In addition, according to the statistics of the number of articles published on 35 research projects in 12 educational journals from 1997 to 1999, only the number of articles on teaching evaluation published in the Journal of Northwest Normal University and foreign educational research ranked among the top 8 in the total ranking. It can be seen that the research on teaching evaluation should further attract people's attention. In addition, how to create a good teaching environment for the implementation of the new curriculum, make full use of the advantages of the potential curriculum to cultivate students' spirit and morality, how to coordinate class teaching, group teaching, and individual guidance effectively, and how to implement a truly comprehensive curriculum under the concept of the new curriculum are topics that need further research and discussion.

## 2.3 A Change of Direction for the Methodology of Chinese Didactics Research in the New Century

Since the 1980s, with the considerable progress in Chinese didactics research, the thinking space of didactics research has been expanding unceasingly, which has exerted an extensive influence on teaching practice. Currently, in the 21st century, both the advancement of modern science and technology and the reformation of diverse domains in social life will inevitably raise new requirements for didactics research, which makes didactics research in the 21st century notably different from previous relevant research.

### 2.3.1 Influence of Basic Discipline Theories on Didactics Research Intensified

*Philosophy as Guidance for Didactics Research*

The major influences exerted by philosophy on didactics research are as follows: Firstly, from the theory of human nature, philosophy furnishes not only the substantive characteristics of students and teachers as members of humankind but also the latest understanding concerning the teacher-student mode of existence in the teaching process, which makes didactics research take human characteristics into adequate consideration and promotes the realization of humanized education. Secondly, from the angle of epistemology, philosophy can not only provide new perspectives and methods of understanding teaching phenomena, but also increase the rationality of didactics research methods, thereby grasping the essence of teaching activities and relevant matters through numerous and complicated phenomena. Thirdly, in terms of knowledge outlook, philosophy raises diverse standpoints pertaining to knowledge-related forms, values, essence, structures, etc., which provides guidance for selecting valuable knowledge from teaching activities.

The preceding influences of philosophy on didactics undoubtedly will urge didactics researchers to assimilate all the outstanding philosophical achievements from human history extensively. Firstly, we must persevere in the directive function of Marxist philosophy. Demonstrating the laws of the development of history in human society, Marxist philosophy is the most advanced philosophical thinking so far, which acts as powerful media of thinking for us to know and transform the world. Consequently, it is necessary to persist in the directive function of Marxist philosophy in didactics research. Secondly, it is necessary to assimilate valuable Western philosophical thinking. Marxist philosophy is not all-embracing. Its understanding of the world is based on that of productive forces and relations of production. As both the philosophy of production and the philosophy of combat, Marxist philosophy incarnates the limited directive function regarding education and teaching. Therefore, reasonable viewpoints of other philosophical schools must be imbibed.

Merely embodying the basic principles for us to know and transform the world, philosophy guides didactics research in both the theoretical and the thinking aspects. Nevertheless, the transformation from philosophical concepts into educational concepts cannot be realized through simple linear logic deduction; moreover, directly requesting philosophy to answer specific teaching issues is based on a misconception about philosophy.[13] Demanding that philosophy give guidance on concrete teaching issues is not only detrimental to the development of didactics but also results in the oversimplification and vulgarization of philosophy.

*Strengthening Psychology's Foundation*

As the effective and suitable origin and basis of didactics research, psychology takes studying the nature and characteristics of learning as its general mission. Although those who research learning theories do not conduct research into teaching issues and phenomena directly, given that learning is the foundation of teaching, research on teaching must be based on that of learning. In the long term, China has not assimilated sufficient psychological research achievements in the field of didactics research, i.e., the psychological foundation of pedagogy is vulnerable. One major and delicate problem confronting the educational circles of didactics is how to utilize the research achievements of modern psychology actively and effectively so as to lay a solid foundation of natural science for Chinese didactics and raise the accuracy and depth of our ability to reveal the laws of teaching.[14] In consequence, didactics research should consolidate its psychological foundation and accelerate the transformation from psychological research achievements into teaching theory and practice. Existing theoretical achievements should be comprehensively utilized, such as behaviorism, cognitivism, humanism, constructivism, and other positive and rational theories in the schools of psychology. Furthermore, newly developed theoretical achievements should be incorporated, such as brain science, artificial intelligence, and developmental psychology. Secondly, the transformation of learning theories into teaching practice ought to be highlighted in the assimilation process. Characterized by the individual behaviors of students and the inherent activities of human beings, learning cannot be equated with teaching. Despite the fact that learning conducted by human beings is more intricate than learning conducted by animals, as a kind of natural phenomenon, they are the same by nature. Research on learning theories is solely factual research. Nevertheless, bearing artificial characteristics, teaching is a joint activity for both teachers and students, with its purposiveness involved in the entire teaching process. Accordingly, didactics is not only factual research but also value research. Therefore, before applying learning theories to teaching practice, didactics researchers must effectuate the preceding transformation.

The guidance provided by psychological study for didactics research mainly concentrates on the following aspects of practice research: teaching strategies, teaching methods, teaching models, etc. Philosophy raises the theoretical standards of didactics research, while psychology facilitates the actualization of didactics research.

***Standardizing the Theoretical Basis of Didactics Research***

Presently, there is a tendency to generalize the theoretical basis of didactics in the field of Chinese didactics research. Such a trend will debilitate the scientific rigor of the didactics discipline, making didactics turn into assorted cold dishes composed of diversified academic disciplines and "a territory dominated by other academic disciplines." Additionally, not all academic disciplines can be regarded as the basic disciplines of didactics. On the one hand, psychology is the father of education. On the other hand, philosophy is the mother of education. In contrast, the other academic disciplines can merely exert limited facilitating influence on didactics research, with the major influence lying in broadening the researchers' horizons so as to present a new train of thought for didactics research. In consequence, standardizing the theoretical basis of didactics research in the 21st century has become an indispensable component.

### 2.3.2 Integrating Humanistic and Scientific Paradigms in Didactics Research

Chinese teaching studies in the 20th century expanded by leaps and bounds. Nevertheless, under the influence of cultural tradition and contemporary mainstream values, there was a scientific and rational research orientation, which not only made didactics become trapped in the so-called "non-scientific" predicament in the late 20th century but also made practitioners and theoretical researchers raise diverse questions concerning didactics and didactics research. To tackle various practical problems and theoretical puzzles, didactics research in the 21st century should combine the humanistic paradigm with the scientific paradigm and integrate rationalism values with empiricism values so as to assimilate multi-aspect nourishment.

***Balancing Scientism in Didactics: Critique and Incorporation of Scientific Methodology***

"The scientific paradigm of didactics refers to the fact that under the guidance of the positivist conception of philosophy and with the studies of natural science as the quintessence, didactics researchers underline the cognitive function of empirical perception. Furthermore, they apply diversified methods, such as meticulous observation, rigorous experimentation, and statistical analysis, in order to conduct the quantitative analyses of teaching phenomena, with the expectation that the knowledge concerning both the causality of teaching phenomena and the corresponding laws can be acquired."[15] On the basis of the world outlook of mechanical atomism and reductionism, the scientific paradigm reckons that the connection between various things and phenomena is uncomplicated, linear, and conveyable in terms of causality, with a keen emphasis on empirical research. The scientific paradigm enables the mechanism to infiltrate didactics research, neglecting the holism, complexity, and non-reducibility of teaching phenomena. Simultaneously, only the instrumentality of humankind has been underlined, while the emphasis on human life and the solicitude for human values have been ignored, which may result in the vicious expansion of utilitarian pursuits and the eclipse of the humanistic spirit in teaching activities and research.

However, on the other hand, scientism has value as well. Firstly, it can extricate researchers from the habits of scholasticism that are characterized by thinking profoundly and following the authorities like sheep. Additionally, it enables researchers to stress the point that factual information can be collected via observations, experiments, etc., and that a conclusion can be drawn through conducting analyses of and calculations on the information.[16] Secondly, on the initiative of scientism, the research methods of natural science are applicable not only to natural science but also to teaching research after appropriate transformations, which can exert an undeniable influence on enriching the system of research methods in didactics. Thirdly, embodied in the preceding paradigm, the scientific spirit, which is characterized by being realistic and pragmatic, refraining from any subjective and groundless conclusion, and letting the facts speak for themselves, is indispensable in any era and for conducting any research task. Without scientific spirit, any research result will lose its deserved value due to excessively strong subjectivity.

As far as China is concerned, this is especially significant. The reasons are as follows: since Descartes, the values of scientism have governed the ideological world of human beings in Western society. Moreover, forsaking subjectivity and advocating objectivity are constantly pursued by humankind. It is scientism's having so fully developed as to arrive at the level of mechanization that leads to combat against and repudiation of scientism in social science studies, including educational research. Nevertheless, in

China, scientism has not yet taken root and sprouted to such an extent as to reach the level of becoming ossified, i.e., it is still at the rudimentary stage, and deserved importance has not yet been attached to the scientific spirit in our studies. As remnants of the tendency towards speculation and idle talk, mechanized and rigid research styles and tendencies in Chinese didactics research are still under the influence of historical and cultural traditions instead of scientism. It is evident that empirical studies are not abundant but instead are deficient among studies on teaching and education.

*Emphasizing Humanistic Paradigm in Didactics Research*

"The humanistic paradigm of didactics is referred to as a paradigm in which didactics researchers, under the influence of the ideological trend of humanistic philosophy, consider the research traditions of the humanities as nonesuch, and apply diversified methods such as interpretation, subjective experience, field study, and participant observation in order to grasp the teaching phenomena naturally, holistically and qualitatively."[17] "Representing an ideological trend of philosophy, humanism highlights human value and dignity, regarding humankind as autonomous beings with self-esteem which can function as the yardstick of all things on earth."[18] The initiation of humanism in Western countries was initially aimed at humanity's being fettered by medieval feudal theology. Incarnated in the field of education, humanism embodies a naturalistic outlook on education, with importance attached to a variety of irrational factors, such as emotions, experience, and intuition. Humanistic teaching theories and all other related theories pertain to the schools of humanism.

The humanistic paradigm is put forward in the light of human mechanization, which is caused by the scientific paradigm's neglecting of human emotions and human values. Because of the empirical approach adopted by scientism, the analytical teaching research method underscores the striped segmentation and quantitative analysis of the teaching ensemble in order to pursue a universal explanation of teaching. The preceding research orientation not only results in ignoring the properties of the teaching ensemble but also gives rise to the tendency towards temporality, practicality, and even utilitarianism in teaching research. Furthermore, various non-quantitative factors, such as human nature and the human spirit, can be neglected, impairing the holistic development of humankind. Therefore, researchers advance the humanistic paradigm in the domain of study in the social sciences. Underlining a holistic mode of thinking, they not only deem teaching and human beings as an ensemble in the process of conducting relevant studies, but also adopt a tolerant and understanding attitude towards the behaviors and thoughts of the objects of study. Moreover, they highlight situational and individual differences, reckoning affective experience as the nature of teaching activities. Accordingly, stressing the researcher's experience of teaching contexts will make diverse research methods arise, such as action research, field observation, and interviews.

Didactics is regarded as a subject of social sciences. Additionally, the humanistic paradigm plays an indispensable role in didactics research. Respecting individual values and differences is required in the humanistic paradigm. Respecting, understanding, favoring, and tolerating the objects of study contribute to converting both the ideology in which official rank is considered to be the sole criterion of one's worth and the style characterized by feudal patriarchal domination, setting a good example for implementing the democratic style of work in teaching practice. The autocratic style in the domain of the study of Chinese didactics does not originate from the influences exerted by rationalism or technological logos. There has always been the ideology in which official rank is considered to be the sole criterion of one's worth. Reflected in the domain of education, such ideology is the Chinese-style "absolute authority of the teachers" in the domain of education. In contrast, embodied in the domain of educational studies, such ideology is an "authoritarian" style in which numerous researchers consider themselves to be the experts who can pick fault with practitioners and disrespect their opinions. In consequence, practitioners are unwilling to coordinate with researchers, resulting in a lack of research fidelity. Thus, it is an utterly pressing task to assimilate the values of the humanistic paradigm in the Chinese domain of teaching practice and educational studies. Secondly, the teaching contextualization cognized by the humanistic paradigm requires researchers to penetrate into the grass-roots of teaching practice, which is conducive to transforming the divergence of Chinese educational studies from teaching practice. Thirdly, the research methods advocated by the humanistic paradigm have been extensively applied in Western countries by considerable numbers of researchers, exhibiting their distinctive attractiveness. Hence it is highly necessary for didactics researchers in China to master various methods in the initiative of the humanistic paradigm.

### *Promoting Quantitative and Qualitative Research Integration*

The speculative method dominates didactics research in China. The scientific paradigm attaches importance to quantitative research, while the humanistic paradigm lays emphasis on qualitative research. The preceding two research methods are complementary. On the one hand, quantitative research claims the quantization, replicability, and generalization of research results. On the other hand, qualitative research results, which are contextualized, can be signified by linguistic description. Nonetheless, the practical foundation of research has been underscored regardless of paradigm, which differs essentially from the speculation-dominated research method in China. The research methods applied previously in China operate mainly under the guidance of a linear and mechanical world outlook and values. Despite the fact that such ideology and values are identical to the values of scientism, both the research methods of scientism and the scientific spirit incarnated in the research process have not been embraced. The humanistic paradigm esteems the subjective experience and value orientation of both the researchers and the research participants. In contrast, only the researcher's value has been embodied in Chinese didactics research. Accordingly, as far as didactics research in China is concerned, there should be not only an integration of quantitative and qualitative research, but also an implementation of empirical research in conformity with solicitude for humankind. Simultaneously, it is highly necessary to enhance the accuracy of qualitative research and to transform the research tendency which currently gives priority to theoretical speculation.

### 2.3.3 Balancing System Establishment and Practice Exploration in Didactics Research

*Didactics Research: Returning to Teaching Life*

As a kind of life, teaching is the life of both teachers and students, i.e., teaching signifies a life world. The teaching world is characterized by a dual nature. "As a world subordinate to both nature and human beings, the teaching world is both objective and ideological, both causal and purposive, both inevitable and liberal."[19] The complexity of the teaching world determines that didactics research cannot concentrate solely on theoretical research. "Although a theoretical system is capable of revealing life from a certain aspect, and can even demonstrate a certain aspect of life penetratingly, a system is not equivalent to life; furthermore, it can never be a substitute for life."[20]

The main aim of Chinese didactics research in the 20th century was to structure a theoretical system. Intense "consciousness of system" has led didactics research to "structure system only for the sake of the system" while ignoring the world beyond the system,[21] especially the authentic world of teaching life. Consequently, the research results of didactics are unable to furnish teaching practice with effective guidance; in addition, a gap is engendered between research and practical needs, which results in existential crises in didactics. Though some studies entitled "The Theory of Teaching Art" lay particular emphasis on practical research, they still cannot fulfill the urgent needs for complex teaching practices to be guided by effective theories. Therefore, reinforcing the researchers' consciousness of showing solicitude for practice and laying emphasis on summarizing and promoting the wisdom of practice are the main development orientations of didactics research in the 21st century. Moreover, with a more profound significance of noumenon, the value of the practice is both the foundation and the cornerstone of the existence of the didactics discipline. If the research is conducted merely to structure a consummate theoretical system, didactics research will inevitably lose its vigor.

*Strengthening Didactics Discipline System*

Despite the fact that didactics research in the 20th century was mainly aimed at system establishment, the theoretical system of didactics is still not integrated, which can be concretely manifested in the following three aspects:

Firstly, the curriculum system of didactics becomes ossified. As far as the published teaching materials of didactics are concerned, they are all organized on the basis of a fixed order, i.e., from fundamental theories to specific practices. In terms of the concrete composition of chapters, each chapter can be stated in accordance with the following pattern: nature (properties), meanings, tasks, contents, principles, methods, types of organization, etc. Upon reading numerous books entitled "Didactics," the reader will be deeply impressed by their "being the same in essentials while differing in minor points."[22]

Secondly, there are a large number of vague concepts. For instance, heurism is not only a concrete teaching method but also a guiding ideology. In terms of the viewpoint indicating that "teachers should play a dominating role while students should function as the subject," can the teachers, who shoulder the responsibilities as the "dominator" of teaching activities, actually be rated as the subject?

Thirdly, there is a lack of understanding of the explicit logical origin of the didactics discipline. On the one hand, some scholars believe that the logical origin of didactics research is self-explanatory, i.e., "teaching" can be deemed as the logical origin. On the other hand, some scholars think that as a concept in need of further explanation, "teaching" cannot be considered the logical origin of the didactics discipline. Therefore, it is highly necessary to pursue a logical origin beyond "teaching."[23]

### *Integrating Information Technology in Teaching*

The influences exerted by information technology on teaching are profound. Information technology can influence teaching activities via new teaching methods and content. More importantly, the values of teaching can be transformed due to the dissemination and application of information technology. Firstly, the application of information technology converts the conventional teacher-student relationship, in which teachers no longer monopolize knowledge, and the establishment of a democratic and equal relationship is expected to be truly fulfilled. Secondly, information technology transforms the traditional outlook of teachers, the conventional outlook of learning, and the appearance of classroom teaching. In other words, it enables learning to become autonomous activities implemented by students to a larger extent, with teachers existing only as supporters. In consequence, the traditional phenomenon in which "one teacher alone has a say" will be exchanged for a better approach. Thirdly, information technology also changes the traditional knowledge outlook, which equates knowledge with the truth and deems that the knowledge imparted through teaching must be incontestable. Diverse characteristics engendered by information technology, such as the enrichment and complexity of knowledge and mutual contradiction among various branches of knowledge, enable researchers to realize the relativity of the value of knowledge and the true nature of knowledge so as to establish a new knowledge outlook. It is difficult to predict the influences of the aforementioned changes in perceptions of teaching activities.

The development of Chinese information technology in the 20th century was at the rudimentary stage. In the domain of teaching, information technology is considered a kind of teaching method with the potential changes it can bring about having not been really recognized in a rational way. Furthermore, integrated studies, which aim at exploring the relationship between information technology and teaching content and methods, have not been conducted. Accordingly, one important problem for didactics research in the 21st century is how to realize the integration of information technology and teaching activities from the dimension of form to the dimension of perception.

### 2.3.4 Emphasizing Localized Didactics Research

In the early 20th century, the development of Chinese didactics was always at the stage characterized by "widely adopting Western learning." After the Opium War opened the gate of China, Chinese learning declined gradually while Western learning flourished gradually. It was the same case in the domain of education. Chinese theories of teaching and education mainly learned and drew lessons from Western research results. All the relevant Western theories, from the theory of Herbart to the theory of Dewey, were once all the rage in China. After the establishment of China as a republic, the teaching theories of China were comprehensively influenced by those of the Soviet Union. "Normal universities either directly adopted the Chinese version of the original work or simply compiled the original work into teaching materials."[24] Didactics material written by educational experts in the Soviet Union, with Kairov acting as the representative, had become the model for us to learn from and draw lessons from. "The didactics research in the early 1960s posed numerous teaching principles, such as imparting knowledge and cultivating people, to the benefit of both teachers and students, dual-foundation teaching, heuristic teaching, advancing gradually in due order, teaching only the essential and ensuring plenty of practice, putting into practice what one has learned, and teaching students in accordance with their aptitude, all of which bore a strong sense of localization."[25] However, the preceding principles had not fundamentally overcome the doctrinairism embodied in the didactics of the Soviet Union. In the 1980s, although numerous scholars had made outstanding contributions to the development and intensification of Chinese didactics, overall, the approach of our own had not yet been established, i.e., Kairov's mode of didactics system still dominated. In the 1990s, because didactics researchers started to introspect the problems existing in didactics research, combined with the introduction and recommendation of learning-centered or student-centered teaching theories in the UK and USA, the collision of Eastern and Western cultures broadened our horizon of research. We began to rethink profoundly the ways to pursue an approach for the development of didactics, which conforms to the situation in our country. "Nevertheless, regretfully, didactics research in China so far has not really established theoretical schools with distinctive features. Even worse, there is still a lack of self-awareness of didactics schools with Chinese characteristics.[26]

The practice of each country in the world testifies that only the teaching theories originating from their own cultural ground are of maximum vitality. Despite the fact that drawing lessons from the theories of other countries is a shortcut to development, the traits of teaching practice differ distinctly due to differences in historical and cultural conditions, geographic environment conditions, and economic and political conditions of each country. Hence teaching research conducted on the basis of the teaching practice of one's own country is generally only effective in the practice of one's own country. If applied in another country, such teaching research must be transformed. Otherwise, this will inevitably result in the consequence of "changing the orange in the south into the trifoliate orange in the north" (or "trying to grow wheat on stony ground"); moreover, the requirements of the teaching practice of one's own country cannot be fulfilled. Additionally, with the acceleration of international economic and cultural exchange, there is a tendency towards quickening academic exchange in the domain of didactics research. Whether a didactics system conforming to national conditions and characteristics can be established is the crux of the desire for Chinese didactics to come to possess its own small space in the worldwide research domain of didactics. Therefore, we propose the following practices. Firstly, excellent educational thinking embedded in traditional Chinese philosophy should be unearthed, which can be interpreted in a modern-day framework rather than be followed rigorously. Secondly, traditional Chinese culture should be adopted as the basis for absorbing didactics research from the Western world. Thirdly, researchers with a deep understanding of Chinese culture should be cultivated to be the backbone. This is the foundation on which didactics research in China can gain independence.

## 2.4 The Value of Inductive Inquiry Teaching in Contemporary Pedagogy

After WWII, the development of pedagogy marched into a completely new stage, and the study of teaching theory and teaching practice in each country became more in-depth and fruitful than ever before. In addition, the scientific and modernized degree of teaching theory has also been continuously strengthened and improved. Although there are still, to a certain extent, debates between different schools of teaching theory, that is to say, teaching practice is still influenced to varying degrees by certain pedagogical ideas, which hold different emphases on teaching objectives, teaching methods, the status of teachers and students, the focus of the curriculum and teaching evaluation. However, it should be clear that after more than 50 years of theoretical research and practical or experimental exploration of pedagogical reform, a clear common feature has emerged in the development of contemporary pedagogy. Moreover, the impact of its research findings on teaching reform and teaching practice has become increasingly significant.

According to examining the representative teaching reform experiments in China since the 1980s and the theories and models they have developed, it is not difficult to find that they all reflect the basic characteristics of the development of contemporary pedagogy from different perspectives. In terms of theory formation, these teaching reform experiments have been able to deal precisely with the relationship among criticism, inheritance, and innovation, between theory and practice, between localization and internationalization of teaching theory, and between diversity and unity in constructing their own theoretical systems. They have both a common feature—the focus on students as the subject of teaching and having distinctly individual characters—various implementation strategies. From the point of view of theory and practice, these teaching reform experiments place particular emphasis on the developmental nature of teaching and the diversity of teaching objectives, the dialectical unity of the teacher's leading role and the students' subjectivity, and also emphasize the scientific and operational nature of teaching models, the inspiration and flexibility of teaching methods, the diversity of teaching information delivery, and so on. These experiments in teaching reform not only provide scientific theoretical guidance for the teaching practice of classroom teachers at the front line, but also greatly enrich and promote the development of contemporary pedagogy.

"Inductive inquiry teaching" is one of the most influential teaching reform experiments in our country, which originated and was hosted by Zhang Xiongfei, a professor at Shaanxi Normal University. When analyzing and evaluating the theoretical and practical value of inductive inquiry teaching from the perspective of contemporary teaching theory and its practical characteristics, we can easily find out that the theory and practice of inductive inquiry teaching not only have national features, but also accord with the basic spirits of contemporary quality-oriented teaching. This experimental research not only has a wide and profound impact on front-line classroom teaching, but also has significant achievements in promoting the development of contemporary teaching theory. From the perspective of the basic direction of education reform in primary and secondary schools in China and the basic conditions of education and teaching practice, it is undoubtedly one of the effective theories and strategies to implement quality education.

### 2.4.1 Inductive Inquiry Teaching: Inheritance and Innovation

History is inseparable, national conditions are objective, and any educational and teaching reform that leaves history and national conditions aside will ultimately be unsuccessful. In the historical process of education and teaching reform in the world, in the process of pedagogical theory moving towards scientification and modernization, there have been two different choices between critically inheriting the previous teaching theory and basically or totally rejecting the previous teaching theory, thus leading to two different ideas of teaching reform: one is to reform and innovate in the process of inheriting the essence of traditional teaching theory and establish a teaching theory system that meets the requirements of cultivating talents in contemporary society; the other is to basically reject the traditional teaching theory and put forward a viewpoint and new theoretical system that is fundamentally opposed to traditional teaching theory. Although there are still different schools of thought in teaching theory circles, the common trend in the development of contemporary teaching theory aims to reform and innovate while inheriting the essence of traditional teaching theory and eliminating its dross, so as to establish a system of teaching theory that meets the requirements of contemporary society in the cultivation of talents. In the process of international teaching reform, many educators have adopted a combination of inheritance and innovation in their reforms and theoretical constructions. They are characterized by deep theoretical background and reforms in line with national realities. As one of the three major schools of contemporary pedagogy, the famous Soviet educator Zankov's theory of 'promoting general development' is a reformed and innovative theory based on a critical inheritance of the reasonable elements of traditional pedagogical thinking. Therefore, his theory and reform practice not only have a wide and profound influence, but also strong vitality. Although the theory of inductive inquiry teaching and its reform experiments cannot be compared with Zankov's theory of "promoting general development," it can be said with certainty that it is a theory with Chinese characteristics that is gradually formed and developed through long-term experimental research on the basis of inheriting the essence of China's traditional teaching ideas and absorbing the research results of contemporary pedagogy. The inheritance attributes to its emphasis on inspiration in the teaching process and the organic combination of learning and thinking, which is the core of China's excellent teaching ideas. The inheritance of the essence of traditional teaching ideology and the innovation according to the requirements of quality-oriented education are reflected in its "elicitation teaching ideology theory, inquiry teaching process theory, and three-dimensional teaching goal theory."

The succession and innovation of inductive inquiry teaching lie in the fact that it scientifically demonstrates the dialectical relationship between teaching and learning in contemporary classroom teaching, and suggests the connotation and characteristics of the student's subject status and the leading role of the teacher. It is proposed that the core feature of the leading role of teachers is heuristic, that is, the implementation of inspirational teaching.

As we all know, heuristic teaching is the essence in the treasury of our outstanding teaching theories, and whether ancient Confucius, Mencius, or the great modern educator Tao Xingzhi, etc., strongly advocated heuristic teaching. It can be seen that heuristic teaching is not only the soul of traditional teaching in our country, but also a summary of our long-term teaching experience. Professor Zhang Xiongfei sees "to lead without giving, to open without reaching, to be adept at indicating and inducing; to promote thinking in an approachable way" as the essence of the teacher's leading role, highlighting that "to change teaching into inducing, to change teaching into guiding," which is in line with the contemporary teaching theory's positioning of the teacher's role in teaching activities.

While affirming the leading role of the teacher, the theory of inductive inquiry teaching believes that the leading role of the teacher should ultimately be implemented to "promote students' lively and active all-round development and become a generation of people with subjectivity."[27] Thus, "the subjective status of students is the starting point, basis and destination for conducting teaching, and is the core of the implementation of quality-oriented education in the process of subject teaching."[28] The theory also demonstrates that students' subjectivity has four main characteristics, namely, mobility, independence, creativity, and fundamentality.[29] Among them, independence is the core characteristic of students' subjective status; that is, students complete their learning tasks independently under the inspiration and guidance of teachers, and obtain development actively. The independence of students' subjective learning is prominently expressed in the independence of thinking, i.e., independent thinking.[30] Advocating independent thinking and emphasizing the combination of learning and thinking have always been valued by educators in China.

The theory of inductive inquiry teaching not only inherits the essence of Chinese traditional teaching theory, but also fully affirms the dialectical relationship between teaching and learning in the modern sense. And it also scientifically analyzes the basic problems of realizing the true dialectical unity of teaching and learning and promoting the development of students' vivid and lively initiative according to the basic theories of modern brain science, cognitive psychology, information theory, and the basic principles of modern pedagogy, that is, students devote themselves to learning activities wholeheartedly. In addition, the teaching guiding ideology and strategy of "training as the main line" and "thinking as the main attack" are put forward, emphasizing that intensive training is the fundamental way to achieve the status of students as the main body, and the development of thinking ability is the main direction of training. It is advocated that students devote themselves to the classroom learning life through "seven actions" (do by hands, see by eyes, listen by ears, read with emotion, discuss actively, write diligently, and think positively).[31]

From the above, it is easy to see that the theory of inductive inquiry teaching serves as a teaching theory with contemporary characteristics constructed on the basis of inheriting the idea of inspiration, developing it, and gaining a comprehensive understanding of it. It organically combines inheritance and innovation. As experts from Shaanxi Province said when they appraised the subject, "the theory of inductive inquiry teaching" is "theoretically broad-based and has obvious Chinese characteristics, making our traditional inspirational teaching scientific, theoretical, systematic, and concrete. It has made the teachers' teaching transform from the current injection to induction, and the students' learning change from passive receptive type into an active inquiry type of full immersion."

### 2.4.2 Inductive Inquiry Teaching: Refined from Practice

In terms of the theoretical formation of contemporary pedagogy, experimentation plays an important role in the formation of scientific theories, and the emphasis on long-term experiments to reach scientific conclusions has become a developmental trend. Take the formation of Zankov's theory of teaching and development as an example, its experiments lasted for 18 years, and the number of experimental classes in the country reached 1,281 at the maximum. In terms of the process of experimentation, Zankov's experiments on teaching reform went through three stages for 18 years, starting with the selection of one experimental class and two regular classes for a controlled study in the first year of Moscow School No. 172 in 1957, and ending with the publication of his book *Teaching and Development* in 1975.[32]

In their evaluation of Zankov's teaching theory, our scholar argues that Zankov's reputation is due to the fact that his "experiments" are the longest and largest, and his theory and curriculum the most complete.[33] The theory of induced thinking inquiry teaching lasted for 18 years from the investigation and experience in 1981 to the publication of the book *Lure Thinking Investigation—Quality-Oriented Teaching* in 1999.

After exploring the formation process of this theory, we can get that its guiding ideology is: "Practice riches scientific research, and scientific research forms theory, finally theory guides practice and so on to run in circles." The specific route is like this: practical experience, experience conclusion, trying to explore, theory formation, experimental testify, theoretical sublimation, re-experiment, systematic theory formation, guiding practice, such a process deepened step by step, promoted little by little. It can be said that this theory comes from practice and serves practice, always maintaining the close integration of theory and practice. Thus, inductive inquiry teaching has strong vitality because of the case that the idea is refined in practice, and the theory is sublimated in experimentation.

As the old saying goes, it takes ten years to grow trees but a hundred years to cultivate people, which means cultivating people is a long-term job. Likewise, the labor of studying the laws and methods of cultivating people is also a long-term process. "The research on inductive inquiry teaching, as a prototype, can be traced back to the exploratory student experiment in physics teaching in 1963, trying to make students the main body of the teaching process."[34] And conscious, formal investigation and experimentation began in 1981. Looking back at the history of inductive inquiry teaching, it is easy to understand why the Shaanxi Provincial Education Commission formally promoted it in the province in 1996, why there are now 64 formal experimental research bases with more than 1,300 formal experimental teachers in the country, and why 300,000 primary and secondary school teachers across 31 provinces, municipalities, and autonomous regions use it in a variety of subjects. The key to the widespread influence of inductive inquiry teaching, especially its popularity and acceptance by front-line teachers, and the remarkable results achieved in the nearly twenty years of repeated experiments, is that the theory has a deep practical foundation and has been tested in practice many times. It is not only scientific in nature with the reflection of objective teaching laws, but also operable for its sublimation of rich teaching experience.

### 2.4.3 The Scientific Model of Inductive Inquiry Teaching

The teaching model based on the idea of inductive inquiry not only prominently embodies the fundamental idea of modern inspirational teaching, but also makes modern inspirational teaching more operational through the design of specific teaching procedures and steps, which has been recognized by experts in China. Analyzing the teaching mode of inductive inquiry with the main elements of the scientific teaching mode, it is easy to see that this teaching mode not only has certain theoretical guidance, and a goal-oriented, operational procedure with a strong focus on quality education, but also proposes evaluation criteria and practical conditions for realization in line with quality education. It reflects the systematic nature of the scientific teaching model, and also has its uniqueness and innovation. The following is a brief analysis of the teaching mode of inductive inquiry based on the constituent elements of contemporary pedagogical theory.

Theoretical basis. Contemporary teaching theory believes that any teaching mode is a relatively stable and specific teaching structure formed around a certain theme in teaching activities under the guidance of certain teaching theories. And it is a transformation form of teaching theory, a basic framework for designing courses, selecting teaching materials, and prompting teachers for activities.[35] In the long-term practice and experimentation, the teaching mode of inductive inquiry has gradually formed its own theoretical guidance system. Following the spiraling research path of "practice enriching scientific research, scientific research forming theory, theory guiding practice and so on to run in circles," after 18 years of efforts, the logical starting point of the subject teaching theory has been analyzed as "learning," and then three basic subject teaching categories are screened out: "teaching," "psychology," and "development," forming a self-contained teaching function view, teaching mechanism view and teaching values.[36] Its teaching thought can be concluded as teachers are guiders, students are subjects, training is the main line, and thinking is the fundamental goal. Here, the words guider, subjects, main line, and fundamental goal properly reflect the words "induction," "thinking," "research," and "investigation." "Induction" and "thinking" show the inheritance and development of excellent teaching thought in our country, while "research" and "investigation" are the new requirement of contemporary quality-oriented education.

Target orientation. Inductive inquiry teaching believes that subject teaching in class should promote students' all-round development, and to achieve this goal, it has to adhere to the three-dimensional teaching target: "acquiring knowledge, developing ability and cultivating morality." In turn, the achievement of the three-dimensional target has to abide by the basic guiding thought: "teachers as leaders, students as subjects, training as the main line, thinking as the fundamental goal," and it's also necessary to find out the primal developing height of knowledge, ability, morality, and conditions that can promote students' potential ability to become a reality. The three-dimensional teaching objectives advocated by inductive inquiry teaching not only break through the knowledge-centered traditional teaching objectives, but also conform to the contemporary trend of diversifying teaching objectives in pedagogy.

Fulfillment conditions. Any teaching mode has its own specific conditions for realization, such as personnel, means, organization, time, equipment, environment, etc. Each of these factors affects the achievement of teaching objectives to varying degrees. The inductive inquiry teaching model takes into account the realities of China's primary and secondary schools and grasps classroom teaching as a basic form of teaching organization, creating a set of procedures and methods for teaching subjects that are not limited by too many factors and enabling both urban and rural schools to use this model effectively. It is for this reason that inquiry-inducing teaching has now been extended to all subjects taught in primary and secondary schools, and has achieved significant social benefits. "All teachers and schools that have persistently conducted experiments in induced inquiry teaching have achieved the two specific tasks of improving the quality of teaching on a large scale and producing scholarly teachers."[37]

Operational procedures. The guidance of teaching theory to teaching practice mainly embodies by the medium of the teaching model, while the specificity of the operational procedures reflecting the external activities of the teaching model directly affects first-line teachers' effective application of a teaching model. The reason why inductive inquiry teaching is able to be promoted to a large extent is not only because it prominently embodies the idea of inspirational teaching and the requirements of quality education, but also that it has a set of operational steps and specific training methods that can adapt to subject teaching, implement the idea of inspiration and quality-oriented education effectively. On the basis of emphasizing the dialectical unity of regularity and flexibility, the dialectical unity of truth, goodness, and beauty, and the dialectical unity of induction and deduction, inductive inquiry teaching puts forward the process of teaching structure, which takes training as the principle line and thinking as the fundamental goal, and it sets up some effective teaching strategies such as practical inquiry (specifically: experimental inquiry, experiential inquiry, empirical inquiry, and image inquiry) and theoretical inquiry according to different disciplines. In class teaching, the teaching content is arranged, and the teaching process is organized according to the cause-and-effect hierarchy of "exploration-research-application" or "observation-thinking-transfer" to achieve the purpose of changing teaching into inducing and learning into thinking. In primary and middle schools, teachers can effectively achieve a "three-dimensional" teaching target based on two cross-cutting elements and three levels of elements, namely, "create and stimulate situation; explore actively and observe seriously; research painstakingly, think dynamically; apply widely, shift frequently; give feedback in time and promote assimilation."

Evaluation standard. On the one hand, the evaluation advocated by the inductive inquiry teaching adheres to the basic guiding ideology based on whether students have achieved the main position in teaching activities, whether they have actively participated in learning and implemented the "seven actions," and whether they have developed their thinking ability. On the other hand, the combination of traditional evaluation methods and modern evaluation methods makes the evaluation results not only scientific, objective, and fair, but also comparable and beneficial.

### 2.4.4 Inductive Inquiry: An Effective Quality-Oriented Teaching Strategy

Having stridden into a new century, the comprehensive promotion of quality-oriented education and new curriculum has become the main melody of China's basic education reform. After getting out of the practical misunderstanding of quality-oriented education in recent years, it has become a consensus that classroom teaching is the main site for implementing quality education and comprehensively implementing the new curriculum, focusing on the development strategy of basic education in China in the 21st century. From the very beginning, the experimental research of "inductive inquiry teaching" has focused on class teaching, firmly grasped the main position of classroom subject teaching, and explored the dialectical connection and value position of various factors in the classroom teaching system. The teaching theory proposes a center of inducing thinking and exploring research and three-dimensional objectives of knowledge, ability, and morality as a trinity. It completely discusses the three basic issues in contemporary teaching reform: subjectivity, dynamics, and process theory. On this basis, the basic principles for the implementation of quality education in subject classroom teaching are proposed, namely the principle of overall optimization, the principle of teaching harmony, the principle of intensive training, the principle of enriching affection, the principle of multi-directional feedback and the principle of promoting transfer. This system of principles is not only an accurate reflection of contemporary research findings in pedagogy, but also a dialectical and interrelated whole.

Meanwhile, inductive inquiry teaching's view of developing students' thinking ability through training corresponds with the core thought of quality-oriented education. *The Decision of the State Council of the Central Committee of the Communist Party of China on Deepening Educational Reform and Comprehensively Implementing Quality Education* states clearly that "intellectual education should change the concept of education, reform the mode of training talents, actively implement heuristic and discussion-based teaching, stimulate students' awareness of independent thinking and innovation, and effectively improve the quality of teaching." Throughout the reform experiments, inductive inquiry teaching has always emphasized on "the practical development of imaginative thinking skills" and "the emphasis should be on developing creative skills."[38] It can be seen that from the very beginning, inquiry teaching has captured the main line and is key to the development of contemporary teaching reform.

Although there are endless teaching reform and practice modes in the world, careful analysis reveals that many teaching reform experiments, which are guided by theoretical interpretation, tend to be detached from specific national conditions in the process of implementation, so that the seemingly exciting theories fail to blossom in practice. In contrast, the practice of inductive inquiry teaching has always grasped classroom teaching, which is now, or will remain for some time to come, the basic form of teaching and learning in China's primary and secondary schools, and has explored and constructed a theory and strategy that can be adapted to classroom teaching in modern urban schools, but can also be universally applied to classroom teaching in the vast number of underdeveloped rural schools.

In the process of using the inductive inquiry teaching model, teachers can combine modern teaching techniques and make full use of computer technology to aid and organize teaching. For example, in a mathematics lesson observed by the author at Li Xiang Secondary School, a key experimental research base in Shenzhen, the experimental teacher made full use of multimedia to assist the teaching process and achieved satisfactory teaching results. At the same time, they can also fully exploit the potential of traditional teaching media to improve the effectiveness of teaching through vivid language, well-designed boards, and the choice of appropriate methods to reflect the idea of inductive inquiry thought in teaching. The substantial improvement in the teaching quality of a large number of experimental research bases, such as Qingzhou No. 2 Middle School in Shandong Province, Handan No. 1 Middle School in Hebei Province, and Zhidan Middle School in Shaanxi Province, is the best example.[39] This also reflects the flexibility and creativity of contemporary teaching models. As Professor Zhang Xiongfei said: "There is a standard model, but it is not the only model. It is a dialectical unity of commonality and diversity, a dialectical unity of 'law' and 'indefinite law,' and a harmonious unity of scientific and artistic aspects in teaching activities."[40]

The theory and model of inductive inquiry teaching come from practice and are refined and sublimated in practice; thus, it is inevitable that it meets the conditions for implementation in Chinese schools. The practice has shown that there is no international path that can be adapted to any context and achieve the best results in educational practice, and exploring the localization of teaching theory and practice is one of the trends in the development of contemporary pedagogy. In this regard, the value of the experiment in inductive inquiry teaching reform is self-evident.

# Hot Issues in Contemporary International Teaching Theories

This chapter mainly studies the hot issues of contemporary international teaching theory research, which is divided into four research topics: Constructivism, Multiple Intelligence Theory, Effective Teaching Theory, and Reflective Teaching Theory. Constructivism believes that teaching should be committed to making students the main body of learning. Teachers should create complex and real learning situations, and provide technical and cultural support for students' autonomous learning. These concepts challenge traditional teaching, which emphasizes the truth of knowledge and the acceptance of learning.

The Multiple Intelligence Theory puts forward eight types of intelligence of human beings. This theory advocates that classroom teaching should offer development space for people with different intelligent inclinations. It regards "teaching by multiple intelligence" as the basic tactic, and "to develop students' multiple intelligence" as a starting point of contemporary teaching.

The Effective Teaching Theory consists of four fundamental value orientations, which include teaching objectives, teaching skills, learning achievement, and the whole process of teaching. And it has various research paradigms, such as the background-process-product (BPP) analysis paradigm, surface analysis paradigm, psychological analysis paradigm, and the knowledge-based analysis paradigm of teaching. Moreover, this theory applies different methods in studying its characteristics. These methods include Speculative Seasoning Study, Desire Analysis Study, and Empirical Investigation Study. The impact of this strong concept on the classroom teaching reform of primary and secondary schools in Britain and the United States is obvious. As an effective way for the sustainable development of contemporary teachers' teaching profession, reflective teaching has attracted extensive attention.

## 3.1 Constructivist Learning Theory and Teaching Idea

Constructivism is a theory about knowledge and learning developed on the basis of philosophy, psychology, and anthropology. It focuses on what knowledge is and how one obtains knowledge.[1] The main representatives in the early stage are Jean Piaget, Lev Vygotsky, and Brunner, and in recent times the representatives are Howard Gardner, Nelson Goodman, Jacqueline Grennon Brooks, and Martin G. Brooks.

After years of development, constructivism has formed different schools of knowledge and learning, among which the most representative schools are: radical constructivism, social constructivism, social cultural cognition, social constructivism, information processing constructivism, and cybernetic system.[2]

Although there are different schools of constructivism in practice, its core idea, "knowledge should be constructed, not taught," has been well known by more and more educators, and is affecting or changing their classroom practice.

### 3.1.1 Learning Theories and Teaching Ideas of Constructivism

Different from the traditional view of knowledge, constructivist theory regards knowledge as temporary, developing, nonobjective, internally constructed, and mediated by society and culture. Therefore, learning is regarded as a process of contradiction between an individual's existing view of the world and new situations and stimuli. Constructivism holds that the learning process is not a process in which students passively accept knowledge, but a process in which students actively construct knowledge.

In traditional classrooms, learning is usually seen as a kind of imitation activity, in which students need to do a lot of repetitive work, and exams or tests are the only way students can reveal new information. Students are regarded as a container for passively receiving knowledge. They rarely have the opportunity to inquire, debate and conduct their own research. Even learning cooperation between peers is very rare. Most of them practice independently after listening to the teacher's teaching and reviewing in order to get good grades on mid-term and final exams or quizzes.

Constructivism regards learning as a process in which teachers help students internalize existing knowledge or convert it into new information. In this process, learning is regarded as a process of actively constructing knowledge and forming new cognitive structures. Repeated learning and test scores are no longer a concern, but the creation of a learning environment and positive evaluation feedback.

An educational environment that focuses on encouraging students to engage in positive meaning construction has four basic characteristics. First, it breaks the traditional boundaries of the curriculum oriented to mastering basic knowledge and allows students to think freely. Secondly, students have more opportunities to practice. They can learn what they are interested in, find the connection between things, reconstruct concepts, and draw conclusions. Thirdly, teachers share information with the students and make them realize that the world is complex, people's views on the world are diverse, and the truth can often be explained. Fourthly, the students can realize that learning and the evaluation of the learning process is not a simple matter. It requires time investment and unremitting efforts. To truly understand the theory of constructivism, educators must focus on students. Only by fully understanding the active role of the students can teachers become true practitioners of constructivism.

Regarding the difference between traditional classroom teaching and constructivist classroom teaching, we can get a deeper understanding from the comparison of Brooks' and Good's ideas (After Good) in Tables 3-1 and 3-2. Although the constructivist theory is not the perfect teaching theory in the world today, it is one of the most influential theories. Because constructivism's new interpretation of the five core concepts in the education system: knowledge, learning, curriculum, teaching, and evaluation has indeed injected new vitality into the reform of education and teaching in the new century. In the following, according to the research results of constructivism by scholars at home and abroad, a brief overview of constructivism's view of knowledge, view of learning, view of students, and view of teachers is given.

*Constructivist view of knowledge*: Knowledge is not a purely objective reflection of reality, nor is any kind of symbolic system conveying knowledge a representation of absolute truth. It is nothing but an explanation, hypothesis, or assumption of the world. It is not the final answer to the question. It will inevitably change, sublimate and rewrite with the deepening of people's understanding, and new explanations and hypotheses will appear. Knowledge cannot generalize universal laws exactly, or provide practical methods for an activity or problem-solving. It's impossible to use knowledge to settle a problem at once in actual problem solving. Rather, it needs re-handling and reproducing the intrinsic knowledge in accordance with the actual situation of the problem.

*Constructivist view of learning*: Constructivism holds that learning is not a process in which teachers simply transfer knowledge to students, but a process in which students construct knowledge themselves; Learning is not a process of passively receiving information stimulation, but a process of actively constructing meaning; Learning is a process in which learners select and process the external information actively according to their own experience, so as to obtain their own meaning and understanding. Learning is a process in which learners re-understand and encode new information and construct their own understanding based on their original knowledge and experience. Learning process is not a process that simply involves information input, storage, and extraction. It is an interactive process between old and new knowledge experiences, that is, an interaction process between learners and the learning environment.

*Constructivist view of students*: Constructivism emphasizes that learners do not enter the learning situation with an empty mind. They have had relevant knowledge and experience in their daily life. And they have their own views on the outside world. Teachers should not ignore students' original knowledge and life experience and simply implement cramming education. They should take students' knowledge and experience as the starting point of teaching and guide students to acquire new knowledge based on what students have learned. Teaching is not to transfer knowledge, but to process and transform knowledge. Teachers are not only the presenters of knowledge, but also the symbol of intellectual authority. They should pay attention to students' understanding of various phenomena and students' opinions and think about why students have those ideas. On this basis, teachers can guide students to enrich or adjust their interpretation.

*Constructivist view of teachers*: Constructivism holds that teachers should help learners construct knowledge, and they should change their traditional role of knowledge transmitter to the prompter, students' partner, and cooperator. Teachers should provide students with complex questions that they may encounter in real life and create a dynamic and supportive learning environment for learners so that they can learn through experiments, independent exploration, and cooperative learning. In addition, teachers should help and guide students to construct knowledge actively. They should stimulate students' learning interest, trigger and maintain their learning motivation, and help them construct the meaning of knowledge by creating certain learning contexts and clues that promote the connection between the new and previous knowledge. In order to make students' meaning construction more effective, teachers should organize collaborative learning activities as much as possible, such as discussion and communication, and they should guide the process of collaborative learning, so as to make it conducive to students' meaning construction.

**Table 3-1** Comparison between Traditional and Constructive Classroom Teaching

| Traditional classroom teaching | Constructive classroom teaching |
|---|---|
| The transmission of course content is from part to whole, and it stresses the mastery of basic skills. | The presentation of course content is from whole to part, and it stresses the mastery of core concepts. |
| It emphasizes that teachers should adhere to the sequence of course content. | It encourages teachers to answer students' questions. |
| Teaching activities should be organized according to the teaching material and the exercise book. | Teaching activities should be organized according to the learning materials. |
| Students are seen as a whiteboard, and teachers are people who etch information on this whiteboard. | Students are regarded as thoughtful people who have their own views on the world around them. |
| Teachers are regarded as a preacher who imparts information to the students. | Teachers are regarded as persons who create a supportive learning environment for students. |

*(Continued)*

| Traditional classroom teaching | Constructive classroom teaching |
|---|---|
| Teachers usually promote students' effective learning by asking students to look for the answers. | In order to understand the effect of concepts that students have mastered on future learning, teachers often actively inquire students' questions. |
| Assess students' learning through tests that are separate from teaching activities. | Assessment is carried out with teaching, and the methods of assessment include not only observation, but also students' portfolios which record their performance and learning. |
| Learning is students' own business | Learning is usually done in small groups |

Source: C. T. Fosnot, ***Theory, Perspectives, and Practice*** (New York and London: Teachers College Press, 1996), 17.

**Table 3-2** Comparison between Behavioristic and Constructive Classroom Teaching

| Behavioristic classroom teaching | Constructive classroom teaching |
|---|---|
| Review: review what students learned yesterday and check their homework. | Encourage students to solve problems by themselves. |
| Knowledge presentation: emphasize the objectives of the course, provide learning materials for students step by step, and keep pace with students' development. | Help students form the habit of inquiring by inducing them to solve problems. |
| Purposeful practice: students practice under the supervision of teachers, and teachers check students' understanding. | Develop students' reflective ability by asking students to solve problems and explain answers. |
| Feedback: teachers offer fast and strict feedback to students. | Through case studies, students can understand the methods of dealing with problems and avoiding wrong concepts. |
| Individual practice: students finish the assignment by themselves. | If the students can't solve the problem, the teacher should consult with the students to formulate a possible scheme and guide the students to think about it; If students encounter setbacks, teachers should lower the difficulty level of the problem. |
| Review: students need to review what they have learned systematically once a week or a month. | Once students solve the problem, teachers should encourage them to reflect and evaluate the solution to the problem and point out what students have done well. |

Source: R. I. Arends et al., *Exploring Teaching: An Introduction to Education*, 2nd ed. (Boston: McGraw-Hill Higher Education, 2001).

### 3.1.2 Constructivist View of the Basic Principles of Classroom Teaching

Why should teachers be encouraged to choose the theoretical paradigm of constructivism in today's classroom teaching? Brooks's view is that once teachers realize the impulse of human beings to construct knowledge and new understanding, students will create limitless possibilities for knowing things.[3]

Therefore, in the classroom guided by constructivism, teachers' teaching ideas and the application of teaching strategies are very different from traditional teaching. The comparisons in Tables 3-1 and 3-2 have provided us with a framework for understanding the difference. The four basic principles of constructivist classroom teaching proposed by Brooks provide theoretical guidance for our further understanding of constructivism. The four principles are:[4]

Create appropriate contexts. Although not all students who come to the classroom have a primitive interest in learning verb structure, movement and machinery, biological cycle, and historical events, most students can construct an understanding of these topics under the guidance of teachers. As long as teachers can create appropriate contexts for students, students will be affected by such contexts, and then actively participate in the corresponding learning and practical activities.

Deal with the relationship between learning time and learning scope. In general, the amount of time spent on learning is proportional to the scope of learning. Of course, requiring teachers to transmit more knowledge to students in a short period of time has always been characteristic of the traditional teaching method, but traditional teaching features fragmented teaching of knowledge, and it relies on tests to evaluate students 'learning results. In this way, the fragmented learning content and the limited scope of the test content will affect the students' overall grasp of knowledge. Therefore, in the constructivist classroom, teachers are required to deal with the relationship between learning time and the learning scope, and advocate expanding the scope of learning through big questions within a certain period of time to deepen students' understanding of problems.

We should teach for the transfer of knowledge. Bruner, the early representative of constructivism, actively advocated promoting the transfer of students' learning through the teaching of the basic structure of the discipline. Brooks, the representative of constructivism recently, emphasizes learning for transfer. In fact, there are many strategies that can be used to promote students' learning transfer activities, such as early "structural learning" and "advance organizer model," recent "big concept" learning, and "anchor" learning. As a teacher who applies constructivism theory in classroom teaching, the key is to reasonably select appropriate strategies according to the characteristics of students and the requirements of learning tasks in order to achieve the goal of learning transfer.

Understanding the value of changing students' original thoughts. Constructivism deems that student' thought and their concepts are not all right. Teachers are bound to recognize the meaning of changing students' original recognition through teaching.

### 3.1.3 Constructivist View of Teacher's Teaching Behaviors

Becoming a constructivist teacher is the title used in many books and articles about education in the United States. Thus, educational researchers pay attention to the application of the constructivist theory in classroom teaching and the expectation for teachers.

Although not all classroom teachers in public primary and secondary schools in the United States have the concept of constructivism and consistent practical ability, the strong impact of this theory on classroom teaching reform is no less than that of multiple intelligence theory and reflective teaching theory.

Of course, in primary and secondary schools in the United States, not all teachers are willing to accept the theory of constructivism and practice it in their own classrooms. On the one hand, it is due to the influence of traditional ideas; on the other hand, it is challenging to become a constructivist teacher who can help students explore the truth rather than just let students accept the knowledge passively. So, what are the characteristics of constructivist teachers' teaching behavior? Based on the research of others, Brooks summarizes 12 characteristics of constructivist teachers' teaching behavior, which provides us with a useful framework for understanding constructivist teaching. These 12 characteristics are as follows:[5]

(1) Constructivist teachers encourage and allow their students to be their own masters and keep autonomy in the process of teaching.

(2) Constructivist teachers usually use firsthand data and materials for teaching.

(3) Constructivist teachers always use terms like "classification," "analysis," "prediction," and "creation" to construct learning tasks.

(4) Constructivist teachers allow students to control the process of classroom teaching and change teaching strategies and teaching contents.

(5) Constructivist teachers usually ask students to seek their own understanding before they teach students the meaning of the concepts.

(6) Constructivist teachers encourage communication and dialogue between students and teachers and between students.

(7) Constructivist teachers encourage students to inquire about the nature of things through thoughtful and open questions and mutual questioning among students.

(8) Constructivist teachers encourage students to achieve the best understanding of a problem by inquiring into the details of the problem.

(9) Constructivist teachers encourage students to experience things they are not familiar with and then develop their own understanding through further discussion.

(10) Constructivist teachers always give students time to think after asking questions.

(11) Constructivist teachers leave more time for students to comprehend the relation of knowledge and encourage them to innovate.

(12) Constructivist teachers often use the cycle of learning activities to satisfy students' curiosity.

The above-mentioned twelve characteristics give expression that the teaching orientation and teaching target of constructivist teachers is to help students shape their own understanding of knowledge rather than meditate and act in the wake of others' logic. These twelve characteristics can also be regarded as the goals for constructivist teachers and the basic standards to evaluate constructivist teachers.

### 3.1.4 The Proper Attitude toward Constructive Theory

There exists an extreme tendency in the understanding of educational theories: one is to only pay attention to the advantages but ignore the weak points, and the other is the reverse. In other words, some people are likely to change from this extreme point to another in treating problems.

In other words, some people tend to go from one extreme to the other when looking at problems. When a theory becomes popular or becomes the mainstream theory, it is usually overestimated, especially in Chinese people's understanding of Western educational theories.

Undoubtedly, it is very necessary to learn from foreign theories, but we must keep a clear mind and evaluate and learn from foreign theories with a proper attitude. We should see the importance of enlightenment of constructivist learning and teaching theory to China's basic education curriculum reform. Its brand-new concept of knowledge, learning, curriculum, teaching, and evaluation has brought us the theoretical basis for re-understanding and positioning the curriculum and teaching of China's basic education. But at the same time, we must also know that constructivist theory is not perfect. It can only be regarded as one of the theories that inspire us to reform, and the application of this theory in primary and secondary school classrooms in China still needs the support of various conditions.

In the process of implementing the new curriculum standards, schools should not only create possible conditions for the classroom practice of constructivism, but also give full play to the advantages of traditional teaching strategies in combination with practice, so that teachers can achieve the goal of the new curriculum on the basis of appropriate selection of teaching strategies. As the American scholar said: "What does this new teaching theory mean for a normal student who is about to take the post of a teacher? It means that you should master not only the traditional teaching methods, such as direct method and lecturing, but also the new teaching strategies, such as problem-solving and cooperative learning advocated by constructivism."[6] It can be seen that although Americans emphasize the new learning and teaching theory, they do not completely deny the role of traditional teaching methods. This is the proper attitude we should take towards the theory and practice of constructivism.

## 3.2 Multiple Intelligence Theory and Classroom Teaching Reform

Intelligence, as an important factor affecting human development and success, has always been a concern in the field of psychology and education. "Defining intelligence has taken a lot of time and effort."[7] As early as ancient Greece, the famous philosopher and educator Aristotle pointed out that people have two kinds of mental abilities: one is the ability to quickly understand the causes and situations of things, and the other is the ability to make appropriate moral choices.[8] Since modern times, researchers have paid more and more attention to intelligence in the field of psychology, and psychologists from various countries have made various definitions of intelligence and its structure. For example, Spearman's two-factor theory and Funan's intelligence level theory in Britain, Seton's group factor theory and Milford's wisdom structure theory in the United States, Gardner's theory of multiple intelligence, Professor Zhu Zhixian's three-factor theory of intelligence and Professor Yan Guocai's five-factor theory of intelligence. Among the theories about intelligence and its structure, the theory of multiple intelligence put forward by American education professor Gardner is favored by people. After entering the new century, Gardner's theory of multiple intelligences has attracted more and more attention from not only educational researchers, but also classroom teachers. In the United States, "interest in the theory of multiple intelligences has been increasing in recent years. You will see a lot of information on this topic on the Internet."[9] At present, multiple intelligences and constructivism have not only become two important theoretical bases for many American schools to guide students' learning and teachers' classroom teaching reform, but also have an impact on the classroom teaching reform of primary and secondary schools in other countries.[10]

### 3.2.1 Comparison between the Theory of Multiple Intelligence and Traditional Intelligence

The theory of multiple intelligence was put forward in 1983 by the educational professor Howard Garnder at Harvard University in his book *Frames of Mind* and was further improved in his later studies. After studying the traditional theories of intelligence, Garnder pointed out the traditional concept of intelligence, which is based on the intelligence quotient (IQ) test has great limitations. Because according to the traditional definition of intelligence, most people believe that: ① human cognition is unitary; ② individual intelligence is single and countable. On the contrary, Gardner regards intelligence as ① people's ability to solve problems encountered in real life; ② people's ability to put forward new problems to be solved; ③ people's ability to create the value of certain cultural products.[11] For the comparison between traditional intelligence and multiple intelligence, please see Table 3-3. Based on the analysis and criticism of traditional intelligence theory, Gardner defined human intelligence as seven distinct types in 1983. Ten years later, Gardner put forward a new type of intelligence in 1993, which constitutes his theory of multiple intelligences.

**Table 3-3** Comparison between Traditional Intelligence Theory and New Intelligence Theory

| Traditional view of intelligence | New view of intelligence |
|---|---|
| Intelligence is fixed. | Intelligence can be developed. |
| Intelligence can be measured by numbers. | Intelligence is not measured by numbers, but in the process of completing an activity or solving a problem. |
| Intelligence is unitary. | Intelligence can be demonstrated in many ways—multiple intelligences. |
| Intelligence can be measured in isolation. | Intelligence can be measured in real-life situations. |
| Intelligence can be used to distinguish between good and bad students and to predict their success. | Intelligence can be used to understand people's abilities and the different abilities that students can acquire. |

Source: *So Each May Learn*, 7.

According to Garnder's multiple intelligence theory, human intelligence may include the following eight types, namely Verbal-Linguistic Intelligence (V), Logical-Mathematical Intelligence (L), Spatial Intelligence (S), Musical Intelligence (M), Bodily-Kinesthetic Intelligence (B), Interpersonal Intelligence (P), Intrapersonal Intelligence (I), and Naturalist Intelligence (N).[12]

(1) Verbal-Linguistic Intelligence (V) is the ability to express ideas both orally and in written form. A person with strong linguistic intelligence can freely communicate with others and engage in writing activities. Politicians, press spokesmen,

storytellers, program hosts, journalists, writers, poets, editors of magazines, and teaching staff can show their distinctive linguistic intelligence. People with high linguistic intelligence can not only effectively engage in listening, speaking, reading and writing activities, but also further develop their linguistic intelligence in these activities. Shakespeare, the world-famous writer, can be regarded as a typical representative of people with strong linguistic intelligence.

(2) Logical-Mathematical Intelligence (L) is the ability to go on the digital operation and statistics. This kind of intelligence is critical for those who engage in hard science and all kinds of activities about math and science. Such people as mathematicians, statisticians, tax calculation experts, computer procedure designers, and scientists all possess strong logic ability—mathematical intelligence. People who like to use logic-mathematical intelligence mostly value reasoning. They are usually able to build a model between the cause and effect of how things develop, and then draw a final conclusion through scientific investigation, experimentation, and argumentation. They prefer to think deeply on the basis of existing concepts and problems, then verify their ideas by testing them. Einstein and Galileo are two typical representatives with strong logical-mathematical intelligence.

(3) Spatial Intelligence (S) mainly refers to the ability to perceive, create and recreate pictures and imagine pictures. People who have good spatial intelligence and often use spatial intelligence can often extract some basic or even abstract ideas from complex pictures, graphics, and charts. They can also express a profound idea in the form of art. Generally speaking, photographers, painters, engineers, architects, and sculptors have good spatial intelligence. For example, Picasso is a representative in this regard.

(4) Musical Intelligence (M) refers to people's ability to create beautiful tunes and rhythms, understand and appreciate beauty, and form a feeling and evaluation of beauty on this basis. People who like singing and using music to express their thoughts and feelings can show their special musical intelligence. People with good musical intelligence will show different sensitivity to all kinds of nonverbal sounds and rhythms they hear in their daily life. Music lovers, composers, and instrument players all have good musical intelligence.

(5) Bodily-Kinesthetic Intelligence (B) is the operation ability in relation to individual physical strength. People who obtain this kind of intelligence can not only express their views and emotion with their bodies, but also can make themselves more comfortable carrying out different physical movements. In addition, these people may prefer to challenge their own bodies; in other words, they keep enhancing their bodily-kinesthetic intelligence in activities and sports. Actors, athletes, dancers, surgeons, mechanicians, painters, sculptors, comic performers, and acrobats have good bodily-kinesthetic intelligence.

(6) Interpersonal Intelligence (P) refers to the ability of a person to quickly understand the tone, intention, motivation, and emotion of others, and communicate with others. People with good interpersonal intelligence are usually able to get along with others in harmony, and can quickly perceive and grasp others' moods, attitudes, and wishes in the process of getting along with others. People of this type often display the characteristics of being friendly to people and extroverted. Most people with good interpersonal intelligence know how to get along with others. Generally speaking, excellent team members in a group and excellent managers in a company can show their good interpersonal intelligence.

(7) Introspective Intelligence (I) refers to one's ability to understand himself or herself and to adjust his or her emotion properly. People with good introspective intelligence prefer to choose work that they can accomplish independently, because they fully trust their understanding of things and adjust their actions accordingly. They are always able to perceive their inner feelings and achieve their goals. They can not only comprehensively estimate their advantages and disadvantages, but also have strong self-discipline ability.

(8) Naturalist Intelligence (N) is the latest intelligence proposed by Gardner in 1999 in his work *The New Structure of Intelligence: Multiple Intelligence for the 21st Century*. It refers to a person's appreciation and understanding of the natural environment in which human beings live. People with good natural intelligence are inclined to outdoor activities and observation. They are unwilling to destroy the relationship between human beings and the natural environment. They like natural things, such as rocks, clouds, and stars. They also like to explore the characteristics, laws, and irregularities of the development and change of nature. The world-famous scientist Darwin is a typical example.

Each of the above eight types of intelligence has its own distinctive features, which are shown in Table 3-4. However, these kinds of intelligence are not fixed for everyone. As professor Gardner has underlined that all of us are possible to own these kinds of intelligence and use or develop them in different situations.[13] Of course, most people may display their distinctive intelligence levels in one or several domains.

Although many scholars have emphasized the need to understand and define intelligence from a broader perspective, Gardner's theory of multiple intelligences is indeed a very convincing theory, mainly because of the rich subject knowledge as the foundation of his research. He not only applies knowledge and principles from anthropology, cognitive psychology, developmental psychology, biology, psychometric testing, physiology, and neurology to the study of human intelligence, but also uses a rigorous system of criteria to identify and classify human skills and talents.

**Table 3-4** Characteristics of the Eight Types of Intelligence

| Type of intelligence | Characteristics (Sensitive aspects) | Tendency (Love aspects) | Ability (Things be good at) |
|---|---|---|---|
| Verbal-Linguistic Intelligence (V) | Sound, Semantics, Structure of Language, and Ways of Language | Listening, speaking, reading, and writing | People with this intelligence are able to communicate effectively (e.g., teachers, religious leaders, politicians) and write effectively (poets, novelists, editors). |
| Logical-Mathematical Intelligence (L) | Mode, number, data, cause, result, objective, and quantitative reasoning | Establishing models, conducting calculus, proposing and verifying hypotheses, and applying scientific methods to inductive and deductive reasoning | People with this intelligence are able to perform effective numerical operations (e.g., accountants, statisticians, economists) and effective reasoning (e.g., engineers, scientists, and computer programs). |
| Spatial Intelligence (S) | Color, shape, visual network, symmetrical graphics, lines, and imagination | Expressing visual ideas, creative imagination, paying attention to visual detail, painting, and sculpture | People with this intelligence are able to perform effective visual creation (e.g., painters, photographers, engineers, and decorators) and accurate visual orientation (e.g., tour guides, scouts, rangers). |
| Bodily-Kinesthetic Intelligence (B) | Touch, exercise, self-adjustment, and athletics | Activities requiring strength, speed and flexibility, activities requiring hand-eye coordination | People with this intelligence are able to effectively use their hands to repair or for creative activities (e.g., mechanics, surgeons, and masons) and participate in physical expressive activities (e.g., dancers, actors, track, and field athletes). |
| Musical Intelligence (M) | Melody, striking sound, beat, tone, and sound | Listening, singing, and playing musical instruments | People with this intelligence are able to create music effectively (e.g., lyricist, composer, musician, and orchestra conductor) and analyze music (Music Analyst). |

*(Continued)*

| Type of intelligence | Characteristics (Sensitive aspects) | Tendency (Love aspects) | Ability (Things be good at) |
|---|---|---|---|
| Interpersonal Intelligence (P) | Body language, mood, voice, and emotion | Paying attention to other people's emotions and personalities and being able to respond on time | People with this intelligence are able to get along well with others (e.g., managers, managers, psychological and educational counselors, and teachers) and help others analyze and solve problems (e.g., psychiatrists and psychologists). |
| Intrapersonal Intelligence (I) | One's own strengths, weaknesses, goals, and aspirations | Setting goals, evaluating individual abilities and responsibilities, and checking one's own thoughts | People with this intelligence are able to think deeply, reflect, and have self-discipline, and they are good at keeping calm. |
| Naturalist Intelligence (N) | Natural objects, animals and plants, problems occurring in nature, ecological problems | Identifying and classifying natural objects and living things | People with this intelligence have the ability to analyze natural and ecological phenomena and data (e.g., ecologists and foresters), to study living organisms and obtain relevant results (e.g., zoologists and botanists), to work or act in the natural environment (e.g., hunters and investigators) Can work and live in the natural environment (such as hunters and investigators). |

Source: Harvey F. Silver et al., *So Each May Learn: Integrating Learning Styles and Multiple Intelligences* (ASCD products, 2000), 11.

### 3.2.2 Enlightenment of Multiple Intelligence Theory to Teaching Reform

Though multiple intelligence is not a study or teaching theory, experts have already given kinds of explanations of intelligence and its composition. Gardner's theory of multiple intelligence immediately attracted a great deal of attention from the psychological and educational communities in the United States and around the world, and soon evoked positive reactions in the field of classroom teaching practice in American primary and secondary schools.

After entering the new century, many teachers at the front line of education maintain a high level of enthusiasm for the theory of multiple intelligence and its guiding role in classroom teaching reform, which is certainly a need to reform traditional teaching. As the American professor Thomas Armstrong says: "At present, the great thing is that the theory of multiple intelligence has attracted the attention of many educators, and lots of schools are applying the physiological thought of this theory to redesign their teaching methods. Unfortunately, however, thousands of schools have yet to move away from the traditional approach. Dull lectures, tedious exercise books, and textbooks that fail to interest pupils still abound." So, what exactly does Gardner's theory of multiple intelligence tell us about classroom reform in American primary and secondary schools?

### *Revamping Teaching Objectives: Updating Concepts for Educators*

According to Gardner's theory, all human beings, provided they are normal, may be born with some of the eight types of intelligence, which are not only variable but can be nurtured and developed through education and teaching. However, in Gardner's view, American schooling and culture always focus on verbal-language intelligence and logical-mathematical intelligence but ignore other types of intelligence. He thinks that it is necessary to respect people with clear pronunciation, fluent language, and strong mathematical logic, but also to value people who demonstrate talent in other areas of intelligence, such as artists, architects, musicians, naturalists, designers, dancers, psychiatrists and those who enrich the world in which we live. As a saying goes that "In practice, there are indeed many different types of excellence, and a wise society should encourage not only scholarly people but also bricklayers."[14] Unfortunately, many children with developmental talents in these areas do not receive more reinforcement in the schools where they are being educated. Instead, what they may receive is frustration or discouragement. Some children may even end up in the category of 'learning disabled' and lose their opportunities for development because of teachers' stereotypical attitudes and the use of single-issue teaching strategies.[15] Thus, according to the theory of multiple intelligence, Gardner asks teachers to change their traditional teaching views to establish the idea that every child has a different intellectual development space, to reflect on their teaching activities and teaching strategies constantly, and to adopt multiple strategies to conduct teaching based on a full understanding of the students' intellectual development so that every child has the opportunity to choose the way of learning according to his or her own intellectual characteristics.

### *Enhancing Learning: Innovative Concepts and Strategies for Teachers*

In fact, there is no single theoretical solution or convention that can be adapted to a wide range of situations and achieve optimal teaching and learning outcomes. To make a theory more instructive, you must use more methods or ways to implement it. In practice, effective teaching always strives to use a variety of strategies to achieve its goals. And the same should be true of using multiple intelligence theory to guide teachers' teaching and students' learning. The important revelation of multiple intelligence theory to teaching lies in: Teachers should choose the appropriate learning methods and teaching strategies according to the content of teaching and the practical flexibility of students, making teaching practice more effective.

As professor Armstrong pointed out: "One of the distinctive features of the theory of multiple intelligence is that it offers students eight potential pathways to learning. If a teacher has a problem in teaching within the traditional linguistic or logical method, he should vary the methods so as to facilitate effective learning with regard to the theory of multiple intelligences."[16] In addition, the theory of multiple intelligence provides teachers with a strong theoretical support for the use of diverse assessment and the design of integrated and interdisciplinary curricula. In other words, according to the theory of multiple intelligence, teachers should assess not only the cognitive abilities of students but also their other abilities, so that students can develop in a holistic manner.

### 3.2.3 Classroom Teaching Practice of Multiple Intelligence

The significance of Gardner's multiple intelligence theory in teaching can be concluded into two sides: one is that classroom teaching should keep an eye on the development of students' multiple intelligence, i.e., teaching for the sake of developing students' multiple intelligences. The other is that teachers should design and organize teaching activities on the basis of multiple intelligence, that is, to teach through multiple intelligence. The former can be regarded as Gardner's new idea about the orientation of teaching objectives. And the latter can be seen as the teaching strategy teachers should pursue and select under the guidance of the new idea.

#### *Theme-Based Teaching for Multiple Intelligences*

Silver et al. suggest that the theory of multiple intelligence can be used to design content and activities when teaching themes. Teachers can use a graph or Curriculum Wheel to combine multiple intelligences with course content, in which way they can not only get to use and develop students' multiple intelligences, but also help to strengthen the links between the content. For instance, when a teacher teaches the topic of "endangered species," he can design a Curriculum Wheel based on multiple intelligence to carry out his teaching. This is done by dividing the content of the topic into eight aspects, each of which is linked to one intelligence, so that students can apply and develop multiple intelligences when learning about the topic. The following is the specific design of eight aspects:

(1) Let students discuss the subject of "endangered species" and then consult materials to create a tabloid on this topic (Verbal-Linguistic Intelligence)
(2) Let students analyze a case of endangered species, and make sure the reasons causing this phenomenon, then to further analyze and compare two animals, such as tigers and pandas (Logical-Mathematical Intelligence)
(3) Organize students to watch a tape named live in nature and draw animals in the field study (Spatial Intelligence)
(4) Ask students to do role play or organize them to travel in the wild environment (Bodily-Kinesthetic Intelligence)
(5) Let students think about the following two questions: "why the natural environment is important for your existence?" and "How do you feel about a species that is endangered?" (Intrapersonal Intelligence)
(6) Let students sing songs about the topic of "endangered species" (Musical Intelligence)
(7) Divide students into groups to complete a themed newspaper and design a plan to protect animals in their groups (Interpersonal Intelligence)
(8) Allow students to take a field trip to the local ecology or organize a trip to a primeval forest (Natural Intelligence)[17]

According to Professor Armstrong, many thematic activities can be designed according to the theory of multiple intelligence, which not only helps to increase students' interest and motivation in learning and develop their multiple intelligences, but also integrates the knowledge and principles learned through multiple intelligences. For example, to teach students the topic of the moon, teachers can ask students to read books about the moon (using and developing linguistic intelligence), calculate the distance from the earth to the moon (using and developing logical mathematical intelligence), to observe pictures of the shape of the moon at different times (using and developing spatial intelligence), to listen to songs about the moon (using and developing musical intelligence), recalling memories or impressions of the moon from childhood (using and developing introspective intelligence), building a model of the moon revolving around the earth (using and developing physical movement intelligence), making a plan with a friend to observe the moon through a telescope (using and developing interpersonal intelligence), studying and examining the topography and landforms of the moon (using and developing naturalistic intelligence).[18] Of course, teachers do not have to use all eight methods, but they should at least select from those which are appropriate to the characteristics of their students and that they think are effective. This is because different teaching methods can be used to develop different intellectual abilities. For example, the didactic method is good for the development of verbal and mathematical and logical intelligence, while role-playing is good for the development of linguistic, interpersonal, and introspective intelligence.[19]

***Leveraging Prior Intelligence for Effective Learning***

People often use their strongest intelligence to consider and complete the work they are going to do. This phenomenon is called "Translation." In practice, some people cannot read a road map described in words, but when they look at a map of the route, they can immediately point out exactly how to reach their destination. Perhaps this is the opposite for you. Obviously, different people could choose different types of intelligences to complete the same task because they have different intelligence structures. In this way, according to the theory of multiple intelligences, teachers should allow students to use their superior intelligences to carry out learning activities when organizing or guiding students to study. The teacher's task is to provide students with as many options and methods as possible to help them master the content they are to learn effectively. For example, in American primary classrooms, many teachers are using a strategy known as Visualizing Vocabulary to teach language. The gist of this strategy is: if a teacher teaches spelling the way of showing pictures, then a student with higher Spatial Intelligence would learn better than a student with higher Verbal-Linguistic Intelligence. This strategy is characterized by making full use of students' superior intelligence to support their own weaker intelligence in learning, thus achieving twice the result with half the effort.

***Exploring Broader Themes with Multiple Intelligences***

The new strategy of applying multiple intelligence theory into teaching is advocated by Gardner in his book *The Disciplined Mind: What All Students Should Understand*, which was published in 1999. That is to say, teachers should take this theory as the main approach for students to understand a broader theme field. In this book, Gardner advocates that the school curriculum should be designed around themes or phenomena that he calls 'icebergs' topics—such as human evolution, Mozart's music, and so on, which are all rich resources for learning. Gardner believes that the current school curriculum should be designed around these broad, life-giving themes. Teachers and students should have a deeper understanding of these themes, which are linked to truth, goodness, and beauty. From this perspective, multiple intelligence would be an effective tool or pathway to help students access these themes, explore their complexity, and understand and argue for them in depth.

Although there are still a number of social science research scholars who adhere to the traditional view of intelligence and have raised some doubts about the theory of multiple intelligences, Gardner's theory has indeed gained widespread acceptance among educationalists, learning theorists, sociologists, and psychologists. Some study results show that the theory of multiple intelligence is valued by most people not only because it provides new thoughts and ways to deeply understand intelligence in a broader meaning, but also because it provides a wide range of teachers with new ideas for changing traditional teaching methods such as using lectures, textbooks, written assignments, and formulae operations, and it also opens up teachers' vision in applying teaching strategies and using a variety of teaching methods to conduct teaching activity. It is undoubted that Gardner's this theory would make great enlightenment for Chinese primary and middle school classroom teaching reform in the new century.

## 3.3 The Concepts and Characteristics of Effective Teaching

Nowadays, in the study field of international teaching theories, the study of effective teaching has already been one of the four hot spots in the international study of teaching. The other three are the study of constructive teaching, the study of multiple intelligence teaching, and the study of reflective teaching. The reason why people are so concerned about effective teaching research is that teaching is the basic way to achieve educational and curriculum goals. With an advanced curriculum concept and ideal curriculum plan, there must also be teaching concepts and strategies to implement the curriculum effectively; otherwise, the curriculum will not be able to achieve its intended ideal goals, not to mention its effect of creating and adding value. Some experts have pointed out that although China's new round of basic education curriculum reform has entered the stage of full-scale promotion after extensive experiments, our primary and secondary school teaching still faces the outstanding problem of "teachers teaching hard and students learning painfully" to a large extent. In regard to this phenomenon, the experts suggest that one of the solutions to get out of this dilemma is to equip our teachers with the concept of effective teaching and master the strategies or techniques of effective teaching. Then, what is effective teaching? What features does it have? How to study and understand effective teaching appropriately? These are all questions we should resolve one by one. In recent years, even though there have been some studies and investigations in this field in our country, the results still cannot meet the demands of guiding teachers in the effective implementation of the new curriculum. This section attempts to explore a basic understanding of several issues of effective teaching based on a systematic examination and analysis of Western research on effective teaching.

### 3.3.1 The Concepts of Effective Teaching

After the 1950s, with the rise of the Western movement for the scientification of teaching and the approval of teaching effectiveness, a range of concepts to describe good teaching emerged in research on teaching. Typical examples are good or excellent teachers, veteran teachers, good enough teachers, good teaching, effective teaching, creative teaching, quality teaching, expert teaching, and so on.[20] However, a systematic review of the literature reveals that effective teaching/instruction is an early and richly researched area of contemporary Western teaching research.

Thus, what is effective teaching? This question is generally considered the first question to be answered in the study of effective teaching. And this seems to be a custom in teaching research at home. However, in contemporary Western discussions and research on effective teaching, scholars have defined and analyzed the concept and nature of effective teaching far less than they have listed the characteristics of effective teaching (including the characteristics of effective teachers). We read 96 studies (including papers, books, and chapters) with the terms "effective teaching," "effective teaching and learning," and "effective teachers" as their subject matter and found that only a small number of scholars had provided a brief description or analysis of 'what effective teaching is' or 'what effective teaching entails,' accounting for about 20% of the total literature. This means that not all the scholars who study effective teaching would define or analyze its conception. The possible reasons are as follows: firstly, some scholars think that effective teaching as an accepted term through common practice has been universally known, and it doesn't need to be explained in detail. Secondly, it is considered more difficult to define effective teaching conceptually than to list a range of characteristics of effective teaching. Thirdly, people also think it is not an easy job to conclude effective teaching by using just one sentence since teaching is a rather complex activity. In addition, it is argued that it is not important to explain what effective teaching is, but rather to study its features as this is more meaningful for further practice. There are some scholars who argue that good teaching is difficult to define because different teaching institutions and different teachers have different standards, and that a uniform model of the ideal teacher or teaching does not exist.

Though it is a hard job or an extremely arduous task to explain exactly the concept and the essence of effective teaching, there are still some researchers who have tried to define it. Here, based on the research literature available to the author, we can summarise Western scholars' explanations of effective teaching into four basic orientations.

### *Definitions Focusing on Teaching Objectives*

Some scholars hold that effective teaching means teachers encourage students to get a high grade through a series of variable quantities. Effective teachers always have the achievement of the teaching target in mind. It has also been argued that effective teaching and learning is teaching and learning that leads to active participation in intellectual learning; effective teaching and learning is teaching and learning that stimulates students' desire to learn, promotes their appreciation, active acquisition of knowledge, communication and teamwork skills, problem-solving skills, acquisition of critical thinking skills and lifelong learning attitudes.[21] Some other scholars consider effective teaching as teaching in which students successfully achieve predetermined learning objectives under the guidance of the teacher. There are two factors essentially restricting effective teaching. One is that teachers have to be clear about what kind of study they want to promote; the other is that teachers should arrange and provide learning experiences for students to obtain this kind of study.[22] It is easy to see that definitions focusing on teaching objectives emphasize the achievement of the intended teaching objectives. In other words, effective teaching is judged by the extent to which the teaching objectives are achieved.

### *Definitions Looking at Teaching Skills*

George Brown and his fellow's definition of effective teaching in his work *Effective Teaching in Higher Education* is mostly from the complexity of teaching and teaching skills of teachers. They argue that effective teaching should be understood in at least two ways: firstly, that effective teaching is complex, intellectually demanding, and socially challenging work; secondly, that effective teaching is accomplished by a range of accessible, refinable, and developable teaching skills. They further state that effective teaching is a requirement for intelligence. It requires teachers to have an extensive and profound grasp of their subject content. If teachers are to teach effectively, they must have good thinking skills, problem-solving skills, the ability to select and analyze the topics they teach, the ability to reflect on whether they have used appropriate teaching strategies, and the ability to select optimal teaching strategies and sound teaching materials, as well as the ability to organize and construct their own ideas, information, and tasks. All of these do not occur in a vacuum, but are requirements of authentic teaching situations. Further, they argue that effective teaching is a social challenge because it takes place not only within certain organizational structures, but also in the context of challenging traditional teaching purposes and teaching values. Above all, effective teaching requires teachers who are well informed about the intellectual background of their students, who are able to communicate clearly with them, and who are able to stimulate students to actively learn and think, and thus to ask valuable or challenging questions of their teachers.[23]

It is clear that Brown et al. believe that effective teaching relies on the teacher's mastery of subject knowledge, understanding of student learning, and choice of appropriate teaching strategies. However, they also know that effective teaching depends not only on teaching but also students' active learning.

### *Definitions with an Eye to Academic Achievement*

With the intense voice of American and British governments and ordinary people to the improvement of students' academic achievement in the late 1980s, studies in this field started to increase. Especially since 2000, under the press of President Bush, the US Congress has demanded that all states should place a high priority on improving student academic achievement and try to achieve that no child is left behind. In the UK, "raising standards for student achievement in mathematics through effective mathematics teaching is now high on the national agenda."[24] This has led researchers to throw their sights on the relationship between effective teaching and students' academic achievement.

In addition, some scholars deem that effective teaching is fundamentally about teachers creating learning activities, organizing learning tasks, and providing learning experiences for students so that they acquire the desired knowledge, skills, understanding, and attitudes. It encompasses both effective teacher behavior and effective teaching and learning management.[25] They argue that the emphasis on different domains leads to different definitions or interpretations of effective teaching and learning. If the key point is put in the factor of teaching input, then the judgment standard must necessarily point more to the characteristics of teachers and students, such as the size of the class, educational background, educational experience, and teachers' individual quality. Provided that the key point is put in the factor of process, effective teaching is often judged by the teacher's classroom organization, classroom management, and classroom activities. If the emphasis is on the industrial element of teaching, then effective teaching is judged by student achievement. However, in Braskamp et al.'s view, none of these aspects can be the only factor in measuring effective teaching and learning, and the correct approach is to think and judge in a holistic manner.

***Definitions with a View to the Whole Process of Teaching***

The book *Evaluating Teaching Effectiveness: A Practical Guide* by Cosme Porras and his fellows who work in the center of educational measurement and evaluation at the University of Illinois not only gives reflection and criticism of the former different definitions and research results of effective teaching, but also puts forward a new view of effective teaching with a view to the whole process of teaching.

They argue that defining good teaching either in terms of teacher quality or in terms of teachers' use of teaching strategies is single-minded and incomplete. And they believe that the definition of good teaching should be analyzed from the perspective of teaching assessment. Accordingly, effective teaching should be interpreted and defined in terms of three dimensions (domains). These three domains are the input of teaching, the process of teaching, and the output of teaching.[26]

**Input**

(1) Students' features (e.g., class level, area of expertise)
(2) Teachers' features (e.g., title, gender, teaching subjects)
(3) Features of course (e.g., size and scope)

**Process**

(1) Classroom atmosphere
(2) Teachers' behavior
(3) Students' learning activities
(4) Course organization
(5) Evaluation steps

**Output**

(1) Outcomes of a course of study, changes in attitudes, development of skills

(2) Outcomes of a semester or academic year of student learning, changes in attitudes, acquisition of skills

We can at least get a conclusion after a review of the literature: There is no single interpretation of effective teaching and learning, and it is equally difficult to find an optimal definition or framework for defining it. The developing trend is explained from the perspective of students' successful learning achievement. For this reason, we can assume that effective teaching is a teaching method that can improve students learning and development in the view of Western scholars. In other words, effective teaching is a teaching method that promotes students' learning and development through the effective preparation of teaching, effective teaching activities, and effective teaching assessment.

### 3.3.2 The Historical Exploration of Effective Teaching Study

In order to further illustrate the different definitions of effective teaching by Western scholars mentioned above, it is necessary to examine the historical development of the research, from which not only the different perspectives of the research can be found, but also the basic direction and development trajectory of the research. According to research literature, since the early 1930s, western scholars have begun to identify and describe the characteristics of effective teachers in experimental studies. Based on the author's review of the relevant research literature, we can broadly divide the development of its study into three basic stages.

*Studies of the Qualities of Good Teachers (from the Early 1930s to Late 60s)*

As early as 1931, Cattell conducted interviews with educational administrators, teacher trainers, school teachers, and students about the characteristics of a good teacher. The method was to ask people to write down what they considered to be the most important qualities of a good teacher, and a frequency analysis was carried out to identify the following qualities of a good teacher:[27]

(1) Good personality and strong will

(2) Intelligence

(3) Compassion and wit

(4) Broad-minded

(5) Sense of humor

Soon, educational theorists criticized this attempt to find a relationship between teachers' qualities and educational goals through interviews, calling it a "black box" study.[28] The reason was that such studies totally ignored the fact that teachers' work took place in the classroom, and that it was too simplistic to attempt to extrapolate an output factor of student learning outcomes on the basis of an input factor of teacher characteristics. However, such kind of studies did not stop with criticism. For instance, in 1951, Gilbert Highet presented clearly in his book *The Art of Teaching* three necessary qualities a good teacher must possess: Firstly, teachers should own solid subject knowledge and keep studying; Secondly, teachers have to love his/her teaching subject and be full of enthusiasm to teaching; At last, teachers must love students. If a teacher has no good feelings for his/her students, he/she'd better abandon teaching.

In the 1960s, Ryan and his colleagues carried out a program of observational research in which they observed teachers in the classroom and identified the following bipolar factors corresponding to three aspects of effective teaching and learning:[29]

(1) Enthusiasm and understanding—indifference and detachment
(2) Being well organized and properly arranged—no plan and sluggish
(3) Stimulation and imagination—clumsiness and dullness

According to Ryan, the closer a teacher's characteristics are to the positive end of the spectrum, the more effective his or her teaching will be. Conversely, the closer a teacher's characteristics are to the negative end of the spectrum, the less effective his or her teaching will be.

*Studies of the Features of Food Teaching (from the Early 1970s to Late 1980s)*

In the 1960s, there were scholars who started being against the studies of teaching efficiency. As in their viewpoint, "Teaching is a complicated activity conducted in a complicated situation, and it's difficult to confirm teaching efficiency, since the influential factors of effective teaching are various, intricate and complex."[30] However, after entering the 1970s, Western scholars continued to study effective teaching and put forward some propositions about features of good teaching based on their rethink of the research in the 1960s. Some scholars believe that the qualities of good teachers cannot totally represent effective teaching, and the standard to judge effective teaching should be searched in teaching practice. This has led to the study of teachers' classroom behavior, i.e., the characteristics of good classroom teaching. Some representative studies include those by Flanders, Rosenshine and Furst, and Doyle.

The research of Flanders and his colleagues has focused on teaching efficiency. Their study method is to observe two different ways of teaching, namely direct instruction and indirect instruction. According to Flanders, direct instruction is a teaching method in that teachers instruct knowledge to students by ways of lectures, criticism, analysis of authority thought, and impart knowledge to students. Indirect instruction means teachers conduct teaching by asking questions, accepting students' affective responses, admitting their viewpoints, and giving them praise and encouragement. Flanders' research suggests that indirect instruction is more effective than direct instruction in arousing students' interest in learning, reinforcing their attitudes to learning, and making them learn better. However, Flanders also suggests that both direct and indirect teaching are necessary for good teaching.[31] Flanders' study does not exclude direct teaching while emphasizing indirect teaching. However, it is clear that the aim of such research is to determine the effectiveness of teaching by examining the effectiveness of the teaching methods employed by teachers in the classroom.

Rosenshine and Furst (1973) put forward five features of good teaching after systematic observation and research of teachers' classroom teaching behaviors:[32]

(1) Teacher's teaching is full of enthusiasm.
(2) Teachers are quick-witted in teaching and have clear task orientation.
(3) Teacher's expression of teaching content is explicit.
(4) Teachers apply various teaching materials and teaching strategies.
(5) Teachers provide the opportunity for students to learn teaching content.

It's easy to get that the first two features have something in common with the study of Ryan in the 1960s. Features from the third one to the fifth one mainly pay attention to teachers' classroom teaching behaviors, which include the ability of language performance, the ability of selecting teaching materials and teaching strategies, and the ability of arranging teaching activities.

In the late 1970s, there was a new shift in research on good teaching, from the study of teachers' teaching behavior to the study of students' learning behavior. A representative study is a larger study led by American scholars Berliner and Tichenoff in 1976.[33] This study is conducted under the observation of students' learning situation in reading and math classes of elementary and middle schools. The aim is to explore the changes in student learning behaviors induced by effective teaching and learning, and thus to reveal the correlation between teaching behaviors and learning behaviors and outcomes. Researchers take the observation of changes in students' learning behaviors in elementary and middle schools as an effective way to study teaching quality. And after the study, researchers find that there are two fundamental elements that decide teaching efficiency, which is teaching intention (target) and students' achievement. If teaching has no objective, the achievement of students can be said to be occasional, and if students get no achievement, then teaching is far from effective.

Doyle (1987) sums up a set of teachers' behaviors that influence students' study after studying the effects of teachers' teaching behaviors on the learning achievement of students. He thinks if a student has good academic achievement, his/her teacher's teaching would have the following features:[34]

(1) Emphasizing the academic purpose of teaching
(2) Having clear educational goals and hoping students to master what they have learned
(3) Being able to organize and put into effect carefully teaching courses
(4) Being able to explain and illustrate clearly teaching content
(5) Being able to check up students' progress and their comprehension of learning content through direct and concrete quizzes
(6) Providing practice opportunities for students
(7) Ensuring students' success by means of promoting their learning strategies and teaching feedback
(8) Correcting students' false and allowing them to use a skill until they comprehend completely
(9) Reviewing and grasping questions students consider regularly

The study by Doyle shows that effective teachers always accelerate students learning through planning and organizing their teaching effectively.

*Synthetical Study of Effective Teaching (from the 1990s to Present)*

Since the 1990s, research on effective teaching in the West has begun to develop in the direction of synthesis. Specifically, when examining the characteristics of effective teaching and the criteria for effective teaching, scholars have moved away from the single-minded mode of thinking, breaking away from the old circle of focusing only on teacher quality or teacher behavior in the classroom, and attempting to examine effective teaching from various aspects and perspectives. Typical studies include those by the OECD (1994) and Kyriacou (1997).

The study data of OECDO about effective teaching are from five countries: Britain, America, France, Japan, and Australia. The study by this organization shows that teaching quality should be a synthetical conception, and the observation of teacher's teaching efficiency ought to consider at least the following five elements:[35]

(1) Teacher's knowledge of the actual curriculum area and the content to be taught
(2) Teacher's teaching skills, including the awareness and ability of applying effective teaching
(3) Teacher's abilities of teaching reflection, self-criticism, and the quality of their professionalism
(4) Teacher's empathy and his/her morality of respecting others
(5) Teacher's ability of academic administration

In comparison with the above-mentioned studies about effective teaching, the study by OECD first puts subject knowledge into consideration. As in the first two stages of research, subject knowledge isn't regarded as one of the effective teaching standards. But now, curriculum and subject knowledge are taken for precondition and foundation of effective teaching. In addition, the study by OECD cites teachers' teaching reflective ability as one standard of judging effective teaching, which is a newly developed view in the early 1990s. The following is the study by Kyriacou.

Kyriacou concludes ten features of effective teaching in his study after analyzing the kinds of variables affecting teaching as follows:[36]

(1) Clarifying teaching expectations and task orientation
(2) Establishing a classroom atmosphere that regards teaching tasks as a benchmark
(3) Carrying on teaching activities in varied forms
(4) Maintaining the dynamics and consistency of teaching
(5) Encouraging all students to take part in teaching activities
(6) Monitoring students' progress and meeting their needs
(7) Having good classroom structure and order
(8) Providing students with positive and constructive feedback
(9) Ensuring the achievement of students' goals
(10) Using effective skills when asking questions

The above features of effective teaching by Kyriacou put a strong point on teaching activities and students' learning rather than teacher's qualities and their characteristics. This shift in emphasis should be approved in light of current trends in teaching theory and practice.

### 3.3.3 Some Basic Paradigms of Thinking about Effective Teaching

Why are there different findings in Western research on effective teaching? One of the reasons is that people have different ideas of its paradigms. These various paradigms all have their own developing progress, and each of them offers a type of perspective to understand effective teaching. Some representative ones include the context-process-outcome paradigm, surface paradigm, psychological paradigm, and paradigm of knowledge basis of teaching. A brief review of these paradigms is presented below.

*Context-Process-Outcome Paradigm*

Research shows that as early as the 1950s, some young education professionals in the USA used the process—outcome analysis model in an attempt to create effective teacher training programs. They summarize the American training methods of soldiers during WWII, and design training program in order to make all teachers become effective ones.[37] Kyriacou draws lessons from such idea and pose out the context-process-outcome paradigm. He points out that the reflection of effective teaching should take such factors into consideration: teacher's characteristics, interaction between teachers and students in classroom activities, and the resulting pedagogical effects. Finally, he put forward three major variables of effective teaching: context variables (input variables), process variables, and outcome variables (output variables).[38]

Context variables include kinds of input elements that affect teaching and learning activities, which are teacher's characteristics (including personality, social class, and training level), student's characteristics (such as knowledge background and family background), features of subjects, features of class, school, and community. These all can be influential factors in teaching.

Process variables are such influential factors of effective teaching in the process of actual teaching activities. They are as follows:

(1) Teacher's enthusiasm
(2) Clarity of explanation
(3) Application of questioning
(4) Application of encouragement and criticism
(5) Management strategy
(6) Discipline
(7) Classroom atmosphere
(8) Organization of lessons
(9) Types of feedback that students accept
(10) Interaction between teachers and students
(11) Students' learning strategies

Output variables (outcome variables) refer to some elements related to the educational target that teachers hope to achieve, which include teachers' teaching plans and their judgment criterion of teaching result. Some important educational targets students should obtain are as follows:

(1) Increase of knowledge and skills
(2) Increase of students' interest towards subject knowledge
(3) Increase of intelligent motivation
(4) Increase of confidence of subjects and increase of ability of self-criticism
(5) Increase of self-management
(6) Increase of sociality

It's not hard to see that Cyriacou's study tries to build a basic framework for scholars to think and predicate effective teaching via his all-round observation. Some data also show that Cyriacou's study does have an influence on numerous studies about effective teaching. At the same time, however, this paradigm of thinking poses some difficult questions. For example, what are the most important factors that influence the determination of effective teaching? How can we think about the three variables in an organically integrated way? These questions remain to be explored further.

*Surface Paradigm*

The surface paradigm is proposed based on the analysis and observation of the studies about effective teaching. The representatives are Creemers (1994) and Fisher (1995). This kind of paradigm stresses two constructive elements affecting effective teaching, which are active learning time and quality of teaching.[39] The first element emphasizes the quality of learning tasks and activities with an eye to the educational objectives. In nature, this paradigm makes effective teaching equal to time investment in maximum learning activities of students. In other words, the more the actual time investment of students, the higher the quality of learning and the more effective the teacher's teaching will be. The amount of time students actually spend on learning tasks is one of the factors that has been highlighted by previous researchers. Creemers has argued that the actual time investment of students in learning is closely related to the achievement of the educational target. If teachers are able to give students more learning time in the classroom in line with the teaching objectives, rather than wasting time, then the achievement of the teaching objectives will be assured. Accordingly, Clemence indicates that the actual amount of time spent on learning is an important factor in determining whether teaching is effective or not. The second constructive element to judge effective teaching is the quality of teaching, which means making students' learning easier through teaching activities and finally reaching the intended learning targets.

As can be seen, this paradigm emphasizes the complementary relation between actual teaching time and teaching quality. i.e., the more time students actually devote to learning, the easier it is to ensure the quality of teaching. And a teacher's rational teaching arrangement guarantees that the students are actually engaged in their learning, and thus time is not wasted. All in all, this paradigm essentially focuses on the variables of the teaching process.

*Psychological Paradigm*

The psychological paradigm tries to find out the psychological variables related to effective teaching, in order to determine the factors that influence effectiveness. If we say that the surface paradigm analyzes influential factors from the perspective of teaching activities and their process, then the psychological paradigm mainly analyzes effective teaching deeply according to some major psychological concepts in order to identify the psychological conditions necessary for learning activities to occur and develop. According to the basic view of this paradigm, if certain process variables influence the achievement of educational targets, then these variables must influence students' mental states and processes.

Slavin and some other scholars argue that the psychological concepts and principles of effective teaching include attention, memory, information processing, learning transfer, reinforcement, feedback, motivation, competence, expectation, and self-concept. These can be summarized as follows:[40]

(1) Students have to focus on learning and have active experience.
(2) Students have to be good at accepting learning experiences.
(3) Learning experience must be adapted to the intended learning goals.

These three aspects are the basic conditions under which student learning occurs and develops. An analysis of effective teaching according to the basic principles of psychology must focus on these three conditions and the associated factors that facilitate or hinder learning.

***The Paradigm of Knowledge Basis of Teaching***

This is the latest paradigm in the Western analysis of effective teaching. This paradigm asserts that much of the previous research on effective teaching has ignored the subject matter knowledge that teachers teach, which is an important criterion for judging the effectiveness of teaching. It is logical and common sense to assume that a teacher who does not understand the subject matter cannot teach students well at all.

Shulman at American Stanford University is one of the pioneers of this paradigm. He lists seven types of knowledge that teachers should have in relation to effective teaching in his book *Knowledge and Teaching: Basis of Reform*:[41]

(1) Knowledge of subject content
(2) Basic pedagogical knowledge
(3) Knowledge of the curriculum
(4) Knowledge of pedagogy
(5) Knowledge about learners' features
(6) Knowledge about the context of education
(7) Knowledge of the goals, outcomes, and values of education

Professor Graeme Clark at the University of Michigan says the most outstanding contribution of this analysis is putting teachers' subject and pedagogic knowledge into a prominent position. He deems that a good teacher should not only know how to manage and offer feedback to students, carry out actual plans, and make sensible decisions, but also be a practicing scholar, a constant gainer of knowledge. Especially in such a knowledge society, a teacher has to be a lifelong learner to study and update his/her subject knowledge constantly. Only in this way can he/she be sure of the sustainable development of the effectiveness of teaching.

Rosie Turner-Bisset, a British academic, analyses and summarizes previous research on the knowledge base of teaching and proposes the following knowledge that teachers should have:[42]

(1) Solid subject knowledge
(2) Solid language knowledge
(3) Knowledge of subject belief
(4) Curriculum knowledge
(5) Basic pedagogical knowledge
(6) Knowledge of teaching models
(7) Leaner's knowledge—cognitive domains
(8) Learner's knowledge—experiential domains
(9) Knowledge about oneself
(10) Knowledge about educational context
(11) Knowledge about education goals
(12) Knowledge about pedagogical content

Such a paradigm that analyzes the knowledge basis of teaching to study effective teaching is regarded by some scholars as the latest paradigm, and its developing direction is to replace effective teaching with expert teaching. This expert teaching is not something that can be achieved by teachers with several qualities in the traditional sense, but is based on solid knowledge of the subject matter and educational theory, as well as on the wisdom of educational practice.

### 3.3.4 Research Approaches and Methods of Effective Teaching

In Western countries, why studies of effective teaching have various results. There are two reasons: besides the effect of researchers' educational philosophy, teaching values, and considerations of effective teaching, another important reason is their different research approaches and methods. After the systematic investigation of effective teaching in the west, we can find that the research ways and data resources mainly include the following aspects:

The first one is to study teachers' or students' views on effective teaching. The usually used ways are questionnaires and interviews.

The second one is to observe teachers' classroom teaching by external observers, usually using recorders, magnetic tapes, videotapes, rating scales, and participatory observation (it refers to researchers participating in students' learning activities as a learner and observing the classroom at the same time).

The third one is to let headmasters, colleagues, teachers, students, and other personnel describe effective teachers' teaching behaviors, usually in the form of open questionnaires, to collect data and then draw a conclusion after sorting and analyzing.

The fourth one is to let teachers describe their own teaching behavior, teaching activities, and teaching effect. The usual ways are analysis of teaching notes, case interviews, teaching seminars, and so on.

The fifth one is to apply and analyze the above several approaches and methods systematically.

We can conclude the methods of effective teaching research in major Western English-speaking countries into three types when examining methodology and research methods: first, speculative and inferential study; second, descriptive and analytical study; third, empirical study. Among these three study methods, the third one is not only the main body of study methods, but also the source of research results. This kind of original research results provides a good reference and enlightenment for later research. The following seven cases are typical in the Western studies on effective teaching (see Table 3-5 for details):

(1) Case study 1: Study teacher's quality by open questionnaires (such as Ryan's study in 1962)
(2) Case study 2: Study effective teaching by observing teacher's classroom teaching behavior (such as Flanders' study in 1970)
(3) Case study 3: Study effective teaching by observing students' learning (such as Rosenshine's study in 1973)
(4) Case study 4: Study effective teaching by a graded questionnaire (such as Kyriacou's study in 1982)
(5) Case study 5: Study effective teaching and learning by interviewing students (such as Brown's study in 1993)
(6) Case study 6: Research on background-process-outcome analysis (such as Kyriacou's study in 1997)
(7) Case study 7: Research on the combination of multiple methods (such as Brand's study in 2000)

**Table 3-5** Examples of Effective Teaching Methods

| Researchers | Time | Research subjects | Research methods |
|---|---|---|---|
| Cattell, R. B. | 1931 | Teachers' quality | Open questionnaire |
| Ryan, D. | 1960 | Effective teaching | Structural observation |
| Taylor, P. H. | 1962 | Good teachers and bad teachers | Open questionnaire |
| Flanders, N. A. | 1970 | Teacher's effectiveness | Make a structural observation of the two opposite teaching methods |

*(Continued)*

| Researchers | Time | Research subjects | Research methods |
|---|---|---|---|
| Rosenshine and Frust | 1973 | Good teaching | Participatory classroom observation |
| Beerliner and Tichenoff | 1976 | Effective teaching | Structural observation |
| Bennet | 1976 | Good teaching | Grade questionnaire |
| Kyriacou, C. | 1982 | Teacher's effectiveness | Grade questionnaire |
| Perrott, E. | 1982 | Effective teaching | Structural observation |
| Brown and Mcintyre | 1993 | Effective teaching | Interview and structural observation |
| OEECD | 1994 | Teaching quality and effective teaching | Case study (structural and non-structural, observation interviews, and workshops among teachers) |
| Cooper, P. | 1996 | Effective teaching and learning | Interview and participatory observation |
| Kyriacou, C. | 1997 | Effective teaching | Factor analysis method (background-process-outcome analysis) |
| Green, B. P. et al. | 1999 | The implementation framework of effective teaching assessment | Case study (observation, interview, and questionnaire) |
| Brand, B. F. | 2000 | Strategies for effective teaching and learning | Case study (observation, interview, and questionnaire) |

Note: The effective teaching research methods listed in this table are limited to empirical research, excluding literature review research and speculative research.

### 3.3.5 Characteristics of Effective Teaching

Theoretical research of teaching serves to guide and promote the development of teaching practice. For it has more guiding value to cite characteristics of effective teaching than to define the definition of effective teaching, in a large number of studies on effective teaching in the west, people's conclusions point more to the characteristics of effective teachers and effective teaching. Although the theoretical thinking framework adopted by researchers is different from the research methods, the generalization of the characteristics of effective teaching is their common pursuit of research results.

In the part of historical investigation, we have already mentioned some corresponding research results, but they are only some typical examples that aim at explaining the historical development of effective teaching research. In this part, the author will use the method of factor analysis to screen out the most representative features (classified and counted according to the frequency of occurrence) from sixteen research conclusions for some analysis and discussion.

What needs to be mentioned here is that such kind of classification analysis is not an easy job because there is no reference classification standard framework for reference up to now, and the differences of words used by researchers in the research results and the differences of emphasis. We can only make a tentative analysis of the classification factors according to our basic understanding of these studies and professional judgment developed by years of teaching theory research.

Because of the differences in words used by researchers in expressing research results and the limited number of research papers (or books) used in this classification, manual classification and manual statistics are adopted. At the same time, effective teaching preparation, effective teaching process, and effective teaching evaluation and results are taken as the basic analysis framework. This is not only our three-dimensional thinking on effective teaching, but also the integration of the research results of effective teachers and effective teaching. According to statistics, the twelve features with high frequency in the study of effective teaching characteristics are as follows (the numbers in brackets are the frequency of occurrence):

(1) Clear expression (10)
(2) Flexible methods (8)
(3) Being enthusiastic in teaching (6)
(4) Stressing goals and task orientation (6)
(5) Can arouse students' interest in learning (5)
(6) Being good at creating a good classroom atmosphere (4)
(7) Promoting learning by making use of appraising actively (4)
(8) Having high expectations of students (4)
(9) Effective classroom management (4)
(10) Stressing problem-solving (4)
(11) Being good at asking questions (4)
(12) Possessing good personal qualities (4)

The above-mentioned 12 characteristics are not only the summary of researchers' basic confirmation of effective teaching characteristics, but also the basic reference factors for evaluating effective teaching, as well as the direction and goal of teachers' teaching professional development.

### 3.3.6 Understanding Effective Teaching: The Enlightenment from Western Studies

Although up to now, western scholars have adopted different thinking paradigms and research methods to study effective teaching, and they also have different views on the definition and characteristics of effective teaching, from the above-mentioned systematic investigation of western effective teaching research, we can at least draw the following inspirations:

(1) The basic trend of effective teaching research in the west is from single method to comprehensive method, from the study of the effectiveness of teachers' teaching to the study of the effectiveness of students' learning, from general to specific (subject teachers and teaching), from single to comprehensive(emphasizing a certain aspect), from qualitative research to quantitative research to qualitative and quantitative combination research, from the study of traits of effective teachers to the study of effective teaching and further to the study of effective teaching and learning. At present, it has developed into effective learning and teaching; that is, it pays more attention to students' active and effective learning inspired and guided by teachers in the classroom.

(2) Effective teaching depends to a great extent on teachers' understanding and grasp of educational objectives, especially curriculum objectives and standards. In other words, the better teachers' understanding and grasp of educational objectives and curriculum objectives and standards, the stronger the effectiveness of teaching. Because in essence, effective teaching is a process in which teachers guide students through various activities, so as to achieve curriculum goals and educational goals. If a teacher' s teaching deviates from the educational goal and curriculum goal, then his/her labor can only be regarded as ineffective labor. Specifically, in the process of China's new basic education reform, it is necessary not only to establish new curriculum plans and standards that conform to the quality education policy, but also to make the front-line classroom teachers clear the objectives of the new curriculum through various ways and methods, so as to teach them to achieve the objectives of the new curriculum.

(3) Effective teaching is always achieved through teachers' good teaching qualities, teaching behaviors and skills, and appropriate teaching strategies. If a teacher ardently loves teaching, has superb teaching skills, and can use optimized teaching methods, then his/her teaching efficiency will be guaranteed. This is why people have studied the qualities of good teachers and the characteristics of good teaching for many years.

(4) Effective teaching is always connected intently with teachers' reflection inquiry on teaching practice and reflection on their own professional development. If a teacher can constantly reflect on his/her teaching philosophy and teaching

practice, if he/she can constantly explore new teaching methods and boldly carry out his/her teaching reform, or if he/she can promote his/her sustainable development by reflecting on teaching, then his/her teaching effectiveness will be fundamentally guaranteed in practice. In short, an effective teacher must be a reflective practitioner.

(5) The effective evaluation standard of teaching depends not only on teachers' teaching behavior, but more importantly, on the concrete progress or development of students after a period of teaching. In other words, the core of effective teaching to evaluate teaching effectiveness is to look at students' progress or development. As some scholars in our country have pointed out: "Whether teaching is effective or not does not mean whether teachers have finished teaching content or whether they are serious or not, but whether students have learned anything or whether they have learned well." If students don't want to learn or learn nothing, even if teachers work hard, it is ineffective. Similarly, if students study hard, but they don't get their due development, it is also ineffective or inefficient teaching.[43] According to this standard, judging today's classroom teaching in China, we can easily find that ineffective or inefficient classroom practices still exist in large numbers. Therefore, according to the goal of the new curriculum to promote students' learning and development, we must pay attention to the effectiveness of teaching.

(6) Effective teaching is not a fixed notion or pattern. It is a dynamic conception influenced by the changes in curriculum objectives and teaching objectives and the development of students. People's views on effective teaching are changing and developing. For instance, people focused on teachers' quality in the 1960s, but stressed teaching behavior in the 1970s. In the 1980s, they paid attention to teaching activities, and in the 1990s, they changed to emphasize the interaction between teaching and learning. And in the 21st century, people all over the world are generally concerned about how to promote students' learning and development through effective teaching. Therefore, we have reason to believe that effective teaching should be a dynamic concept, and the research on effective teaching must be endless. (Note: we retrieved 4963 research papers (1994–2003) by keywords "effective teaching/instruction" and "effective teaching and learning" in the British database Mimas, while only retrieved 56 research papers (1994–2003, including some introductory articles) in Chinese Social Science journals with the keyword "effective teaching."[44])

## 3.4 The Theory and Practice Mode of Reflective Teaching

Since 1983, D. A. Schon proposed and advocated that teachers should be reflective practitioners with regard to their professional development, the theory and practice of reflective teaching have made rapid progress and have been accepted by more and more educational researchers and teachers.

Although, from the current evaluation of this theory by western educational researchers and the role of this theory in practice, it still needs to be continuously studied and improved in practice. But it should be recognized that this thought has indeed had an important impact on the development of contemporary teachers' teaching specialization. Currently, the major assessments of reflective teaching by Western scholars are as follows:

(1) Reflective practice helps teachers liberate from impulsive and impetuous behavior.
(2) Reflective practice makes teachers act in a cautious and firm way.
(3) Reflective practice regards teachers as educated people and distinguishes them from others in different occupations, for it is one of the signs to checkout wisdom. In addition, as people have noticed, reflective practice is conducive for classroom teachers to strengthen themselves. However, the most important thing is that reflective practice is a tool for individual teachers to improve their teaching practice and become better, more effective, and more creative experts within their purview."[45]

It is obvious that reflective teaching is not only a kind of teaching thought, but also its practice is very important to ensure the effectiveness of teaching. At present, with the comprehensive implementation of the new curriculum of basic education in China, as a classroom teacher who goes hand in hand with the new curriculum reform, knowing the basic characteristics and practice mode of reflective teaching and putting it into reflective action in combination with her own teaching will undoubtedly contribute to the realization of the new curriculum objectives. The following is a brief review and comment on the basic characteristics, value orientation, and practice mode of reflective teaching, based on the research of domestic and foreign scholars on reflective teaching and personal thinking.

### 3.4.1 Basic Features of Reflective Teaching

In the field of educational study, the notion of reflection was first put forward by Dewey, a famous American pragmatic educator who was called the father of reflection. As early as 1933, Dewey, who was called the father of reflection by American scholars, discussed the function of reflective thinking and reflective action in improving teaching practice in his book *How We Think: Reconsideration on the Influence of Reflective Thinking on the Educational Process.*

Even in the United States, from the 1930s to 1940s, many American educators haven't fully recognized the great function of reflective teaching in teachers' professional development because of war and economy. However, according to studies by Western scholars, the view of education and teaching reflection posed by Dewey was very helpful for people to know and understand reflective teaching, and it inspired people to understand the features of reflective teaching from at least the following six sides:[46]

(1) Reflective teaching includes teachers' positive interests in teaching objectives, teaching results, and the consistent teaching methods and efficiency of teaching technology.
(2) Reflective teaching is a circulatory process when applied in reality rather than a disposable action. In this circulatory reflective process, teachers continuously monitor, evaluate and revise their own teaching practice.
(3) Reflective teaching requires teachers to have the ability to question teaching methods, and this ability is the foundation to support teachers' professional development.
(4) Reflective teaching requires teachers to have an open mind, a strong sense of responsibility, and persistent pursuit of teaching.
(5) Reflective teaching is a kind of activity based on teacher's professional judgment. It not only relies on teachers' self-reflection, but also relies on their understanding of educational science principles.
(6) Through cooperation and communication with peers in teaching practice, teachers' reflective teaching, professional learning, and personality improvement will be further strengthened.

Scrutinizing carefully the above-mentioned six features of reflective teaching, it is not difficult to find that it is not an easy job to reflect teaching practice. It requires teachers not only to have a strong sense of teaching responsibility and positive awareness of improvement, but also to have basic teaching reflection ability, rather than just knowing how to teach students knowledge and skills. In this sense, the early understanding of the role of reflective teaching has laid a good theoretical foundation for the new idea that later people regard reflective teaching as the basic way of teachers' professional specialization.

Indeed, if a teacher wants to keep a strong driving force for sustainable development of his/her profession, he/she should not only get the necessary knowledge and skills through professional training like doctors and lawyers, but also constantly reflect on the process and results of his/her teaching activities in the later teaching practice, and constantly improve his/her teaching on the basis of reflection, so as to meet the basic requirements of sustainable development of schools and students.

### 3.4.2 Value Orientation of Reflective Teaching

Even though reflective teaching has been widely recognized as an effective strategy for the development of the contemporary teachers' teaching profession, there are still different value orientations in practice. From the historical point of view, there are four orientations that have played a dominant role in different stages, namely, academic tradition orientation, social efficiency orientation, developmental orientation, and social reconstruction orientation.[47] These different orientations were formed and developed with the reform of American teacher education in the 20th century. They have not only influenced teacher education in the United States and the teaching practice of primary and secondary school teachers, but also influenced the practice of reflective teaching in other countries in the world.

*Academic Tradition Orientation*

Reflective teaching, which focuses on the academic tradition, focuses on the role of humanities and subject knowledge, and emphasizes that the study of academic knowledge should be the first priority in teacher education, supplemented by teaching practice and other clinical experiences when preparing for future teachers' careers. This reflective orientation of teacher education focuses on the fact that teachers should be scholars and textbook experts. In teaching practice, teachers should often reflect on their mastery and understanding of subject knowledge, so as to better impart the knowledge they have mastered to students and promote the development of students' understanding ability.

Among many scholars who support and advocate reflective teaching in the academic tradition, Lee S. Shulman is a typical representative. Schulman and his colleagues have always been concerned about the core educational problem: What knowledge should teachers have and teach students in order to develop students' understanding ability? Under the guidance of this thought, Shulman comprehensively discussed the basic issues of teaching in his book *Knowledge and Teaching: The Foundation of Neo-Reform*, published in the 1980s.[48]

After entering the 21st century, American scholars put forward view of knowledge and teaching methods leading education development on the basis of reflecting their own educational system and stressed that American teachers teaching and teachers training should pay more attention to the grasp of subject knowledge and teaching methods which were uses to support teaching.[49]

In short, reflective teaching of academic tradition orientation underlines that teachers should frequently reflect on their teaching content and applied methods in order to see whether teaching content is right or not, whether teaching methods are proper or not, and thus to make sure whether teaching value and teaching efficiency are accord with the requirement of society and state or not. This orientation is seemingly traditional, but it clearly represents a new trend of thought in the reform and development of Teacher Education in the United States since the late 1980s.

***Social Efficiency Orientation***

Social efficiency orientation is initiated by progressivism education in the process of American teachers' teaching reform. Scholars advocating social efficiency orientation hold that the effective curriculum program of teachers teaching is mapped out only by scientific teaching study. That is to say, what and how to teach is concluded through scientific study. As a result, the reflection by teachers should combine closely with their teaching study rather than their subjective and groundless imagination in mind.

We cannot get scientific results of teaching reform without scientific teaching study, and under this situation, the teaching reform can be said to be blind, invalid, or at least inefficient. It can be clearly seen that a teacher should not only be a practitioner of reflection, but also be a researcher who regards study as a precursor to conducting teaching reflection. Undoubtedly, this orientation influences the later study of classroom action and new ideas of teachers being researchers.

*Developmentalism Orientation*

After the 1960s, with the popularity of cognitive psychology in the field of American teachers teaching, the developmentalism of teaching reflection has attracted more and more attention. The constructivism theory formed on the basis of cognitive psychology has further strengthened the reflection orientation of developmentalism with its anti-traditional view of learning and knowledge.

The biggest difference between this orientation and the above two is that it shifts the focus of teaching reflection from teachers to students. Under the basic ideological framework that learning is not passive but active, and knowledge is not transmitted but constructed, this orientation believes that the focus of teaching reflection is to see whether it promotes students' learning and development, rather than the process of teachers' teaching and students' learning achievement.

*Social Reconstruction Orientation*

Social reconstruction orientation considers when teachers do teaching reflection, they should not only focus on teaching practice, but also pay attention to the appropriateness of the social environment and external conditions supporting their teaching. From a large scope of view, teachers' reflections should partly focus on resolving conflicts between the development of society and teaching so as to make teachers' teaching practice meet the needs to the maximum extent of rebuilding a new social structure and new order.

From a small scope of view, teachers' reflection should not only consider their own professional development, but also pay attention to the overall development of their working schools with interest. In addition, focusing on the basic view that teacher education should strive to create a learning community, social reconstruction also emphasizes that teachers' reflection should be a daily social activity with the nature of the obligation. In other words, teachers' reflection on teaching should not be regarded as a private event, but should be closely linked with the creation of social justice and equality of opportunity.

All in all, the above four kinds of reflective orientations have their own key point: academic orientation emphasizes that through teachers' reflection, we should reprocess and express the content of teaching materials, so as to promote students' understanding of the content; social efficiency orientation underlines to advance students' intelligence through scientific teaching; developmental orientation emphasizes that teachers should focus on the development of students' learning methods and comprehensive ability; The orientation of social reconstruction emphasizes the promotion of social justice and equality of opportunity through the reflection on the social environment and conditions of school education.

These four orientations not only provide a certain reference for us to understand and implement reflective teaching from different angles, but also tell us that reflective teaching is not easy. When we want to reflect on our own teaching, we should clearly realize that reflection is a personal thing on the surface, but from the result, the action after reflection will affect the development of students and the development of school and society.

### 3.4.3 Practice Model of Reflective Teaching

Being a reflective teacher has been a common slogan in the worldwide educational field and teaching practice field. More and more educators and educational practitioners agree that teaching is a complex rational and intelligent activity. In order to ensure teaching effectiveness, teachers have to conduct continuous introspection and perfection in their teaching activities. Why do teachers have to reflect on their teaching? What features do reflective teacher possess? How do teachers conduct reflective practice? People have different answers to these questions.

What is the significance of teaching reflection? Why do teachers have to reflect on their teaching idea and practice? The general reason is for teachers' professional development, but the American scholar Ross, D. D. and his fellows put forward seven basic reasons to reflect teaching according to the missions of school teaching and teaching profession in the book *Reflective Teaching Focusing on Students' Educational Rights*. Next, I will analyze the reasons for their reflection in combination with my own understanding briefly:[50]

**Teaching not only bears the duty of ethics, but also needs the guidance of value.** Although there are many features in common in worldwide teaching activities, from the perspective of the basic relationship and mutual restriction between teaching and social, political and economic, teaching is not and cannot be an activity of value freedom. Any society and country will always infiltrate its required values through teaching.

To form a kind of value needed by a specific society is the basic goal pursued by every social educator all through the ages. For example, citizens having democratic values in America is one of the criteria to measure whether American education is successful or not. Because making a good citizen have democratic values is the cornerstone of American education. Teachers have the responsibility to help students grow into authorized citizens who can and are willing to fully participate in social activities in a democratic society. To achieve such a target, teachers should reflect on their teaching constantly, and view whether their teaching is in accord with the requirement of American democratic values, thus grasping a better understanding of their teaching direction.

In a democratic society, a reflective teacher will choose the correct teaching content and appropriate teaching methods according to the ethical standards of this society, and will use this ethical standard to evaluate his teaching process and teaching results.

**Teaching needs to understand students' views.** Knowledge is constructed rather than transferred. Students' thought and their views on objects directly affect their learning content and learning process. According to opinions from cognition psychologists and constructivists, knowledge is constructed rather than transferred. Learning is not only a simple process of absorbing knowledge transmitted by teachers. Instead, it is a process of constructing knowledge in their minds according to their own existing experience.

Teachers have to know about students' thoughts, design proper teaching activities, and organize teaching practices for them in order to help students correctly understand what they have learned. But to achieve this target, the teacher has to first reflect on his/her own teaching practice. At the same time, he/she should possess the ability to master whether his/her teaching could promote students' positive development, but such ability, to a large extent, is formed through the successive reflection of his/her teaching practice rather than through books.

**Teacher's thinking affects the changes in classroom activities.** Teachers' views on problems in teaching and education directly influence their classroom decision-making and the ways to deal with classroom problems. For example, a teacher who regards teaching as displaying information to children will deal with teaching very differently from a teacher who regards teaching as exchanging information with children. The former may apply methods of lecture and demonstration to make students listen and observe his/her teaching; the latter may use conversation and talk to promote students' understanding of information. As a result, if a teacher advocates interchange with students in his/her teaching, he/she has to reflect on his/her teaching frequently. This is also one of the reasons that reflection is a significant part of teaching.

**Teachers' acquiescence to invalid beliefs will affect the efficiency of the classroom.** Many teachers' views on teaching and learning belong to intuitive judgment, which is often not tested by practice or science. However, teachers always organize their own teaching activities according to such unconscious subjective judgments. Beyond doubt, some opinions or judgments are efficient, but some are not. Even if they are excellent teachers, some of their views and ideas are still harmful to promote students' learning.

Generally speaking, teachers' beliefs about teaching, learning, and children are formed in long-term teaching practice. No teachers can be fully aware that their tacit teaching beliefs may affect kids' development. The constant reflection on teaching will help teachers further know well about their tacit teaching beliefs and check out whether their teaching ideas are correct. Teachers can examine the effectiveness of their tacit teaching ideas by means of collecting evidence of different teaching opinions, so that to change their teaching opinions consciously to adapt to the requirements of promoting kids' learning and development.

**Actually, there is no regular method that can solve all the problems in teaching and learning.** Since teaching is an activity of complexity and uncertainty, it requires teachers to make proper judgments and decisions unceasingly in light of the changes in teaching. Focusing on the diversified characteristics of contemporary school education objectives, classroom teachers are faced with the task of considering how to achieve these diversified objectives at any time in teaching?

It is of vital importance as well as difficult for teachers to select a suitable strategy for students to achieve the corresponding target. Because teaching is a dynamic process, there is no strategy that could adapt to any teaching situation. For educational problems that have no fixed answers, teachers have to constantly judge the effectiveness of their strategies. Because of this reason, teachers' reflection on teaching theory and practice appears to be essential.

**Educational research cannot answer all the teaching problems.** For the past many years, a large number of educational studies have focused on solving the actual teaching and learning problems, and have played a very positive guiding role in teaching and kids' development. However, it is obvious that educational study cannot answer all the teaching problems.

Although, in the view of many people, research is more difficult and complex than practice, in fact, the complexity and diversity of teaching activities are unmatched by the Institute of education. Moreover, research usually pays more attention to the common and hypothetical standard environment, while teachers must individualize and realize the results of educational research according to the students and situations in their own classrooms. This makes the reflection on teaching the only way to improve the pertinence and effectiveness of teaching.

**It is teachers' responsibility to maintain the sustainable development of the teaching profession.** In reality, it is difficult for any education schemes by pre-service teachers to make all-side preparation of knowledge and ability for teachers' future teaching. With the development of society, renewal of knowledge, and variation of teachers' practice, teachers in working posts have to face tasks of continuing studying and improving their practical ability.

That is to say, if a teacher wants to provide perfect teaching for his/her student, he/ she has to develop his/her professional ability, and through reflection, he/she can make the teacher clear what he/ she should learn and improve in his professional life, which is conducive to maintaining the driving force of teaching and improving the quality of teaching. George J. Posner (2000) brought forward a formula about reflection: experience (practice) + reflection = professional development.[51]

It tells us that for the sustainable development of teachers' teaching profession, only experience (teaching practice) is not enough. However, perhaps more importantly, teachers are role models for students. If they expect their students to learn actively and actively, they should first regard learning improvement as an obligation and responsibility. If students can often see their teachers taking advantage of possible opportunities to learn new knowledge and explore new things, and regard learning new things as a happy thing, the positive impact on them is self-evident.

In a word, teaching is a complicated intelligence activity. With regard to variable situations and children with different personalities, the already accepted theories and people's experiences cannot provide all the answers to teaching problems for classroom teachers in reality. Teachers can make correct decisions to successfully apply the existing theories and research conclusions to specific teaching situations.

***Practice model of Reflective Teaching***

According to the process of teaching, teaching reflection can be divided into two basic types: Reflection on teaching and reflection in teaching. The former can be called result reflection, while the latter can be called process reflection. The prevalent one in current is a reflection in teaching, or we can say it is reflection accompanied by action research. This kind of reflection model is more systematical, and its effect is more obvious. This reflection mode is more systematic than daily reflection, and the effect will be more obvious. Action research can not only help teachers form reflective attitudes, but also guide teachers to innovate knowledge and transform teaching. Of course, such reflection not only requires teachers to have a strong sense of teaching responsibility and reflection, but also requires teachers to have the knowledge base of educational theory and certain research abilities.

This kind of reflective model consists of seven basic links: planning, research preparation, action, data collection, analysis, evaluation, and reflection decision-making, and they form a circular process.[52] See them in Figure 3-1.

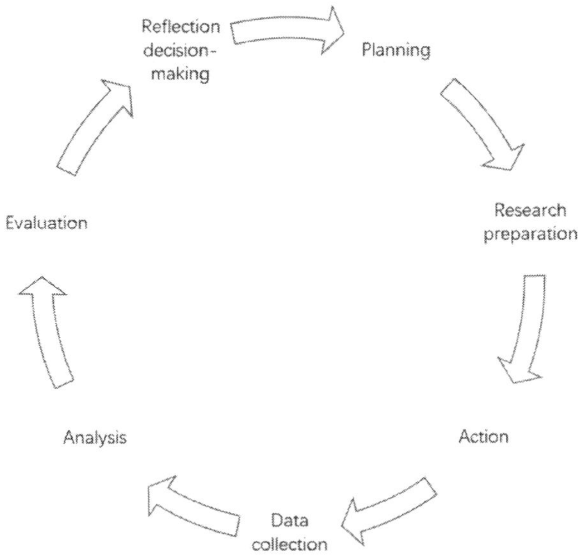


**Figure 3-1** Reflective Teaching Process Based on Action Study

General teaching activities usually only require teachers to plan, prepare and take action, but reflective teaching requires teachers to conduct self-monitoring on the basis of the above three links, observe and collect data on their own and children's learning intentions, learning methods, and emotional changes, and then make decisions to revise and improve their classroom teaching policies and strategies through the analysis of these data. This model provides a dynamic guide for teachers' teaching reflection, and its working has a great influence on high-quality teaching.

The following is a brief analysis of each sector:

**Planning stage:** In the planning stage, a reflective teacher should always consider the unity of his/her teaching program and reflective plan. For example, when you make lesson preparation, you can devise a lesson list that has certain blank space (often on the right side of the paper), the left side can be left for your course content and teaching process, but on the right side, you can write down your teaching impression and thought in order to make tips for your reflection after class.

**Research preparation stage:** Since reflective teaching is based on action study, teachers cannot only consider the question of how to teach. You have to make full psychological and material preparation for the study. For example, if you plan to record a video for your class so that you can make a careful analysis after class, you should prepare all equipment in advance. If you want your colleagues to listen to your class, you should discuss your plan with them and make your students understand the purpose of your action. Whether these works are perfect or not directly affects the effectiveness of your teaching reflection.

**Action stage:** As the reflective teaching base on action study is carried out along with actual teaching practice, it should be the core section of this model. The process of action does be the process of the program being put into practice. A plan would be a mere scrap of paper without action. So, in this stage, teachers must put their passion into teaching and work with high responsibility. Generally, in the process of reflective teaching based on action study, teachers' choice of course content and teaching method with purpose and direction, and their dependent teaching consciousness would be further enhanced.

**Stage of collecting data:** In the process of reflective teaching based on action study, the collection of data and materials is completed by the individual teacher. Usually, teachers should use the proper time to record some classroom activities of themselves and their children. Of course, it is very critical to choose an appropriate method to collect information for improving the effectiveness of action research and ensuring the scientificity of reflective decision-making.

**Stage of analyzing materials:** In this stage, teachers should summarize and sort out the materials they have collected, and select the information through certain classification methods, so as to lay a good foundation for the further decision of evaluation and reflection.

**Stage of assessing materials:** Assessment is actually a process of value judgment, and the correct evaluation of the effectiveness of material is the concrete embodiment of teachers' theoretical teaching level and teaching experience. Generally speaking, the evaluation of material should rely on the objectives of teaching and action study. On the one hand, it should take factors affecting the achievement of students' learning targets into consideration. On the other hand, we should also consider the factors that have positive significance for future actions.

**Stage of reflecting decision:** Decision-making is a rational judgment process of selecting and determining the best scheme among multiple resolving schemes. The teaching reflection and decision-making on the basis of action research are actually not carried out at the end of research work, but have already started with the progress of research.

The reason why we divide this model into seven stages, one is for the convenience of study and narration, and the other is for the explanation of this problem: Decisions made in the late stage would affect the good beginning of the next study circle. As any action study can't settle all the problems in teaching, the action study which sees from the angle of teaching improvement and sustainable development should be continuous.

# Basic Strategies of Contemporary Teaching

This chapter mainly focuses on the basic strategies of contemporary teaching, including four subjects: teaching method, forms of teaching organization, classroom teaching art, and seminar methodology. The teaching method refers to a series of specific activity modes and technical means adopted by teachers and students in the teaching process for certain teaching objectives and specific teaching tasks. The adoption of the teaching method must take the eight factors into consideration: teaching rules and principles, teaching objectives and tasks and teaching content, etc. Teaching organization form is a kind of activity that can make full use of teaching time, space, intelligence, and objects. In terms of our current national condition, classroom teaching is a basic teaching organization form used in elementary and secondary schools and also a basic way and place for quality education and new curriculum reform. Reforming the classroom teaching method is an important step in achieving basic education curriculum reform goals. Teaching is both scientific and artistic. Teaching art refers to a set of teaching skills by which teachers creatively organize the teaching process to achieve teaching objectives to get the best teaching effect. Classroom teaching art is the center of teaching art, including teaching organization, giving lectures, using teaching language, classroom questioning, blackboard writing, and the use of multimedia. Seminar methodology is a kind of teaching method used widely in western colleges. Its main function is that it is beneficial to mutual communication, interaction, and complementation between teachers and students and among students, and it can fully express the nature of teaching activity as a process of communication and interaction.

## 4.1 The Classification and Adoption of Teaching Method

### 4.1.1 The Meaning of Teaching Method

As for the definition of teaching method, scholars at home and abroad have different perspectives. Traditionally, it is defined from the perspective of teaching, so teaching method is regarded as the way of teaching. Instead, western progressive educationalists regard it as a way of learning from the perspective of learning. From the research results of contemporary pedagogy, our interpretation of teaching methods should be defined from the perspective of dialectical unity of teaching and learning; that is, teaching is the interaction between teachers and students. According to this point, teaching method refers to a series of specific activity modes and technical means adopted by teachers and students in the teaching process for certain teaching objectives and specific teaching tasks. Contemporary teaching method includes the way of teaching and the way of learning under instruction. Modern teaching theory and its practice focus more on the unity of teaching and learning, emphasizing that teachers should not only consider how to teach but, more importantly, how to make students learn in a better way. In other words, efficient teaching makes efficient learning.

Any teaching mode is inseparable from the participation of a specific teaching method. The teaching method is a major factor in the teaching system, and it is a bridge between teachers, students, and course content. An efficient teaching method is of great importance for making students actively take part in teaching activities, achieving teaching objectives, improving teaching efficiency and quality, and easing the learning burden of students. In order to make sure teaching scientificity and artistry, teachers must combine teaching content and students' actual condition to create and recreate teaching activities. Because teaching quality cannot be improved without effective teaching methods nowadays, one of the reasons why students who are burdened with excessive learning work cannot develop in an all-round way and fail to get improvement in their ability is that teachers cannot adopt appropriate teaching methods and lack teaching art. Therefore, it is very important for teachers to study and choose the proper teaching method and improve teaching art. Especially, it is of great significance to realize the importance of teaching method reform and choice based on the current goal of contemporary national basic education curriculum and teaching reform, as well as the implementation of curriculum standards.

### 4.1.2 Classification of Teaching Method

Teaching method varies in nation and time, and so does the classification of it. Some claim to classify it based on teaching tasks, some on the source of knowledge and information, some on the form of thinking logic, and some on the combination of the three. No matter how to classify, there is one thing in common, i.e., to provide convenience for teachers.

Modern teaching theory insists that the teaching method is a method system, a sub-system of the teaching system, composed of a teacher, student teaching content, teaching means, etc. Its basic elements include teaching of teachers, learning of students, the interaction between teachers and students, object of recognition and carrier of information (like language, characters, etc.), and teaching aid (general aid and audio-visual aid, like TV, audio aid, computers, etc.). Any teaching method contains three aspects of meaning: it concerns working mode of teacher (like the selection and organization of information, the carrier and tool of information, and the transmission of information), it also concerns the learning mode of students (reception, organization, storage, recurrence of information in a selected way) and the way of interaction between teachers and students. Based on this view, we believe that it is more appropriate for teachers to select teaching method based on the classification of teaching method according to the relationship between teachers and students and the mode of information exchange. We will divide teaching method into four types:

(1) Teaching method system centered on teaching activity
(2) Teaching method system of teacher-student interaction
(3) Personalized teaching method system
(4) Teaching method system centered on practice

The features of each type are shown in Table 4-1.

The purpose of classifying teaching method is not only to make teaching ways more systematic and clearer, but also to provide convenience to teachers. A famous educational scholar of the Soviet Union, Zankov, once said, "When choosing a teaching method, what's important is to have the concept of comparing effects of the different solutions to certain tasks," which tells us to make proper teaching method, we have to make clear classification of teaching method and the features of those. Only this way can provide broad background for choosing. Classifying teaching method and identifying the features of each of them is beneficial to the option of teachers.

**Table 4-1** The Classification and Features of Teaching Method

| Type | Ways of information exchange | Thinking pattern | Specific method | Feature |
|---|---|---|---|---|
| Teaching method system centered on teaching activity | One-way | Polymerism | Instructing | Teachers instruct, students listen; large informative, not good for development of thinking ability |
| | | | Questioning | Teachers ask, students answer; questions are informative |
| | | | Reasoning | Teachers instruct, students listen; students accept passively |

*(Continued)*

| Type | Ways of information exchange | Thinking pattern | Specific method | Feature |
|---|---|---|---|---|
| Teaching method system of teacher-student interaction | Two-way or even multi-way | Divergent thinking or critical thinking | Class discussion | Teachers as class members; teachers and students, and students and students form multi-way communication |
| | | | Group discussion | Same as the "class discussion" (more effective for high-level learners) |
| | | | Peer teaching | Students' strengths can be exerted by encouraging students to join teaching activities. |
| | | | New teaching methods: discovery method, suggestion method, guiding-learning method, heuristic method, three-link teaching methods, reading, discussing talking, practicing teaching | From the perspective of modern teaching theory, give consideration to the effect of teaching and learning; attaching importance to the leading role of teachers and the principal role of students; imparting knowledge and developing students' ability |
| Personalized teaching method system | One-way (having feedback function) | Independence and volatility | Procedural instruction | Students are involved in learning process; suitable for individuals; students can make progress based on their own plan, but somewhat mechanical. |
| | | | Simulation teaching | Students are involved in the learning process, which is flexible but time-consuming. |
| | | | Independent learning (reading, designing) | Suitable for higher-level learners; in favor of self-learning ability and operational ability |
| | | | Computer-aided teaching, multimedia, internet teaching | flexible, provide feedback based on their own progress |

*(Continued)*

| Type | Ways of information exchange | Thinking pattern | Specific method | Feature |
|---|---|---|---|---|
| Teaching method system centered on practice | One-way or two-way | Creativity | Camping, field research, Clinical diagnosis | Learning in practice can motivate students' interest; beneficial for a combination between theory and practice; it needs a detailed plan. |
| | | | Laboratory study | Students' learning is active, which is good for practical skills. |
| | | | Case study; role-play | Ditto |
| | | | Imitation and game | Ditto |
| | | | Exercise and homework | It is good for consolidating knowledge and cultivating ability. |

### 4.1.3 Choice of Teaching Method

The teaching method is the approach and means adopted with the aim of fulfilling teaching goals and tasks. It is an integral part of the structure of the whole teaching process and occupies an important position.

An educational scholar of the Soviet Union, Babanski considered that in the teaching process, teaching goals and tasks cannot be fulfilled without proper teaching methods. The American educational scholar L. H. Clark believed that choosing a teaching method is very important in teaching. Teaching tasks will not be accomplished with improper teaching methods. We can draw the conclusion that proper teaching method is crucial to teaching.

However, choosing a teaching method is never easy. It must follow certain rules and standards. According to the research fruits at home and abroad, we must choose teaching methods according to the following eight standards.

(1) Teaching laws and principles

Teaching laws and teaching principles are the rationale of the process. All teaching activities must stick to teaching principles. Choosing the teaching method, as an important part of the teaching process, is no exception. To make the proper choice, teachers have to make teaching laws and principles clear. Only in this way can the choice of method be proper.

(2) Teaching goals and tasks

The method serves goals and tasks. So, when choosing methods, one must have a clear understanding of aims and tasks. Only when making clear the goals and tasks and analyzing the possibility and utility of the tasks can the best selection be gained.

(3) Teaching contents and features

Teaching contents and features are important variables affecting the choice of teaching methods, because teaching methods serve to teaching content. Only when teachers can independently reconstruct teaching materials and truly master their features can they choose the proper teaching methods.

(4) Students' age characteristics and learning level

Teaching objects influence the choice of teaching methods. Teaching methods are adopted according to students' age and learning level. E.g., the teacher-centered teaching method proves effective in junior grade and students of lower learning levels during the clinical study and independent learning in middle school students and undergraduates.

(5) Teachers' possibility

When choosing teaching methods, teachers should also consider their own possibilities in the implementation of all teaching methods. We should try to choose teaching methods suitable for our own reality. At the same time, we should also make preparation and training for those teaching methods that could have achieved good results but could not be implemented due to their own ability constraints, carry out "micro-teaching" and strengthen the practice of teaching methods.

(6) Time and space

Time and space are also factors that must be considered when choosing teaching methods. That is, whether there will be a contradiction in time between a series of teaching methods you choose and ensuring the completion of teaching tasks, and whether space is allowed. This is also very important. In terms of time, we should try to get twice the result with half the effort according to the teaching progress; In terms of space, it should be arranged appropriately according to the size of the site.

(7) Class features

The scale and academic level of the class can influence the choice of teaching methods. American educationalists once proved that when practicing the guided discovery method, the scale should be small (less than 15 is the best); when practicing the lecturing method, the scale should be relatively large (30–50 is the best). Soviet educationalists once considered if the academic level is higher, independent work should be increased in a simple and intuitive way decreased and vice versa.

(8) Teaching environment and modernization of teaching media

The geographical environment, production and social environment, and modernization of teaching media all influence the choice of teaching methods. E.g., without the audio-visual facility, audio-visual teaching would be impossible.

All in all, there is no all-powerful method in reality. Different objectives, different teaching materials, and different students call for different teaching strategies and methods. Therefore, in the teaching process, teachers will face an important task, that is, choosing teaching methods appropriately. Only in this way can expectant results be achieved.

## 4.2 The Applied Research of Teaching Organization Form

Teaching organization form is a kind of teaching activity that can make full use of teaching time, space, intelligence, and objects. The teaching model is a relatively stable teaching process and methodology system which is designed and developed for the intended teaching objectives under the guidance of certain teaching ideas and teaching theories. In theoretical research, teaching organization and teaching model are often regarded as two concepts, but they are connected in practice, for any practice of teaching model cannot be separated from certain teaching organization forms.

Although there are all kinds of teaching organization forms around the world, the primary and middle schools in China still practice classroom teaching in light of our current conditions. Scene teaching, individual instructing, and team teaching are the aid forms, and compound teaching is a special aid form.

### 4.2.1 The Basic Organization Form—Classroom Teaching

Although the basic education curriculum reform puts forward many new concepts and calls for the change of traditional teaching forms to independent, cooperative, and research-style teaching methods, classroom teaching is still a major part of quality education and new curriculum reform. Traditionally, classroom teaching is to practice department instruction in which students of similar age and academic level are divided into the same class, and teachers give classes according to the standard course content, teaching hours, and school timetable, which is also called classroom teaching system or classroom teaching. One salient feature is that one teacher can give a class to a whole class at the same time, which greatly improves efficiency. However, teachers cannot teach students in accordance with their own aptitudes. So traditional classroom teaching calls for reform to adapt to the demand of New Curriculum Learning.

It should be noted that classroom teaching is the product of social history. Schools of feudal society at home and broad adopted individual teaching. Since capitalist production was established, it is recommended that teaching objectives be increased, teaching contents enriched, and teaching schedules be quickened. Western European schools began to try a class teaching system in the 16th century. In the 17th century, Czech educationalist Comenius once expounded a class teaching system theoretically based on the practice of his predecessor and himself and confirmed its advantages. Since then, classroom teaching has been generally adopted in western schools. The first school in China to adopt a classroom teaching system was Imperial Tung Wen College in Beijing, founded by the Qing Regime.

The advent of classroom teaching is a big shift in teaching organization form as well as historical progress. Compared with individual teaching, it has many advantages: the leading role of teachers can be fully exercised, which may improve the teaching organization, planning, and systematicness; it can expand the teaching scale to speed up teaching and improve teaching efficiency. Dividing students into groups in which they can learn from and have a discussion with each other, students have classes according to the school timetable on the same day, which will regulate their brains and arouse learning interests and strike a balance between work and rest. Meanwhile, it is convenient to practice collectivist education. However, every coin has two sides. Classroom teaching also has many disadvantages. It overemphasizes sameness while ignoring individual characteristics; it centers teaching, which easily results in the detachment between theory and practice.

*The Types of Class*

The classification of the class is based on teaching tasks. The division and practice of class type have significant meaning to teaching practice. In the teaching process, if the teacher has the ability to choose and adopt different types of classes based on teaching tasks, contents, students' age characteristics, and the link between different classes, he will make class form a whole system in order to guarantee the unity of teaching process, make students master skills and knowledge in an all-round and firm way and develop intelligence. There are mainly two types of classes:

Single class. It means only one teaching task is accomplished in a single class, which can be further divided into the class which imparts new knowledge, which consolidates former knowledge, which is aimed to cultivate skills, which checks the knowledge, etc. Senior class often adopts this kind.

Comprehensive class. It is also known as a joint class, which means two or more tasks will be fulfilled in a single class, and it is often used in primary or junior students in the middle class. This is because the contents in primary and junior schools are relatively simple and do not need a whole class to finish a single goal. And it is also because students' attention may not concentrate on a single item for a long time. For these reasons, imparting new knowledge, reviewing and consolidating, checking and questioning, and homework and practice are exercised in one class.

*Structure of Class*

The structure of a class refers to the components and their order and allocation in a class. The structure varies in different types of classes. A comprehensive class composes of teaching organization, review and check, imparting new knowledge, consolidation, and homework. A single class is comprised of lecturing, review, practice, etc., in which each one has its own organization. But generally speaking, any type of class has three parts: It begins with teaching organization, centers on teaching tasks accomplishment, and ends with a consolidation of new knowledge.

The factors impacting class structure include not only teaching objectives and contents, but also students' learning ability and teaching methods adopted by teachers in class. Therefore, the class structure should be diverse, not uniform.

### 4.2.2 Assistant Organization Form

*Individual Instruction*

In classroom teaching, teachers give personalized instruction is a useful assistant form of classroom collective teaching, which has existed for thousands of years in China. And Chinese ancient educator has accumulated lots of valuable experience in this field.

Teachers in classroom collective teaching often give lectures from the similarity of students in age and learning level. However, every student is in his own special condition to be given special attention. In this way, individual instruction is quite necessary for classroom teaching, which plays a positive role for both outstanding students and underachievers.

The individual instruction includes the following parts:

(1) Personalized answering, tutoring, and remedial work
(2) The guidance of extracurricular reading
(3) Guidance and check of extracurricular homework
(4) The instruction on learning methods
(5) Employing relative personnel as assistants to provide help for students regularly

With the popularization of modern teaching means, teachers can also use such tools as recordings, videos, books, and computers to give individual guidance to students. Students can choose the learning content and time according to their own needs and conditions. Such kind of optionality and flexibility give individual instruction strong adaptability. Currently, such kind of organization form has become an important part of primary school teaching, and its effect is becoming more important.

*Group Teaching*

Sine the 1960s, with the reform of teaching organization form, group teaching has received more and more attention from western educationalists, and it even has become the fundamental form of primary school teaching in some developed countries. However, group teaching is still viewed as an assistant form as far as the actual situation of primary and secondary school teaching in China is concerned. With the comprehensive promotion of quality education and the deepening of basic education curriculum and teaching reform, its significance will be highlighted in the teaching activities of primary and secondary schools in China.

The advantages of group teaching are that it is beneficial to teaching democracy, arouses the enthusiasm and initiative of students, and forms a favorable teacher-student relationship and student-student relationship. The forms of group teaching are various, which can be generally included as the following eight types:[1]

(1) Group cooperative learning. Partners can share out and cooperate with each other on some issues with difficulty. Such as, when looking something up in the dictionary, students can do the work each with a certain amount and then exchange it with each other. When making up sentences, they can make a sentence each and then choose the best. Everyone gives a solution to a multi-solution math question and then selects the best one.
(2) Group attempt. Teachers help students to master some attempting ways, such as how to attempt to master a character, to read, to write, and to solve a problem. When they meet difficulties in the process, they can communicate with each other. "Little teacher" can help break through difficulties.
(3) Group discussion. Group members can communicate in a low voice or through body language and written units or signs to discuss to find out the right answer.
(4) Group homework. Group members can do difficult work together, have a discussion, and gain inspiration. "Little teacher" can offer help.
(5) Group correction. Some homework can be corrected in the group each other, by a certain member or the "little teacher."
(6) Group reading and reciting. Members do the reading and reciting work and then make role reading and check recitation by the group leader.
(7) Group gaming. We can properly carry out silent or quiet game learning and homework required for teaching, such as new word-moving games, crossword puzzles, looking at pictures to find mistakes, solving mathematical problems, intelligence games, etc.
(8) Group competition. It can be carried out within or among groups, such as writing down characters, words, passages from memory, or oral arithmetic problems.

*Scene Teaching*

It is a kind of teaching in which teachers combine a certain product scene and social life to teach students with relevant personnel on the spot. It can provide direct knowledge for students and enrich their perceptual knowledge, which is important for combining theory and practice. Through scene teaching, students will more deeply understand and master the book learning and improve their exercising skills. Students can keep in touch with the material in person, which will firmly memorize and keep what they have learned.

There are roughly two types of scene teaching: One is to organize students to teach at relevant sites according to the needs of learning knowledge and skills of a certain discipline; another is that students need to go to the relevant site to learn relevant knowledge and skills in order to engage in some practical activities. In scene teaching, students can better understand society and reality. Going to revolutionary sites, cultural relics, and the construction fruits of our nation will exert a great impact on students' ideology, morality, and political attitude. Such special educational influence can hardly be achieved in pure classroom teaching. Therefore, it is necessary to have scene teaching.

The following points should be noticed in organizing scene teaching:

(1) The objectives should be clear. Teachers, students, and involved personnel must make clear what will be achieved through scene teaching and what tasks should be fulfilled. Only in this way can a good subject and proper scene be chosen to ensure the cooperation and connection between scene teaching and classroom teaching.
(2) It must be well-planned. Scene teaching should be under the guidance of teachers and carried out in a prepared, well-planned, and well-organized way. It must gain the cooperation and support of the personnel on the spot. It is advisable that the plan is made with field staff.
(3) The importance should be attached to theoretical guidance. Scene teaching is a good way to combine theory and practice, and it provides plenty of practical knowledge and perpetual material, which demands that teachers emphasize theoretical guidance, lead students to abstract and generalize based on perpetual material, from perpetual knowledge to conceptual knowledge, to analyze and know practical issues theoretically.
(4) Make a summary of the scene teaching. The summary can be talked about by teachers or talked about in a group.

### 4.2.3 The Special Teaching Organization Form—Compound Teaching

Compound teaching is a kind of organization form in which students of different level of more than two grades are organized in a class, and one teacher employ over two teaching material to give lectures to those students in the same classroom at the same time. It is a special organization form in primary school.

Compound teaching maintains all essential characteristics of classroom teaching, such as class, classroom, and the same time. What is different is that teachers have to organize several grades and teaching activities in the same period. It is proper for badly-equipped areas with litter students, teachers, and small campuses. In rural areas of China, many remote villages with large spaces but litter population, with poor transportation have only one teacher and one classroom. Therefore, this kind of form is adopted by many such schools. It will exist as indispensable for a period for the current rural economy and culture are not well-developed while primary school education is urgently calling for development to improve the rural population's quality.

Compared with a single teaching system, compound teaching has some innate disadvantages. For example, students of compound teaching have less instruction time from teachers; students may interfere with each other in the same class, and the teacher will encounter more difficulties both in the classroom and in lesson preparation. The practice has proven that well-organized compound teaching can also achieve good effects, especially if it is good for students' basic training, independent learning, and independent working skills.

With the comprehensive implementation of quality-oriented education, more and more demands have been raised for primary and middle school teaching organization forms. Based on classroom teaching, multi-organization forms co-existing have become mainstream in teaching organization form.

## 4.3 The Cultivation and Improvement of Teaching Art

Teaching is a science as well as an art. Early in the 17th century, Czech educationalist Comenius said in the preface of his book *The Great Didactic* that "education is an art to teaching everything to all human beings." As to the art, he further explains that "To find out a teaching method by which teachers can teach less, while students can learn more, in this way, the school has less noise, troubles and useless labor but more leisure, happiness, and solid progress." British educationalist A. N. Whitehead also considered that education is an art of applying knowledge. When talking about teachers' culture, Albert Einstein once said three basic demands: the first is morality, which is lofty character; the second is intelligence, a wide range of knowledge; the third is skills, excellent teaching skills. He believed teachers should combine creativity with independence to master teaching art. The great educator of the Soviet Union, Sukhomlynsky, said, "Who wants to lead the teaching and educating process has to master the science, skills, and art of teaching and education." He further pointed out that "the art of education first includes speaking art and the art of communication." Mr. Yu Ziyi once said in his *The Scientific and Artistic Outlook on Teaching Method* that teaching without scientific theory is dangerous, just like a blind man on a blind horse rushing headlong to disaster; but if only with theory but no artistic skills to handle problems, it is almost impossible to cope with ever-changing students.[2]

So, what is teaching art? Teaching art is a set of teaching skills by which teachers creatively organize the teaching process according to teaching rules and teaching objects and use teaching methods flexibly to inspire students to arouse their enthusiasm in learning to fulfill teaching tasks to achieve the best effects.

Teaching art is comprehensive, which exists in every step of teaching, such as the art of lesson preparation, lecturing, and homework checking. Among them, lecturing art, that is, classroom teaching art, is the most important part and is also the key point for teachers to study and master.

### 4.3.1 Classroom Teaching Art

Its major parts include: teaching organization, lecturing, use of teaching language, classroom questioning, blackboard writing, etc.

*Art of Teaching Organization*

Teaching organization is a major step in classroom teaching, which plays an important role in attracting students' attention, stabilizing classroom order, and making sure of the progress of teaching. It generally has initial organization and process organization.

Initial organization, the organization before lecturing, aims to lead students into a teaching situation, which utilizes all methods to organize students to learning activities as soon as possible.

Progress teaching is organizing teaching through the whole process of classroom teaching. It aims to maintain students' attention and interest to make teaching progress smoothly. So, how to make teaching progress smoothly?

The first is to use common practice to organize teaching; second, to organize emotionally; third, to use body language; four, to use attention rules; five, to handle accidents in teaching in a proper way.

*Lecturing Art*

Lecturing is also called lead-in. A good lead-in can enhance students' learning desire and arouse their learning interests. Therefore, teachers must pay attention to it. How to begin lecturing? The common ways are as follows:

(1) Guiding an interesting type of lecture. It means using vivid and attractive content and forms to arouse students' interest before lecturing. It requires that the forms be original and vivid, the contents be well-directed, having cognitive value and educational value.
(2) Question lecture. Questioning before lecturing will attract students' attention, arouse their thinking activities and produce a thirst for knowledge, which opens the neural pathway for lecturing content.
(3) Description lecture. Teachers making a vivid description of the teaching material with brief diction and ardor will heighten the classroom atmosphere,

arouse sympathy, and make an association, which paves the way for receiving new knowledge.

(4) Situational lecture. Before class, teachers create a situation by all kinds of methods to arouse questions and lead thinking to make them feel excited. Creating a teaching situation needs a combination of teaching content and the current level to make it inspiring.

(5) General lecture. It is the most common way, that is, to summarize the main content in brief language and point out the key points and difficulties of the class to make students understand and listen to the class around the key parts.

(6) Suspense lecture. It means to create suspense before lecturing, to arouse students' desire for new knowledge and make them concentrate.

There are many ways to begin a lecture, and each has its own advantages. The teacher should design it creatively according to content and reality.

*Art of Using Teaching Language*

Teaching language is a special form of language. It is scientific, thoughtful, and artistic. It is the modification of written language and extraction of oral language. Good teaching language should have the following five criteria:

(1) Clear and scientific. Scientific knowledge should be expressed through scientific language, which is thoughtful and precise, with accurate meaning, precise wording, and no ambiguity.

(2) Brief and logical. Teaching language should be brief and logical. Teachers cannot give lectures by repeating what the books say. They should process and refine it, trying to avoid modifiers and long sentences with too many adjectives to use the simplest sentences to express the most content.

(3) Vivid and figurative. Figurativeness is an important demand for teaching. Teachers should try to make the lecturing more interesting by the vivid and visualized description with rhetorical devices or quotes, allusions, and idioms.

(4) Easily understandable and popular. Teachers should use language in an easily understood, clear, fluent, and standard way. They should try to give lectures in mandarin rather than the local dialect and vernacular.

(5) Cadenced and tuneful. Teachers should not master the language art but also the speaking skills. Tone changes which mean speaking loudly, pronouncing clearly and accurately with moderate speed, and natural intonation with ups and downs.

All in all, the use of language is the essence of classroom teaching art and the key to achieving good teaching effects, so teachers should try to improve language art.

### *Questioning Art*

Questioning is a way to conduct heuristic teaching and improve teaching quality. Questioning may prompt students to think, cultivate their ability to find and solve problems, consolidate knowledge, check and evaluate learning effects and provide feedback to teachers.

Questioning in class is an art, and it demands as follows:

(1) Questions should be clear. First, the aim should be clear, which means the question does exist among students; second, the range of answers should be clear, which generally means only giving a question from one perspective.
(2) Questions should be inspiring. It means teachers should ask in a skillful way that can evoke deep thinking and arouse association and imagination. Next, give some enlightening guidance and key directions for deepening their thinking.
(3) Questions should be moderate. It means the questions should be proper for students' actual level, which can be answered with the guidance of teachers. Questions that are too simple or too difficult do not work.
(4) Questions should be universal. It means it should be aimed at all students, giving more students the opportunity to answer. Meanwhile, the questions should also be individualized, which means students of different levels have questions of different difficulties.

Teachers should listen to the answers carefully. Teachers must give enough attention to the answers, no matter whether they are correct or not, and give impartial and proper judgment.

### *Art of Blackboard Writing*

Blackboard writing is an aid to classroom teaching, and it is an important teaching art. An elaborate blackboard writing will not only highlight key and difficult points to help students understand the stream of teaching contents but also enhance the teaching atmosphere to give students aesthetic enjoyment.

The fundamental requirements are to show the structure of teaching contents and teaching process, highlight key and difficult points, have a clear layer and reasonable layout, make the language clear, and combine blackboard writing and drawing.[3]

Forms of blackboard writing vary in different subjects. The common ones are as follows:

(1) Outline type. This is to summarize the contents and extract the main points, and arrange them logically, which shows the inner connection between the thesis and arguments to form the outline of teaching material.

(2) Abstract type. It is the most common type in Chinese, which shows the structure and change in meaning with key characters and words.
(3) Clue type. It is to grasp the clue of development and then to understand the main body of the whole passage, which is commonly used in teaching novels in Chinese class.
(4) Graphic type. It is to combine blackboard writing and drawing with lines to draw simple graphs and diagrams to help students understand knowledge in the simple links.

Blackboard writing has no fixed form and has no need to form a pattern. The same subject and teaching material may have different blackboard writing. In practice, in order to give full play to it, teachers have to make creative designs according to contents and students' actual level.

### 4.3.2 The Cultivation and Improvement of Teachers' Teaching Art

The practice has proven that the teaching art of teachers has a direct influence on teaching effect and quality. Teachers should try to improve it. So, every teacher should love his subject, understand and study his students, and then practice his basic teaching skills. Basic teaching skills are the prerequisite of teaching art. Without solid basic teaching skills, it is impossible to improve teaching art. Every teacher should stress the training of basic teaching skills. Blackboard writing and drawing should be practiced according to rules and should not disobey the requirements.[4] Form a decent talking manner, pronounce clearly, and express accurately to improve the oral expression ability. And teachers should learn mandarin and pay attention to tone and intonation. In addition, they also should make summary and reflection on teaching ideas and teaching practices and improve teaching arts to further advance career development by teaching reflection.

## 4.4 Seminar Methodology: Origin, Structure, and Function

Seminar has three meanings in modern English-speaking countries: the paradigm or way of teaching, the study and discussion of academic conferences, and a training course for teachers in universities. What we talk about here is the seminar as a teaching method with its origin, structure, and function. It aims to help people to know something about it and provide helpful references to the teaching practice in higher education schools in China. At present, some teaching staff has done research on seminar methodology and creative experiments in postgraduate and graduate teaching.[5] A typical case is the key research topic of the Ministry of Education, "The Structure and Function of Seminar Methodology, Its Application, and Creative Research in Chinese Higher Education Teaching" by Pro. Ma Qinmin in Shaanxi Normal University in the 15th

Five-Year Plan of National Science and Education. In order to fit the Chinese culture and language tradition and habit, and to make it more understandable with Chinese characteristics, we decide to translate "Seminar" into "shuangjiangzhi" (double talk teaching paradigm), making it correspond to the "single teaching method" in which teachers dominate teaching.

### 4.4.1 The Origin of Seminar Methodology

As a teaching method, Seminar originated from traditional universities of the European continent in the Middle Ages. It was first used in German universities and then spread to America and Britain. Until the early 20th century, it was widely used by many college teachers in different countries. "Seminar" originated from the word "seminarium" in Germany, which means the seedbed of academy. Early in the 17th century, the well-known Czech educationalist Comenius argued that the word "seminar" should be used in schools. Although at that time, European countries founded the seminary or seminarium to train priests, it also cultivated college teaching personnel.[6] In fact, at present, Seminar in German still has the same function. However, people think differently about the function of seminar in early times. Some think seminar is an academic discussion and research for seeking truth, democracy, and freedom. Some think the early seminar has the function of teaching students to learn and recite. Others believe the seminar of the 18th century has the double functions of research and teaching in colleges.

Literature shows that in the University of Hall, founded in 1694, Seminar was employed to develop a free academic atmosphere rather than to teach students curriculum knowledge. In addition, literature also manifests that the advocate of mass education A. H. Frank, the Greek professor conducted his teaching research by combining lecturing and informal German. However, the most influential Seminar practice is F. A. Wolf's practice of using seminar methodology in philosophy in 1786, which is regarded as the reform of traditional philosophy teaching. He made students prepare a written and oral presentation on a certain subject and then led them to make discussion on it. After that, people followed the example, and the typical Seminar methodology in German universities took shape. Meanwhile, it retains the early meaning that it is a specialized research department or institution where the material for research and teaching are stored, and students discuss and do scientific research in a group under the guidance and instruction of the professor.

With the increase in the academic atmosphere in universities and the demand for the academic ability of students since the 19th century, the traditional method of teachers' lecturing was challenged. Seminar came into vogue in German and other European universities in order to train elites in classical disciplines. Usually, the students who want to attend the seminar should be qualified with enough academic knowledge and make preparations both in written and oral forms under the requirements of the instructor. Although seminar was applied differently in universities, it was regarded as the most effective method of learning and academic exploration at that time. And literature indicates that Seminar as a teaching paradigm had formed its popular pattern in the mid-19th century: the instructor puts forward a proposition or an issue, then the student makes up an outline or a scheme, does a pre-class preparation or initial research, and makes a presentation based on it to his fellows and the others give questions and advice. At last, the student writes a complete report based on the advice, talks about it in class, and has a discussion with his instructor and classmates. At that time, the basic structure of Seminar can be summarized as the following process: the instructor gives an argument proposition, some students make a presentation, the others give advice and criticism, write a complete report, and make a topic discussion in the end. Such structure shows the following features: students discuss about a specific topic or subject given by the expert instructor by reading, writing, and discussion. Apparently, seminar at that time already has the feature of research.[7]

To sum up, the characteristics of Seminar Methodology can be summarized as the following three aspects:

First, the research character of orientation. It means the goal of Seminar is to research some issues rather than the impartment of knowledge of a certain subject; it is mainly used in subjects with high speculativeness, such as philosophy and logistics.

Second, the limited participants. Only students with higher ability, skills, and enough knowledge can be entitled to attend seminar, which is particularly obvious in German. In the early and middle 19th century, seminar methodology was only used for sophomore in Germany, and students had to pass a certain qualification exam to be enrolled.

Third, the definiteness of topics. The topics in seminar were chosen by experts and instructors according to their expertise. Students' task is to prepare and discuss these topics. The self-service topic system has not yet appeared.

Compared with Germany, at the end of the 19th century, traditional American universities (such as Michigan University, Yale University, and Harvard University) used Seminar in a wider and more flexible way, despite that they borrowed it from German. Many scholars believe that the Seminar in America is more proper to be called seminary method of teaching rather than academic seminar. The historian Charles Adams at Michigan University was the first to introduce Seminar to American universities from Europe, and in 1869, he exercised it in the course "Advanced Course in History." He thought students should be explorer and finder of truth and devote their time to doing research rather than stay at the library reading books. Teachers should guide their students to carry on research. Seminar is an effective way to put this into practice. Adam's idea was indicated in his lecture on history. He did not put much emphasis on systematic knowledge and clear knowledge structure, but he chose some topics worthy of discussion, had a discussion with some qualified students, and then shared the fruits with students through Seminar.[8]

However, Seminar was not advocated and carried out before the 20th century in Britain. Teachers in Britain who were used to traditional teaching methods, tutorial systems, and tutorials or supervision did not consider Seminar as a valuable teaching paradigm. This is because Britain has a long tradition of strict examination system, so the German paradigm featured research and open conclusion cannot meet such demand. Just as Pro. Ian Watt, the fore-leader of the English Department at the University of East Anglia in Britain, once pointed out that the traditional exam encouraged students to master and retell the knowledge that can be tested, so what cannot be tested cannot be called knowledge. Apparently, in written tests of three or four hours, facts that can be memorized and intelligent skills to solve problems are readily tested.[9]

After the 1930s, with Seminar beginning to show its advantages in cultivating students' research spirit and ability, Seminar was gradually accepted by British scholars and combined with other methods to be used in college teaching. After the 1960s, with the expansion of British higher education and the increase in enrollment, Seminar paradigm was used more frequently from graduate education to postgraduate education. Meanwhile, theoretical research of Seminar began to mushroom, with various implementation plans appearing.[10]

### 4.4.2 The Basic Structure of Modern Seminar

In the long-time practice of college teaching, Western Seminar has formed different structures, like the University of Leicester, which divides the Seminar into five major types: teacher's prescribed topic seminar (48%), students' self-choose topic seminar (37%), report and discussion seminar (66%), discussion seminar (37%), and problem-solving seminar (44%) Apparently, Seminar does not have a fixed pattern. We can divide Seminar teaching in Britain and America into two types according to who leads the class: tutor-led seminar and student-led seminar. Next, we will introduce the basic parts of the teacher-led report and discuss seminar based on the study of research literature and the writer's personal experience in foreign universities.

(1) Introduction

This part takes about five minutes. It mainly includes a brief introduction and arrangement of the topic of the presentation, participants, and process. Sometimes, the host—the teacher makes a brief review of the last lecture and further explains the theoretical and practical value of the current topic.

(2) Report (20–30 minutes)

This part is the major part of Seminar. The presenter will make a speech to the class about the topic prescribed by the teachers or self-chosen, which is usually called a presentation. The reporter can be on behalf of himself or the team. It is quite common that team members will work together on a research report or topic report in universities in Britain or America. No matter what the topic is, the reporter has to make a brief literature review and then give his own perspective. He should make the audience feel that he has referred to lots of literature and knows cutting-edge information about this field, and the major reference should be listed at the end of the report. Nowadays, students mainly give reports with self-made PowerPoint or CD-ROM, which can achieve good effects generally.

(3) The speech of the response person (10–15 minutes)

At this stage, If the reporter represents the whole group, his fellows can give some compliment then others can give a statement of various forms such as questions, criticism, and advice. The reporter just gives a brief explanation.[11]

(4) Discussion (10–20 minutes)

Based on the report and the speech of the response person, the host leads students to have a targeted discussion on one or more issues. If it is well-organized with an active atmosphere, in many cases, this part will become fierce debates or criticism and counter-criticism. Students will show their intelligence and critical thinking based on this academic accumulation. Teachers play the role of leading the discussion and managing the limited time.

(5) Summary (5 minutes)

The host teacher will give his assessment and summary of the seminar, including the gains or analyze what can be further discussed, meanwhile giving his assignment and requirements.

(6) Student assessment (3–5 minutes)

At the end of a Seminar class, many teachers give assessment lists to students to get students' assessment of the seminar. The list usually contains the report content, the way of a report, the use of verbal and non-verbal language, and aid methods that provide feedback for improving students' report ability.[12]

### 4.4.3 The Function of Modern Seminar Methodology

Since its appearance in Middle Ages, Seminar has been gradually known and used widely, and it is still a popular way in college teaching abroad. What function does it have? The writer believes its major functions are as the following:[13]

First, Seminar will develop students' skills in listening, speaking, reading, and writing. When it comes to the four skills, people will think about foreign language teaching. In fact, every subject has the function of developing the four skills of students. In traditional teaching, we just ignore this point so that the four skills develop separately so the students cannot develop in an all-round way.[14] Seminar methodology covers such shortage. It demands students not only listen to others but also make their own ideas understood by others and write reports. In brief, the seminar teaching paradigm requires the student to understand (be able to understand), speak (to say everything clearly), read (be able to read and understand), and write (be able to write well). Why was the seminar first used in philosophy teaching and then used in other humanistic and social sciences? This is because every scholar of humanistic and social sciences should be equipped with the four basic skills, and seminar is aimed at developing the four skills as a whole. This is the prominent feature and basic function of Seminar, and the reason why it is stressed by many college teaching scholars.[15]

Second, seminar methodology can cultivate students' exploring spirit, habit, and ability. Different from traditional teaching and individual instruction, seminar requires students to explore and study the issues in their own field. To fulfill the tasks, students have to read, think and study, and make pre-class preparation, presentation, and participation in the class. In order to make their reports more scientific and convincing, students use scientific research methods and experience the scientific research process, which is good for the form of exploring spirit and improvement of exploration ability.

Third, Seminar can help achieve teacher-student and student-student interaction. It changes the one-way communication in cramming teaching, realizing the multi-exchange and cognitive interaction between teachers and students and between students and students. It integrates learning with teaching, making classroom teaching more active. Moreover, students can master, think about, assess, and innovate knowledge while reading, writing, speaking, discussing, criticizing, and assessing.[16]

In brief, seminary method of teaching helps to achieve mutual communication, mutual effects, and mutual complement between teachers and students and between students and students in knowledge, thinking, and emotion, which demonstrates the nature of teaching activity as a process of communication and interaction.[17] In the current reform of college teaching, if it can be used when combined with other ways according to course characteristics and students' actual situation, the desired effects can be achieved.

# CHAPTER FIVE

# The Evaluation of Contemporary Teaching

Targeted at the evaluation of teaching as the research subject, this chapter includes the following four sections: The first section expounds on such characteristics of the evaluation of teaching in contemporary quality education as the evaluation objectives toward promoting the overall development of students, the evaluation content on diverse factors of teaching system, the systematic integration of various forms of evaluation, the comprehensiveness of the evaluation criteria, the diversification of evaluation methods and assessment tools, along with multiple channels gathering evaluation information.

In the second section, a discussion about the evaluation of teaching in the network environment is administered, thus promoting the fundamental perspectives where the effectiveness of choosing media-supported systems and teaching behavior should be adopted in order to evaluate classroom teaching in the network environment.

The third section investigates the history of evaluating teaching development in American universities and demonstrates the characteristics of the evaluation standard of teaching at different stages.

The theoretical and practical issues concerning the evaluation of teaching in American universities have been covered. It indicates that the basic researchers' view toward students' evaluating teaching, i.e., students' evaluation is not only reliable but also valid. The following developmental tendency for the evaluation of teaching in American universities in the early years of the 21st century will still exist in applying the students' evaluation to promote the sustainable development of college teachers' teaching and assist it in becoming scientific and modernizing constantly.

## 5.1 The Characteristics of the Evaluation of Contemporary Quality Education Teaching

As the new curriculum to promote the deepening of quality-oriented education in the new century has been implemented, it has been the main melody of the foundation education reform and development in our country. The implementation of quality-oriented education involves many theoretical and practical issues, such as strengthening leadership, changing concepts, improving teachers' quality, using scientific evaluation, and so on. What is accomplished can meet the requirements and objectives of quality-oriented education only with a clear mind. This section places special stress on the basic characteristics of evaluating the teaching of equality-oriented education, hopefully providing some references for the first-line teachers in practice.

### 5.1.1 Focusing on the Evaluating Objectives of Promoting Students' Comprehensive Development

For students, the teaching evaluation of the "exam-oriented education" is an isolated system, with the exam as the core, promotion as the direction, and scores as the assessment. The way that merely exam scores are regarded as the sole criteria to evaluate students has severely impaired students' initiative, enthusiasm, and creativity, thus taking a toll on the improvement of students' comprehensive quality and the development of students' personalities.

However, the teaching evaluation of quality-oriented education is a developing evaluation system, focusing on the direction of comprehensive development, the core of developing intelligence, cultivating ability and creativity, as it widely collects material to measure the students' progress comprehensively. In terms of teachers, the "exam-oriented education" evaluation system is based on only one information source (their leaders or the students' achievements) to determine the quality of teaching and judge the quality of teachers' work by the graduation rates. While the quality-oriented education evaluation system advocates collecting information all-roundly and assessing teaching comprehensively.

On the whole teaching process, aimed at the teaching system, the evaluating teaching of quality-oriented education is a complex system with the characteristics of multi-level, multifaceted, multi-angle, and comprehensive overlapping. The quality-oriented education evaluation system keeps eye on improving the evaluation of both teaching and learning, and it emphasizes the following goals:

(1) The evaluation cannot derive from the teaching goal. Namely, the evaluation works very well only when the teaching goals are analyzed specifically, and the achieving process is pursued.

(2) The evaluation should be continuous. In order to help constantly changing children, it is not enough to only depend on regular tests or measures. Instead, all accessible measures should be conducted constantly so as to get an accurate evaluation.
(3) Only based on arousing the initiative of teachers and students' self-assessment, the evaluation can achieve the best effect. Teaching evaluation should wisely explain the best effect of evaluation and make full use of the results to take the guidance activities after evaluation. Only by incorporating evaluating into guidance can the evaluation play its proper function.

### 5.1.2 Focusing on Evaluating the Various Factors of the Teaching System

The evaluating teaching of traditional "examination-oriented" education is intended primarily for students, while other factors in the teaching system are rarely evaluated. The sacredness of the classroom and the freedom of teachers' domination have been institutionalized. However, the teaching evaluation of modern quality education advocates analyzing the teaching under the guidance of principles of system theory. Within the teaching system, the following factors matter a lot, such as teachers, students, teaching targets, teaching contents, teaching media, teaching environment, and so on, all of which are supposed to be included in the evaluation process, instead of mere students. We must evaluate the teaching system widely as a whole in order to obtain various aspects of feedback, regulate the teaching process in the best state and achieve the teaching results successfully.

All in all, teaching evaluation of quality education not only emphasizes evaluating students (their knowledge, intelligence, ability, character, etc.), but also stresses that of teachers (teachers' quality, teaching ability, teaching proficiency, preparation state of teaching, teaching art, creativity of teaching and psychological factors, etc.). It not only emphasizes evaluating the teaching process (the choice of teaching methods, the application of teaching skills, and the presentation of teaching art), but also advocates the teaching input (the establishment of teaching targets, the preparation of teaching materials, and the selection of teaching contents) and teaching output (the quality and effect, and the achievement of teaching targets). It places emphasis on evaluating individual students (to know the differences) as well as the students as a whole (to know the common problems). It is fair enough to say that the objectives of the teaching evaluation of quality education involve all the factors in the teaching system, and it even expands to the entire field of teaching. Of course, teachers and students as the core teaching subjects are undoubtedly the focal points.

### 5.1.3 Focusing on the Systematic Integration of Diversified Evaluation Forms

From the perspective of the types of evaluation, the evaluating teaching of the "exam-oriented education" mainly emphasizes the summary assessment, with the advocate of the disposable evaluation to assess students. The teaching evaluation of quality education advocates the use of various types of evaluation, which organically combines the diagnostic evaluation (pre-teaching evaluation) used to understand students' knowledge background and learning criteria, and the final evaluation (post-teaching evaluation) used to understand students' learning, identify and grade students, so as to give full play to the various functions of teaching evaluation. In terms of teachers, the evaluation should not only function as gradation and identification. More importantly, it should play a role in promoting teachers to reflect on themselves so as to make improvements in teaching.

As for students, the evaluating teaching of quality-oriented education should play the following parts: diagnosing learning problems, evaluating teaching effectiveness, guiding students' learning, foreboding the development of students, marking students, grouping and resettling in teaching, etc. As far as teachers are concerned, the functions of quality education teaching evaluation are as follows: the improvement of teachers' teaching, personnel decisions, curriculum development, evaluating the quality of school teaching, etc. According to the requirements of quality education, the ultimate goal of the teaching evaluation is to guide learning and improve teaching. At present, one of the most prominent features of evaluating teaching of quality-oriented education is applying various evaluation types, especially formative evaluation.

### 5.1.4 Focusing on Comprehensiveness of Evaluation Criteria

In view of the evaluating standards for the teachers and students, the traditional "exam-oriented education" mainly emphasizes the results (the students' test scores), which obviously do not adapt to the principle of cultivating an all-round personal development. While under the guidance of cultivating all-round development people, the modern evaluation of teaching focusing on quality education actively advocates formulating a comprehensive standard to evaluate the quality of teaching and learning roundly. For teachers, it should not only inspect the quality of the teaching output (students' marks and improvement), but also the quality of the teaching process and the quality of their instructional design, which aims at directing teachers to improve their teaching. In terms of students, competence education requires that teachers should lay down the evaluation standards of students' achievements and they should formulate the evaluating criteria on the development of intelligence, ability, interests, hobbies, critical mind, creativity, and individuality as well, aiming at guiding the students to achieve comprehensive development.

### 5.1.5 Focusing on the Diversification of Evaluation Methods and Assessment Tools

From the perspective of the historical development of evaluation methods plus techniques, centered on the subjective qualitative method, the traditional evaluation of teaching lacks objective quantitative indicators. While in the stage of measuring movement, the quantitative methods have become the center, putting low emphasis on the function of qualitative methods. Thus, the evaluation of "exam-oriented education" excessively emphasizes the exams and the "hundred-mark system." In the view of the modern evaluation of teaching, it is inappropriate to take either biased qualitative or quantitative methods. The idea integrates qualitative methods into quantitative methods, soft evaluation into hard evaluation, experiment design into the non-experiment design, and that emphasizes applying all kinds of emerging measurements such as multivariate statistical methods, hierarchical analytic processes, and comprehensive evaluations of the fuzzy mathematics technology been advocated.

Besides, the traditional evaluation of teaching mainly makes use of exams to gather information, and following that, here comes the preference of teachers and students for the scores. While the modern evaluation of teaching focusing on quality education advocates collecting information through many kinds of feasible technology and tools, such as achievement tests, intelligence tests, questionnaires, conversations, rating scales, diary examinations, behavior observations, self-report, case analyses, works analysis, and talking. Teachers and students are mainly concerned with obtaining feedback so as to make a scientific teaching decision, effectively control the teaching process, and improve the quality of teaching. It also pays great attention to play computer technology in the designing of evaluation, the material collection and the result settlement, etc.

### 5.1.6 Focusing on Assessing the Sources of Information through Various Ways

In the traditional evaluation of teaching, the approach to collecting evaluation information and material is usually single. The teacher is the only judge of the learning quality, while the leader is the main committee for the teaching effect. Conversely, in order to approach a scientific objective and right evaluation conclusions, the modern teaching evaluation of quality education advocates gathering information through multiple channels and ways. The evaluation of teaching effect should consist of various aspects of evaluation information ranging from their leaders, peers, students, themselves, teaching achievements, alumni, society, and so on. While for the evaluation of the learning quality, the related information should be collected in such a multifaceted way as the teaching team, their teachers, classmates, themselves, and so on. The modern evaluation of teaching focusing on quality-oriented education claims the multi-channel sources of information and the diversity of evaluation methods. The main reason is that the results of comprehensive evaluation based on all-round collected information can balance the limitations of one way or aspect with the advantages of another way and method, which will greatly increase the fairness and accuracy of evaluation. The more impartial and accurate the evaluation is, the more valuable the feedback becomes so that teaching improvement is more guaranteed.

## 5.2 The New Thinking on the Evaluation of Teachers' Classroom Teaching in the Network Environment

In today's information society, the wide application of network, a brand-new technology, and its expansion in all fields of social life have made itself beyond the scope of technical achievements. As a result, it has become the cultural characteristic of the learning era. Its penetration into education has caused profound reform on the material plane, the conceptual plane, and the institutional plane. With the further development of information technology, this kind of permeation must be strengthened and diffused to each corner of education. As the main position of curriculum implementation and creation, classroom teaching activities cannot be free from the infiltration and challenge of new technology. Teaching networking is an inevitable trend in classroom teachers' teaching activities in the 21st century.

Under such circumstances, the traditional evaluation system of classroom teaching effect is hard to continue to deal with the new situation and will lose the existing foundation due to the changes in the teachers' role and teaching activities within the new Internet context, even though the evaluation of teachers' classroom teaching aims at improving the ultimate purpose without radically changing. Therefore, we must build a new system of contemporary evaluation of classroom teaching, adapt to the network environment, and conform with the value orientation of the new curriculum.

### 5.2.1 Changes of the Teachers' Roles in the Classroom Teaching of the Networking Environment

"The role is a part or a segment of the behavior patterns in one's daily life." The teachers' roles are the reflection of themselves in the behavior patterns of the teaching activities. In traditional classroom teaching, teachers mainly play the following roles:

(1) The conveyors of knowledge, which are the teachers' central role, and who other roles service
(2) The classroom discipline administrators who are responsible for dealing with emergencies to ensure the order of the teaching activities
(3) The decision-makers, who have the authority not only on the behavior of "teaching" but on "learning"
(4) The models and the agents of parents who confer various iconicity to students from the following aspects knowledge, emotion, morality, and so on. They are also important ways for school students to gain information about the adult world, realizing students to be socializing
(5) The artists of interpersonal relations who should communicate with students comprehensively, coordinating relations between students and teachers, stu-

dents and students to construct a good classroom learning environment, and it also can promote students' socialization to a certain extent
(6) The scholars and learners
(7) The clerks who are responsible for some things that are not directly related to classroom teaching activities, such as grading, marking, scores registration, etc.

Represented by the Internet, the involvement of information technology has made fundamental changes in students' learning. In other words, the learning was transformed from being controlled by teachers to autonomous learning by students themselves. The learning process has also changed from passive knowledge accumulation to self-constructive acquisition. Therefore, the teachers' inherent role in the traditional classroom teaching environment cannot meet the demand of the new form of network teaching. As a consequence, teachers must reshape their roles in line with the characteristics of new teaching activities in the network environment. In general, there will be four changes in the existing role of teachers.

*Teachers' Roles Fading as Knowledge Conveyors and Clerks*
Essentially, teaching activity is the interactive communication process among subjects. While in the network environment, the communication mode of human-human interaction will be replaced by multiple composite communication modes such as human-machine communication, human-human communication, and human-human communication based on the machine. "An experiment from Kulek, an American psychologist, showed that students who learn with computers can save 30%–50% of the study time compared to those who learn in a traditional teaching way." The main reason is that technological support facilitates the integration of multiple teaching methods in the Internet situation. Contrary to the traditional classroom teaching that is only congruous to those students who acquire information mainly through visual approaches and who perceive the process mainly by the intuitive ways and are good at understanding knowledge orderly, it overcomes those defects and achieves essentially for teaching students according to their aptitudes.

From this point of view, in the network environment, the position of the teachers must transform from the center of teaching activities into the "edge" part. The role of the knowledge conveyor, the teacher's central role in the traditional classroom, will fade and disappear subsequently, and the related role of the classroom policymakers will lose its foothold. Instead, teachers' general affairs have been replaced by various facility software so as to lead the disappearance of the role of the clerk.

*Updating Teachers' Role of Classroom Administrator*
In the network environment, students are still in breach of discipline that impacts the teaching order to some extent, but due to the students' stages and methods of

autonomous learning and self-deciding study, new teaching activities are in a disordered state. The traditional violation of discipline is no longer the main unconventional behavior that interferes with learning. The unconventional behavior of students caused by the changes in environment and learning style has become the main factor affecting the achievement of teaching objectives. Therefore, it requires teachers must update the role of classroom administrators.

### *Strengthening Teachers' Roles of the Relationship Artists, Models and Parents' Agencies, Scholars and Learners*

Essentially, teachers' work is a kind of spiritual production activity. The lowest education goal is to help students' cognitive development, while the real ultimate goal is to further develop students' emotional, moral aspects, and so on. "Interpersonal emotion on the ontology is a kind of social need that can be achieved essentially by more direct social interaction activities through person-to-person." The necessary condition for students to master a series of social rules and become social people is that students take part in social interaction activities with peers and adults represented by teachers.

As "social representatives," teachers behave so important because they reflect the social rules which can guide the students. But the machine has the characteristics of linear and non-emotion. The virtual network world will also pull the real distance between adults and people, resulting in a lack of students' emotions and obstacles to socialization. In this case, teachers must strengthen emotional communication activities between teachers and students and between students with their own morality and personality charm with the help of interpersonal artists, role models, and parental agency roles so as to fulfill the cultivation of the "whole" person.

It is an inevitable requirement for teachers to strengthen these roles of the learners and scholars in the network environment. Teachers monopolize knowledge in traditional teaching, and the learner's identity is more symbolic of providing students with imitable models, relying on the scholars' identity. While in the network environment, it provides teachers and students with unprecedented equal learning opportunities and conditions, and the scholars' identities are supported by the learners' identities. When teachers fail to identify themselves as learners, they face a survival crisis, especially to be scholars, so teachers must strengthen their roles as scholars and learners.

### *New Roles for Teachers: Network Administrators, Developers, Researchers, Helpers, and Supporters*

(1) As helpers and supporters. The condition for teachers to improve teaching effect is to reorient their dominant roles according to the changes in the activities in the classroom. Although the network environment has largely eliminated the institutional authority of teachers as social spokesmen, the knowledge authority as knowledge monopolists, and the leading role as knowledge imparters, it does not mean the

complete elimination of teachers' activities in network classroom teaching. Because of the character of independent learning in the network environment and the tendency of education democratization and personalized, teachers are no longer the center of teaching activities, and teaching process has also become the democratic collaboration between teachers and students. The teachers' activities are mainly auxiliary rather than controlling the students' learning activities. Therefore, teachers' dominant roles have changed into helpers and supporters.

(2) As network administrators. Such a role provides a technology guarantee for normal teaching activities. No matter how advanced a technological instrument is, if teachers cannot recognize and use it correctly, that will be useless for teaching.

Thus, better recognition and application of the Internet is the premise for the Internet to be the basic tool of classroom teaching. If teachers cannot solve the technical problems in the process of students' learning, teaching activities will stagnate due to the interference of external factors, and the quality, efficiency, and benefit of teaching cannot be guaranteed. That is the reason why teachers must be equipped with the basic knowledge of network hardware and software technology that enables them to cope with students' inquiries and equipment maintenance so as to ensure the normal order of teaching.

(3) As the developers of the network resource and the researchers of the curriculum content. What counts an important practical value is that the development of network resources and the research of course content are combined in network classroom teaching. The instrument on the Internet is a double-edged sword. On the one hand, its abundant resources and friendly interfaces can stimulate students' interest, improving the efficiency of classroom learning; on the other, it still has some insurmountable weaknesses.

From the quantity of information, the network provides rich resources along with huge information pressure. In the face of overwhelming information, people's self is obliterated. As for the storage form of information, the information in the network is randomly piled up together, no matter how powerful the search engine it is, while the results are mixed with effective information and invalid information. The information provided by the network is generally integrated information, especially less targeted, and a large amount of inefficient and repetitive information. From the perspective of acquiring the approach of information, the same information can be gained from the different paths owing to the cross links in the network information. The efficiency of obtaining information through different paths is different, and people can't know the efficiency of this path before choosing it. Only after many times of practice can they choose the best path. Therefore, in order to improve the efficiency of teaching, teachers must study the curriculum content, restructuring and integrating the network resources so as to effectively guide the students' learning.

### 5.2.2 Changes in Teachers' Behavior on the Classroom Teaching

Based on the characteristics of the management activities in the class, teaching behavior in the classroom can be divided into the flowing three types: the main teaching behavior, auxiliary teaching behavior, and management behavior. Directly pointing to the teaching objectives and teaching contents, the main teaching behavior is manifested in the language and behavior that is closely related to the teaching objectives displayed by teachers, such as blackboard writing, explanation, questioning, and other teaching behaviors. Auxiliary teaching behavior is used to deal with situational problems and indirectly promote teaching objectives, such as stimulating and maintaining students' motivation, strengthening students' real behavior, creating classroom atmosphere, and so on. Classroom management behavior services for classroom accidents, and improve the efficiency of classroom teaching. The difference between the main teaching behavior and auxiliary teaching behavior is that the former has been prepared before serving the teachers' dominant role. In contrast, the latter cannot be prepared before owing to the differences in scenarios, obeying teachers' non-dominant role. Roles conform to their behavior so that in networking classroom, the transformation of teachers' roles inevitably bring changes in teaching behavior.

Firstly, teachers' main teaching behavior in traditional classroom teaching has lost its central position. That is the inevitable cause of the loss of the central role of the knowledge conveyor.

In the traditional classroom, the main character of teachers occupies quite a large quantity of time. The teaching objective is the motivation of various student-teacher activities. While in network-based classroom teaching activities, the whole process of imparting knowledge is completed through the interactions of person-machine, ranging from presenting the target and explaining the content to appraising the learning. As teachers' main teaching behavior in the traditional classroom has lost its active main position, it becomes developing into the auxiliary behavior of "leak checking and vacancy filling" for the functions and problems of teaching software. This is not only the embodiment of the requirements of the leading role of teachers' helpers and supporters for teachers' behavior, but also the inevitable result of the disappearance of the role of teachers' knowledge instructors.

Secondly, the traditional auxiliary teaching behavior becomes the teachers' main teaching behavior. Such a turn in their roles is in line with the leading role of teachers as helpers and supporters. In traditional classroom teaching, what auxiliary teaching should do is only promote the effect of teachers' main teaching behavior. There are many reasons for the improvement of its status and value in the networked classroom:

(1) Students' learning is highly personalized in the network environment, and the problems in the teaching process are more situational if teachers make

preparations in advance. Trying to cope with the problems in the classroom will make themselves in trouble, so teachers' teaching can only be situational behavior.

(2) Machine teaching lacks pertinence and flexibility. The so-called "treat each student as an individual" is just to provide as many choices as possible and obtain pertinence and flexibility with diversity; however, it is still rigid in the face of vivid specific practice. Of course, with the development of technology, the function of teaching software will become more and more powerful, but machine can never reach the degree of pertinence and flexibility that people can achieve. It is impossible to judge that the root of students' wrong responses is a congenital defect or lack of motivation. Therefore, teachers' auxiliary teaching behavior becomes the key to solving substantive issues.

(3) Teachers' non-dominant role in traditional classroom teaching has been strengthened. In classroom teaching activities, teaching and educating are unified. The ultimate goal of teaching should be to focus on the generation of one's spiritual world instead of the physical one. During the process, the interaction of person-machine mostly has an effect on the learning of knowledge, especially instrumental knowledge, while it is powerless in the following aspects, such as people's morals, personalities, socialization, and so on. That is why it fails to create the generation of human's whole spiritual world. In contrast, teachers are able to play the roles of the non-dominant role, such as interpersonal artists and models, which is a significant approach for students to generate their spiritual world and personality in education. In the meantime, the simple work in the network classroom that ever toke teachers' large energy in the traditional classroom was replaced by the machine so that the cultivation of the complete person has a reality foundation. And the reinforcement of the behavior of the non-dominant role becomes a necessity to teach on the Internet.

(4) The content and direction of management behavior of teachers in the classroom have changed. In the network environment, the management in the classroom can be classified into the following three aspects: information source management, time management, and behavior management of students. Resource management refers to the complexity of the information in the repository of the network resource. Everyone seems to have the same experience that they are attracted by irrelevant information when surfing the Internet. Students are growing people, and their self-control and management ability has a low degree of development, so it is difficult to consciously resist the attraction to irrelevant information. That is why teachers must control the source of information to reduce the "unconventional" behavior of students.

Teachers' behavior time management in network classroom teaching is more valuable than in traditional teaching. In the traditional classroom, time management is the teachers' job, fusing in the main teaching behavior; however, in the process of autonomous learning, time management becomes the students' behavior.

However, not all students are able to administrate time effectively; especially for primary and middle school students, it is difficult for them to administrate time effectively owing to their low level of self-awareness. So, it is an essential condition to improve teaching efficiency by assisting students or directly taking time management by teachers. An effective way to deal with general disciplinary actions and prevent students from absorbing irrelevant information is to administrate students' non-normal behavior directly.

### 5.2.3 Relocating the Evaluation of Teachers' Classroom Teaching in the Network Environment

In the traditional evaluation of classroom teaching, the focus is placed on the main teaching behavior embodied in the teaching skills and techniques, which mixes the evaluation of people with the evaluation of classes, thus judging teachers' teaching ideas and teachers' quality with the quality of a class. As a matter of fact, "these teaching skills and techniques, such as blackboard handwriting, language, teaching posture and so on, cannot present the whole quality of teachers, and it is also difficult to determine what is the good or bad standard." Particularly, in the network environment, the defects of this evaluating model are hard to ignore. On the basis of the change in teachers' roles and teaching behavior in the network environment, the evaluation of classroom teaching of teachers is divided into the following two major parts: the evaluation of the effectiveness of choosing media-supported systems and the evaluation of the effectiveness of classroom teaching behavior systems.

#### *The Evaluation of the Teaching -Supported Systems*

The teaching-supported systems indicate the tool systems chosen by teachers to interact with students, including hardware-supported and software-supported. The process of selecting a support system is an important role behavior of teachers' supporters and helpers. Therefore, the effectiveness of the evaluation support system is an important aspect of evaluating teachers' teaching in the network environment. According to the basic principle of the evaluation of modern teaching and the change of teaching in the network environment, we believe that the evaluation of the effectiveness of the teaching-supported system can be conducted from the following several aspects:

(1) The effectiveness of selecting teaching software. The interaction of teacher-student was replaced by the interaction of person-machine. The routine evaluation of teachers is mostly transformed into the evaluation of software effectiveness. As the core of the assessment of support system evaluation, teaching software usually includes the evaluation of internal effectiveness and external effectiveness.

Internal effectiveness refers to the evaluation of the availability and reliability of the teaching software, inspecting from multiple perspectives, concretely analyzing and assessing the following characteristics: the interface intuition of the software; the clarity of the navigation system; the models and efficiency of the content links between models (linear or radial?); the simplicity of operation; the effectiveness of the help module, the error rate of text materials; the failure rate and the flexibility of the whole program; its interactive level and so on.

External effectiveness refers to the matched degree of the software with the users' need, and the integration degree of the teaching content and teaching goal. The important indexes to evaluate the external effectiveness of the teaching software are as follows: its load of the inspiration of the content, transferable degree, logic system and the matched degree with students' physical and mental characteristics, the load of the diversification and effectiveness of the teaching strategies and methods, the reliability and timeliness of assistance and feedback, and the quality of the recording, storing and dealing with students' study data, etc.

(2) The effectiveness of the learning resources provided. The learning resources provided by teachers to students are an important support system for students' autonomous learning. Conversely, the effective information obtained by students mainly comes from the resources provided by teachers. The evaluation of learning resources can be carried out from the following aspects: the relevance of the resources and the target, namely existing any irrelevant information or not; whether the organization structure and the presenting method are reasonable, conforming with the characteristics of students' age and the network learning; whether the resources are rich enough to meet the needs of different students; whether the individual resources provide for personalized students can be shared enough, influencing the result of the interaction among students to cause the Matthew effect; whether it provides a personalized approach to obtain resources, and it is a highly efficient way or not.

(3) The effectiveness of online learning tools provided for students. The premise of mastering effective tools is to apply resources effectively. Resources on the Internet are very complicated. Students' online resource search is like looking for a needle in a haystack if they lack effective instruments, which leads to hinders for them from achieving their teaching goals. At the same time, the students can directly enter the high-quality online resource database to improve learning efficiency. So, whether we can provide flexible and convenient online learning tools is also an important index for the appraising support system.

(4) Whether the old and new media can integrate reasonably. Not all new things are the most effective in teaching. "We cannot totally reject the traditional teaching mode and methods, because after all, they are effectively going through several generations of education workers summary from their hard work." We should

hold the view of "taking advantage of what is good from multiple directions." Whatever can promote students' development should be reasonably used in the process of teaching. This indicator should contain the following elements: the advantage of the network has been played fully and reasonably; whether it is reasonable to apply the traditional media in accordance with the teaching content, teaching goal, and students' physical and mental characteristics; whether the old and new media form complementary situations to each other, etc.

***The Plate of Teachers' Behavior System***

Composed of teachers and students' direct interaction, teachers' behavior systems can be divided into two parts of management behavior and teaching behavior in the network environment. Within the category of teachers' behavior, the evaluation behavior implemented by teachers to students has irreplaceable value. Thus, we can construct the evaluation index of teachers' behavior system from three aspects: teachers' management behavior, teaching behavior, and evaluating behavior.

(1) The effective evaluation of teachers' management behavior. Although the direction and content of teachers' management behavior in the network environment have changed, whether teachers deal with unexpected things in the classroom timely and appropriately is still the fundamental index to evaluate the effectiveness of management behavior. Specifically speaking, it contains the efficiency of the management behavior, the reasonableness of management strategy, the efficiency of the management behavior effectiveness, the reasonableness of time management, the rationality of the resource management, etc. Students' violations in the network environment have three conditions: caused by the wrong operation, immature software is not mature, and interference of irreverent stimulus. Therefore, it should appraise whether teachers can handle properly violations caused by different situations.

(2) Evaluating the effectiveness of the teacher's teaching behavior. It is complex to appraise teachers' teaching behavior because of the transformation of teachers' main teaching and the strengthening of the auxiliary teaching behavior, which generally include two kinds of evaluating teaching: the form of interaction among teachers and students and the form of support system. In terms of the former one, some indices in the traditional evaluating system are still available, for example, the following evaluation elements related to the following behaviors: motivating and maintaining students' learning motivation, communicating and cooperating with students in the aspects of the cognition and emotion, promoting exchanges and cooperation among students, analyzing diagnosis and timely responding students' questions, and so on.

Whether teachers can effectively communicate with students at different levels, whether they can prevent students from "information loneliness," and whether they can help and guide students' misoperation are new problems brought about by information technology. For the evaluation of teachers' teaching behavior pointing to the support system, whether teachers can make up for the defects of human-computer interaction with the advantages of human-human interaction, choose the appropriate behavior mode according to the function of the software, organize and sort out learning resources according to the specific situation of students' learning, provide processing strategies for the cognitive load caused by excessive information, and carry out collaborative construction of teaching resources in learning activities are the basic points of evaluation.

(3) The evaluating of the rationality for teachers' evaluating behavior. The machine can only make a simple factual evaluation, but cannot make a value judgment. The factual evaluation only lies in judging whether the students' knowledge is correct or not, which is a lack of pertinence and enlightenment; and as for the evaluation of students' thinking method and process, students' motivation, attitude, and values, it is not within the scope of the machine. The purpose we evaluate students is to promote students' complete development. To make up for the defects of the machine, teachers must take the evaluating task relating to students' senior moving target so that rationality of the evaluating of teachers' evaluating behavior mainly relates to the teachers' rational evaluating of students' high activity.

The following can regard as the basic elements to appraise the rationality of teachers' classroom behavior: the rationality of the evaluating ways, the effectiveness of the content, pertinence, and inspiration of evaluating behavior, stimulating students' interest in learning by evaluating behavior, the promotion effect to students' overall development, seeing "learning" as the center, and so on.

In a word, with the popularization of the Internet and the networking of classroom teaching, we must take theory research for teachers' classroom evaluating teaching in the network environment, aiming to indicate the direction of the practice. I hope these preliminary discussions in this article can provide a beneficial reference for building a new scientific and reasonable network classroom evaluating teaching system.

## 5.3 The Developing Characteristics of Evaluating Teaching in American Colleges and Universities

The theoretical research and practical activities of evaluation teaching in American colleges and universities (hereinafter referred to as evaluating teaching) started relatively early in the world. The research and practice of teaching evaluation in American colleges and universities have been going through a history of over 100 years since the beginning of the 20th century. In the 1960s, with the progress of society and the development of higher education, improving the quality and efficiency of university teaching has become a topic of general concern. At the same time, teaching evaluation, which plays an important role in improving teaching and improving teaching quality, has also been greatly developed. In the mid-1970s, under the impetus of the higher education reform movement, the studies of evaluating teaching theory become more and more active. There are not only many monographs on teaching theory, but also many monographs on the theory and technology of university teaching evaluation, emerging with lots of articles, new evaluating models, and projects.

At present, evaluating teaching has become an indispensable part of the whole teaching process in American colleges and universities. It has been a convention to evaluate the teachers' teaching work. Most colleges and universities not only have a relatively complete theoretical system of teaching evaluation, but also specialize and institutionalize it in practice. In order to strengthen the evaluating teaching research, and ensure constantly improving in the quality of university teaching, many colleges and universities have built specialized research institutes on evaluating teaching (some also said teaching improvement centers). For decades, American colleges and universities have accumulated a lot of successful experience and concluded useful teaching evaluation mode and methods, gradually formulating their own style and characteristics. Of course, some shortcomings and insufficiency are extant. As regards the research and practice of teaching evaluation in colleges and universities in China, these successful experiences and historical lessons have certain reference values.

These successful experiences and historical lessons have certain reference value for the research and practice of teaching evaluation in Colleges and universities in China and the continuous improvement of teaching quality. In order to search for some enlightenment for the evaluation of Chinese higher education teaching, the translator in this paper tries to inspect the history of evaluating teaching in American higher education and the characteristics of evaluating teaching at all stages.

We can start from different angles in order to study the historical process and changes in teaching evaluation. It is possible to investigate the development and change of evaluating teaching in American colleges and universities and divide it into three main stages according to the content and standard of evaluating teaching. The first evaluating stage is based on teachers' characteristics as the main standards (the beginning of the 20th century to the late 1950s). The main standard in the second stage is teachers' classroom teaching behavior (in the early 1960s to the mid-1970s). The third stage is to evaluate teachers' teaching all-roundly by comprehensive standards (the mid-1970s to the present).

Since there lacks a systematic discussion on the stage division of the development process of teaching evaluation in American colleges and universities at home and abroad currently, this article is the first attempt. The purpose of stage division is to better understand the characteristics and trends of the development of teaching evaluation in American colleges and universities through this stage division, so as to be used by me.

### 5.3.1 Regarding Teacher's Personality as the Main Standards

Although the germination of education evaluating research and practice activities in the United States can be traced back to the end of the 19th century (beginning with Rice's research in 1894), evaluating teaching research and practice activities in high education did not attract university education workers' attention until in the 1920s, due to the influence of the traditional education system and ideology. The traditional education system (before the 20th century) only assessed students' scores instead of formal school teachers. It has become worse, especially in higher education institutions. "The idea of the sanctity and inviolability of classroom and the freedom of teachers to dominate teaching has been institutionalized." The old education system that only evaluates students rather than teachers has seriously hindered the development of the evaluating teaching theory research and practice activities in American colleges and universities.

However, with the development of the modern education evaluating movement and the change in education concepts, college educators came to realize that it is difficult to improve the teaching quality only if the main aspect of the teaching process—teaching effect—is assessed. Therefore, evaluating teaching research and practice in institutions of higher learning entered the early stages of development in the 1930s. The study of the theory of evaluating teaching in colleges and universities did not make huge progress until the end of the 1950s for social and historical reasons and the constraints of traditional education, though some pedagogy experts have made a lot of effort in evaluating teaching. By investigating the research and practice of teaching evaluation in American colleges and universities at this stage, we can conclude the following characteristics:

(1) From the perspective of contents and standards of evaluating teaching, during this period, evaluating teaching emphasize the traits or personalities of "good teachers" and "bad teachers." Teachers' traits are considered as the content and standard of evaluating teaching. "But in the actual evaluating, managers' subjective impression is still the most important."
(2) From the point of the evaluating method, some experts and scholars have put forward the means of evaluating the teaching effect by students' achievements, and began to explore the ways that students rate scales of teaching. For example, Purdue Teaching Rating Scale showed up in 1926. But actually, it was managers (the dean or director) that listened to few lessons, recorded the results according to the requirement of the evaluation, and collected them in the teacher's file, which plays an important role in teachers' personnel decisions, such as teachers' ascending, reward, employment period or removing duties, etc. Managers do not make decisions mainly on the basis of this factor, because they generally

understand that there are some limitations. We can see that evaluating teaching work at that time was subjective and formalistic.

(3) In order to distinguish the difference between "good teachers" and "bad teachers," the researchers mainly pay attention to finding the relationship among different inventory, and hope to be able to find out the relevant variables so that work out the unified standard of judging teachers.

(4) Many educators have repeatedly pointed out that the teacher's teaching effect should be an important standard for teachers' upgrade, but in the actual university evaluating teaching, the proportion of research results usually greatly exceeds the proportion of teaching effect, which has close relation with the evaluating of teaching effect not being standardization and quantification to a large extent.

In a word, at the beginning of the end of the Second World War, the United States was an era of "planning and enjoying a 'better life.' Society rarely requires educators to show efficiency and effectiveness in their efforts for development." Therefore, the college evaluating teaching had not achieved new breakthroughs.

### 5.3.2 Regarding Teachers' Behavior of Classroom Teaching as the Main Standards

Since the 1960s, the status of education in social development has been increasing, due to the economic development and changes in social life brought by the development of science and technology. Especially in the late 1960s and the early 1970s, education gained reduplicated attention and support. At the same time, the United States higher education had greatly developed. The number of American community college students had increased from 660,000 to 2,500,000, nearly three times. However, the quality reduction came immediately after the great development of higher education. Although the shortage of education funds counted as one of the main reasons, teachers' poor quality and low teaching efficiency did also matter a lot. Since the 1970s, how to improve the quality and efficiency of university teaching has become a general concerned research subject for education workers. In this case, the study of evaluating teaching was more and more active, and brought a series of changes. Its characteristics are as follows:

(1) Classroom Teaching becomes the important content of evaluating teaching. From the 1930s to the 1950s, teaching evaluation is actually the evaluation of teachers' characteristics. The educators' research point mainly focuses on how to find out the relevant variables in order to make sure the traits and personality of a good teacher. Since the 1960s, the research has transformed into studying specific classroom teaching behavior. If comparing *The Handbook of Research on Teaching I*, published in 1963, with *The Handbook of Research on Teaching II*, published in

1973, it can be seen that over this period of time, the characteristics of teachers have not been a strong research problem. *The Handbook of Research on Teaching I* discussed teachers' characteristics, while *The Handbook of Research on Teaching II* just involved a little about this topic. Educational researchers clearly believe that such research is unlikely to achieve much. Therefore, education researchers began to search into the classroom to find the characteristics of "Good Teaching" or "Effective Teaching," especially the interactions between teachers and students. One important reason to emphasize the interaction relations of teachers and students is that "since 1950 the number of the enrollment has hiked up by about 400%, while the number of higher schools only increased by 60% in the United States ... Unfortunately, the larger the size of the school, the more complex and bureaucratic the university is, the fewer opportunities each student must devote himself to rational life and the less personal contact between teachers and students." Thus, after the 1960s, emphasizing the interaction between teachers and students (including inside and outside of the classroom) became a common concern in evaluating problems for education researchers. Teachers' classroom teaching behavior and teaching effect were the most important standard for evaluating teaching during this period.

(2) There are more and more methods of rating teaching by students. Students' evaluation of teaching has begun to become an integral part of the function of evaluating teaching staff in American colleges and universities. As reported in the literature, more than 50% of colleges and universities used students to grade the teaching effect in the 1970s. Some scholars began to study the reliability and validity of students' evaluating teaching and the correlation of assessment among students, leaders, and peers and obtained some preliminary research results.

(3) Some educators have come to realize that the fundamental purpose of evaluation should be to promote teachers' self-renewal, which helped self-evaluation gain emphasis again.

(4) Many educators have deeply realized after their evaluating practice that different situations need various approaches to evaluation, because there are many modes of successful teaching, and it is obvious that one mere use of the evaluation method is not enough. Therefore, some new evaluating models and methods emerged one after another, such as Miller evaluating model, clinical guidance model, formation-finality model, target management model, and so on. These patterns later had been further enriched and developed.

(5) The first monograph on researching university evaluating teaching standards—*The Evaluating of University Teaching*, came to publish in 1971. In this book, Wilson and others reported their evaluating teaching project spanning three years of study in the University of California higher education research and development centers. Based on the factor analysis, this project established the

standard evaluation system and was divided into two different kinds of scale: peer evaluation and student evaluation. Each scale is composed of five sub-scales. The research results have great effects on the practice of evaluating teaching in American colleges and universities.

### 5.3.3 Evaluating Teaching Effect Comprehensively with Multiple Standards

Since the mid-1970s, all the countries have started to intensify the reform of higher education in order to meet the challenge of the new technology revolution and the era of a knowledge economy. The key point of this reform is how to improve the teaching efficiency and teaching effect of university education as soon as possible. In this aspect, the United States government and educators not only put forward many measures. For example, in terms of training objectives, those talents who meet the requirements of the times should be cultivated; curriculum structure and knowledge structure should be reformed; the form of teaching organization and method should be changed. And they clearly pointed out that there are three important terms to improve the quality of higher education; namely the students' putting into learning, strict requirements, evaluation, and feedback. At the same time, schools are required to conduct normal and regular teaching evaluations so as to use feedback information to adjust teaching direction and continuously improve teaching quality. The evaluating teaching of theoretical research and practice is becoming more and more active in American universities and colleges under the impetus of the reform wave.

In addition, in the mid-1970s, it was widely realized that the teacher played a key role in improving teaching quality. For example, the United States Gallup poll in 1979 showed that about choosing what measures to improve the quality of public schools, the voice in favor of improving the quality of teachers is the highest. In Colleges and universities, in order to improve the quality of teachers and curriculum teaching, teaching researchers have also carried out a lot of research and practice on teacher evaluation. This stage was regarded as the active period of evaluating teaching in American colleges and universities. Compared to before, the evaluation concept got further updated, and there appeared to be a diversified situation. Various new evaluation models and theories, monographs, and papers on teaching evaluation have emerged in large numbers. The integration of evaluation approaches, methods, and standards has become a prominent feature of teaching evaluation research in this period. From the perspective of evaluation practice, teaching evaluation in universities has become a practice. Many universities have organizations or institutions specialized in teaching evaluation technology and processing teaching evaluation results. Teaching evaluation has not only become an essential link in the teaching process of colleges and universities, but also developed into an interdisciplinary subject integrating multi-disciplinary knowledge and technology.

Throughout this phase of evaluating teaching theory and practice, it can be seen that the main change and development trends are as follows:

(1) With a new understanding of what is excellent teaching or successful teaching, the content of teaching evaluation is more extensive, and the standard is more comprehensive. Educators have deeply realized that factors affecting the success of teaching are various. Teaching quality must be analyzed systematically and comprehensively evaluated in order to get an objective and scientific evaluation of teachers' teaching effect. They clearly put forward that the three main variables considering successful teaching are input variables, process variables, and result variables. And it was advocated that a comprehensive and comprehensive evaluation of teaching from the aspects of teaching design (preparation), teaching process, and teaching results, which required that both explicit and implicit standards should be taken into consideration.
(2) The requirement of comprehensive evaluation has not only become a common voice of educational researchers, but has also been widely used in practice. In the Education Measurement and Evaluation Center of the University of Illinois, the evaluating teaching scheme put forward and carried out by Porrasker and others was a typical example. They divided the purpose of evaluating teaching into self-improvement, personnel decisions, student course selection, and course development; the appraisal standard with obvious, implicit, process and output standards; evaluating teaching information sources from leadership, students, peers and self, alumni and records; evaluating teaching methods including conversation, test, rating, and paper.
(3) People pay more attention to formative evaluation because the ultimate goal of teaching assessment is improvement. The reliability and validity of students' evaluation of teaching effects have been further recognized. The method of using students to evaluate teaching and obtain specific information to improve teaching has become an important means of teaching evaluation in many colleges and universities.
(4) Value judgment has become the central part of evaluating teaching. More and more educators realized that evaluation was an extremely complicated work. Evaluation needs not only description, but also value judgment and analysis of evaluation results.
(5) Modern teaching technology is fully used in the practice of evaluating teaching. Audio and video recording have become important tools for evaluating teaching, especially the teachers' self-assessments. Using various statistical techniques and computers to process evaluation data and results has become a common practice.
(6) Remarkable characteristics of the development of teaching evaluation in American colleges and Universities are complicated, combing qualitative evaluation and

quantitative evaluation, hard evaluation with soft evaluation, and formative assessment and summation assessment, using the evaluation scheme of multiple purposes.

In summary, the theoretical research and practical exploration of teaching evaluation in American colleges and universities are gradually moving towards scientization, institutionalization, and modernization since the beginning of the 20th century. It has improved a lot moving from the evaluation of teachers' traits to the overall evaluation of teacher's teaching process, from the single evaluation purpose, standard, content, and model to the diversified and comprehensive evaluation, from the qualitative evaluation to the combination of qualitative and quantitative evaluation, from the emphasis on summation evaluation to attach importance to formative assessment and student teaching report for the improvement of teaching. The characteristics and trends of this series of development and changes have important reference significance for the teaching evaluation of colleges and universities in China.

## 5.4 Theory and Practice on Students' Evaluating Teaching in American Universities and Colleges

The theoretical research and practical activities of American College Students' evaluation of teaching can be traced back to the 1920s or earlier. The first published rating scale used to collect information on students' evaluation of teaching is the Bodeau teaching rating scale (Purdue Rating Scale of Instruction, 1926). By the 1960s, students' evaluation of teaching had greatly increased in American universities and colleges, and special institutions began to appear to study students' evaluation of teaching effect. At the beginning of the 1970s, a survey by American Council on Education indicated that about 65% of the 669 colleges and universities surveyed allow students to evaluate teaching in department-level institutions. Seldin once conducted a comparative study on the development of information sources of teaching evaluation in the 1960s and 1970s. The method administered was a questionnaire conducted to the president of the university and the dean of the college. It showed that the obvious change in evaluating teaching in the 1970s was the increase of "the system of student assessment." Since the 1980s, student evaluation has become an important part of university teaching evaluation, and the technology of evaluation has become more and more modern. By the early 1990s, there were thousands of research literature and data on students' evaluation of teaching effectiveness. Marsh's studies have manifested that students' evaluation of teaching had the most literature in all the personnel evaluation research and also was one of the most supported evaluation ways. At present, systematical and multidimensional student evaluation has formed a system. That is to say, the review and assessment of teaching performance about the university teachers' employment and upgrade must collect students' opinions. Before the end of every course or the last two weeks of every semester, it requires students to evaluate this course and the teacher's teaching (including a rating questionnaire and open questionnaire), in order to provide feedback for further improving teaching or the basis for personnel decisions.

### 5.4.1 Educators' Basic Attitude to Students' Evaluation of Teaching

A large amount of literature shows that the majority of American educators keep a quite consistent view of the students' evaluation of teaching. They think that students are the teaching objectives, and the basic participants of teaching activities. Thus, their evaluation of the teaching process and its effect are quite vital and unique. If the evaluation criteria are appropriate and well organized (for example, explain the purpose of the evaluation, use anonymity, etc.), students' evaluation can reflect the real situation of the teaching process. Students' evaluation of teaching can serve multiple purposes, such as improving teaching, providing the basis for judging the teaching effect, helping students to choose courses and teachers, encouraging students to think about their educational activities, providing leaders the basis for personnel decisions, and so on.

In every class, students observe teachers' teaching activities and feel teachers' learning attitude through the work judging and examination marking, even the process of interaction among them. Researchers in US colleges reckon that there are many advantages to using students to evaluate the teaching of university teachers, such as economy, implementation, regularity, and continuity. The evaluation of the same teacher and the same course in the past students and current students can be compared with each other, which can provide teachers with specific improvement letters, etc.

Some educators believe that "students are not in the best position to judge the suitability and progressiveness of course content and the academic level of teachers." But most researchers believe that the students generally can gain a better description in the following aspects, such as the relationship between teachers and students, teachers' professional conduct and ethical views, students' learning burden, what their learning in the class, the teachers' grading errors, and teachers' language communication ability. Decades of research have shown that it has achieved great development in the practice of students evaluating teaching effects. There are still some doubts and discontent about it, but certainly, students' evaluation is effective and credible. Cashin has studied more than 1,300 articles on student evaluation of teaching (including special discussed in the books), and one of the basic conclusions is that the students' evaluation result is reliable and stable.

### 5.4.2 Methods and Tools of Student Evaluation of Teaching

In American Universities and colleges, there are many methods and tools to collect evaluation information through students. Among them, mostly used ones are Systemic Student Ratings (or student evaluating teaching reports), written assessments, conversations, and tests.

*Systemic Student Ratings*

Systemic Student Ratings began in the 1920s and are still a popular evaluation method at present. The vast majority of colleges and universities have adopted different forms of rating scales or checklists. A large number of studies on whether students' grade evaluation of teaching is credible and effective followed. Rating Scales are commonly used in practice. The rating scale includes a student rating questionnaire and checklist. Because the rating scale is the most effective method to collect evaluating information, it is the most common method to evaluate teaching in most schools.

American educators think, as a basic tool for evaluating teaching, the rating scale has advantages and disadvantages. Advantages are as follows: firstly, it is easy to list and statistical analysis; secondly, it is easy to be standard and preserved, and can collect a large amount of information quickly and efficiently; thirdly, it can be designed in advance, and there is a lot of technical literature which can be taken as a reference to design and use of the scale. The disadvantages are that: first, because students are required to reply to a lot of problems in a short time, they can't have a more profound view of teachers; secondly, it cannot encourage valuers to think carefully; thirdly, appear duplicate projecting; fourthly, unable to realize direct communication between student and teachers. In spite of this, because there are no more effective tools, rating scales still continue to play a major role in evaluating teaching.

There are a variety of rating scales used by American universities to evaluate teaching. The most commonly used are the blanket checklist, cafeteria system, target check table, etc.

(1) Blanket checklist. The Blanket checklist is usually used for the same inspection and evaluation of all the teachers in the same schools and the department. This checklist is generally designed based on the study results of classroom evaluating teaching standards. Because educators have different views on "successful teaching" or evaluating teaching standards, they designed different checklists. The "student teaching report" designed by the United States education test service center is one of the representative checklists for teaching examination evaluation. The checklist is divided into the following four parts:

The first part is the ratings about teachers' teaching design, teaching process, and evaluating teaching (refers to the examination and grading) rating. The second part is the ratings about the class content and the teaching effect. The third part is the total evaluation of teachers and curriculum. The fourth part is specially added to the important problems about teachers' and students' thoughts. As is shown, the scale designed by Educational Testing Service testing respectively includes the evaluation of teachers' teaching and curriculum evaluation. In fact, in the American university, it is very common to use curriculum evaluation instead of teacher evaluation.

(2) Cafeteria system. The cafeteria system is not a simple tool or checklist. It is used to make the student's rating adapt to the needs of the individual teacher- teachers are allowed to select their own traits in a series of originally used items (or their class character) in order to construct a checklist. The first cafeteria system was created in the early 1970s by the University of Purdue. Later, the University of Michigan professor Jams A. Kulik developed it. At present, this method has become one of the most common methods for rating in many universities.

In order to obtain feedback correlating with their teaching, the prominent characteristic of the cafeteria system is that teachers can make rating scales by themselves. At the University of Michigan, all the questionnaires contained five ordinary center projects listed in the scale. In addition, the teacher can also select over 25 projects from a total of nearly 150 useful problems, and even can increase a few more items. Therefore, teachers can obtain precise feedback on their special interested problems. It can be seen that the main purpose of using the cafeteria system is for the needs of adapting teachers to improve their teaching.

(3) Target check table. This checklist focuses on investigating students' learning situations in various fields of courses. Students make a rating on their own progress according to the curriculum and the target, such as the acquisition of knowledge, the development of specific skills and abilities, and the application ability of knowledge.

On the basis of this view, Hoyt at Kansas state university designed a students' questionnaire about students' reactions to teaching and courses called the IDEA evaluation checklist. The checklist contained three parts: the evaluation of teachers, the evaluation of the curriculum, and the evaluation of their progress. It leaves an instructions column for teachers' additional questions. By students' rating of their learning, it not only provides teachers with useful information for improving teaching, but also takes the formative assessment for teachers' teaching effect so as to help teachers improve their teaching.

### *Written Appraisals*

Written appraisals, as known as paper evaluation, refers to the method of promoting a series of open questions for students to answer or giving a general topic for students to answer freely to obtain more profound evaluation information. Written assessment has two forms: one is independent written evaluation, and the other is mixed with the rating, which means being a part of students' rating checklists. The main purpose of utilizing written evaluation is to encourage students to deliver profound opinions about these outstanding problems in the process of teaching. For example, what are the main advantages and disadvantages of the teacher? How do you think this course should be improved? What is your favorite content in this course? What is the most useful part of this curriculum for you?

In the evaluating teaching of American universities, written appraisal mainly aims at teaching improvement. Because this method has a simple procedure, it may take at any time. However, it requires teachers to have the self-restraint and mentality to accept different views bravely.

*Discussion*

In American universities evaluating teaching, it is also a common method to organize students to have a discussion in order to collect more information about courses and teachers' teaching. The discussion has two types: individual discussion and group discussion. The discussion is organized by specialized staff, who usually are peers and people responsible for the development of teaching. According to the content of the discussion, there are three types of discussions: structured, general structure, and free conversation without structure. The information collected through discussion is mainly for personnel decisions, but what is more important is used for the progress of teaching.

*Test*

It is a traditional method of teaching evaluation in the United States to check and evaluate teachers' teaching effect through students' examination results. Student achievement is a reliable measure of teaching effect. People, however, have realized that as one kind of appraisal standard, student achievement has its intrinsic value, but it can only be regarded as one of the important pieces of information to evaluate teachers' teaching ability, not the only index. Students' scores are influenced by many factors, such as students' variability, regression effect, and the limitations of the current achievement test. So, the vast majority of American educators have a negative opinion on simply utilizing students' test scores to evaluate teachers' teaching effect.

So far, there are still some people studying the reliability and validity of student evaluation of teaching. But most research and practice show that student evaluation is reliable and effective. What is more, it will still be a development trend of American university teaching evaluation in the 21st century to continue to use student evaluation and make it scientific and modern.

### 5.4.3 Some Implications

Taking the American university student evaluation of teaching theory and practice, and the reality of evaluating teaching in China into consideration, the author thinks that we should change ideas, set up a system, and remove the obstacles urgently in order to strengthen the university students' evaluation of teaching practice in our country, and constantly improve teaching efficiency.

First of all, university administrators and teachers should change their ideas. And they must admit that students at the university stage have strong value judgment ability along with their convincing and precious evaluation towards teaching, especially in the following aspects: teachers' teaching attitude, professional spirit, ideology and knowledge size and strength, teaching organization ability, the choice and application of teaching methods and means, classroom management and the impartiality of the marking, and so on. At the same time, university teachers should clearly recognize that the final result of the teaching is to help students obtain knowledge, develop themselves and form good moral character. Thus, it is very important that students' information of evaluating teaching for improving teaching, and realizing the above purposes. Modern pedagogy especially emphasizes that the student is the main body of teaching, the study master, and adhering to the use of student assessment to improve teaching actually embodies this point of view.

Secondly, a system of student evaluation of teaching should be established and formed as soon as possible. In recent years, the author's college has learned from the practice of American universities, independently strengthened the establishment of the student evaluation teaching system, and equipped with a modern computer data entry and processing system. Every semester, the teacher's teaching is evaluated, and the evaluation results are made full use of to make it play a positive role in year-end evaluation, award payment, curriculum arrangement, and professional title evaluation. Among others, special attention is paid to the use of formative student teaching evaluation reports to provide specific feedback information for teachers, encourage teachers to reform teaching, and continuously improve teaching quality. There is no denying that attaching great importance to student assessment not only can provide the right decision-making basis for the scientific and standardization of teaching management, but also that it improves the practice value of teaching effect.

Thirdly, various psychological obstacles of students in the process of evaluation of teaching should be tackled. We should try to eliminate evaluation error, so as to ensure the objectivity of evaluation results. On the one hand, students as the main body of teaching activity. Guiding them to understand the significance of evaluating the teacher's teaching, improving the consciousness of students' participation in evaluation, and the attitude of filling in the evaluation questionnaire is quite important. At the same time, let the students know the purpose of the evaluation, and master the usage of the evaluation tools. On the other hand, a harmonious relationship between teachers and students should be established, and teachers should clearly realize the purpose of implementing student assessment aims to improve teaching, and believe that there are great degrees of correlation between student evaluation and peer evaluation. In the evaluating teaching in American universities, a large number of studies have shown that there is objective consistency between the student evaluation of teaching results and the teacher peers. Teachers don't have to doubt the reliability and validity of the student evaluation, and should regard students evaluating teaching as important information sources for improvement.

# Contemporary International Basic Education Curriculum and Teaching Reform

In this chapter, the contemporary basic education curriculum and teaching reforms of Canada, America, Britain, and China are mainly analyzed by the author, making a comparison among the four countries. Before the 1980s, the curriculum in the British Columbia Province (B.C. Province for short) of Canada gradually could not meet the demand of contemporary development, which thus triggered an educational reform in the 1980s. Seven aspects are included in the content of the reform, such as curriculum structure, curriculum design, curriculum management limits, and teaching assessment. The British government issued the *1988 Educational Reform Act* in 1988, and the national curriculum begins, by which curriculum and teaching practice in primary and secondary schools are changed, especially in four aspects, curriculum control, teacher autonomy, teaching center, and teaching assessment. Generally speaking, China's new round of basic educational curriculum's main line is seeking balance and harmony. It aims to seek a balance between experience exploration and scientific overall planning in the process of curriculum reform and generalization, which includes a balance between each district's economy and culture and balance among these seven aspects such as curriculum structure, curriculum content, curriculum management limits, curriculum reform's subject structure and model of curriculum reform and development, so as to build up basic education curriculum's theory and practice system with Chinese characteristics. The curriculum reforms in China, Britain, America, and Canada are influenced by different educational backgrounds, all including adjusting reform goals, optimizing curriculum structures, and improving evaluation methods. However, the differences can be seen obviously in the specific operating process.

## 6.1 General Education Curriculum Reform in B.C. Province of Canada

In any one of the education systems, curriculum issue occupies the central position, and curriculum reform is usually the breakthrough point of education reform. Looking back in history, it is easy to find that curriculum reform is almost the beginning of every important education reform. This is because specific curriculum content arrangements must be the basis to make the education goal achieved and reflected. Curriculum content determines the school education system, teaching method, and teaching organization mode, which in return serves it. The level of curriculum content and how much it accomplishes are mainly the judgment of assessment of education quality and teaching quality. Since the 1980s, the curriculum issue remains to be the emphasis of general education curriculum reform in B.C. Province of Canada. This section intends to briefly introduce and analyze the reform of the general education curriculum reform in B.C. based on the report of the Royal Education Commission of B.C. and related materials, which may be a reference for the curriculum reform of primary and secondary schools in my country.

### 6.1.1 Basic Situation

During the last 20 years, quite a lot of achievements have been made by general education in B.C. Province, especially in students learning basic skills. Compared to students in other provinces, students in B.C. Province performs better in their scores. However, with the development of the times and changes in society, the problems in general education are increasingly exposed, and the public's complaints about education and teaching quality are also increasing day by day. To deal with this situation, the government of B.C. Province formed the Royal Education Commission in March 1987 to comprehensively examine all aspects of public school and non-public school education, and to propose reforms and recommendations on how to guide the province's general education toward the 21st century.

Members of the Royal Education Commission have done a lot of work in order to investigate the education situation. All over the province, they traveled 2,400 kilometers, going around 139 schools and 89 social organizations and participating in 66 public assemblies, 53 teacher meetings, and 23 students rallies. Students in various schools, as well as their parents, teachers, and students' managers, are visited by them, who receive 2,350 opinions both in written and oral form. The commission completed the survey report in August 1988, and put forward a total of 83 reform proposals on curriculum, quantity and quality of teacher demand, school management, education funding, etc. Among them, there are 15 suggestions for curriculum reform, which involve the planning of curriculum content, the implementation of curriculum, the evaluation of curriculum, etc.

### 6.1.2 Curriculum Structure of General Education in B.C. Province

To introduce the old basic curriculum structure in B.C. Province before the reform implemented on January 27, 1989, is the first thing in order to illustrate the curriculum reform situation of general education in B.C. Province. We can illustrate this in terms of planned courses, implemented courses, and completed courses.

*Planned Course*

The so-called planned courses refer to a series of pre-arranged courses or programs that are officially determined, formal and authoritative, and have unified textbooks, auxiliary materials, and teaching guidance. In other words, the planned curriculum for general education in B.C. is the curriculum determined by the provincial education department or school district board according to the school system, including coursework (subject categories) and time allocation and progress.

(1) Planned course in primary school

In *Education Management Guide*, the provincial education department of B.C. Province has clearly stipulated the implementation time of all subject teaching plans for primary schools (Grades 1–7). That is, a maximum of 1500 minutes (25 hours) per week, but at least 1325 minutes must be guaranteed. The time allocation for each subject in elementary school is roughly as follows:

| Subject | Language Art (%) | Mathematics (%) | Fine Arts (%) | Science (%) | Social Study (%) | Sports (%) | Local Course (%) |
|---|---|---|---|---|---|---|---|
| Time Ratio | 42 | 14 | 13 | 7 | 7 | 10 | 7 |

We can see from the primary school's present course planning in B.C. Province that the time proportion of Language Art is relatively large, and from the time allocation, we can see the provincial education department of B.C. Province requires primary students to learn what kinds of subjects. It is clear that French is not included in the program as a second language and that courses such as domestic affairs, industrial education, and health issues are not arranged. The Royal Education Commission thinks that this kind of time allocation emphasizes the subject of Language Art (reading, writing, listening, and speaking), reflecting the importance of the development of language competence of primary students. However, they also think that it cannot be ignored to develop students' language abilities combined with other courses.

(2) Planned course in secondary school

In B.C. Province, secondary schools contain the 8th grade to the 12th grade. All five grades are included in most schools, while some schools just set junior high grades (from the 8th grade to the 10th grade) or senior high grades (from the 11th grade to the 12th grade). Compared with the curriculum design of the primary school, the curriculum design of the secondary school is more complicated. The provincial education department requires that more courses and learning programs should be provided for middle school students in order to meet the growing interests and requirements.

The two parts, the compulsory course and optional course, are included in the secondary school courses in B.C. Province. The proportion of these two courses varies with the increase in grades. In the 8th grade, it is required that six main courses be learned by students, English, French, Mathematics, Social Study, Science, and Physical Education. Besides Housekeeping and Industrial Study, they also need to select one course. Music, Art, and Drama are usually their optional courses. Students continue learning the above five main courses except for French and optional course in the 9th grade and the 10th grade. Students must continue learning English, Mathematics, Science, and Social Study in the 11th grade. In the 12th grade, English is still a required course, and students can arrange their learning time through elective courses. Moreover, no less than 10 hours of Family Life Education must be guaranteed by these five grades.

There is no significant difference in the time distribution of the main subjects in secondary schools, unlike the focus of primary school is language art. In secondary school, the curriculum implementation is in the form of department instruction and different subjects taught by different teachers.

(3) Scheme selections

In order to make students' special demands, abilities, and interests satisfied, some education schemes that can be chosen from primary schools and secondary schools are also provided by the *Education Management Guide* of B.C. Province. These optional schemes are also part of the planned curriculum.

- Special education scheme
  Each school district has a corresponding education scheme to adapt to different students' situations and to meet the special needs of some students. The following special schemes are mainly included: genius education, second language education, correction of bad behavior, education of children with learning disabilities, education of children with mental retardation and physical disabilities, education of children with disabilities, correction of aphasia, and Indian education.
- Career guidance program
  The purpose of this program is to prepare students for entering the labor market or vocational education after secondary school.

- Cooperative education program
  This program refers to the cooperation between schools and employers in training plans, personnel exchanges, and training evaluations. Generally speaking, about 200 hours of training for middle school students need to be conducted on the spot.
- Correspondence education program
  The program is designed primarily to provide communication education for students who are far from school, those who have long been ill at home, those who live abroad, or those who enter other schools but are unable to choose their own courses. Some schools also stipulate that they can apply to study correspondence courses in other schools in the following situations: a. if they want to acquire credits for the courses that their school cannot set up; b. if they want to acquire credits for the courses not listed in their curriculum schedule; c. if they want to acquire credits for the extra courses that are not concluded in the general curriculum design. The correspondence education department of the provincial education department mainly manages this program.
- Native American education program
  This program is a special education program designed specifically for native Indians, which is different from regular courses. To adapt to Indian culture, history, and present life, the provincial education department of B.C. Province encourages each school district to develop a local curriculum.

In addition to the above five main programs, there are such as community school programs, adult secondary education programs, and summer school programs for school choices.

Above is the planned course of general education's general situations in B.C. Province. Although courses in primary school and secondary school and the optional programs are generally confirmed by officials, in the implementation process, there are some differences between each school and each school district to some extent.

*Enforced Course*

The enforced course refers to what teachers actually teach students in class and how they teach them. Some differences are allowed between the planned course and the enforced course. As teachers have all received special training, they also have the right and ability to decide what content to teach students, what teaching materials are most suitable for their students, and what teaching methods are most effective. Besides, one of the teachers' duties is to conduct creative teaching. However, although teachers have their freedom when giving classes, the education department requires that they must ensure the continuity of the content of the provincial course.

General education curriculum design has two basic forms in B.C. Province: semester system and streaming system.

(1) Semester system

The semester system is taken by most secondary schools in B.C. Province as the curriculum design form. Every semester, students in 8th grade must learn courses of four subjects with a guaranteed 75 minutes of each subject per day. This is basically consistent with the requirements of the education department.

Setting up courses of 4 to 5 subjects in the same period is characteristic of the semester system, which is comparatively easier for students to learn. However, the study in the second semester could be influenced if the student didn't get good grades in one subject in the first semester.

(2) Streaming system

The streaming system is another curriculum design form chosen by some secondary schools in B.C. Province. That is, students are divided into different classes according to the results of the ability test. Provincial junior high schools mostly use this model. Several primary schools also include streaming methods but mainly stress mathematic learning.

As the *Curriculum Guideline* of the B.C. provincial education department does not clearly stipulate which form the school should adopt to implement the curriculum, different curriculum implementation modes have emerged in practice. Each school or school district's own streaming method has developed, which no doubt leads to differences.

Streaming theory and practice have long existed in B.C. Province. However, research has shown that the streaming method is good for high-ability students. Putting students of different abilities in one class can improve the academic performance of most students. That's why the Royal Education Commission offers blended learning groups.

*Finished Course*

To put it simply, the finished course is the result of school education. The consequence involves a series of questions as follows: What did the students learn through the implementation of the course? What habits have they developed? Have they made progress? Have their personalities developed? What value system do they hold?

Information on the achievement of curriculum objectives comes from a variety of sources, including teachers reporting student progress to parents; various educational notes from principals to district officials; final exams in the 12th grade; provincial learning assessment programs, etc. Some studies and data show that students are doing well in a prescribed course studying in B.C. Province. However, most evaluations lack the evaluation of students' interests, attitudes, affections, values, and personalities, but focus on academic goals (i.e., the right-hand target).

(1) Teacher's report to student's parents

Class teachers report students' progress to their parents regularly in B.C. Province, which is an important way for parents to understand how course goals are being achieved. However, the vast majority of these reports are about how far students have progressed relative to past learning in some schools, especially primary schools. This is a typical assessment of intra-individual differences without comparison with external standards. Such reports are useful for students, their parents, and teachers to understand the situation, but because of their subjectivity, coupled with the influence of teachers' personality characteristics, such reports are difficult to use for other comparative purposes. For example, student-to-student, class-to-class, school-to-school, district-to-district comparisons.

In B.C. Province, as a student can only enroll in the next subject if he has achieved the minimum required score in a subject, a quantitative evaluation method is used by secondary school teachers. This is also reflected in the report to the parents of students.

(2) Learning evaluation program

In the mid-1970s, B.C. Province developed and promulgated this program. The main purposes are as follows:

- Through evaluations, professionals and the public are informed of the strengths and weaknesses of the public school system
- Help the Education Department, school districts, and schools to make decisions on the development of the school, adjustment, correction, curriculum implementation, and teaching resources' development and utilization
- Help the Education Department to make decisions about educational resources' allocation
- Determine the scope of teacher's teacher pre-service and in-service training
- Provide basis and guidance for conducting educational research
- Check students' learning situation
- Provide useful information for improving teaching

In B.C. Province, the evaluation of each subject in the primary and secondary curriculum was jointly conducted by the Provincial Bureau of Student Evaluation and the Curriculum Development Bureau according to predetermined procedures. Usually, one subject is assessed a year, and in exceptional cases, two subjects are assessed. The Education Department has already conducted at least one assessment in subjects such as reading, writing, mathematics, natural science, French and social studies since the establishment of the learning evaluation program.

Student evaluation programs' implementation process takes a lot of time, and it generally takes at least 15 months for the evaluation of major subjects. Besides, the assessment happens every four years, which can also be said to be the flaw of this program.

(3) Final exam in the 12th grade

In 1983, the final exam in the 12th grade was introduced to B.C. Province. High school graduates were required to attend this exam before 1988. This can be said to be a compulsory exam, and its grades account for 50% of the students' final graduation grades, and the other 50% are assessed by teachers based on students' records in middle school and test scores in each semester.

Since a new curriculum structure was proposed by the Royal Education Commission in August 1988, the flaws of the original 12th-grade final exam were clearly shown. The new curriculum requires that the 12th-grade humanities and natural sciences courses must be subject to provincial examinations. The proportion of students' scores in the provincial examinations in their graduation grades has been reduced from 50% to 40%. The purpose of this is to emphasize teachers' evaluation of students' learning in the classroom.

From the above, we have introduced the general education course's general situation from three aspects in B.C. Province before 1989, planned course, enforced course, and finished course. It is not difficult to see that the planning, implementation, and completion of courses are not completely consistent in practice. As officials at the Royal Commission for Education have pointed out, in some schools, the three are largely aligned, but in most schools, the planned curriculum is not well implemented. In addition, the planned curriculum itself has some social problems that cannot adapt to the ever-changing society. Therefore, it must be reformed and adjusted.

### 6.1.3 Reform Measures of General Education Course in B.C. Province

The Royal Education Commission of B.C. Province has conducted an extensive investigation and solicited opinions from personnel at all levels on the current situation of the general education curriculum in the province. After a comprehensive inspection and analysis, it has put forward reform measures and suggestions to guide the general education curriculum in the province to the 21st century. It mainly involves the following seven aspects:

*Identify a New Curriculum Structure for Grades 1 to 10*

The Royal Education Commission proposed a new unified curriculum plan for students in Grades 1–Grade 10, based on the survey and analysis of the province's primary and secondary school curricula. The program consists of four major areas of learning that relate to students' knowledge, abilities, and attitudes. The four learning areas are given as follows:

- The Humanities, including English, social studies, and French
- The Natural Science, including mathematics, biology, chemistry, and physics
- The Art, including music, art, dance, and drama
- The Art Practice, including sports, industry education, housekeeping, and life education

In addition to the identification of a new curriculum structure, The Royal Education Commission made specific recommendations on the learning requirements for each subject. For example, the new curriculum suggests that English teaching is best to start with students' life experience, and let students speak and write about people or things in their memory. It also proposes to expose students to a wide range of reading materials, such as classical, popular stories, articles, poems, and knowledge about other subjects.

The new curriculum emphasizes that learning the methods of investigation, understanding the relationships among people, and understanding the culture, politics, legislation, and economic conditions of the region should be the focus of the social study courses. It encourages students actively lecture on social issues and make predictions about the future. Let students know how they should fit into society as a member of society and how to participate in social life.

*Strengthen the Local Curriculum*

Survey of The Royal Education Commission of B.C. Province shows that many teachers and parents feel that the development and utilization of local curriculum were ignored by the Education Department. Thus, in addition to the unified curriculum, the local curriculum accounts for 20%, which is nearly three times more than the original 7% in the new curriculum structure. Of course, the development of a new local curriculum is not just a matter for local governments. As the upper education management department, they should encourage and create conditions for local governments and school districts to develop their own curriculum.

*Strengthen the Integration of the Curriculum*

One of the reasons why the current curriculum structure does not reflect the connection with the actual life situation is that the curriculum is arranged in subject-curriculum mode, which is subject-oriented. When designing the curriculum, curriculum compilers mainly consider the internal connection of the discipline, and less consider its connection with other disciplines and real-life situations. This not only causes "overloading of courses," but also is not conducive to students' adaptability to future life. Therefore, the new curriculum structure proposed by the Royal Commission of Education paid attention to the integration of the curriculum. Practicing the arts, for example, strengthens the link between physical education, industrial education, housekeeping, and health education.

*Advocate Interdisciplinary Teaching*

In the past, the interdisciplinary teaching model had already been adopted by primary school teachers, especially teachers teaching in lower grades. For example, math is taught in science classes; spelling and reading skills are taught in other classes. Teachers still have the opportunity to illustrate links between disciplines to the children, although the compilation of the primary curriculum is subject-oriented. This teaching mode continues in the teaching of all subjects in Grades 1–10. The recommendations of the Royal Education Commission are as follows:

- Teachers should appropriately use interdisciplinary teaching in their teaching and make the connection between different disciplines strengthened.
- Further study should be done by educational administrations and research institutes, and living examples of interdisciplinary teaching should be provided to teachers by them.
- Relevant educators should develop methodological courses which emphasize curriculum integration.

*Build a Mixed Learning Group*

At present, many primary and secondary schools in B.C. Province still adopt the streaming system, and establish study groups or education classes; that is, students with basically the same ability are arranged in a group to study according to the results of the ability or ability test. Research and practice show that students' learning outcomes cannot be effectively improved by this kind of system. Instead, it is more effective to organize students of different abilities in a mixed group for collaborative learning and peer mentoring. California in the USA has achieved remarkable results in this regard. Therefore, the Royal Education Commission recommends that in primary and secondary schools, especially primary schools, there should be more use of cooperative learning and peer mentoring in mixed classes, which can not only play the leading role of outstanding students, but also provide more opportunities for teachers to provide individual guidance.

*Improve Classroom Evaluation*

One of the main responsibilities of class teachers is evaluating students' learning. Teachers must implement effective evaluation activities to obtain feedback in order to know whether students are meeting course objectives.

However, exams and tests are the main focus of previous evaluations. The Royal Education Commission believes that in order to make a comprehensive and objective assessment of students, teachers should collect assessment information from multiple sources. For example, observing the participation of students in class discussions, designing activities, conversations, oral exams, and additional writing. Evaluation should be continuous, and attention should be paid to the use of diagnostic evaluation. Whether the course objectives have been achieved is the most important goal to see.

*Enhance Extracurricular Activities*

In B.C. Province, a necessary part of students' school life is extracurricular activities. A variety of extracurricular activities are the main complement to students' regular coursework. In 1988, the Royal Education Commission concluded that students need extracurricular activities after a comprehensive survey of extracurricular activities conducted in primary and secondary schools in B.C. Province, especially in modern society, through which extracurricular activities can develop students' interests, hobbies, and talents, expand students' knowledge and vision, also help students to know and understand school life, society, and others, and cultivate the ability to adapt to society. In the past, some achievements in conducting extracurricular activities have been made by many secondary schools. However, due to the traditional examinations' influence, people's awareness of extracurricular activities is insufficient (for example, some teachers think that it is not worth spending a lot of extra time on things beyond the curriculum goals), coupled with insufficient funding for extracurricular activities, extracurricular activities in primary and secondary schools in B.C. Province are not optimistic in terms of form and type. In response, The Royal Education Commission of B.C. Province required that the organization of extracurricular activities should be further strengthened by schools, and various forms should be adopted to develop students' abilities in all aspects.

In addition, Grade 11 to Grade 12 are very important for students since they are the last two years of general education. Therefore, Grade 11 to Grade 12 directly affects or decides whether students can adapt to the next stage of continuing study or enter society smoothly. To this end, ideas of curriculum reform for Grade 11 to Grade 12 were specifically proposed by the Royal Education Commission of B.C. Province, such as: strengthening the flexibility of curriculum, establishing the core curriculum and basic academic courses, providing various options, and reforming exams of Grade 12. It is very clear for the purpose of doing so. On the one hand, it is to ensure that more students continue to choose higher-level academic courses. On the other hand, it lays a foundation for the student who can become a knowledgeable, competent, educated, and creative citizen in the changing society.

## 6.2 Curriculum and Teaching Reform of Primary and Secondary Schools in Contemporary Britain

In order to analyze and discuss the changes in primary and secondary schools' curriculum and teaching practice in the UK since the promulgation of the Education Reform Act of 1988, the author reviews the relevant research papers by using the opportunity of studying in the UK in the early 2000s, conducted an open interview with some adult college students in the School of Education, University of Leicester. The results of the study are that since the late 1980s, with new education laws and regulations promulgation and implementation, basic education in the UK has changed greatly in many ways, such as policy orientation, school management, students' enrollment, financial control, curriculum setting, teaching strategy, and evaluation system, etc. Among them, four aspects manifest the most prominent changes in primary and secondary schools' curriculum and teaching practice: the change of curriculum control from school-based curriculum to national curriculum; the change of teaching activities from teacher's autonomy to target orientation; the change of teaching mode from children-centered to subject-centered; the changes of teaching evaluation from formative evaluation to final evaluation. By examining the reform plans and implementation strategies of the curriculum and teaching of contemporary primary and secondary schools in the United Kingdom, and comparing the new basic education curriculum and teaching reforms implemented in China since the early 1990s, it can be found that there are many issues worth thinking about. Based on the results of document research and interviews, this article's intention is to analyze and discuss the changes in these four aspects. On this basis, considers the reasons for the similarities and differences between the basic education curriculum and teaching reform in China and the UK.

### 6.2.1 Changes in Curriculum Control: From Emphasizing School-Based Curriculum to the Implementation of National Curriculum

Since the late 1980s, the enforcement of a new national curriculum, including both core courses and basic courses by legislation, has been one of the most prominent changes in the UK's basic education reform. The fundamental purpose of implementing the National Curriculum is to improve the standard and quality of education, which is regarded by the government as an indispensable part of the current British education system.[1] This strong reform not only ended the long history of no unified curriculum in the UK, but also broke the school curriculum pattern dominated by the school-based curriculum in primary and secondary schools in the UK for a long time. Moreover, the reform speed was so fast that British schools and teachers accustomed to a free curriculum felt hard to accept, especially primary school teachers. Although the government had already revised its national curriculum in 1994–1995 and lowered the requirements of some content, which were welcomed by teachers, there are still many debates about the national curriculum and its assessment standards, especially among Educational Theorists, where criticism of the national curriculum is still widely seen. In his book *National Courses: National Disaster?* Griffith criticized the current educational system that implements the National Curriculum as becoming less and less relevant to real life and future social progress, and this will cause irreparable damage and destruction to the capitalist economy and democratic social fabric.[2]

However, due to the reasons of education legislation and the unswerving implementation of reforms by the British Conservative Party and Labour Party, the national curriculum has now become the main body of the primary and secondary school curriculum. Moreover, due to the fact that the mastery of subject knowledge and the evaluation system of academic performance of students are focused on by the national curriculum, its status in primary and secondary schools is still unshakable, although various criticisms continue. In fact, since the national curriculum has been implemented in Britain, the academic performance of primary and secondary school students has indeed improved substantially. Take England as an example. According to its statistics, the number of students whose scores in graduation general examination achieved level ABC in all English schools was 23.7% in the 1978/1979 academic year, and in the 1988/1989 school year, it rose to 32.8%, and in the 1999/2000 school year, the number rose to 49.2%.[3] The national curriculum's strong implementation and its assessment criteria is an important factor undoubtedly, although the reasons for the rising are not singular. Looking back on history, British schools have always had the right to set their own curriculum. Although local education authorities and local curriculum management committees also had basic regulations on the school curriculum in the past, the real power lies in the hands of school management committees and principals. Especially from the 1970s to the 1980s, the school-based curriculum had always occupied a dominant position in primary and secondary schools. It became a trend to encourage teachers to participate in the preparation and development of school curricula.[4] Each school could formulate a set of curriculum plans and basic requirements of the curriculum according to its own reality. On the other hand, teachers had the power to choose specific teaching content and a wide free space for teaching. It can be said that teachers have absolute decision-making power in what to teach in the classroom, how to teach and how to judge, etc. However, since the introduction of the national curriculum, the teaching of schools and teachers has to be carried out around the standards of the national curriculum. The national curriculum has replaced the school-based curriculum. The policies mentioned in the government education documents that a certain degree of freedom should be given to schools to develop the curriculum completely become a story on paper. In addition to consulting the relevant research documents, the author also adopted an empirical approach to do an open interview of the adult students in the Education College of the University of Leicester in order to test this huge change and its impact through front-line teachers' practice. These teachers from primary and secondary school students basically have the same view: Now national curriculum is actively implemented by all schools because the results of students' learning of the national curriculum will be examined and assessed by the government, which also evaluates and announces the ranking to society and parents. Therefore, teaching activities must be conducted by schools and teachers in accordance with the national curriculum's requirements and standards. As the state has already arranged well for the school, it is generally agreed by these teachers that schools now have less power and freedom in curriculum setting than before. Most teachers believe that the characteristic of the national curriculum is that it indicates what you should teach and what standards you should meet. Students can indeed grasp more systematic knowledge about the subject through the learning of the national curriculum. But at the same time, the national curriculum also makes teachers have greater psychological pressure and work. Due to the pursuit of academic performance, it also leads to cramming teaching. In the interview, many teachers believe that the loss of teachers is one of the reasons for the shortage of teachers in the UK. The reasons for the loss are not only because of poor wages, but also because of the national curriculum and its strict external assessment of students' learning achievements. Teacher pressure has a lot to do with it. Nevertheless, the demand for teachers did not decrease after the British Labor Party came to power in 1997. Under the guidance of former Prime Minister Blair's repeatedly stressed thinking that education will always be the core of government work, higher career development requirements for new teachers have been put forward by the government education administration department, which constantly increases the training of teachers. Requirements for teachers to master the national curriculum standards and to promote their students' academic performance effectively are included in all of them. During the interview, adult students also said that the content of national curriculum standards and effective strategies for how to implement them is a considerable part of their present training courses. The national curriculum has not only raised the requirements for teachers' teaching, but has also made the standard of students' learning raised. So, some students cannot learn at all at school or do not have an interest in learning. In this situation in the past, in order to make students interested in learning, the school could try to adjust the curriculum's content. However, because of the present pressure caused by established curriculum content and regular assessment, the school has to give up those students who did not study well, which makes the national curriculum's goal to promote each student's development equally cannot be fully implemented in practice.

### 6.2.2 Changes in Teaching Decision-Making: From Advocating Teacher's Autonomy to Emphasizing Goal Orientation

In view of the relationship between contemporary curriculum and teaching, the way to achieve the curriculum goal is by teaching, so the goal of teaching activities and the goal of the curriculum should be consistent. Once the course objectives are clear, the teaching activities' goals should be close to the course objectives as much as possible. As mentioned above, before a unified national curriculum is formed, the curriculum of primary and the curriculum of secondary schools in the UK are quite different. The running thought of the school and the educational philosophy of the principal could be presented in the school's curriculum. At the same time, educational thoughts and educational values of the class teachers could also be reflected in the class teaching activities' design. Although each school had its own curriculum guidance program, teachers still had a lot of freedom in the determination of the teaching objectives and teaching contents. In other words, on the basis of their own teaching decisions, teachers who were the organizers, managers, and evaluators of class teaching, could exercise a high degree of autonomy in class activities. They could formulate their own teaching plans according to children's interests and needs, choose teaching materials, design teaching activities, and determine the evaluation standards and the goals that students should achieve. In some primary schools, a flexible class period system could also be adopted by teachers, and some teachers could also teach in an open style, which means, they could change the teaching objectives and teaching activities arrangements with the development of teaching. Sometimes, it might last for several afternoons to do a comprehensive thematic activity, and the actual achievement of its goals might be beyond the teachers themselves expectations. However, since the establishment of national curriculum standards and subject teaching objectives, this phenomenon of teachers' autonomy has changed. Especially in the early stage of national curriculum practice, there was an irreconcilable contradiction between teachers and the national curriculum. Some scholars pointed out that the social and historical tradition of teacher autonomy in the curriculum field was an important reason for the tension between teachers and the national curriculum.[5] In the conversations with adult students, many people said that now they have to spend a lot of time studying the requirements of the national curriculum for the subjects they teach and the standards that should be met. They believe that the current classroom teaching objectives and classroom activities are closely considered around the subject goal that is required by the national curriculum. Although the goal of the national curriculum is to promote the full and harmonious development of all children in the spiritual, moral, cultural, intellectual, physical, emotional, and social aspects, in practice, the overemphasis on the academic curriculum leads to subject knowledge-based rote learning.[6] At the same time, the teacher-autonomous classroom has also become a goal-oriented classroom. This change also directly caused the transformation of classroom teaching mode.

### 6.2.3 Changes in Teaching Mode: From Advocating Children's Center to Emphasizing the Discipline Center

This teaching mode's shift has been particularly salient in primary schools. Currently, the United Kingdom implements the national curriculum, which is subject-based or knowledge-based, requiring sub-discipline-centered curriculum design. The previous pattern in primary schools of the United Kingdom focused on integrated courses and comprehensive thematic teaching. This is quite different from that. The transmission of this established teaching content determines the change of teaching mode from the center of children's needs to the center of subject knowledge. In many British scholars' view, the British basic education reform in Britain since the 1990s has been seeking to return to the traditional teaching paradigm. There are several typical formulations that have increased in educational theory and practice to describe this phenomenon, such as teacher-centered, subject-based, knowledge-based, whole-class teaching, direct teaching, and "chalk and explanation." Obviously, the orientation of the government in teaching strategies is to enable students to master the system and contents of subject knowledge effectively and improve their academic achievements continuously. In the conversations between the author and adult students, most of them mentioned that in the past, teachers could use a lot of time to arrange a subject-teaching activity, and students could carry out various types and methods of activities around this subject. Now teachers must teach step by step according to the knowledge system of each subject, which is difficult to find more time for special subject teaching, and the task of knowledge imparting in course teaching is relatively large, and teachers must complete the teaching task on time. They believe that teachers are now paying more and more attention to the teaching of subject knowledge, rather than carrying out various activities according to students' interests. From a historical point of view, since the 1960s, British basic education, especially the mainstream education of primary schools, has been influenced by the American progressive educator John Dewey's Child-Centered Theory, and has carried out a series of teaching reforms. For example, grouping by ability, mixed grade system, open classrooms, learning resource centers, instructional package, integrated curriculum, integration day, collaborative group learning, comprehensive thematic teaching, and the return of children with special needs to the mainstream. These reforms are aimed at the cultivation of children's interests, needs, personality formation, and practical ability. For a long time, the teacher's center, knowledge center, and whole-class teaching for all students were subjected to criticism and attack. The organizational forms of teaching are mostly group teaching, individual teaching, and students' individual practice activities, and the whole class teaching for all students only accounts for about 30%. The main theme of teaching is focusing on individual differences and the development of students' personalities.[7] However, since the national curriculum's implementation in the early 1990s, the conservative government has advocated that teachers should no longer be influenced by progressive educational ideas, and should develop toward more structured, standardized, and responsible classroom teaching.[8] At the same time, the function of Child-Centered Theory to improve students' academic performance has been questioned and challenged, while subject-specific teaching and direct teaching for the whole class have been re-recognized by the government and its think tanks. There are two main reasons for this. One is the related research results' support, and the other is the government education policy's orientation. For example, four basic requirements were proposed by Professor Bogorghes for effective mathematics teaching in the report entitled "Effective Mathematics Teaching," which is a preliminary research result of his studying topic, "Strategies for National Mathematics Teaching." Encouraging whole-class teaching while reducing individual activities was the first of these. This is the result after researchers make a comparative study on teaching in Hungary, Poland, Singapore, Japan, and the United Kingdom. In particular, at the end of 1999, after the promulgation of the *National Teaching Strategy for Reading and Writing* and the *National Arithmetic Teaching Strategy* by the Department for Education and Employment (DfEE), the teaching methods of comprehensive subjects and integration days have been restricted to a certain extent.[9] The document, *Strategies for National Mathematics Teaching*, also requires teachers not to affect the direct teaching of other subjects because of organizational integration days.[10] Also, it requires teachers to take good direct teaching as an effective teaching strategy to improve students' literacy and math abilities and grades. From the perspective of the government's reform, the teaching strategy for the whole class has been paid more attention to, and the model orientation of teaching is very obvious. A typical example is that the above-mentioned national arithmetic teaching strategy not only puts forward the requirements of good direct teaching, but also suggests that the basic structure of classroom teaching should be composed of three parts, that is, the first part (5–10 minutes) for whole-class teaching; The main part that focuses on the whole class but also combining the group activities and individual activities (30–40 minutes) and the end part (10–15 minutes) for the whole class summary.[11] A comparative study of English primary school class teaching in 1996 and in 1976 conducted by Galton, M. and some other people found that compared to the classes in 1976, exchanges between teachers and students increased significantly in the classes (mainly mathematics classes and science classes) in 1996, while the time for students' independent learning and practical activities significantly decreased.[12] Although facing the country's teaching reform goals, many educators have proposed a partnership teaching model of teacher-student cooperation on the basis of reflecting on the advantages and disadvantages of traditional teaching and Child-Centered Mode. However, at present, the teaching practices with a focus on subject knowledge teaching and summarized evaluation in UK Primary schools have clearly moved towards Children-Centered Mode's opposite.

### 6.2.4 Changes in Teaching Evaluation: Emphasis on Formative Evaluation to the Terminal Evaluation

In modern British primary and secondary schools, three basic types of teaching evaluation are diagnostic evaluation, formative evaluation, and terminal evaluation. The main purpose of the diagnostic evaluation is to know the students' learning background and their preparations for learning before teaching so as to formulate a targeted learning plan. The formative evaluation mainly aims to understand students' learning progress and learning problems in the process of teaching to effectively improve learning; the function of the terminal assessment is mainly to evaluate students' learning results after teaching, and to give students a grade-level identification. In recent years, the evaluation guidelines and evaluation practices of primary and secondary schools in Britain have changed significantly from the emphasis on diagnostic evaluation and formative evaluation in the past to the current emphasis on the final evaluation. have changed significantly from the emphasis on diagnostic evaluation and formative evaluation in the past to the current emphasis on summative evaluation, whose content and way are also formulated by schools themselves. The center of the school's learning assessment system had always been the teacher's self-compiled tests, oral exams, and reports on learning and progress for each student. However, now the situation has changed a lot. A series of standards have been set by the government for schools and teachers. Teachers must not only teach according to the goals of the national curriculum, but students must also take regular and standardized examinations. In Dr. White's study, a new teacher put it this way: Since I started teaching the new curriculum, the government's expectations of us and the actual workload have increased significantly than before, and all students have to take external examinations so that we have to focus our teaching on improving students' achievements.[13] As we all know, in the past, a unified national examination in primary and secondary schools did not exist in the United Kingdom. But now they not only have but also make a classification in a detailed way. In the past, the British education circles' subject of criticism has always been the entrance examinations of all levels in Eastern countries. Now from primary school to secondary school in the UK, the unified national examination is divided into four grades: Grade Two (7 years old), Grade Six (11 years old), Grade Nine (14 years old), and Grade 11 (16 years old).[14] Moreover, schools and students should be ranked according to the test scores and reported through the media, as the basis for parents to choose schools and government funding for their children. Although basic education in the UK is compulsory and there is no pressure on students to go to school, strict external examinations and inspections have caused a series of debates and problems. As some scholars have said: "Nowadays, the market economy's competition mechanism has been introduced to schools by the government, although the former Conservative government's education and science department once pointed out in earlier education consultation documents that appraisal is the servant of curriculum and provides service for curriculum, not the owner."[15] However, after 1997, the education management department of the Labor government continued to strengthen the summative assessment of students' academic performance and regular inspections of schools. To a large extent, the formative evaluation of students by classroom teachers is gradually replaced by strict external examinations and inspections, and the purpose of evaluation to improve students' learning ability has been greatly weakened. Student-to-student, school-to-school competition is intensifying. At the same time, the criteria by which the education sector evaluates good or effective teaching have also changed. Test score has become an important criterion for evaluating teachers' teaching. Teachers who can help students achieve good marks in the unified examinations of English, Mathematics, Science, and ICTs will be rated highly by the management.[16]

### 6.2.5 Comparison and Inspiration

Inspecting the primary and secondary school curriculum and teaching reforms implemented by the British government since the 1990s, combining with the comparison of China's new basic education reforms, and re-examining the basic education reforms in other countries in the world, the enlightenment given to us is that the basic education reform in the world has entered a new stage of "reflection and deficiency." Everyone's eyes point to the new century, and the goal of education reform is to improve the quality and cultivate high-quality talents. However, its reform path and implementation strategy are not the same, and even completely opposite in some aspects. For example, while the government of China begins to shift its power downward, the UK is constantly strengthening the central government's management and evaluation of schools. Although from various types of education reform documents, it is not difficult to find that the educational reforms in China and the UK are consistent in their pursuit of goals, that is, to cultivate comprehensive and harmonious development of high-quality talents with individuality. However, studies have shown that the implementation strategies used to achieve this goal are quite different. The author's feeling is: It can be said it is hypercorrection, or to say, all roads lead to Rome. Why is there such a situation? The reasons for this are many. The main reason is that the Chinese and British governments and educational circles have different results in reflecting on their past educational gains and losses before the arrival of the new century. The focus of the British government and the education community's reflection is why the academic performance of British students has been declining, especially in the international educational achievement evaluation and international primary and secondary school academic competitions (such as International Olympic Competitions) always falling behind, which will undoubtedly affect Britain's future international competition. How to improve and promote students' learning achievements? This is obviously the starting point of British education reform. However, the focus of our government and educational circles' reflection is not on the academic performance of students, but on the high scores and low abilities of Chinese students compared with students in developed countries such as the United States and Britain, especially the backwardness of creative awareness and creative ability.

Elementary education in Britain has been influenced by American educator Dewey since the 1960s, especially primary education, which always emphasized the Children-Centered model and Activity-Centered model. Group teaching and individual teaching are mainstream teaching strategies. The biggest advantage of this educational paradigm is that it can stimulate students' interest and initiative in learning, which is conducive to the cultivation of children's exploratory ability and creative ability, but is not conducive to the mastery of systematic subject knowledge and the improvement of academic performance. Numerous international comparative studies have confirmed this. Therefore, the focus of the British basic education reform is constantly shifting to the learning of subject knowledge and effective direct teaching. On the contrary, since the 1960s, China's basic education has been influenced by the former Soviet Union educator Keluofu since the 1960s. Concerning the teaching model, it is basically a Teacher-Centered model and a Knowledge-Centered model. The mainstream teaching strategy is direct teaching, which faces the entire class of students. Although this kind of teaching is beneficial to the mastery of scientific knowledge of system culture and the improvement of students' academic performance in subject courses, it affects the cultivation of students' practical ability, especially the development of creativity, to a considerable extent, and its drawbacks are obvious. Because of this, China's basic education reform in recent years has emphasized the need to change the tendency of the previous curriculum to focus too much on knowledge imparting, emphasize the formation of a proactive learning attitude, and make the process of acquiring basic knowledge and basic skills equally important. Therefore, different characteristics of the educational reforms in China and Britain have been shown. Since the early 1980s, a lot of education reforms have presented waves by waves in the world, and more and more countries have learned from each other. A considerable part of both Chinese and foreign education circles has become the attempt to integrate East-West educational thinking and teaching strategies. In fact, this point has also been clearly reflected in the practices of education reform in various countries. However, mutual learning among countries is not only very sensible, but also completely feasible. It is hoped that my country's basic education reform can take new steps with Chinese characteristics while learning from the experience of other countries.

## 6.3 Characteristics of the New Round of Basic Education Curriculum Reform in China

At present, the new round of basic education curriculum reform in our country has steadily advanced to the second stage—the pilot experiment stage—and has achieved pioneering progress. The gradual expansion of the national and provincial experimental areas and the accumulation of reform experience have laid a solid foundation for the all-around promotion of the reform in the autumn of 2005. If we go deeper into the background, objective, concept, and development tendency of the practice of basic education curriculum reform, it is not hard to find that it significantly distinguishes itself from the previous curriculum reform and presents its basic characteristics. According to the author, this curriculum reform generally focuses on "seeking balance and harmony," trying to find a suitable balance between the curriculum theory and the reform practice, which were previously considered to be contradictory to each other, and constructing the best basic education curriculum theory and practice system which are in line with Chinese characteristics. Specifically, the following features are significant:

### 6.3.1 Balancing Science and Experience in Curriculum Reform

Most previous curriculum reforms in China belong to the experiential type, which is short of rational guidance. The intent of curriculum reform was hard to accomplish, leading to the fact that some curriculum forms like "elective courses" and "activity classes" only appear in government curriculum documents and school curriculum plans.[17] The new round of basic education curriculum reform has stepped out of the tradition of experience-based curriculum reforms, combining scientific and strict implementation steps with experiential exploration, and proactively exploring effective experiences under rational guidance. First of all, they are fully prepared before the implementation of the reform, with full investigation and reflection on the successes and failures of the previous curricular reforms, and they conduct a comparative study of representative curricular reforms in other countries around the world to formulate a scientific guidance plan for the implementation of the new basic curriculum reform. Secondly, they attach great importance to teachers' training, strengthening teachers' understanding of the new curriculum to achieve a radical change in their teaching philosophies and teaching methods to clear the key obstacles for the implementation of the new curriculum. Finally, the development of experimental research has greatly strengthened the scientific nature of this curriculum reform. Large-scale pilot experiments were never seen in previous curricular reforms. They not only provide us with feedback on curriculum reform plans, but also explore and accumulate effective experiences to promote the mutual penetration of experience and rationality to make curriculum reform completely shake off the experience model.

### 6.3.2 Balancing Internationalism and Nationality in Requirements

The balance between internationalism and nationality refers to the fact that the new basic education curriculum reform should be established on national conditions to go with the trend of global development. It is an excellent tradition of China's curriculum reform to gain advanced experience in foreign curriculum reforms. In the history of China's curriculum reforms, foreign advanced theories and experiences indeed played a vital role. However, any foreign theory and experience will be likely to grow into "geeks" without local transformation. As some Chinese scholars have pointed out, "Our country's curriculum begins with learning from the Soviet Union in the early days of new China to introducing Western theories in the 1970s. It lacks criticism and innovation upon foreign theories and experience so that gives rise to many problems in the current curriculum system."[18] Therefore, how to handle internationalism and nationality properly is a problem that cannot be neglected in China's curriculum reform. During this curriculum reform, China has drawn on and incorporated foreign theories and experiences in many aspects, such as the concept of curriculum reform, curriculum structure, curriculum content, curriculum implementation, and evaluation, etc., and mainly draws on recent curriculum reform experiences of countries in the following three cultural regions: Western Europe, East Asia, and North America. However, this reform, based on the status quo of China's curriculum, is committed to building a new curriculum system with Chinese characteristics.

The balance between unified requirements and local characteristics means that local differences should be fully considered under the unified national requirements to increase the adaptability of the curriculum and establish a curriculum system that can meet the different needs of different regions. The local adaptability of the curriculum is a neglected part of China's previous curriculum reforms. Although the political, economic, cultural, and educational levels across the country vary widely, the curriculum standard is unified. In order to change this situation, the basic education curriculum reform has made adjustments in many aspects. For example, it increases the proportion of local curriculums, sets school-based curriculums, advocates the utilization and development of local curriculum resources, expands the local curriculum management authority, and requires curriculum in rural elementary schools to serve the local economy, etc. All of these above are aimed at resolving the contradictions between the unified requirements and local characteristics.

### 6.3.3 Improving Curriculum Structure with Subject Diversity

According to different standards, courses can be classified as follows: branch course and integrated course; elective course and compulsory course; national course, local course and school-based course; imparting course and discovery course; etc.[19] Different types of courses possess different values. The proportion of different types of courses has a direct impact on the types of talents cultivated by a country. Therefore, the adjustment of the course types becomes the most important content of the curriculum structure adjustment in any country. The current basic education curriculum types in China are single, in which subject courses, compulsory courses, national courses, and imparting courses occupy absolute dominance. Although activity classes and elective courses were added during the curriculum reform from the late 1980s to the early 1990s, the issue has not been radically solved. Coupled with the overemphasis on Chinese, mathematics, and other so-called key subjects' structure, the comprehensive development of students is difficult to implement in practice. The curriculum reform now focuses on correcting the deviation of the old curriculum structure, increasing integrated courses and reducing the proportion of national courses and compulsory courses, and reducing the proportion of traditionally advantageous subjects like Chinese, mathematics, etc., striving to construct a structure-balanced curriculum system. Especially in terms of integrated courses, we set up an integrated practical activity curriculum that runs through the entire school system from elementary school to high school and has been included in the compulsory courses, making it an important part of the school curriculum system. At the same time, two kinds of curriculum plans have been designed, branch-type and integrated-type, and the integrated curriculum plan is also advocated everywhere. These measures indicate that the new basic education curriculum reform is a breakthrough change from the previous curriculum system. It will lead to fundamental changes in learning and teaching methods, and eventually achieve changes in the types of talents.

### 6.3.4 Balancing Social Needs, Development, and Knowledge in Curriculum

Society, students, and knowledge are three basic sources of the curriculum's contents. Education's ability to effectively perform its intended function depends on whether the three can build a reasonable equilibrium relationship. As we all know, the current curriculum in China belongs to the knowledge-based curriculum model, which is characterized by emphasizing the logical system of knowledge itself and paying attention to the learning of systematic knowledge and the teaching of contents in books while lacking due care for the interests and social requirements of students. In addition, the curriculum contents are famous for being "Difficult, Complicated, Partial, Old." On the one hand, it fails to meet the needs of the comprehensive development of students' personalities; on the other hand, talents cultivated in this model cannot meet the needs of social development due to their poor social adaptability. To this end, the new round of basic education curriculum reform has made major adjustments to the current curriculum: First, delete outdated and difficult knowledge contents, absorb new knowledge such as information technology knowledge, integrate too complicated knowledge contents, and adjust the proportion of knowledge based on different values. The second is to add more social life-related content to the curriculum and set up courses like social practice and community, labor, and technique education to make the curriculum more socially adaptable. The third is to integrate the knowledge of different subjects and different types, present students with the knowledge in its natural state of existence, and promote students' comprehensive development. Meanwhile, it provides students with curriculum knowledge of different levels and more choices to meet the various needs of students. The above reform measures not only coincide with the reform trend of international curriculum contents in the 21st century but also effectively promote the modernization and adaptability of the curriculum contents in China.

### 6.3.5 Balancing Centralized and Decentralized Curriculum Management

Overviewing the global reform of curriculum management systems, there is a general tendency to seek the harmonious unity of centralization and decentralization, and initiate multiple forces to participate in curriculum management and decision-making. At present, very few countries completely adopt a single mode of centralized or decentralized curriculum management. From the early days of New China, our country began to follow the centralized curriculum management system of the Soviet Union. This model adapted to China's national conditions in the early days and played a positive role at that time. Today, however, the centralized curriculum management mode increasingly shows its drawbacks, like inelasticity and cannot meet the requirements of different regions, which has seriously hindered education development in China. Some forward-looking scholars have recognized that since an early time. Mr. Lv Da, a Chinese academic scholar, first proposed the three-level curriculum management mode in 1990 and preliminarily discussed the authority and duties of the three parties—state, local, and school—in curriculum management.[20] In the early 1990s, Shanghai, Zhejiang, and other regions made the first attempt to decentralize curriculum management.[21] In 1999, for the first time, the national government proposed a three-level pilot system of managing curriculum at the state, local, and school levels.[22] In the current curriculum reform, the Chinese government begins to popularize the three-level curriculum management system across the country and attempts to construct the framework for the respective duties of the three-level authorities. Based on the status quo that schools in China lack subject awareness in curriculum management and teachers lack experience and ability to develop school-based curriculum, the government continues to follow the strategy that gives priority in curriculum management to state and local while the curriculum management authority of schools can be extended to a limited extent.

In addition, it also has relaxed the management authority of textbooks and gradually changed the traditional situation where the state monopolized the compilation, publication, and selection of textbooks, giving local, educational, and book publishing agencies greater autonomy.

### 6.3.6 Balancing the Structure of Curriculum Reform

The balance of the main structure of curriculum reform is associated with the accomplishment of the curriculum reform intention. An unreasonable main structure affects the quality of curriculum reform and hinders the accomplishment of the curriculum reform intention, while a reasonable main structure can mobilize the enthusiasm of all parties to participate in the curriculum reforms. All the previous curriculum reforms in China have primarily been government behaviors. Government is the initiator, designer, and promoter of curriculum reform. The officials who are the spokespersons of the government are the absolute power corpus. During the process of curriculum reform, the government must consult with experts and organize think tanks to design and develop the curriculum. Expert is an important part of curriculum reform in China. Teachers are only the executors of curriculum reform. The community staff, students, and parents are outsiders with no voices in the curriculum reform. The curriculum reform only reflects the will of the government and the value orientation of experts, which makes other parties hold negative, indifferent, and even hostile attitudes towards curriculum reform. Therefore, even if the new curriculum reflects the direction of curriculum development, it is difficult to achieve the expected results. The way to solve this problem is to change the main structure of curriculum reform so that the main body of curriculum design and development can be integrated with the main body of curriculum implementation. If compared to countries with relatively perfect curriculum systems, the integration between the main body of the new basic education curriculum and the main body of curriculum implementation in China is insufficient. However, compared with the previous curriculum reform in China, the new curriculum reform clearly pays more attention to teachers' participation in curriculum design, which can be embodied in the following appearances. In the brewing stage of curriculum reform, some teachers are involved in the overall planning process; In the pilot experimental phase, experience summaries are regularly held to listen to the opinions and suggestions of teachers. School-based curricula are added to the curriculum structure to give teachers direct control over curriculum development. All the above shows that teachers are not only the subject of curriculum development and design but also the subject of curriculum implementation. Besides, the new curriculum strengthens education's function to serve local economic and cultural development, mobilizes the enthusiasm of local people from all fields to participate in the curriculum reform, and further improves the structure of the main body of curriculum reforms.

### 6.3.7 Integrating Compilation, Implementation, and Evaluation in Curriculum Reform Model Development

Any curriculum reform is carried out under the guidance of a certain concept. Curriculum compilation is the embodiment of a curriculum concept. Curriculum implementation is the realization of a curriculum concept. Curriculum evaluation, which includes the evaluation of the curriculum itself and the evaluation of the teachers' teaching and students' learning, is the process of criticism and reflection upon the rationality of the curriculum concept, the scientificity of the curriculum compilation, and the adaptability of curriculum implementation. It is also the information feedback and quality supervision system in the curriculum reform. One of the drawbacks of previous curriculum reforms in China is that several links like compilation, implementation, and evaluation of the curriculum are disjointed with each other severely. Although there are cultural traditions, the more important reason is that there is no integrated curriculum reform model, and the reform only emphasizes curriculum compilation but neglects implementation and evaluation. Although the compiled curriculum is perfect, the curriculum actually implemented does not necessarily reflect the intention of the compiled curriculum; it is just the perfect curriculum considered by teachers personally. What's more, the curriculum evaluation system does not reflect the concept of curriculum reform correctly and even contradicts the concept of curriculum reform. The contents of the evaluation are not the stress advocated by the curriculum reform, resulting in few achievements of the curriculum reform. However, this curriculum reform has not ignored any link, and has taken various measures to increase the conformity between the implemented courses and compiled courses, emphasizing the transformation of the curriculum evaluation methods, reforming and perfecting the examination system, and establishing a curriculum evaluation system that reflects the concept of the curriculum reform, that is, a developmental curriculum evaluation system. By doing so, the curriculum evaluation can promote students' progress and also enhance teachers' teaching ability and the continuous improvement of the curriculum itself.

It can be seen from the above characteristics that the new round of basic education curriculum reform is the most advanced, scientific, and urgent curriculum reform in the history of China's curriculum reforms. It is not just revising the existing curriculum programs or teaching plans, nor merely publishing a new set of textbooks, but a fundamental curriculum revolution that focuses on economic globalization and the socialization of learning in the 21st century. Its success will surely drive China's basic education to a higher step.

## 6.4 Comparing International Education Reform: China, US, UK, Canada

At the turn of the century, humanity stepped into a new era of transcendence and revolutions: intelligence of production activities, informatization of life interactions, and political and economic globalization have constantly inspired people to renew themselves actively to keep in line with changes in the world. Therefore, educational activities have increasingly become the focus of people's common concerns. Corresponding to this, as the axis of educational activities, the curriculum becomes the main entry point for balancing the conflicts of interests of political groups, coordinating the contradictions between humans and nature, and participating in international competitions. Overviewing the trajectory of education reforms in different countries, we are not hard to find out that basic education curriculum reform has become one of the core events in the education affairs of all countries around the world. It has become inevitable for all countries to face the following questions in their basic education curriculum reforms: One is how to make basic education curriculum exert its full function on personal development, social progress, and national power improvement; the other is how to make the curriculum effectively realize the mission of inheriting culture, spreading civilization and inspiring national pride. In the face of common issues and common times, curriculum reformers in all countries provide their own answers from their own cultural traditions and propose different curriculum reform programs. It is obligatory for this study to offer vivid and diverse experiences of the "new curriculum reform" in China as well as to promote the modernization of the curriculum with Chinese characteristics, referring to the reform practices in all countries in the horizontal direction. After careful consideration, we select the United Kingdom, the United States, Canada, and China as the study objects, intending to explore beneficial reform experiences through horizontal comparison and guide the steady progress of "new curriculum reform" in China. At the same time, in order to enhance the comparability and draw a useful conclusion, this article attempts to base itself on the common background analysis of curriculum reforms in the four countries and analyze from three degrees which respectively are the basic education reform goal, curriculum structure, and curriculum evaluation. Therefore, the basic education curriculum reforms in these four countries not only communicate with each other but also reflect their own characteristics so as to provide a comprehensive and objective basis for the cross-cultural grafting of other countries' curriculum reform experiences into China.

### 6.4.1 The Common Background of the Basic Education Curriculum Reforms in the Four Countries

The trend of basic education reform that orients to the 21st century takes precedence over its practice. Since the 1990s, China, the United Kingdom, the United States, and Canada have taken precautions in the first step, considering and planning the blueprint for basic education curricula in the 21st century. Certainly, these measures are not absent-minded but are based on their insights and sensitivities of the era. To conclude, on the threshold of the new century, education reformers in all countries must consider the following three issues:

#### *Science and Technology Revolution and the Curriculum Content Adjustment Issue*

Since the late 20th century, the revolution in science and technology has occurred one after another, with a rapid change of knowledge, forming the so-called "third wave," according to Alvin Toffler. In this wave, information technology plays the leading role, which makes the informatization and networking of human life an issue that every ordinary person must deal with. Consequently, educational reformers in all countries have to make careful choices of educational content and allow for a large amount of popular science knowledge to ensure the modernization and informatization of curriculum contents. Otherwise, consumers of basic education will doubt educational activities.

***Conflicts between Personal Freedom and Curriculum Management***

The 20th century was an era of educational exploration. Dewey's experiential curriculum theory gives rise to a rebound towards the concern for social efficiency of the 20th-century curriculum, as can be seen as follows: The United States has witnessed a "pendulum" curriculum; the curriculum management in Britain has been placed under the command of "liberalism"; the Canadian curriculum has struggled hard for "informal" and "basic" curriculum management, while China is striving to get rid of the barriers of "exam-oriented education" by the trend of "children-centered" and "free" curriculum reform. However, by the late 20th century, especially since the 1980s, the stimulus of economic competition caused by economic globalization and the thought of "reflection" in the education circle have brought about a deep exploration of the quality of education. In addition, the American awareness of the secondary school students' decline in academic test scores, the British perception of the ineffectiveness of a "loose curriculum," and the resentment of Canadian citizens over the shortcomings of the curriculum's regional differences, all make education quality closely related to curriculum management. In short, the emergence of the "Global Village" has buffered the conflicts between individual freedom and national interests within the curriculum. It has become a new concept of curriculum management in the 21st century that education can better serve workers and national interests through the state's self-defense intervention. Except for China, which has long been quite capable of education control, the other three countries also put forward the choice of a unified curriculum and the new issue of maintaining the balance and vitality of curriculum.

Secondly, as the knowledge-explosive and information-flooded society is beginning to take shape and the radiating power of curriculum to life is enhanced, new contents have emerged, which can be concluded that the basic education curriculum is not focusing on the inheritance of culture but on the reconstruction of the new curriculum culture which pursues the development of learning abilities and takes curriculum structure optimization as the means. Therefore, the four countries must address two issues in the curriculum reform: One is how to create a sustainable, life-form basic education curriculum, which is designed to meet the new requirements for the basic education curriculum from lifelong education; the other is how to develop a balanced curriculum structure to achieve the integration of multi-functions of the curriculum so that the basic education curriculum can contribute to solving the "global problems" and serving for "leisure life." For this reason, curriculum reform has become a thorny issue. Thus, all four countries have had new discussions on the objectives and structure of the curriculum so as to improve the adaptability of their curricula.

### *Changes in Educational Quality Concepts*

It can be said that how to improve the quality of national education is a universal concern for all countries in the world in the 21st century. The United Kingdom's *1988 Education Reform Act* proposed that education quality and academic achievement as overwhelming tasks. The United States regards the improvement of students' achievements in three major subjects of English, mathematics and science as an important criterion for the success of the reform.[23] Canada has introduced a problem-testing method, and each province has formed a unified examination system. China has formed a subject structure for the college entrance examination, namely "3+X." These various exams and standards aim to emphasize the improvement of "basic learning skills." Therefore, the "basic learning skills" has drawn everyone's attention to the problems with the quality of education in various countries. Needless to say, the improvement of basic learning ability not only reflects the promotion of the intellectualization of human social life but also means that competition over the curriculum quality has entered a substantive stage.

In short, faced with the above three issues, current national curriculum reform in each country must propose new reform measures. Reflections on these issues have become the starting point and entry point of reform in each country. Although the answers and ways to solve these questions differ from country to country, they are closely associated with the common mission of the times. Therefore, a comparative study of them is a fascinating project. The purpose of this study is to explore the subtle correlation between basic education reform and each country's unique national conditions and cultural background in order to understand the strategies and unique thinking modes of basic education curriculum reforms in various countries in general. In the following, the article will analyze the basic education curriculum reforms in China, the United States, Britain, and Canada from three aspects. The rationality lies in the fact that the goal of the curriculum reform is to take a macro-level look at basic education curriculum reform in each country. It means that each government should plan for the ideal state of curriculum reform. The curriculum content structure is the concrete and realistic plan of all its reforms and is the best "text" for us to gain an insight into the contemporary curriculum reform in each country. The curriculum evaluation is the continuation of curriculum management, the tool for achieving curriculum goals, and the ruler for regulating curriculum contents. The comparison of these three dimensions can help us see the structure and essence of the curriculum reforms in China, Britain, the United States, and Canada.

### 6.4.2 Diverse Perspectives on Curriculum Reform Goals

In response to the long-existing weaknesses in education, such as a lack of standards, low-level examinations, vague achievements, and a lack of motivation,[24] the United States set up a series of curriculum reform documents like the *2000 National Education Standards*, the *2061 Plan* and so on, especially the latter as a representative, which contains the following six items:

(1) All children in the United States have been prepared to study when they first go to school.
(2) The high school graduation rate will be increased to at least 90%.
(3) At the end of Grade 4, Grade 8, and Grade 12, American students must demonstrate their outstanding abilities in the following subjects: English, mathematics, science, history, and geography.
(4) American students' achievements in science and mathematics will rank first in the world.
(5) Every adult in the United States is literate.
(6) All schools in the United States have no drugs or violence.

It can be perceived that the education quality concept in the United States is centered on the achievements of the natural science disciplines, taking universal cultural education as the periphery and the solution to the education crisis as the policy bottom line. Its fundamental feature is to make education actively respond to economic globalization and the competition of scientific and technological strength, and meanwhile give full play to the multiple functions of education, therefore achieving the overall pursuit of education quality in the balance between science and technology and humanities.

Britain has formed its own unique value orientation and reform thinking in the education quality concept, which is reflected in the *1988 Education Reform Act* and *Curriculum in 2000*. The *1988 Education Reform Act* proposed the followings:

(1) More opportunities to choose from
(2) Combination of academic courses and vocational courses
(3) Development of key skills
(4) Participating in public activities

If we make a comparison, we may find that the United States stresses more on the quality of education and ultimately makes the academic capabilities of American students stand at the forefront of the world. American education begins at the Scholastic Aptitude TEST of the lowest level in basic disciplines and tool disciplines (English and Mathematics) in Grades 4, 8, and 12 and develops in the form of from both ends (Children's Entrance Examination Education and Adult Education) to the center (Basic Education). The education quality concept in British education is centered on the unified examination, unified curriculum, and unified outline. Its mission is to break the shortcomings of long-standing liberal traditions in basic education in the United Kingdom by strengthening national control over education, therefore helping children seek a balance between life experience and basic education curriculum. It can be said that the British education quality concept is supported by the national curriculum control (embodied in the three core courses and the six basic courses), and the unification of educational standards is based on the summative evaluation and the introduction of competition mechanisms. It can be said that the national curriculum reform in the UK resulted from the underlying education issues, and such an education quality concept can be regarded as a powerful means by which the British government controls education.

Now reviewing Canada again, we may find that the center of its curriculum reform can also be attributed to the education quality issue; the special national condition in Canada determines its education quality should put more emphasis on the double standards between commonality and individuality, as well as between social needs and personal development. On the one hand, establishing a national core curriculum to achieve common goals and meet the needs of society;[25] On the other hand, Canada has set up a series of optional courses like industrial technology, housekeeping, business service, and so on to emphasize that curriculum reform should meet diversified needs of various groups and individuals. In addition, Canada has included the science and technology education curriculum as one of the major contents of the reform and has given priority to improving the quality of mathematics, and science education in the government agenda.[26] Therefore, there are many similarities between contemporary education quality concepts in Canada and those in Britain and America, such as beginning to pay attention to the unified test and the quality of science education. Finally, an education quality concept that is led by science education is formed, combining humanities and science as well as academics and professionalism simultaneously, and advocating STS (science-technology-society) education.

Different from the above views on the curriculum quality, the curriculum reform in China promotes a balanced and ecological quality view based on positive learning, which is mainly embodied in *The Outline of Basic Education Curriculum Reform*: The so-called "balance" means to orientate the goal of curriculum reform toward the formation of a reasonable goal structure, which is reflected in two aspects as follows: One is not only emphasizing the outcomes of education quality which are embodied in the formation of good quality, ability and awareness of students, but also emphasizing the process of education quality which is embodied in the changes of learning styles and the promotion of an independent, cooperative, exploratory curriculum culture; The other is not only emphasizing the education quality of the humanities, which puts the formation of correct "three concepts," environmental awareness and the national spirit in the first place, but also emphasizing the education quality of science, which focuses on the basic scientific knowledge and information literacy in reform. At the same time, the two means, "only exams" and "national reunification," must be opposed when achieving the goal. We should strongly promote process evaluation and powerfully activate the enthusiasm of local authorities, schools, and teachers to improve the quality of education.

Therefore, the curriculum reform goals in the four countries are all to improve the education quality and to meet the demands of the nation, society, and people for quality education. However, there are discrepancies in terms of understanding education quality, ways of improving education quality, and focus on education quality improvement. In general, the United States focuses on the quality of science and technology, China on overall quality, Britain on national unification, and Canada on personalized education. It can be said that it is precisely the different understandings of education quality and the different emphases that result in the fact that all countries have developed their own unique curriculum reforms that are different from each other.

### 6.4.3 Common Trends and Differences in Curriculum Reform among Four Countries

Contemporary curriculum reforms in all countries have cast off the "dualism" of modernism, and no longer puzzle about the dispute between "activism" and "intellectualism," but focus on resolving the above dispute in the reform practice to reach harmony within the curriculum. Therefore, rational curriculum modules are designed to pursue an organic and balanced relationship within the curriculum structure, so that the curriculum will become a powerful tool to balance education and humans and society. For the above reasons, the United States, Britain, Canada and China have designed their own curriculum reform programs one after another. Now the author will analyze each of the above as follows:

Contemporary curriculum reforms in the United States are mainly shown in the following documents: *The 2061 Education Reform Plan of the United States* in 1983, *The National Education Goal of the United States* in 1990, *The 2000 Education Strategy* promulgated by the Bush administration in 1991 and *The Target of 2000: American Education Act* promulgated by the Clinton administration in 1993. Among these documents, the United States has planned a curriculum structure for primary and secondary schools that has three characteristics as follows:

(1) Taking academic subjects as the axis, and non-academic subjects as the periphery, weakening the proportion of ornamental subjects and pursuing a new balance between academic subjects and empirical subjects

Before the 1980s, due to the impact of the progressive doctrine and the trend of career education, the United States regarded life-oriented education as the focus of curriculum reform. However, since the Second World War, due to the intensification of scientific and technological competition, the decline in the academic performance of American students has caused alarm in the educational decision-making departments in the United States. In order to consolidate the United States' status as a world superpower, its basic education curriculum has transformed the center from experience to the academy. This is reflected in the curriculum structure. Contemporary American elementary school curricula include social science (including history, geography, politics, law, etc.), art (including reading, writing, language, speaking, etc.), science (including physics, chemistry, biology, etc.), music arts, sports, health care and so on. Among the above, language arts, social sciences, mathematics, science, sports and health care, music, and art education are the basic core subjects, and mainly take the form of integrated courses, which combine academic courses and comprehensive courses. In secondary schools, for example, the United States has set up two types of courses: common core courses and elective courses. The former type includes language courses, history, civics, science, mathematics, technology, health, occupation, interdisciplinary courses, and so on, while the latter type can be divided into three categories, occupational course, academic course, and integrated course of the above two, accounting for half of the total class hours.[27]

(2) Regarding the core courses as the subject and elective courses as the auxiliary, and pursuing the balance between unity and diversity of the curriculum

Taking the American middle school curriculum as an example. There are seven compulsory courses designed for junior high schools, which are respectively English, sociology, mathematics, science, foreign language, sports, and arts. As for the high schools, the department has designed nine common core courses, including language, history, geography, civics, mathematics, technology, health, and so on. At the same time, a large number of elective courses have been set up in accordance with the core curriculum. It is also stipulated that in the latter two years of high school, students can spend half the time learning the core curriculum, but the other half must be given to 5–6 elective courses, which gives the curriculum structure some freedom to a certain degree and enhances the flexibility and adaptability of the curriculum structure. In the *1988 Education Reform Act*, Britain also divides compulsory education courses into three categories: core courses, basic courses, and additional courses. The former two are national courses. The proportions among the three types will change according to the political power comparison and the theme of the times.

(3) Putting the modern science curriculum at the core while the language and social science curriculum at the edge, and pursuing the balance between modernization and tradition within the curriculum structure

The vitality of a course is that it will establish a metabolic mechanism for it to not only include the newest scientific and technological achievements but also help students accumulate the knowledge and experiences that are necessary for students' growth in the curriculum, so that the curriculum can become the foundation of students' growth and the starting point for students' development. The contemporary United States has constantly incorporated emerging disciplines and top-level disciplines into the school curriculum and has expanded the proportion of the newest achievements of science and technology in the curriculum, which has made the basic education curriculum structure increasingly modernized. In the meantime, the United States has made reading and writing abilities the significant content of the curriculum and has continuously increased their proportion. These measures have created a good combination of inheritance and renewal of the curriculum.

Britain has also made positive attempts in curriculum structure reform. On the whole, its curriculum reform tries to take the national curriculum as a link to achieve comprehensive communication and overall balance within the curriculum. From the aspect of curriculum design in the UK, we may see four characteristics:

(1) Laying a solid foundation for tool disciplines, and emphasizing basic learning ability is the starting point of curriculum reform

Britain has formally launched the new curriculum design, *Course 2000*, throughout the whole of Britain since September 2000, setting 12 compulsory courses, including English, mathematics, science, design and technology, information and communication technology, history, geography, a modern foreign language, art and design, music, sports, and civics. Although tool disciplines such as English, mathematics, and modern foreign languages only account for one-third of the course categories, learning hours of English subjects fully cover the four key stages. The modern foreign language subject will be set up in the third and fourth stages from September 2001. The prominence of these tool courses in the new curriculum structure undoubtedly makes the British curriculum more adaptable to the special requirements of the learning society for learning abilities.

(2) Strengthening science curriculum, attaching importance to information and technology education, and promoting the modernization of curriculum structure

In the new curriculum structure, Britain has listed science, information, and science communication technologies as core compulsory courses at the four key stages since 2000, and devoted to improving students' information literacy and basic science knowledge. They regard the following abilities and skills as the necessary qualities of British facing the 21st century: the application of science, the ability to scientific research, the spirit of scientific thought, the ability to acquire information, and the application skills of information equipment, which undoubtedly make curriculum structure keep pace with the development of science and technology, reflecting the unification of technology development and children's development.

(3) Boosting humanity and social courses, promoting the coordinated development of individuals and society, spirit and morality, and enhancing the humanism of the curriculum structure

In *Course 2000*, Britain includes civics as a compulsory course and makes family education, sex education, school enrollment and career guidance, personality development, and sociality formation the study topics across all disciplines. Therefore, these humanity courses are organically infiltrated into various compulsory courses to improve the education effect of these humanity courses in a more imperceptible way. These reform measures will inevitably make the humanistic characteristics more prominent in this curriculum reform.

(4) Opening design courses to deepen students' participation in the curriculum and to promote the subjectivity of the new curriculum structure

The new curriculum structure includes various types of design courses in the compulsory courses. For example, the design and technology course introduces product development, industrial production, and living environment issues into the class to enable students to become inventors and users of new products; The art and design courses stimulate students' imagination and creativity, encouraging students to design their lives in accordance with the laws of beauty. All of the above have made the curriculum no longer a rational constitution but a visible reality. Therefore, the new British curriculum structure has found a more effective balance point and junction among the various factors that affect it through the connection between curriculum and technology, the connection between curriculum and life, and the connection between curriculum and students.

Due to the large number of immigrants and multiculture in Canada, the formation of the curriculum structure has always been based on the provinces themselves. This is marked by the fact that each province will promulgate its own *curriculum design requirements*, so the curriculum structures of different provinces vary widely from each other. Since the 21st century, because of the common requirements of scientific and technological development, the coordination of educational decision-making departments in Canada, and the frequent exchanges among educational institutions in different provinces, many new features have emerged in the basic education curriculum structure in Canada, which can be summarized as follows:

(1) Finding a balanced relationship between the unity and the flexibility of the curriculum structure

Since the mid-1980s, all Canadian provinces have demanded that primary and secondary schools set uniformly stipulated common curricula with certain teaching contents and teaching hours. Therefore, subjects like English, social science, and natural science are mostly set as compulsory courses, and the proportion increases. At the same time, Canadian provinces continuously increase flexible and varied elective courses. These elective courses are often classified according to categories and are generally divided into three categories: academic elective subject, elective interest subject, and professional elective subject to cater to students' interests and individual development needs. This makes the new curriculum structure moderate flexibility. Take British Columbia as an example once again. The curriculum structure promulgated by the Education Commission of B.C. Province in 1988 can be described as follows: On the one hand, unified curriculum subjects are put forward, which are humanity science (including English, social studies, and French), natural science (including mathematics, biology, chemistry, and physics), arts (including music, art, dance, etc.), and practical arts (including sports, industry, home craft, etc.); On the other hand, it places emphasis on the development of local curriculum, accounting for about 20%, which effectively balances the dialectical relationship between unity and flexibility.[28]

(2) Seeking integration of curriculum structure in courses of science, technology, and society

At the beginning of the 1980s, Canada promulgated a series of curriculum reform plans, creating a big wave of curriculum structure reform. Among these, firstly, the public is particularly interested in the attempt to accelerate the integration of courses in science, technology, and society. For example, Saskatchewan, which is considered the model for curriculum reform in Canada, published the "K-12 Consistent System" plan of core courses and was required to set up a compulsory course—basic learning essentials. This course requires cultivating students' abilities in the following six aspects:[29] language communication ability, mathematical computing ability, commentary thinking ability, scientific and technological concepts, correct social values, and independent learning ability, and these should be taught in various disciplines. Its main orientation is to pave the way to unify and integrate humanity courses and science and technology courses, social concepts, and self-cultivation as a whole. Secondly, another typical sign of accomplishing this combination is the "STS Curriculum Project," among which the most typical one is the "Atlantic Science Curriculum Program." The program emphasizes combining the understanding of natural science, the development of social decision-making skills, and the solution to technical problems, and effectively promotes the totalization and integration of curriculum structure. Thirdly, promoting interdisciplinary education and enhancing curriculum consolidation is another measure to achieve the integration of curriculum structure. For example, the Royal Education Commission in British Columbia demands that primary school teachers adopt an interdisciplinary educational approach and employ practical arts classes to strengthen the links among sports, industry, home crafts, and health. These reforms embody the inevitable requirements for curriculum integration.[30]

(3) Strengthening the communication between curriculum structure and local social life

To make the basic education curriculum a vehicle that inherits and carries forward the culture and customs of their own regions, own nations, and own schools, all Canadian provinces strive to incorporate their basic education curriculum design within the province with the life, customs, and interpersonal relationships of their own regions, own nations, and own schools. For example, Nuwaite Culture Class and Daiwaite Culture Class are classified as basic classes in high schools in the northwestern region. In the Yukon Territory, the flora and zoology classes related to the southern region are excluded. Meanwhile, Yukon is committed to revising the curriculum that reflects the local cultural characteristics, allowing the curriculum structure to maintain diversity and individuality, with typical characteristics of the local culture.[31]

In short, the typical feature of the basic education curriculum reform in Canada is its active exploration of the diversification, individualization, and integration of curriculum.

Finally, the author will analyze the curriculum structure reforms in China. *The Outline of Basic Education Curriculum Reform* clearly stipulates the basic structure of the new basic education curriculum in China. Its basic features are as follows:

(1) Vertical consistency

The overall design of the nine-year compulsory education program has the following requirements: On the one hand, the composition of the curriculum structure is in line with the age characteristics of students. For example, setting up morality and life course in the primary lower grades while setting up moral and society course in the upper primary grades, and the curriculum forms are mainly comprehensive courses. In junior high school, ideology and morality courses are set up to ensure the curriculum design is progressive and scientific; On the other hand, attaching importance to the link between different grades in the core curriculum contents, like Chinese, mathematics, etc., to serve for the spiral expansion process of students' learning.

(2) Highlighting the practicalness of the curriculum

This characteristic is primarily demonstrated by the following measures: Making the comprehensive practice activity a required course; incorporating research-based learning into the curriculum contents; improving the life orientation of the curriculum structure and enhancing students' information technology skills; exploring and promoting innovative awareness to make the curriculum a way for students to cultivate quality and exercise life practices.

(3) Balance of curriculum structure

Paying attention to the comprehensive balance of various courses in the curriculum structure to make them complement each other and bring out the best in each other. This is embodied by the following measures: Arranging reasonable learning hours for each course in some course pairs like compulsory and elective, comprehensive and branch, theoretical and practical, scientific and humanity, and vocational and general courses, so that the course functions are fully arranged, organically integrating the guidance of the learning process and learning method, the cultivation of emotion and attitude, and the delivery of knowledge and skill information together to effectively improve the students' living ability, learning ability, and sensibility. For example, the UK strengthens the integration of general courses and vocational courses in two ways: One is to use "general national vocational qualification" as an intermediary for students to transform between the two kinds of courses; The other is to introduce key skills that run through the two kinds of courses.[32]

(4) Integration of curriculum structure

The new *Curriculum Standards* for every discipline of basic education in China will make all efforts to get rid of the discipline system that is subject-based, fragmented and segmented, and relatively isolated, and will organically connect static subjects together in an integrated systematic curriculum thinking. These integration points are human development, life practice, and social events, and thus form three integration paths. The first is the integration of the main lines of comprehensive practicing activities, including community service, research courses, thematic study, labor technology education, information technology education, etc; The second is the integration of the main lines of quality and attainments, focusing the goal of all learning activities on the formation of students' "all-round" qualities and building a platform for the integration of the curriculum from the perspective of the curriculum objective of human cultivation; The third is the integration of the main lines of the education function, which is mainly embodied in the implementation of "integration of general education, vocational education, and adult education" and "combination of agriculture, science and education" in rural areas, which provides a basis for the rational optimization of basic education curriculum structure and the release of the function of serving rural areas.

Through the horizontal reference to the curriculum structure in the United States, Britain, Canada, and China, it is not difficult to find that the direction of the adjustment of the curriculum structure in the four countries is more common than diverse. From the perspective of commonality, due to the common background of the curriculum reform, the convergence effect of the exchange of curriculum theory, and some other factors, curriculum structures in these four countries show consistency in the following four aspects:

(1) Pursuing the modernization of curriculum structure. This can be reflected in the following aspects: regarding information technology education and the latest basic knowledge of theoretical disciplines as important points of view in curriculum structure reform, seeing the cultivation of scientific quality and innovative awareness in students as the main task of the curriculum structure reform, and improving the status of comprehensive science education. What is especially striking here is the unbridled assertion of the United States that "American students will be number one in science and mathematics worldwide," while Canada promulgated a policy document, *Science Is Happening Here*, in 1986.

(2) Pursuing the localization of curriculum structure. There is violence and drug abuse on American campuses, freedom of illness in British education, diversified orientation in Canadian education, and rural education issues in China. All the above demand responses to the curriculum structure reform. Therefore, secondary schools in the United States set up anti-drug abuse education and safety education; Britain implements a national curriculum; Canada establishes a national curriculum in some areas; and China implements a "Green Education Certificate" curriculum in rural areas. These measures are all beneficial for returning the curriculum structure to localization.

(3) Pursuing holistic education in curriculum structure. In a sense, the curriculum structure and the quality structure of human beings have correspondence and isomorphism, and thus the design of the curriculum structure is the design of human beings. Facing the new concept of "holistic education," all countries have noticed that the curriculum structure should be improved from the perspectives of hand and brain work, learning and creating, and coordination between self and society. Specifically, the United States better considers the dual requirements of learners' comprehensive development and personality development in the overall curriculum structure, which is typically manifested in "James Madison's curriculum program."[33] The program not only fully considers the needs of human beings in terms of cognitive development, emotional development, and cultivation of humanistic and scientific literacy in the overall curriculum structure, but also puts forward the requirements of promoting the holistic cultivation of human beings from the perspective of each subject. For example, the Arts discipline before the eighth grade is given various requirements of artistic appreciation, artistic creation, and artistic evaluation. In the UK, for "offering all students opportunities of studying and making progress" and "promoting students' spiritual, moral, social, cultural, physical and other developments and providing opportunities, a sense of responsibility and life experiences for all students,"[34] a wide range of courses are set up, especially the information and communication technology course (ICT) as the representative, which focuses on the discovery, exploration, analysis, and exchange of information and provides the entire designing course that organically penetrates the importance of information on life and work. This makes the entire curriculum the best "nutrition" for the development of "all people." In addition,

Canada's "K-12 Consistent System" plan and China's emphasis on the requirements for curriculum structure to embody the "three-dimension" goal (i.e., knowledge and skills, process and methods, emotion and attitudes), together with the above American and British examples, all show the common direction of holistic curriculum structure.

(4) The dynamics of the curriculum structure. The separation of curriculum concept and discipline concept is another characteristic of contemporary curriculum reform. The curriculum is not a reproduction of discipline but a product activated by the reorganization of discipline contents. This has become the mainstream concept of curriculum structure reform in the four countries. Take a look at the design of the new curriculum structure for the four countries: On the one hand, they are expanding the traditional curriculum to make them more inclusive and comprehensive. For example, the United States combines the foreign language course with the culture and knowledge course, history with home craft and aesthetics; Britain combines the language discipline with the latest science and technology documents to establish a communicative relationship between the curriculum and real life. On the other hand, promoting the merger of related courses can be considered an important measure to break the stability of the curriculum so that the stable courses can be related to the unstable courses.

In summary, curriculum structure reform is the focus of the basic education curriculum reforms in the four countries. Although they choose different adjustment focuses, different measures, and different strategies, they all base their choices on their own national conditions, trying to respond to competition and wanting to accelerate the reforms.

### 6.4.4 Diverse Curriculum Evaluation Methods among Four Countries

The dynamic operation process of curriculum reform begins with reselecting the curriculum target, then comes the design of the curriculum structure, and finally is conducting curriculum evaluation to propel the process integrally. As an important part of curriculum reform, curriculum evaluation undertakes the important task of providing reform momentum, giving feedback on the reform process, and guaranteeing the direction of curriculum reform. Therefore, facing the 21st century, all countries have put curriculum evaluation reform in a particularly prominent position. From the leading directions of the curriculum evaluation reform in various countries, there are the following characteristics:

(1) The United States: Weakening the shortcomings of the academic achievement test and establishing two levels of evaluation systems, a national evaluation system, and a state evaluation system. Since the "high-quality education" reform in the 1980s, the United States has continuously introduced standard tests to raise academic standards,

resulting in a lack of constraints on curriculum evaluation. In the 1990s, Clinton promulgated the *2000 Goals: American Education Act* and established the "National Education Standards and Improvement Committee," which required to formulate non-mandatory national standards and national non-mandatory student assessment system, and the American academic examination system, raising the graduation standard and setting the "Presidential Award for Outstanding Achievement" in five core courses to reward outstanding students with excellent achievements in the national examinations.

(2) The United Kingdom: Planning the external evaluation of the curriculum comprehensively, improving the evaluation agencies, and implementing stage evaluation. The UK is excluding internal evaluation methods like teacher evaluation and school evaluation while establishing the evaluation target system (discipline achievement targets ATs) and the evaluation institutions (SEAC-School Examination and Assessment Committee), and conducting summative evaluation proactively. The organization of the national examination is carried out in stages; that is, the process of compulsory education is divided into four stages, which are the 1st key stage, the 2nd key stage, the 3rd key stage, and the 4th key stage, respectively implementing examinations for 7-year-old students, 11-year-old students, 14-year-old students, and 17-year-old students. At the same time, the process of discipline evaluation is reasonably designed. The evaluation of each discipline is divided into three parts: achievement, study plan, and evaluation arrangement.[35] Finally, the qualitative evaluation method of the national curriculum evaluation is widely adopted. It requires combining teachers' daily evaluation and "standard mission evaluation" together and suggests the use of the score file tool. The evaluation results should be recorded scientifically in time and then prudently published.[36] This is particularly evident in the *National Curriculum and the Evaluation: Interim Report*, published by Dylin in December 1993. In short, paying attention to summative evaluation has become an important trend in the UK curriculum evaluation.[37]

(3) Canada: Paying attention to the coordination among the three evaluation paradigms. Since the 1990s, Canada has introduced Ryan's three evaluation paradigms: the empirical analysis paradigm, the hermeneutic paradigm, and the critical theory paradigm, trying to make a comprehensive judgment of the implementation of the curriculum. The evaluations of the three types, the planned course, the implemented course, and the completed course, are organically related, and the VOSTS evaluation tool is designed accordingly. The evaluation is characterized by its emphasis on the authentic evaluation of the curriculum, especially science courses.[38] For example, in Ontario, Canada, the curriculum evaluation criteria for mathematics are divided into four parts: the expected achievements of students, the characteristics of students' achievements, the specific indicators of students' performances, and the cases of evaluation activities to understand the students' mathematics learning strategies and learning ability developments accurately. In addition, based on the development of

students' knowledge and skills, Ontario also sets the achievement level chart for the evaluation of science and technology achievements and its accompanying evaluation tasks, which makes the curriculum evaluation standard more specific and operational.[39] For another example, British Columbia attaches great importance to the 12th-grade examinations. In 1988, the Royal Education Commission lowered the ratio of general examination scores in the graduation examination scores from 50% to 40% in order to emphasize the teachers' evaluation of students in the classroom, providing a realistic basis for the balance among the three evaluation paradigms.[40]

(4) China: Adjusting evaluation orientation and enriching evaluation methods. In *The Outline of Basic Education Curriculum Reform*, China clearly points out that the direction of the evaluation reform is to "establish an evaluation system that promotes the all-round development of students," "give play to the educational function of evaluation" and "establish an evaluation system that promotes the continuous development of the curriculum." The core is to confirm three curriculum evaluation orientations: goal orientation, process orientation, and subject orientation. In order to carry out these orientations, the new curriculum emphasizes the authenticity of the evaluation object, the expansibility of evaluation, and the function of qualitative evaluation.

### 6.4.5 Rational Consensus on Basic Education Curriculum Reform in the Four Countries

The basic education curriculum reform practice shows us many regularities of curriculum reform from different aspects so as to provide a clear and rational guideline for the continuous and in-depth promotion of basic education curriculum reform in China. Looking at the basic education curriculum reforms in the United States, Britain, Canada, and China, we summarize four points that have universal meanings to the curriculum reform in all countries:

(1) The consistency of the reform goals and the differences in reform paths

Common reform backgrounds and the common competition of comprehensive national strength contribute to the common idea of creating quality education. As a matter of fact, the curriculum reforms in all countries have been deeply influenced by the times. Therefore, the convergence of the objectives of curriculum reform is a natural phenomenon. At present, facing the impact of the knowledge economy era and the challenge of "global problems" and economic globalization, all countries try to promote talents with a reasonable quality structure to achieve the national development plan by promoting the modernization of the curriculum. Therefore, the reform targets are no more than national citizens with scientific and technological literacy, humanistic spirit, and democratic awareness, as well as villagers in the "global village." However, the common targets do not necessarily lead to the convergence of reform paths. On the contrary, due to the different national backgrounds, different cultural backgrounds, and different understandings of the curriculum in different countries, the path for curriculum reform varies in different countries. It can be said: It is this "difference" that has activated the pressure on curriculum reform in all countries and thus provided rich experiences and paradigms for the world's curriculum reforms.

(2) The ideality of reform implementation and the reality of reform practice

The curriculum reform implementation is a comprehensive changing process from idea to practice. However, this process is apparently bipolar, that is, the perfection of the ideal and the practicality of practice, making curriculum reform in all countries more complicated and arduous. The basic education curriculum reforms in the above four countries have all encountered the test of this conflict. For example, all countries are trying to design a balanced, ecological, and coordinated curriculum structure, but to consider which factors should the balanced, how to balance them, how to choose the balance points, and other issues, it is indeed necessary for curriculum reform workers to base their decisions on their own education, curriculum theory and the developing status of practice to make a targeted response. It can be said that the art of curriculum reform lies in the combination of a perfect curriculum reform blueprint and the solution to the real issues of curriculum reform.

(3) The wisdom of learning from others and localization of the reform program

The basic education curriculum reform is a complex and multi-factor process, which determines that the curriculum reform experience of one's own country is unavoidably unilateral and narrow, making it difficult to promptly respond to the emerging problems in the reform. Through the international exchange of curriculum reform experiences, each country improves predictability and controllability and has taken wise reform measures in the curriculum reform process. Holding the international horizon of curriculum reform and improving the advancement of one's own curriculum reform is the fundamental starting point of curricular reforms in various countries. At the same time, the foreign experience needs to be localized so that it can adapt to its own national cultural background and develop well. Therefore, the acquirement of each reform program is not only an international comparison process but also a localized re-creation process. The combination of learning from others and localization is the basic experience of curriculum reform in each country, which is typically verified by the many materials mentioned above.

(4) The rationality of different roads to the same destination and the selectivity of reflections and filling vacancies

The United States, Britain, Canada, and China started with the unified goal of curriculum reform, moved toward different reform ways, and finally achieved the same goal, which is rational with inevitability and reflects the concept of "Harmony in Diversity," guiding to all countries in the world. The above four countries are all working to improve the quality of education, but their strategies for curriculum reform are diverse. For example, the key points in the curriculum reforms of the above four countries are different, which are science education of the United States, the uniform curriculum of the United Kingdom, the construction of multiple curriculum systems in Canada, and the design of an integrated practice curriculum in China, respectively. All the above embody the reform ideas of filling vacancies and adjusting to local conditions. Many measures of the curriculum reforms in the four countries reflect the direction of "filling vacancies." For example, in the United Kingdom, the right of curriculum management shifted from "delegating power" to "retaking power"; the United States puts emphasis on the errors in curriculum reform, "drug abuse," and "campus violence"; Canada improves the curriculum evaluation paradigm of sole empirical analysis; China takes reforms aimed at the drawbacks of disciplinary courses and a centralized curriculum management system. All the above reflect a reform phenomenon that seeks to achieve the common curriculum goal through reflection and filling vacancies. Therefore, there is neither a standard model nor a unified model for the basic education curriculum reform, but only a reform program that is more adapted to our national conditions. Promoting reform differently should be the basic idea behind curriculum reforms in all countries.

All in all, upon the threshold of the new century, the United States, Britain, Canada, and China all successively raised the topic of basic education curriculum reform as an issue of national importance. Although their explorations of the reform path are unique and their starting points are varied, the common background of the times makes their reform strategies communicate with each other and be relevant to each other. Studying these reform experiences and the momentum will inevitably help promote the advancement of the new curriculum reform in China and ensure its promotion more smoothly and orderly.

# A Comparative Study on the Teaching Thought of the Main Western Pedagogical Philosophy Schools

This chapter mainly reviews and compares the representative schools of teaching thought in the modern West. Six typical representative schools of teaching thought are included: pragmatism, perennialism, essentialism, structuralism, humanism, and social reconstructionism. "Usefulness is truth," as advocated by pragmatism, so pragmatic teaching ideas advocate that in practical activities, children obtain useful experience. The perennial teaching philosophy takes the development of human reason as its goal, believing that the teaching duty is to enable human to obtain eternal truth. Essentialism emphasizes the learning of basic facts and basic subjects and the cultivation of basic skills. Also, it stresses discipline, obedience, and the systematic learning of subject knowledge. For structuralistic teaching philosophy, the development of students' intelligence and the basic structure of the subject are essential. It advocates discovery learning. Humanistic teaching gives priority to the development of individuality and creativity and the direct experience of students, taking psychology as the main orientation. The teaching philosophy of social reconstructionism proposes that the most basic responsibility of schools is to establish a new social order by gradually transforming society. The common point of the above schools is to focus on the development trend of society by trying to reform traditional education and teaching ideas and methods and train the talents needed by social development, but the schools differ in their teaching objectives, curriculum focus, teachers and students views and teaching methods.

## 7.1 Teaching Theories and Schools of Thought in Modern Europe and America

In the history of the development of world teaching thought, Chinese scholars have made outstanding contributions to ancient teaching research and practice. *The Note of Learning* by Zisi-Mencius School, known as the master of ancient Chinese teaching thoughts, is recognized as the world's earliest work on teaching and learning. It makes an incisive summary of ancient Chinese teaching experience, which has laid an important foundation for the emergence and development of systematic teaching theories in the long term. However, the earliest advocates of teaching theory research are Western scholars in terms of the systematic and scientific process of teaching theory. It can be said that systematic research on teaching theory originates from the west. However, in the modern West, the research on teaching theory by scholars (this chapter mainly refers to European and American countries) and the schools of thought formed have had a significant impact on the research and development of teaching theories in countries around the world.

The first to advocate teaching theory in the development of Western educational thought was W. Ratke, a German educator. His study on the "art of teaching" set up a precedent for the study of teaching theory as a theoretical form. The publication of Comenius' *The Great Didactic* in 1632 by a Czech educator marks that the study of teaching theory has entered a systematic stage. As we all know, *The Great Didactic* (1632) by Comenius is a masterpiece. From the perspective of teaching art, he expounded the principles and rules of teachers teaching less while students learn more while developing Ratke's teaching point of view, demonstrated the class teaching system, stipulated a wide range of teaching contents, and proposed the intuitiveness of teaching principles, etc. The German educator Herbart came from behind, and his masterpiece *General Pedagogy* in 1806 pushed the study of world teaching theory to an unprecedented stage. He discussed the four stages of the teaching process based on psychology and ethics, namely, clarity, association, system, and method, emphasizing the educational role of teaching. In the history of Western education, a modern "three-center" teaching ideology system represented by Comenius and Herbart gradually comes into being: teacher-centered, classroom-centered, and textbook-centered. With the formation and development of the independent teaching theoretical form, a great number of bourgeois educators, such as Herbart, Rousseau, Locke, Spencer, Destohui, Fropeier, etc., made studies and discussions on teaching issues from different angles, putting forward many insightful viewpoints that had a profound impact on teaching practice. In particular, the traditional teaching school represented by Herbart, an inspector, has had a significant impact on the teaching practices of many countries in Europe and the world, even more than in Germany. As the U.S. Bureau of Education pointed out in its 1894–1895 report, "Today, America is more committed to Herbart School than Germany in education."[1]

After entering the 20th century, with the improvement of the status of education in social development, teaching as the basic way to cultivate talents has been given more attention, and the research on the theory and practice of teaching activities has also aroused more concerns. In particular, Dewey, an American pragmatist educator, came to the fore and put forward a completely different point of view from the traditional teaching theory, which was the first major conflict between European and American teaching theories. Dewey, in his book *The Child and the Curriculum* in 1902, criticized the Herbart school of teacher-centered theory, emphasizing that the child is the basic element of the educational process. This leads to a profound reflection on the research on teaching theory. At the same time, the teaching theory centered on the formal stage theory of the Herbart School, which once influenced the teaching practices of elementary schools in the United States, gradually lost its dominant position. There are more and more theoretical and experimental studies on teaching reform. Different teaching ideas and theoretical schools appeared one after another in the same period and began to form the first diversified situation of teaching theory research in the early 20th century. However, people are inspired to have a new and deeper understanding of many problems in teaching theory because of the conflict and mutual criticism of various schools of thought. The development of teaching thoughts also began to enter the modern period.

Since the end of the 19th century and the beginning of the 20th century, the development of teaching ideas has also entered the modern period as Western capitalism has entered the stage of diversification from the monopoly stage. The basis and technology of teaching theory research have been further strengthened and enriched, and the research orientation has also begun to show a trend of diversification. On the one hand, especially since the 1950s, the rapid development of society needs to cultivate talents that can adapt to it through reform of education and teaching. On the other hand, more and more educators, psychologists and educational practitioners have realized the drawbacks of previous education and teaching and actively advocate education and teaching reform, which has set off a wave of education and teaching reform again and again. In the reform tide, various schools of teaching ideology systems come into being. They not only played a positive guiding role in the process of educational reform, but also enriched, developed, and even changed during the reform, forming a variety of schools of teaching ideas with different orientations.

From the perspective of the development history of modern teaching research, among the teaching theories and schools of teaching thought with different orientations, the teaching theory or school of thought with philosophy as the main orientation should be said to be the one with the earliest formation, the longest duration, and the widest influence. Its history can be traced back to the three great philosophers of ancient Greece: Socrates, Plato, and Aristotle. Many ancient educators started with the study of philosophical problems and gradually dabbled in the problems of education and teaching. After modern times, under the influence of British philosopher Bacon and others' philosophical thoughts and the promotion of the "Educational Psychology" movement, philosophical-oriented teaching thoughts and psychology-oriented teaching thoughts have gradually become the two main lines of teaching theory research.

Creative educational thinkers and psychologists in the development of modern teaching thought are trying to make their original ideas systematized as an ideological system, common in Europe, especially America. It's believed to be proper that the condition of modern European and American teaching thoughts can be shown by "schools in great numbers." Due to space limitations, this chapter selects six representative schools of teaching thought for comment and comparison. They are pragmatism, perennialism, essentialism, structuralism, humanism, and social reconstructionism. These schools of teaching thought are basically developed and established by educators or psychologists. Of course, there is its core representative in each school. The reason why these six schools of teaching thought are selected for comment is that their theories have had a significant impact on the teaching practice and teaching reform of primary and secondary schools in Europe and America, and even still have an impact so far. In fact, the influence has spread to other countries around the world. Their thoughts affect teaching practice and reform, bringing abundant theoretical support and reflection for a scientific teaching theory. It is undoubtedly of great significance to study and understand the advantages and disadvantages of these schools of teaching ideas for the theoretical construction of teaching theories in the new century.

People have different perspectives and clues about the research on modern foreign teaching theories and schools of thought. In the relevant studies by domestic scholars, it can be found that most of them are introduced and commented based on country, chronological order, or character theory. For instance, the analysis and reviews in *Contemporary Foreign Pedagogy Theory*, edited by Wu Wenkan, and *Western Teaching Thought History* by Liu Xinke, are made according to different representatives and nationalities. Tian Benna's *History of Foreign Teaching Thoughts* includes a chronological review. *Confusion and Choice—New Pedagogy Theory in the Twentieth Century*, authored by Yang Qiliang, is a collection of typical theories to comment on. Mainly according to important content about pedagogy theory, *The Development of Modern Pedagogy Theory*, compiled by Zhong Qiquan, covers an introduction, analysis, and reviews. Others are monographs, such as *The American Schools of Pedagogy* and *The German Schools of Pedagogy*. These reviews are based on the main lines of different research, providing valuable references to understand and learn from foreign teaching thoughts. So, how can it enable men to form a clear framework in their minds for European and American teaching theories and ideologies and, on this basis, have a deeper understanding? This is indeed a problem that is worthy of discussion. Because the teaching theories and ideologies of modern Europe and America are varied and in great numbers. According to the documents, there are at least dozens. Tables 7-1 and 7-2 are carried out in accordance with representative schools of thought and the theories of modern European and American scholars, generally introduced by domestic scholars.

**Table 7-1** Arrangement in Accordance with Domestic General Introduction to Representative Schools of Thought

| Number | Countries | Representatives | Schools of teaching thought | Formation time |
|---|---|---|---|---|
| 1 | Germany America | Meuman. E, W. A. Lay, Binet. A, Edward Thorndike, etc. | Experimentalism teaching thought | First half of 20th century |
| 2 | America | Pierce, James, Dewey, W. H. Kilpatrick, etc. | Pragmatism teaching thought | First half of 20th century |
| 3 | America | Taylor, Dewey, W. H. Kilpatrick, etc. | Progressivism teaching thought | First half of 20th century |
| 4 | America Britain France | Hutchins, Livingstone, Alain, etc. | Perennialism teaching thought | First half of 20th century |
| 5 | America | W. C. Bagley, J. B. Conant, Bester, etc. | Essentialism teaching thought | Early 20th century |
| 6 | Germany France | Suttle, Martin Heidegger, etc. | Existentialist teaching thought | Middle of the 20th century |
| 7 | Switzerland America | Jean Piaget, Brunner, J. J. Schwab, etc. | Structuralism teaching thought | 1960s |
| 8 | America | Watson, E. C. Tolman, F. Skiner, etc. | New behaviorism teaching thought | Middle of the 20th century |
| 9 | America | G. S. Counts, Thedove Brameld, etc. | Social reconstructionism teaching thought | Middle of the 20th century |
| 10 | America | A. H. Maslow, C. R. Rogers, etc. | Humanism teaching thought | 1980s |
| 11 | Britain | D. Lauton, etc. | Cultural analytic teaching thought | 1970s |

**Table 7-2** Arrangement in Accordance with Domestic General Introduction to Representatives' Theories

| Number | Countries | Representatives | Teaching theories | Formation time |
|---|---|---|---|---|
| 1 | Germany | M. Wagenschein | Sample teaching theory | 1960s |
| 2 | Germany | Winkel, etc. | Communication teaching theory | 1970s |
| 3 | Germany | Herman, etc. | Teaching structure analysis theory | 1970s |
| 4 | Bulgaria | G. Lozanov | Suggesting teaching theory | 1970s |
| 5 | Britain | D. Lauton | Cultural analysis teaching theory | 1980s |
| 6 | America | R. M. Gagn | Learning conditions and teaching design theory | 1960s |
| 7 | America | B. F. Skinner | Procedural teaching theory and practice | 1950s |
| 8 | America | J. S. Brunner | Disciplinary structure teaching theory | 1970s |
| 9 | America | B. S. Bloom | Mastery learning teaching theory | 1970s |
| 10 | America | D. P. Ausubel | Meaningful learning teaching theory | 1960s |
| 11 | America | Fred Keller | Personalized teaching system theory | 1960s |
| 12 | America | C. R. Rogers | Non-instructional teaching theory | 1980s |
| 13 | America | R. E. Slavin | Cooperative learning teaching theory | 1980s |
| 14 | America | Eli Corning | Intellectual acceleration theory | 1970s |

In the two tables shown above, modern European and American teaching theories are classified and arranged in accordance with the theories of representative figures that are usually introduced in China. Besides, some theories may not have been translated and borrowed until now. Of course, the theories only in Table 7-1 can be said to be rich in numbers and schools. From chapter two on, we will comment on and compare the six schools of teaching thought that have a great influence both at home and abroad and are represented in certain countries. Through these six representative schools of teaching thought, we cannot only understand the basic situation of modern European and American teaching theory research but also analyze and compare the similarities and differences between different schools of thought and their impact on teaching reform and practice. At the same time, it can also summarize the basic characteristics of the development of modern teaching theory and its enlightenment for the future. In terms of nationality, the six schools of thought selected here are dominated by American teaching theories and are also representative to a certain extent. In terms of theoretical formation, they belong to systems of thought developed by several or many educators or psychologists. Therefore, in the studies, they are mostly referred to as schools of thought. It should be noted that the purpose of this arrangement and combination is mainly to include more content that is easy to compare in a limited space and to enable readers to establish a clear framework for the content involved. In fact, the schools of teaching theory and teaching thought are often used and explained by people as having the same gist.

## 7.2 Education Notion of Pragmatism

The pragmatism school of teaching thought is an important school of American teaching thought that developed with the development of the progressivism educational movement in the United States during the late 19th century and the first half of the 20th century. Dewey, William Kilpatrick, and Konzlts are the main representatives. People often express pragmatic educational thought as progressive educational thought or use pragmatic educational thought to highlight progressive educational thought due to the close relationship between pragmatism education and the progressive education movement. It can be said that the education notion of pragmatism is fostered by the practicability of the progressivism educational movement, and in return, the latter has become the former's theoretical basis. Although the theory and practice of pragmatic education cannot be equated with progressive education, in the first half of the 20th century, the pragmatic education represented by Dewey was indeed a new force emerging from the American progressive education movement.[2]

### 7.2.1 Philosophical Foundation of Education Notion of Pragmatism

The first person to put forward the philosophical concept of pragmatism is Charles Sanders Peirce (1839–1914). A philosophical book named *Pragmatism* was written by Will-Tames (1842–1910), whose influence gradually expanded. In terms of philosophy, Dewey believes in pragmatism, and after that, he forms the pragmatism school of education and teaching by combining it with education. "Usefulness is truth" is Dewey's pragmatist philosophy's main point. The earlier philosophy, which consists of ontology, epistemology, and axiology, answers three questions, respectively. They are "what," "why," and "how" or "what is the value." Dewey holds that it is science, not philosophy, should solve the question "what." "Why" and "what is the value" are the problem's two aspects. Men are prone to learn things starting from their standpoints, with the aim of using them for themselves. Therefore, pragmatism only believes in human experience, denying the objectivity of the law. "Experience" is a keyword in Dewey's educational philosophy. Dewey believes that "experience," generally speaking, is the interaction between the environment and the human body. Thus, education works to cultivate the skills and methods of solving problems, as human life relies on the ability to solve problems. Therefore, Dewey especially emphasizes the process or method of solving problems, while idealism, realism, perennialism, and essentialism emphasize the learning of lots of discipline, teaching materials, and practical knowledge. Solving practical living problems is the meaning of philosophy in Dewey's view, while the educational issue in his time was the biggest problem encountered. "School is society," "education is life," and "learning by doing" are put forward by Dewey, who is guided by this idea. The philosophical basis of Dewey's pragmatism teaching has been formed by these three propositions.

### 7.2.2 Main Ideas of Education Notion of Pragmatism

In Dewey and William Kilpatrick's series of works, the education notion of Pragmatism is mainly embodied. ***The Child and the Curriculum*** (1902), *Democratism and Education* (1906), ***Thinking and Teaching*** (1910), *School and Society* (1923), and *Experience and Education* (1938) are all written by Dewey and Kilpatrick's *Design Pedagogy* is mainly included. The principal teaching thoughts and teaching theories include the following five aspects:

First, pragmatism teaching thought in teaching objectives emphasizes cultivating students' thinking and basic living abilities. The practicability is highlighted for this purpose. Teaching aims at preparing for future life is the view protested against by Dewey, but that teaching itself is part of children's lives is his belief. Teaching is not only for the future but also for the present. In Dewey's view, traditional teaching is teacher-centered, subject-centered, classroom-centered, and knowledge-oriented, which is very unfavorable, even destructive, for training students' thinking abilities and developing students' intelligence. Therefore, he believes that the teaching of thinking should be stressed in modern education, with the basic goal of training and cultivating students' thinking. In ***Thinking and Teaching***, written in 1910, this thought is reflected. Training students' repeated, solemn, and lasting thinking abilities is the essence of Dewey's thinking training, thus developing their intelligence. For traditional teaching, which merely attaches importance to knowledge teaching, it's indeed progress. Dewey has also systematically studied the thinking teaching issues, claiming to cultivate students' exploratory thinking attitudes, realistic thinking processes, good thinking results, and experimental thinking methods. Meanwhile, he combines his views concerning the relationship between education and society, holding that in students' adaptation and contribution to society, strengthening students' basic living abilities' cultivation is of great importance. The teaching method "learning by doing" is put forward by Dewey to achieve this goal. The typical representative is Design Pedagogy by Kilpatrick.

Second, it emphasizes on children-center concerning the relationship between teaching and learning. When commenting on pragmatic educational thought, American scholars believe that all educational activities start with children, but teaching materials or subjects is the greatest difference between it and perennials.[3] "Children-center" thought is not only the inheritance and development of the naturalistic view of children through progressive education but also the challenge of the progressivism education movement to traditional education. If the progressivism educational movement's teaching reform and experiment are examined, it's obvious that the common characteristic shown in most of the reforms is that individual teaching replaces collective one, and having signed a learning contract with teachers, children have the initiative in learning. Under the guidance of progressive education, the teacher just instructs learning activities and provides learning resources in a class. His or her basic responsibility is to seek to promote students' learning, not pass on the so-called eternal truth.[4] Dewey believes that "children" are not only the starting point but also the center or purpose of teaching activities. In light of pragmatism in teaching thought, students' learning needs, interests, and hobbies should be the starting point of teaching, while students should be the focus of the selection of teaching materials and the design of teaching activities. If students were the sun, the planets running around, it should be teachers and the teaching.

Although Dewey especially stresses that the center of teaching activities should be children, the guiding role of teachers is not neglected by him. In schools dominated by pragmatism thought, the role of teachers is to plan to teach, provide students with relevant materials, create a favorable learning environment and conditions, and instruct learning; at the same time, raise appropriate questions that help students discover knowledge and truth for themselves, and introduce students to democratic life. In a class guided by pragmatic thought, the role of teachers is "the instructor standing aside" rather than "the wise man on stage."[5] Actually, in Dewey's view, it is teachers' responsibility to help students learn in any environment, at any time, and at any place.

Third, for selecting and arranging curriculum content, children's interests and experience and their logical order of mental development are focused on. As for the selection of curriculum content, the idea that the center of the school curriculum should be children is emphasized by pragmatism, and children's needs and interests in cognitive, physical, social, and emotional aspects should be taken into consideration in school education and teaching. In Dewey's view, students should be equipped with direct experience in certain environments, learning is positive, not negative, and they can learn best through the process of doing. Therefore, students' interests should be the basis of the curriculum, which should also take children's psychological development order into full consideration at the same time. He also believes that as society is constantly changing and thus knowledge and value orientations learned today may change tomorrow, teaching students to think and cultivating their problem-solving abilities obviously should be the curriculum's principal part. In Dewey's view, developing students' abilities to solve human problems is more important than their knowledge of human problems. Only in this way can students be better prepared to adapt to social life in the future. In addition, the community views pragmatic education as a rich source that provides students with learning experiences and resources. To a certain extent, many of today's efforts to make community service a condition of high school graduation are the product of the pragmatists' belief that "education should have practical social value."[6]

In the arrangement of curriculum, Dewey and Kilpatrick all insist that the system of course teaching materials is different, believing that as the logic of discipline is scientific, it is organized strictly in accordance with scientific knowledge's logic, and while curriculum material systems and logical order are psychological, they should be organized according to children's psychological development's logical order. Only curriculum materials that are in line with students' mental development can truly meet children's needs and interests. Therefore, the interest curriculum and activity curriculum are Dewey's curriculum. In his experimental school, a comprehensive course that focuses on experience, homework, and activities replaces traditional subject curriculum and textbooks.

Fourth, as for the organizational form of teaching, "learning by doing" is advocated, and the flexibility and openness of teaching are stressed. Pragmatism in education advocates that the traditional teaching form is not conducive to the development of flexible and creative thinking because they are so rigid and inflexible with provided and fixed teaching materials, teachers, classrooms, and teaching seats. Therefore, it advocates open education and an open classroom;; that is, schools do not arrange fixed classrooms for students, there are no fixed seats in the classrooms, learning activities are in accordance with teaching objectives, and students have much say in the learning content. The classroom has actually become a center of interest or activity. Through this flexible and open teaching form, students can be helped to learn self-management and cultivation of their awareness and abilities to learn cooperatively with classmates, thus developing their imagination and thinking abilities.

Fifth, in teaching methods, always-solution and design teaching are advocated. Dewey divides five steps of the thinking process. First, to find difficult problems; second, to determine the nature of problems; third, to present the hypothesis of solving problems; fourth, to deduce the meaning of the hypothesis; fifth, to clarify whether the meaning is consistent with fact through experiments, then decide whether to accept it or not. Therefore, he puts forward a "problem-solving method," which is different from traditional teaching methods. While Kilpatrick's design pedagogy specifically applies Dewey's "problem-solving method." There are four stages in his design pedagogy: First, to determine the objective; second, to work out a plan; third, to implement the work; fourth, to criticize the results. In this process, all the work should be done by the students. Students themselves decide the objective, draw up a plan, implement the project, and criticize the results. Teachers just provide some reference materials for them.

### 7.2.3 Commentary on Education Notion of Pragmatism

In terms of pragmatism teaching thought's contribution, limitations, and influence around the world, *History of Foreign Teaching Thoughts*, which is edited by Tian Benna, gives an objective commentary, pointing out that the greatest criticism of this school is its ignorance of systematic, scientific and theoretical teaching, that is, students have more activities but fewer knowledge gains, which makes them unsuited to face the challenge of the new scientific and technological revolution. So, gradually, it has lost its dominant position since the 1950s. However, its effect is profound in America and even other countries around the world. As for America, for almost half a century, the educational experiment has been guided by pragmatism teaching thought. The emphasis on "practicability" in American educational teaching has become a spirit of the times. Dewey's thought, in particular, is "regaining attention." "Many educational practices, which are applied in today's classes, are based on the pragmatism view of Dewey. Cooperative learning, group learning, arranging rooms as centers of interest and activity, allowing children to choose what they want to learn, establishing warmhearted mutual support with students, the curriculum that emphasizes students' self-esteem, and the teaching of skills in conflict resolution and friendly relationships with others are included in these practices."[7]

In addition to America, pragmatism-based teaching has a universal impact on many countries like Britain, Germany, Japan, the former Soviet Union, and China. Around the May 4th Movement of 1919, Dewey gave lectures for a long period in several provinces and cities of China to propagate his pragmatism thought, which greatly influenced quantities of Chinese educators. Some works and reform experiments about his thoughts were then produced. Pragmatism in education and teaching thinking in the 1950s have been severely criticized. It has been restudied since the end of the 1970s. Some useful thoughts about it are being reanalyzed and reevaluated, which in new situations are transformed, referred to, and applied, such as ideas about the relationships between education and life as well as school and society, the standpoint that attaches importance to activities, the status, and roles of students. As for specific teaching theory and thought, it's believed that, like Dewey and William Kilpatrick, the key representatives of this school have proposed some views and thoughts. For example, teaching should put the cognitive subject's initiative and enthusiasm into full play; both children and society should be reflected in teaching materials; the unity of knowledge and practice, as well as the cultivation of children's creativity, should be achieved in teaching; and so on. These thoughts are full of vitality till now.

## 7.3 Education Notion of Perennialism

The education notion of perennialism, which is based on perennialism educational philosophical thought, is established and developed. Robert M. Hutchins (1899–1977) and Mortimer J. Adler (1902–) in America, Rinwingstone (1880–1960) in Britain, and Alain (1868–1951) in France are the main representatives. Hutchins set up undergraduate courses while he was the president of the University of Chicago, which consist of 100 literary masterpieces, including works reflecting Western civilizations such as *The Lliad*, *Origin of Species*, and others. In the process of setting up and applying this curriculum,[8] his perennialist educational thought has permeated. The active supporters of modern education notion of perennialism are scholars at the Saint John Institute, located in Maryland, America.

### 7.3.1 Philosophical Foundation of Education Notion of Perennialism

Mentalism or idealism is the root of perennialism. That truth is long-lasting and perpetual, which is the belief of scholars who believe in perennialism. Perennialism educational philosophical thought is the basis of education of perennialism. In epistemology, it insists on "classical theory," which believes that preceding "individual" and "general things" exist objectively and independently and that truth is universal and common. It has eternal value because it's the same everywhere. As for the theory of human nature, "common humanity" and "unchanged human nature" are advocated by it. Hutohins said, "Man, as a person, as long as in every time or society an educational system existed, its purpose was the same as his function, that is, to improve everyone as a person." Or, in Adler's words, "If a man is a rational animal, and in all historical times, nature is eternal, whatever the culture or time, certain perpetual characteristics must be in each sound educational program."[9] Obviously, from the human being, the eternal nature of education is derived from perennialism. Therefore, it is a big advocate of the restoration of classical educational traditions, which have existed since the Renaissance Movement. Contrary to progressivism educational philosophy, whose emphasis is the thought that change is everywhere, complying with absolute principles is insisted upon by men believing in perennialism. They say that "although in social and political aspects modern history is turbulent, permanence is more real than change eventually. Human nature does not change, basically remaining the same. Therefore, the moral principle should be obeyed by men for a good life, and for the education they received, it's the same with that."[10]

In the process of criticizing progressivism, perennialism as a school of thought has developed. The teaching of classical cultural knowledge can be ignored, which is the view and practice of the latter, which is extremely protested against by the former. Additionally, it holds that the present and instant success is emphasized by pragmatism teaching thought, which renounces the teaching's eternal cultural value. In the 1930s, its criticism has made an influence, but due to pragmatism teaching thought in its heyday, it has never truly been shaken. Until the 1950s, as progressivism educational thought lost its power and influence, the impact of education notion of perennialism gradually increased.

### 7.3.2 Main Ideas of Education Notion of Perennialism

First, the aim of teaching is the development of human reason, cultivating rational men. Perennialism believes that human nature is unchanged and that the essence of education is also the same. As rationality is a humans' significant characteristic, cultivating their rational ability should be the focus of education. Living with rationality and controlling his unbridled instinct is man's bounden duty. For a civilized man, freedom and restraint are complementary. Therefore, as their deeds are not always good, children behaving at will shouldn't be allowed to.

Second, to adapt humans to the eternal truth is the task of teaching. Perennialism holds that the study of those eternal truths is the function of education and educators' task because students' wisdom can be cultivated, and logical thinking abilities can be formed by those eternal truths. Therefore, the aim of teaching is to cultivate students who can adapt to the universal and unchanging truth. Hutchins says: "Education means teaching, and teaching does knowledge. Knowledge is truth, the same anywhere. Thus, education is common anywhere. Between organizations, management, and other local customs, there exist differences, which have never been overlooked because they are all detailed things. I believe that if we correctly understood education, whenever, wherever, and whatever the political, social or economic condition is, any curriculum that is designed for students should share the same core."[11] Therefore, perennialism concerns the so-called truth rather than the changing world.

Third, teaching is to prepare for life, not to imitate it Perennialism holds that the "situation of real life" or the imitation of society can't or shouldn't be provided to students by schools. Education is the preparation for life, which enables students to understand cultural heritage's essence and realize its value in the future. Therefore, to choose teaching content, it must be based on long-term and lasting value, which can never be driven by instant success.

Fourth, it proposes to set masterpiece courses for curriculum content, which emphasizes the study of humanities. Perennialism holds that classical language and ancient masterpieces should be set as the main courses by schools. At the beginning of school age, children can read ancient masterpieces and learn the classical language. "To accept first, then to understand" is characteristic of children's learning that determines it. It is based on this thought that a list of celebrities and masterpieces has been recommended by Alain for children to learn and read, including Montaigne, Corneille, Racine, Hugo, Da Vinci, Rafael, and Beethoven and their works. Additionally, he strongly recommends learning Latin for the purpose of successfully learning and understanding classical masterpieces. In Britain, Livingstone advocates learning classical courses and considers Greek and Latin as the middle school's main courses. As for the purpose of learning these courses, Adler says: "It is to gain wisdom and rationality, with a perfect personality, not for the study of cultural relics or archaeology."[12]

Fifth, in the teaching method, teacher-center instruction and discussion are advocated. According to the perspectives of perennialism, in teaching activities, the roles of teachers are to teach students to accept the eternal truth, and learning foundation subjects must be the start of grasping the eternal truth. These subjects will make the world's permanence familiar to students. Teachers' instruction followed by students' discussion is the best way to learn the contents. Only through truth, value, and critical knowledge taught by teachers and the organization of students' discussion, can students' thinking and logical reasoning abilities be well developed. In the teaching process, applying teacher-centered instruction and Socrates' Q&A is important for students to master teaching materials and develop academic abilities.[13]

Sixth, in terms of teaching management, it is for authority and coercion. Modern Europe's perennialist concept of children entirely restores the traditional one. The management of children particularly emphasizes authority and compulsion. Alain has ever sharply criticized European "new education" and American "progressive education" by pointing out that "for inventions, such as children's parks or education in entertainment, he is in disbelief." "Let children or parents choose to learn this sounds absurd. Blaming the state for forcing him to learn this or that is equally ridiculous."[14] He believes that avoiding being children as early as possible is the greatest aspiration of children. Therefore, the autonomy of children is excessively emphasized by progressive education's children-center method, which is not conducive to cultural learning and knowledge traditions' inheritance. So, that reading and learning is the worship of culture or authority must be made clear to children and require students to study hard. Children should receive strict restraint and discipline in the process of teaching instead of doing anything they like, which is the claim of progressive educators. If learning is easy and pleasant in the beginning, laziness and laxity can be encouraged, and even conduct can be looked down upon, which eventually harms children.

### 7.3.3 Commentary on Education Notion of Perennialism

Its strong revivalism and little attention to modern science and technology knowledge is the greatest criticism of perennialism teaching thought. Ornstein, an American scholar, holds that in the cultural sense, perennialism and essentialism are conservative, which can be viewed as educational traditionalism or conservatism's defense when he criticizes perennialism.[15] However, we should also know that perennialism's strong advocation, strengthening humanistic educational thought, still brings certain enlightenment to the present curriculum system and teaching contents' reform. As Yang Qiliang comments on perennialism teaching thought, "perennialism teaching thought, generally speaking, is like turning the clock back; this is almost overcorrected. Restoring the ancient is the choice of negative confusion, which makes little difference in overcoming social crises and adapting to science and technology. On the other hand, scientism and utilitarianism toward the extreme are alleviated and curbed by it, which enlightens that it can never overemphasize humanistic education at the expense of the other. In turning practical and vocational education into generalized ones, it indirectly plays the function, which in the inheritance of the excellent cultural heritage takes on a certain role."[16] Nevertheless, in both Europe and America's primary and secondary schools and universities, perennialist views about curriculum and liberal education have had a positive impact.[17]

## 7.4 Education Notion of Essentialism

Based on essentialist educational philosophy, the education notion of essentialism was developed at the beginning of the 1930s, with its main representatives including W. G. Bagley (1874–1946), J. B. Conant (1893–), H. G. Rickover (1900–), A. Belor (1908–), etc. Especially Bagley, who is an education professor at Normal Institute at Columbia University, establishes the Essentialism Education Association and *Journal of Essentialism Education* as pioneers, which greatly promotes the spread of education notion of essentialism in America.[18] Essentialism teaching thought is very popular and received great support in America during the turning period between the 1950s and the 1960s, which greatly influenced American educational reform. Due to the one-sided emphasis on instilling knowledge in books and the teaching method that is traditional and outdated, it thus loses its dominant position by the end of the 1960s, as it doesn't meet the demands of the times. But "at the midpoint of the 1970s, with the rise of the foundation restoration movement in elementary and middle schools, the essentialism teaching program once again became popularized.[19] Its perspective, which emphasizes the learning of basic knowledge and skills while catering to man's discontent with Bruner's failed reform, is the main reason.

### 7.4.1 Philosophical Foundation of Education Notion of Essentialism

Essentialism is considered a conservative educational philosophy by American scholars who believe its rise is the response to progressive education. Based on essentialist educational philosophy, the education notion of essentialism is established and developed. Protesting against the lowering of intellectual and moral standards in schools is its original goal. The view that essentialism never belongs to any philosophical tradition or has no fixed philosophical foundation is generally believed by scholars. Some pragmatist perspectives, such as denying the role of teaching materials, or some perennialist viewpoints, like placing much emphasis on revivalism, are protested by it. Because there is no fixed philosophical foundation or unified front in essentialism, not exactly the same viewpoints are shared by men who believe in essentialism. However, the view that human culture contains "joint elements" is their common ideological basis, which should become the core of courses. Although different philosophical points are held by essentialism educators, they believe non-violated "reality" exists in the objective world. Therefore, as an educational philosophy, essentialism holds that all students require learning a community of knowledge existing in practice, which is a prerequisite for students to play an active role in society.[20] In 1938, considering the intelligence and moral standards decline in American public schools, a group of educators got together and briefly described essentialism's basic viewpoints. They appeal: "Should our public schools recommend, through systematic training in a series of subjects such as reading, writing, arithmetic, history, and English, that students, whether men or women, master knowledge? Shouldn't we emphasize discipline and obedience if necessary, making them prepared for taking on adults' responsibilities?"[21] It can be seen that instead of merely considering children's interests and their experiences acquisition, essentialism emphasizes discipline and obedience, and through the systematic learning of subject knowledge, students' abilities to prepare for the improvement of social benefits can be developed.

### 7.4.2 Main Ideas of Education Notion of Essentialism

First, as for the teaching objective, basic facts and disciplines' learning and basic skills' cultivation are emphasized. Unlike perennialism, which advocates learning all classical cultural heritages and cultivating "generalists," essentialism mainly chooses to teach cultural works with "common elements," with the aim of enabling students to master the "elements" of cultural knowledge and then become outstanding experts.[22] In particular, systematic knowledge learning and the cultivation of basic skills such as reading, writing, and arithmetic are the advocation of essentialism. In each sound curriculum in primary schools, the application of basic skills like reading, writing, and arithmetic is required.

Second, as for curriculum, it advocates "curriculum theory of joint elements." To analyze and arrange human cultural knowledge is its aim, and then the contents containing "joint elements" are selected and compiled as a curriculum for children to learn. Based on pragmatism "activity curriculum," this view is put forward. Pragmatism believes that systematic and ordered learning is replaced by activity-based curriculum "movement," which even takes the activity itself as a self-satisfied one without concerning whether through this activity we can learn something or not. That's another question. So, what kind of knowledge that contains "common elements," is worth learning? Essentialism holds that for spiritual training, some strict-demanded subjects that have particular value, such as Latin, algebra, and geometry, should take important status in the curriculum and serve as secondary schools' common compulsory courses.[23]

Third, in the learning method, industriousness, endeavor, and concentration are emphasized. Men believing in essentialism are discontent with the viewpoints and practices of the emphasis on personal learning "interest," and advocating having "interest" replaced by the concept of "hard-working." The reason is that "human is the intelligent soul of the whole universe." Only humans can take present desires into long-term consideration. Children will be hindered from making full use of their talents if their abilities are not encouraged. Self-restraint and self-control abilities are needed in order to achieve purposes of any value. This ability can be developed only through getting children more arduous training."[24]

Fourth, as for teaching relationships and learning styles, teacher-centered receptive learning is advocated. Perennialists' viewpoints about teachers' roles are similar to essentialists' concept of teachers, which consider them to be the possessors of knowledge and truth. Their responsibilities are to provide cultural courses supported by the school's basic disciplines and train students' intelligence and minds to meet social requirements. However, under the teachers' arrangement, it's the students' task to learn the perfect human cultural elements and then acquire and apply cultural knowledge, thus developing their mental abilities. Therefore, in the teaching process, the relationship between teachers and students is that between managing and managed, dominating and dominated, which is advocated by essentialists. As centers of teaching, teachers have decision right of teaching instead of what and how to teach determined by students' needs. In the teaching method, essentialism advocates applying traditional methods and training rigorously, with strict academic performance assessment adopted as the standard of attending the next grade or not. Essentialism is the same as perennialism, also advocating receptive learning and holding that, compared with children, teachers' understanding of teaching is deeper. Teaching activities should be teacher-centered rather than child-mastered, while learning contents should be disciplinarily knowledge-centered.

### 7.4.3 Commentary on Education Notion of Essentialism

The rise of the education notion of essentialism, which is basically conservative, is a reaction to progressive education. Based on the criticism of progressive education and the defense of traditional teaching, essentialism teaching thought is developed, as is perennialism teaching thought. The role of teachers in curriculum teaching is overemphasized by essentialists, who insist on treating teachers and subjects as centers, ignoring the initiative-driven learning of students. Additionally, traditional and strict teaching methods, which are more training but less inspiring, are over-believed by them, and not conducive to students' creative thinking development. Nevertheless, in educational reform in America and even in other countries, a positive role has ever been exerted by essentialism teaching thought.

## 7.5 Education Notion of Structuralism

During the turning period between the 1950s and the 1960s, structuralism teaching thought, as a school, was formed and developed. Its principal representatives include J. Piaget (1896–1980), a Swiss psychologist, and Jerome Seymour Bruner (1915–), an American educational psychologist. By applying structuralism psychology to the study of education and teaching issues, Piaget lays a great foundation for the formation of the education notion of structuralism. Piaget's thought is inherited and developed by Bruner, which makes the education notion of structuralism even more systematic.

Emerging in American educational reform, Bruner has been an influential figure since the beginning of the Second World War. As he establishes and develops Harvard University's "cognitive research center" and makes profound research on cognitive psychology, he becomes well known in the international psychological field. He leads the first large-scale American elementary and high school teaching reform after the war, which makes him enjoy a high reputation in worldwide education even more. His unique views on psychological and educational teaching issues can be reflected in his main psychological works like *The Study on Thinking*, *On Cognition*, *Learning about Learning*, *The Study on Cognitive Theory*, and educational books such as *Education Process*, *The Construction of Pedagogy*, *The Theory of Pedagogy*, *The Relevance of Education*, and *Re-recognizing Education Process*. In the development of contemporary international teaching theories, three typical representative schools include his teaching theory of "disciplinary structure," Zankov's "teaching and development" theory, a former Soviet Union educator, and "sample teaching" theory by M. Wagenschein, a German educator. In the curriculum reform movement, which rose in America at the end of the 1950s and demonstrated the world's tendency in the 1960s, as Bruner deeply explores curriculum modernization and teaching scientification, the first large-scale teaching reform's theoretical foundation is his teaching thought in American primary and secondary schools after the war. *Educational Process* is the main work that reflects this theoretical foundation. It is considered "the most important and influential educational work" and known as "the milestone of educational theory."[25]

### 7.5.1 Philosophical and Psychological Foundations of Education Notion of Structuralism and Its Social Background

The research shows that the developing course of the education notion of structuralism is from philosophy to psychology, then education and teaching. The "structure" and "schema" concepts are put forward by Kant, who is one of the earliest structuralists in philosophy, having had a profound impact on future generations. Structuralism, which formed in the 1950s, is a philosophical thought. The structural analysis and construction of recognition are included in its contents. This thought affects psychology, the main representative of which is Piaget and his epistemology.[26] Bruner's teaching thought is influenced by structuralism philosophy, which has been formed and developed by drawing lessons from Piaget and others' research achievements on psychology, inherits and develops cognitive structure psychology and intuitionism epistemology, and criticizes the empiricist educational thought of Dewey. Additionally, it should be noted that, besides philosophy and psychology's historical influence, the formation of the education notion of structuralism is directly related to the revolution in science and technology and international competition. We believe that structuralism philosophy, especially cognitive psychology's influence, is crucial to the formation of structuralism teaching thought's internal motivation. While American primary and secondary schools' teaching reform, which was stricken by the former Soviet Union's launch of the first artificial satellite in 1957, was the external motivation for structuralism teaching thought's systematic development by Bruner, the later important representative. Therefore, the understanding of education notion of structuralism and research lies in the teaching theory of "disciplinary structure" by Bruner.

***Philosophical Epistemological Basis of Bruner's Teaching Theory of "Disciplinary Structure"***

Structuralism philosophy deeply affects Bruner's philosophical thought from the perspective that *Education Process*, an important work in which American primary and middle schools' curriculum and teaching reform's guiding ideology at the beginning of the 1960s is clarified, shows how Bruner views subject knowledge and comprehends human development process of understanding and the basic method that is applied in education and teaching research. Structuralism is a philosophical school of thought that was popular in the 1950s and 1960s in Europe and America. Analyzed from the history of philosophy, structuralism philosophy is, first and foremost, a kind of methodology. Its basic feature highlights the understanding of the internal structure of things, but the simple study of the external phenomena is protested; whole research but the isolated partial study; mastering knowledge from systems, functions, and relationships but the pure empiricism. It is from a series of structuralism philosophy's basic characteristics mentioned above that Bruner's own knowledge theory and epistemology are formed.[27]

(1) Knowledge comes from experience while they are different

The issue with which philosophers and educators are concerned is the relationship between knowledge and experience. From the point of view of structuralist philosophy, knowledge and the relationship between it and experience are illustrated by Bruner. He holds that "knowledge is a kind of model constructed by which the regularity of experience is made significant and structural. Any view that organizes knowledge systems comes from humans, the aim of which is to make the experience more economical and coherent."[28] Obviously, Bruner views that knowledge comes from experience, which is different from experience. Knowledge is made by arranging experience as a structural model. Therefore, through arranging the knowledge men acquire from experience, they get rid of the original experience and obtain much more common value in its use. "Knowledge is a model" and a conceptual framework for certain assemblages is the view of Bruner, according to which any subject or series of organized knowledge can be understood by man, the ability to understand objective things and their regularity thus formed. It is the philosophical basis of knowledge structure that is particularly emphasized by Bruner.

(2) Understanding is a process but a result

"Understanding is a process rather than a product,"[29] according to Bruner, a process in that the cognitive model is operated by the cognitive subject himself, or the conceptual model of human cognitive achievement is put into his own to improve and develop his cognitive level. Therefore, as for the cognitive subject, a positive rather than a negative or passive meaning must be contained by the cognitive process itself. If a man turns knowledge into his own, in "discovery action" and the process of constructing a model, he must be personally engaged. Accordingly, he regards the cognitive process of humans as a kind of discovery process that is similar to or the same as scientists' work, which is the epistemological guidance that receptive learning, not discovery learning, is protested against by Bruner.

***Psychological Basis of Bruner's "Disciplinary Structure" Teaching Theory***

Although because of leading teaching reform in American elementary and high schools, Bruner has become a famous modern educator, in terms of his research field and achievements, he is undoubtedly a psychologist. The main theoretical basis of Bruner's "disciplinary structure" teaching theory is psychological thought. He inherits and develops the structuralism psychology thought of Piaget, applying his theory of cognitive structure development to American primary and secondary schools' educational reform. Through research in learning and teaching psychology, especially classified studies on the cognitive developmental characteristics of children, Bruner holds that the central thought that guides American primary and secondary schools' teaching reform is that letting students grasp the basic structure is the main part of learning any subject. He believes that "you will be helped to learn and research independently by your insight into the structure of knowledge." It is possible to infer individual things you want to know only by mastering some profound principles, so to deal with everything is needless so as to know its property. You can know many things through understanding, which is a clever strategy, even if the things that are borne in mind are not so many."[30] Cognitive structure theory, children's intellectual development theory, and learning transfer theory are included in Bruner's "disciplinary structure" teaching theory's psychological basis.

***Social Background of Bruner's "Disciplinary Structure" Teaching Theory***

Bruner got a Ph.D. in psychology at Harvard University in 1941, after which he was mainly engaged in research on learning and cognitive psychology and in education and teaching research, making no outstanding achievements. The former Soviet Union launched the first artificial satellite in 1957, which shocked the American government and the public. Having reflected on its education in the competition between it and the Soviet Union, America realized that its education in science and technology was not as good as that of the latter. Therefore, reform of the school curriculum was immediately implemented, which thus set off America's first educational reform after World War II. In 1959, a meeting in Woods Hole was immediately held by the American "Worldwide Academy of Sciences," the lecture being about how to reform the primary and secondary schools' teaching of mathematics and science and cultivate a large number of technical personnel as soon as possible to meet scientific and technological development and international competition's requirements. Bruner served as the president of the general assembly and made a summary report, which became the meeting document named *Education Process*, which guided the American primary and secondary schools' educational reform. Bruner's "disciplinary structure" teaching theoretical system came into being gradually in the process of reform. Therefore, it can be said that an important external impetus to form and develop Bruner's "disciplinary structure" teaching theory is the educational and scientific-and-technological competition between America and the Soviet Union.

### 7.5.2 Main Ideas of Education Notion of Structuralism

At the earlier stage, Piaget, a Swiss psychologist, was the main representative of structuralism teaching thought, but Bruner's "disciplinary structure" teaching theory really demonstrates systematic structuralism teaching thought. In his works like *Educational Process, Re-Research on Education Process*, and *The Theory of Pedagogy*, it is mainly reflected, and the following five aspects are included in its main ideas.

*Paying Attention to Students' Intelligence Development in Terms of the Purpose and Task of Teaching*

What are the purpose and task of teaching? It has been an important issue with which educators are concerned. There existed a debate between formal education and substantive education which is about developing thinking and imparting knowledge of history. That the development of students' intelligence should be given more attention by modern teaching is advocated by Bruner by focusing on the new requirement of social development for talent training. He holds that "to pursue "excellence" is the most general goal of education. This word not only means outstandingly educated students but also means that the best intellectual development is obtained by every student."[31] Besides, children's intellectual development is related to national survival, according to Bruner, indicating that whether children's intelligence can be developed well or not is directly related to a country's survival strength in the world. He believes that "if all students made full use of their intelligence, a democratic country should get a better chance of survival in an age of extraordinarily complicated technology and society."[32] In his view, fully developing the young generation's intelligence is necessary to get better developmental opportunities for individuals and countries in the era of rapid scientific and technological development and social change.

Bruner not only emphasizes that developing students' intelligence in modern society is important but also discusses the phases and essence of children's intellectual development and specific goals in teaching. He thinks that three stages are required by children's cognitive development, namely behavior assurance, image assurance, and symbol assurance. With cognitive structure, which is inherent in this developmental stage, children understand and reproduce the representation of things in the stage of behavior assurance. Behavior assurance is a child's initial cognitive structure, namely the "recognition in behavior" stage. Image assurance is a cognitive style that is more advanced than behavior assurance. To master or reproduce things that are taken as the product of visual and auditory imagination is called image assurance. As a kind of behavioral cognitive style, image assurance is similar to symbol assurance, relying on linguistic signs to show recognition. In the stage of symbol assurance, in which the elements contained become verbalized, children can understand things logically. The relation between the elements of things can be understood by linguistic function, so as to realize logical assurance. The cognitive development of learners is the process from behavior assurance to image one then symbol one in Bruner's view, which is also his viewpoint on children's intelligence development's essence.[33] Three tasks of children's intellectual development in teaching are explained by Bruner, which is based on the discussion on children's intelligence development's essence and stages. First of all, stimulate students' learning motivation to give them the confidence to solve problems with their thinking. Secondly, the cultivation of students' various abilities to observe and imagine objective things and finish symbolic operations is suggested; encourage them to find their assumptions' value and the possibility of improving themselves to make the meaning of experiments and various assumptions recognized by them. Finally, "self-propelled" abilities should be developed with students, with their active roles given full play and dealing indirectly with the teaching contents in the way of problem study, which is used to be mastered by professors' teaching, so as to promote their understandings' development.

In a word, in Bruner's view, helping the improvement of students' abilities in mastering, transforming, and transferring knowledge so as to enable them to acquire better intellectual development is the goal and task of modern teaching.

### *Mastering the Basic Structure of Discipline Is Emphasized in Teaching Content*

Three mainstays are included in Bruner's structuralism teaching theory. They are "disciplinary structure," "early teaching," and "discovery learning." People usually summarize Bruner's teaching theory with the "disciplinary structure" theory, "discovery learning" theory, or "structuralism" theory, mostly due to the fact that different theories and practices have existed on the issue of "what to teach and learn" and "how to teach and learn" for a long time. However, Bruner puts forward a view that is different from previous teaching theories by focusing on knowledge and information's rapid development requirements in modern society and attaching importance to the mastery of the discipline's basic structure, the early teaching of new knowledge, and development of students' intelligence by the "discovery" method. It is the reason that there are widespread concerns about Bruner's teaching theory and its important influence in the world.

Bruner opposes traditional subject curriculum theory that instead of helping students seek the principle that forms the knowledge system and procedures led to the conclusion, there existed objective facts and knowledge's conclusion. He is also not in favor of Dewey's experience curriculum theory, which holds that the basis for selecting teaching materials is children's spontaneous activity experiences, in ignorance of scientific knowledge's systematic nature and children's training in logical thinking. He believes that the most important thing is its basic structure, no matter how complex a discipline's knowledge is. In order to enable students to master knowledge to have a greater value in their future lives, "whatever the subject we choose is, make sure that its basic structure is understood by students. It is one of the most basic requirements for applying knowledge. The problems or events encountered outside class or in the class training can be solved by students only in this way."[34] In Bruner's view, the basic structure of the discipline is the common viewpoint by which the essence of the subject can be best reflected, or those concepts that are extensive and strongly adaptive, which constitute the discipline's basic system. In other words, the system of basic concepts, rules, and principles which play an extensive role in every subject, is the basic structure of the discipline. Not only some specific objective things in this subject can be explained by them, but also the general principle of the discipline can be regularly reflected. Once the basic structure of a subject is mastered, how things are related to each other can be understood by students, allowing them to continuously master deeper and broader knowledge.

Why should master the basic structure of a subject be emphasized? In Bruner's view, in four aspects, the learning of basic scientific structure is meaningful for students. Firstly, by mastering the basic concepts, rules, and principles of discipline, the discipline is made easier to understand; secondly, the basic structure of discipline contributes to memory; thirdly, the transfer of knowledge and skills can be promoted;

and lastly, the gap between advanced knowledge and simple knowledge is narrowed. Certain characteristics of the times can be seen in Bruner's disciplinary theory.

*Advocating the Early Teaching of New Knowledge at Educational Chance*

In *Education Process*, which focuses on American primary and secondary schools' teaching reform thought in the 1960s, two important assumptions are put forward by Bruner. The first highlights that for learning any subject, its basic structure must be mastered; the second indicates that, in a certain way, students at any age can be taught any subject. He believes that "the right way in effectively teaching any child at any stage of development can be any subject that can be used in intellectual education. This is a bold assumption, which is even a necessary one that reflects the essence of the curriculum."[35] At the time, this hypothesis was controversial. But Bruner insists that it is possible for the early teaching of all subjects. For example, students in the lower grades in primary schools also can be imparted advanced teaching knowledge in an intuitive way. He points out in *The Theory of Pedagogy* that "all subjects that are taught in currently existing methods can be imparted to children in a simpler style. It is possible for students in the first grade of primary schools to master preliminary calculus. An important basis for systematical learning will be the preliminary calculus learned at the earlier school ages, which will even make a great contribution in future life."[36] He believes that many important disciplines and the newest knowledge have been put off in the past by schools on the grounds of being too difficult, thus wasting students' valuable time and making the task of "talent cultivation earlier and more quickly influenced fundamentally." Therefore, he advocates early teaching that enables students to master the latest scientific knowledge by applying appropriate strategies in primary schools. In order to facilitate students' mastery of the discipline's basic structure, Bruner, on the one hand, indicates that teachers should begin to teach according to children's own unique ways of observing and understanding the world and that the basic concepts and principles of the discipline should be imparted using intuitive teaching methods so as to make the teaching content intuitive. Meanwhile, in accordance with children's understanding abilities, teaching materials should be provided, making them adaptable to the characteristics of the psychological development of children. For instance, work out your teaching materials spirally in accordance with performance, portrait, and symbol representation, which are children's three programs and characteristics of understanding the world. On the other hand, developing students' intrinsic motivation for learning is emphasized by him in the teaching process, and he advocates that raising students' interest in what to learn as much as possible should be the basis of teaching activities. So, how can we make children's early learning more effective? In Bruner's view, two important aspects exist in early teaching. The first is that intuitive teaching methods should be made good use of by teachers to teach, or students should be guided to learn and master the discipline's basic knowledge through games or activities. A careful analysis of the characteristics of the teaching process and teaching materials' is highlighted by the second, which gives a full estimation of children's abilities.

### *Motivation, Structure, Procedures, and Feedback Are Emphasized in the Teaching Principles*

In *The Theory of Pedagogy*, Bruner points out that at least four aspects are included in the main task and research subject in teaching theory. Firstly, the best experience and situation arising from learning enthusiasm must be ascertained; secondly, the problem with optimal understanding and knowledge structure must be sure; thirdly, the problem displaying an optimal program of teaching materials must be confirmed; fourthly, the problem with the rewards and punishments' nature or transition in the teaching process must be verified.[37] Bruner puts forward four teaching principles, which are named motivation, structure, procedure, and feedback principle, in order to apply these research subjects' results shown above to specific teaching activities.

(1) Motivation Principle. The principle of emphasizing motivation is that children's learning enthusiasm and initiative in teaching activities are required to be mobilized by teachers as much as possible. He believes the primary determinant for successful learning is enthusiasm for learning. As children have a natural curiosity and desire to learn, arousing their enthusiasm to participate in learning is the teachers' task by making full use of children's natural tendencies. That the situation to motivate enthusiasm in learning is various is Bruner's view. Besides school activities, it can also take advantage of the favorable factors of family and society to stimulate students' strong passion for learning. In Bruner's opinion, the real power that promotes learning and the most important psychological tendency that affects children's learning and problem-solving is internal motivation, while the "promotion and regulation" role in it must be played by teaching. The "exploration activities" can go smoothly only when learners have good learning motivation.

(2) Structure Principle. As mentioned above, he especially stresses that any particular learning is mainly the basic disciplinary structure mastered by students, which is the reason why the teaching theory of Bruner is summarized as the "disciplinary structure" theory. He believes that a series of basic concepts can be induced from the subject, even if it is complex, and it can be expressed in the simplest form. The "general understanding of the disciplinary structure is actually the final purpose of learning any subject or teaching any group of related disciplines." To some extent, students must be enabled by teaching to master a set of basic thoughts and principles that constitute the best knowledge structure, which is conducive to understanding for learners. He also puts forward the best knowledge structure's

three organization principles. The adaptability principle of reproduction means that the learning modes of students of various ages must be adapted by the representation of the subject knowledge structure. The economic principle of reproduction also means rational simplification of knowledge, which refers to simplifying subject content as far as possible under the condition that it is conducive to students' advanced learning. That the simplified knowledge structure has vitality, namely transferring that is conducive to students' transfer learning, is highlighted by the validity principle of reproduction.[38] In the course of teaching, only the appropriate knowledge structure that is suitable for students' cognitive structures is selected by teachers, and learners can be promoted to master the complex teaching contents' basic principles.

(3) Procedure Principle. It is required the teaching must provide the most effective order of learning content. Therefore, two basic requirements are put forward by him to design the best order. The first is that, according to students' cognitive development, the order in teaching materials should be presented. The second emphasizes arranging teaching programs by applying economical and effective views. He points out that the task of teachers is not only to make the arrangement of the teaching order adapt to the knowledge representation that learners can understand but also to determine teaching procedures according to economic and effective principles. If the learners' learning process isn't smooth, teachers should make proper guidance or adjustment in the teaching program so that learning direction can be changed by learners according to their own cognitive levels and knowledge background.

(4) Feedback Principle. "Feedback" is information on learning outcomes in Bruner's view, which is an essential part of the teaching process. The teaching process can be carried out effectively only with proper feedback information. At any time, teachers must capture the students' feedback information and mete out appropriate rewards or punishments in order to promote the teaching process, while students should understand learning results that were successful or failed in time and the mastering and applying knowledge's validity to make the evaluation that is beneficial to their learning and then correct or determine the advanced learning activities continuously. Obviously, the strengthening of form and pace in teaching is actually Bruner's feedback principle.

*"Discovery Learning" Are Advocated in Teaching Methods*

As mentioned above, one of the three mainstays of Bruner's teaching theory is "discovery learning." Bruner's teaching theory has become synonymous with the "discovery teaching method." Bruner believes that simultaneous processes are included in learning, namely acquisition, conversion, and evaluation. Students are active information processors, not passive knowledge recipients. He holds that "the purpose of teaching a subject is that they can participate in the process of acquiring knowledge but not that students can become specialists in this subject. Learning is not a result but a process.[39] Therefore, the "discovery teaching method" is strongly advocated by him.

Bruner believes that the application of the discovery teaching method is beneficial for the improvement of students' potential for intelligence, stimulation of students' internal motivation to learn, students' acquiring the way of exploring problems, and helping students remember the learned knowledge. Judging from the guiding thought, the discovery teaching method is advocated by Bruner for three main reasons. The first is that man is not a passive organism and active processes occur when mastering concepts and solving problems; the second believes that the "re-organization" and "conversion" of the mind is the central link in learning so as to make discoveries; the role of "intuitive thinking" in learning is particularly stressed by the third, which considers it a shortcut to leaping forward. Concerning the connotation of the discovery teaching method, Bruner has provided a further explanation. In his view, discovery is not only the behavior of searching for unknown things. Properly speaking, all forms of acquiring knowledge personally in mind are included in it. In his view, the discoveries of students and scientists have the same essence, only belonging to different degrees. He believes merely that human initiative selection, conversion, storage, and application of things that enter his mind or that of active learning from, adapting to, and transforming environment is the learning process from the principle of cognitive psychology. Therefore, initiative and creativity should be given full play by students to discover the learned knowledge and laws personally, making themselves into discoverers. The traditional narrative style is strongly opposed by Bruner, which puts students in a passive state. Teaching should be hypothetic style in his view. Instead of preparing knowledge in the teaching process, teachers should provide students with the discovery situation. Some content that can make students excited should be retained by teachers so as to guide them in their discoveries. Thus, the "discovery" that is advocated by Bruner is actually an exploratory teaching method; that is, according to the materials provided by teachers or textbooks, students are guided by teachers to study, explore and develop some problems' corresponding principles and conclusions. Discovery learning or teaching is not bound to students' exploration of hitherto unknown knowledge and scientific inventions, but a proactive study taken by them and mastery of new knowledge while exploring activities, developing abilities, and forming scientific learning methods.

In a word, students' learning initiative and inquiry and the elicitation and guidance of teachers' teaching are emphasized by Bruner's "discovery" teaching thought.

### 7.5.3 Commentary on Education Notion of Structuralism

A positive commentary has been made by theoretical educational research on Bruner's structuralism teaching theory's meaning and value. In *Confusion and Choice—New*

*Pedagogy Theory in the Twentieth Century*, authored by Yang Qiliang, the excellence of Bruner's "disciplinary structure" thought and his views on mastering it in the teaching process are pointed out as having irreplaceable value. Meanwhile, Yang Qiliang considers one of the typical representatives of new teaching theories as Bruner's teaching theory in the 20th century. *Contemporary Foreign Pedagogy Theory*, which is edited by Wu Wenkan, has evaluated Bruner's teaching theory's contribution from three aspects. It's believed that an attempt at systematic teaching theory is Bruner's teaching theory, which promotes the educational psychology of contemporary teaching theory and illustrates that at the beginning of the 1960s, the teaching theory played an important role in the American primary and secondary schools' curriculum reform, thus promoting the re-establishment of disciplinary teaching materials like mathematics and physics and affecting some countries' teaching reform, to varying degrees. Indeed, "disciplinary structure" pedagogy is one of three typical representatives of modern teaching theories or curriculum modernization, which exerts an internationally acknowledged influence. Men think highly of Bruner's teaching theory, the reason for which lies in that it emphasizes the basic disciplinary structure's learning and mastery and students' intelligence's development, and that his assertion of thoughts like early education and discovery learning that focus on the future, conform to the talent training's requirement for social development. However, as the teaching reform movement advocated by him and centered on curriculum reform fails, finally, there are more and more concerns about the deficiencies or limitations of Bruner's theory.

So, what are Bruner's structuralism teaching theory's deficiencies or limitations? There are lots of comments, even criticisms. Generally speaking, three sides are mainly included in it. First, its basic disciplinary structure and theoretical knowledge are excessively emphasized, and the practical knowledge and basic skills learning are weakened. Second, students' discovery and exploration activities are overemphasized, and the characteristics of their understanding are ignored in the process of mastering knowledge. Third, the learning burden on students is increased by the emphasis on early learning of any disciplinary knowledge, which thus affects their continuous interests in the subject. Undoubtedly, it was the "recovery basis" movement's key cause in American primary and secondary schools at the beginning of the 1970s.

## 7.6 Education Notion of Humanism

With more than a long history, humanism or humanistic educational thought's ideological origin can be traced back to Cicero, who was a scholar in ancient Rome. An Italian scholar, F Gio Leo, first elaborated on "humanism" as an educational thought in the European Renaissance. American humanism psychology is the guidance of the rise of modern humanism teaching theory. It became popular in the 1950s. A. Maslow (1908–1970) and C. Rogers (1902–1987) are included as its representatives.

### 7.6.1 Psychological Basis of Education Notion of Humanism

Basically, in accordance with philosophical and psychological orientations, the development of Western teaching thought is carried out. Philosophy is the basic orientation of quite a few schools, like the education notion of progressivism, perennialism, essentialism, and existentialism mentioned above, while some existentialism philosophical thought has been received by humanism teaching thought, which also inherits the basic thoughts of humanism psychology. It should be said that it is a typical representative, which takes psychology as the main orientation. Four sides are included in the basic thoughts. First, "a healthy man" is the research object of psychology; second, the instinct of humans is growth and development; third, the right to choose initially and creatively is possessed by man; and fourth, the most important content is the emotional experience in human nature. As it is incompatible with traditional psychological viewpoints, humanism psychological thought is called "the third power" or "the third ideological trend," which emerged swiftly in the psychological field.[40] Since the psychological scientific movement began at the end of the 19th century, through the development of structure theory, function theory, behavior theory, psychoanalysis and configurationism, etc., five major endless debate issues exist in psychology. First, what does psychology exactly research? Whether it is the internal "heart" or external "behavior?" Second, what is the psychological research's purpose? Whether it aims at negatively understanding human nature or more actively helping man overcome difficulties and seek happiness? Third, what's the object of psychology, human or animal? Can it explain man according to the animals' research results? Fourth, which explanation is appropriate for psychology—holism or atomism? Fifth, as science, can psychology get rid of valuable research? Its own unique answer has been made by humanism psychology in order to solve the five problems, thus forming a school. Humanism psychology's research results have been applied in education and teaching since the 1960s, so in the field of teaching thought field the school of education notion of humanism is formed. An outstanding contribution was made by Maslow to the research on human needs by putting forward the famous "hierarchy of needs" that several levels are included in human needs like physiology, safety, love and belonging, respect, and self-fulfillment, and from the lowest to the highest level, man meets content. This has provided the basis and direction for motivation research in teaching. Laying emphasis on a student-centered approach, Rodgers applies "patient center" psychotherapy in the teaching, creating the "non-instructive teaching" model, which has had a wide impact on class teaching reform in European and American countries.

### 7.6.2 Main Ideas of Education Notion of Humanism

First, in the teaching objective, the development of students' individualities or personalities is emphasized. In the view of humanism, quite a few psychological qualities like independence, autonomy, and initiative should be included in a human's personality. Through teaching, these psychological qualities in children can be fully promoted and developed. Maslow and Rodgers emphasized the development of individual teaching, believing that achieving self-realization is the fundamental goal of teaching. In the process of teaching, teachers should select the knowledge that can achieve students' self-realization to help students achieve self-realization so as to combine students' cognitive development with emotional development.

Second, as for curriculum content, students' direct experience is emphasized. Humanism holds that various needs are the basis of an individual's self-realization. Individuals can produce the need for self-realization only by meeting these needs and then becoming self-fulfilling men. Therefore, the curriculum should be based on students' needs, taking into account their learning interests and direct experience development. The importance of obtaining knowledge from direct experience has been discussed by Rodgers from the point of view of meaningful learning, who divided children's learning into two categories, namely, meaningless conjugation learning and meaningful experience learning. He believes that the first is difficult to fully mobilize students' enthusiasm for learning, as it is a kind of learning without emotion and personality. Therefore, the second, named meaningful experience learning, is strongly advocated by him.[41]

Third, it advocates applying "non-indicative teaching" in the teaching mode. The core content of humanism teaching theory is the "non-indicative teaching" mode, which fully reflects counter-traditional thought. According to the "self-learning" theory, Rodgers created a more radical teaching strategy for promoting individual "self-realization" called "non-indicative teaching mode." While teachers' "indicative teaching" is characterized by traditional teaching, in a diametrically opposite way, he advocates self-selection and self-discovery for students.[42] He also believes that in students' learning activities, teachers should be the consultants or advisers, and that teaching should not be an instructive knowledge-prescriptive activity dominated by teachers but an assistance activity of "non-indicative" learning.

Fourth, in the teaching of interpersonal relationships, it is advocated that the teacher should be a "facilitator." In traditional teaching activities, Rodgers believes that authority and rulership are the teachers' roles, while students are passive recipients. It seriously depressed students' personality development in such a teaching interpersonal relationship. According to "patient center therapy," Rodgers deduces the word "facilitator" to distinguish the traditional explanation for "teachers" in order to change the traditional teaching interpersonal relationship. In the teaching process, the role of the facilitator includes four aspects. The first is to help students clarify what to learn; the second highlights helping arrange appropriate learning activities and materials for students; the third is to help students discover the meaning of the learned knowledge for themselves; the fourth aims at maintaining some psychological atmosphere, which promotes the learning process. Obviously, Rodgers's teaching style and the traditional teacher-student relationship are completely different. He regards the prerequisite for implementing "non-indicative teaching" as the establishment of a good class atmosphere.

### 7.6.3 Commentary on Education Notion of Humanism

Mainly three aspects are included in the criticisms of humanism as a school of thought. The first is that traditional teaching theory and practice hold an overall negative attitude; the second highlights much emphasis on students' status and roles and a negative attitude towards teachers and teaching's roles; the third is less attention to systematic theoretical knowledge, similar to progressivism teaching thought. Additionally, it is based on phenomenology and existentialism, and subjective idealism can be seen in its views on issues, including curriculum contents. However, the humanism spirit of the times is reflected in humanism teaching thought, a new force in psychology and the teaching thought field. There has been a humanism boom since works that are about humanism teaching thought were translated and introduced into China, the reform of teaching organization management and method promoted, as well as attention aroused on the teaching's special and creative goals.[43]

## 7.7 Social Reconstructionism Teaching Thought

Social reconstructionism, which is also known as social construction or social reconstructionism, is rooted in pragmatism and progressivism educational movement. The views of social reconstructionism and those of progressivism are similar, and many social reconstruction movement's representatives are progressives, highly praising Dewey's philosophy and defining education as the reorganization and restructuring of experience. Meanwhile, the experience means that the meaning of practice can be enriched, and the ability to guide the further process of practice can be enhanced. As the term suggests, social reconstructionism believes that teachers, students, and schools play a key role in transforming society, rebuilding a new social order, and thus forming a more real democratic life. The main representative of this school is George Konz (1889–1974), Dewey's student.

### 7.7.1 Philosophical Foundation of Social Reconstructionism Teaching Thought

In 1932, the masterpiece of George Konz (1889–1974) was finished, which named *Dare Students to Build a New Social Order?* This book puts forward that the basic principle of social reconstructionism is to form a new social foundation and to educate students as the representative of social change. Konz's representation of establishing a new and more equal society is the following.

"The times call for a new situation of American destiny; the chance given by fate should be taken by the profession named "teachers," at least the progressive content as soon as possible. In our school, I would like to introduce the scenes in America during the industrial era. However, it is required that our children learn the priceless cultural heritage, which is the primary content in learning and teaching processes. There are increasing oppositions to the endless social responsibilities that teachers should bear. However, in a time, hard and dangerous era, when past things have lost their importance, like teachers in the past, we will dedicate ourselves without any benefits, if we are content to maintain security and peace but not actively respond to society."[44] As another important representative of social reconstructionism, Theodore Brameld has presented the reconstructionism thought's philosophical foundation from two aspects. First, he believes that living in a crisis-ridden society, men are able to destroy civilization overnight; second, at the same time, a rich, sound, and friendly civilized society can be created by humans as they have wisdom, technology, and moral potential.[45] According to Theodore Brameld's view, in this era, the basic place of planning and guiding social transformation should be schools. In short, schools should not only transfer the knowledge to maintain social order but also seek social transformation ways and means.

It is easy to see that the school curriculum and the relationship between social and economic activities and political progress are concerned by men who believe in social reconstructionism and that they believe establishing a new social order through gradual social transformation is the schools' basic responsibility.

### 7.7.2 Main Teaching Thought of Social Reconstructionism

As for the teaching objective, cultivating students as new citizens is advocated. Men believing in social reconstructionism advocate that "the aim of teaching should be cultivating new citizens, who will apply scientific and technological tools to establish a reasonable and humane society instead of having blind faith in them, and who will apply skillfully 'group discussion' method to reach the consensus to enable a group to solve problems with unified force."[46] In the view of social reconstructionism, a new social order must be created by education with devotion. This new society must be truly democratic. If we were to transform society, the education of social members should be paid attention by us, convincing them to change the living society, which should start from schools. Focusing on the future, schools should cultivate students' minds and character, so as to make them equipped for a new social order, thus paving the way for a new order.[47] That teaching is a social affair and process, which is approved and supported by society, is also believed by men believing in social reconstructionism. Naturally, public schools should be supervised by society, helping them solve various problems, so as to make society better. Therefore, teachers to face society and create a curriculum that is beneficial to themselves and others and social reform is the demand of men believing in social reconstructionism. A teacher, who believes in these insightful views, may lead students to help uneducated adults read, their own learned knowledge and skills applied to solve community problems.[48] It emphasizes curriculum integration and problem-solving for the setting of the curriculum. Men believing in social reconstructionism hold that an important agency that improves human and social conditions, directly guiding social changes, is the school. Mainly by cultivating students' abilities to promote reform, schools can participate in this transformation or reconstruction. Therefore, designing a curriculum system that helps students develop all potential is the advocation of men believing in social reconstructionism.[49] Specifically, it is a regular curriculum that integrates knowledge, and students' abilities to solve social problems are cultivated. Social reconstructionism holds that students should be provided with the curriculum learning by schools, which makes them aware of and participate in seeking the ways by which main social problems can be solved, such as violence, crime, running away from home, sex and social injustice, property disputes, and AIDS. More important, in solving these problems, students spare no effort. For example, students try their best to make the awareness of their peers caring about children with HIV / AIDS improved and help those children suffering from HIV / AIDS by raising funds for family financing centers. Men believing in constructionism hold that social and cultural forces should form schools and education, so making school education aim at these goals is the responsibility of schools and teachers. At present, American public schools make efforts to make that engage students in community service as the requirement for graduation, which is clearly related to the social reconstructionism philosophy.

First, in the relationship between teaching and learning as well as teachers' and students' tasks, teachers' instruction and students' active exploration are emphasized. Social reconstructionism holds that students should be allowed by teachers to study social issues and be guided to participate in seeking problem-solving schemes to face various problems in modern society. Based on equality, social justice, and democratic principle, it convinces students of social reconstructionism's correctness and urgency, which takes behavioral science as the source of the curriculum system. It encourages students and community leaders and organizations to cooperate and help each other, and by combining with all the disciplinary knowledge, which students have learned, it solves community problems. But in the teaching process, considering their interests, students should actively seek ways that solve social problems and study the skills of problem-solving while mastering the ability to evaluate social behavior, thus committing to make basic community problems and global issues solved.

Second, it advocates cooperative learning and problem-solving in teaching methods. Men believing in social reconstructionism hold that improving students' understanding of social problems with the initiative to solve problems is the aim of education. It is required that encourage students to ask questions and to explore debating issues on religion, society, economy, politics, and education in order to improve students' understanding of society. Students will have their choices on traditional knowledge by examining the issues.[50] In a typical class that is under social reconstructionism educational thought's guidance, rather than dictatorial dictators, teachers are often "active facilitators in students' learning activities."[51] The classroom is taken by teachers as the place where students prepare for future social life, not merely to advance a higher grade. The method that in cooperative team, students discuss, design, and make a decision to solve various problems is usually applied by teachers.

### 7.7.3 Commentary on Social Reconstructionism Teaching Thought

It is obvious that social reconstructionism teaching thought and progressive education basically shares the same content. The principal difference lies in the fact that the former is more concerned about a new social order's establishment and transformation than the latter. Social reconstructionism teaching thought that is mainly developed in the cultural confusion is formed by two major social crises is the reason. The first is the economic depression, which started in America in 1929. The second is in the 1950s, scientific and technological revolution's challenge on social life around the world. During two different periods, Konz and Theodore Brameld, the representatives of reconstructionism, respectively put forward through school education to create a new social order and through social members' education to achieve human's better and ideal life. Based on this idea, the social reconstruction curriculum and teaching thought are formed and developed. Although in the commentaries of domestic scholars, it has been considered an "intermediary" school, which is based on criticizing and inheriting progressive education, essentialism education, and housing education, showing an obvious compromise position.[52] But social reconstructionism focuses on teaching's social value, not ignorant of the teaching's role in children's individual personality development, which has a certain significance. Some references have been provided by it for man to reflect on both perennialism teaching thought and progressivism teaching thought's extreme tendency in the early stage and its detrimental effect on teaching practice. Until the late 1960s, some American primary and secondary schools classroom teachers still were in accordance with reconstructionism teaching thought to carry out the teaching activities. Focused on social issues, they integrate with learning contents, guiding students to discuss and work out solutions to problems, thereby students' abilities to solve social problems fostered.[53]

## 7.8 Comparative Study on the Teaching Thoughts of Six Major Educational Philosophical Schools

If the six main educational philosophical schools' teaching thoughts mentioned above were analyzed and commented on in the macro perspective, the focus on social developmental tendency and attempt to reform traditional education and teaching thought and methods to cultivate talents that are required for social development can be seen on all of them. Therefore, in the process of criticizing traditional thought or other schools of thought, most of them are formed and developed, or by separating from a school, then formed an independent system. We can easily find by a more specific study that the above-mentioned schools are mainly derived from respective educational philosophies, originating from philosophical thoughts. The six schools clearly reflected different philosophical thoughts and teaching thoughts, which resulted from various educational philosophical thoughts. Concerning teaching objectives, curriculum focus, view about teachers, concept of students, and teaching methods, the six schools enjoy many differences and few similarities, which can be seen from the introductions and comments above. From the horizontal perspective, the following generally compares different views of six schools regarding teaching theory and practice issues, which is also a summary of this chapter.

### 7.8.1 About Teaching Objectives

Regarding that knowledge is a kind of experience in nature, pragmatists believe that the goal of classroom teaching should be constructing students' experience. Considering that education is life itself, not the preparation for life, they advocate by way of experience educational process should conform to the process of life. Because experience develops continuously and the lives and learning of children should be a continuous whole, pragmatism educational philosophical school believes that by way of fact, educators should construct students' experience in the teaching process, which thus makes children's learning experience connected with that in social life as a whole.

Structuralism educational philosophy inherits rationalism tradition and holds that the learning content of students should be academic knowledge. But as academic knowledge grows rapidly in the era of knowledge explosion, in order to deal with the expanded knowledge, men must have superb intellectual abilities. Therefore, in structuralists' view, the main aims of teaching should be to develop students' intelligence and cultivate their thinking abilities, problem-solving skills, and knowledge-transfer abilities, so as to make exponentially growing knowledge effectively dealt with.

Eternalists hold that human nature is eternal, although society keeps changing constantly. Therefore, regardless of the times, there are some eternal factors in education. Such unchanging virtues as justice, temperance, and fortitude show human's eternal nature. The teaching objective is to cultivate students with these virtues. Contrary to pragmatism views precisely, in perennialism's view, the school mission should be the preparation for future life, not the specialized occupation training for children. Therefore, cultivating children's skills and techniques that distinguish the superior from the inferior of cultural heritage is another important teaching objective, so as to make them able to tell cultural heritage in future life.

The views of essentialism educational philosophy school and perennialism educational philosophy school are similar. Compared with eternalists' opinion that "masterpiece" is defined as the most valuable knowledge field, displaying a narrow understanding, essentialism expands the worthy knowledge's connotation, holding that the cultural elements, which pass on in human history, are all valuable. Education should aim to equip them with all human cultural elements in order to enable the young generations to adapt to social life better. Teachers should try their best to make these cultural elements understood and mastered by students, especially core ones in the process of teaching. Due to pragmatism, American education's current situation is weak and feeble, which can be changed only in this way so as to improve the quality of education.

Social reconstructionism educational philosophy school believes that human civilization is in crisis, facing possible extinction, which can be saved not by political reform but by education. Education should be committed to establishing a new social order, that is, a truly democratic society, working out a social reconstruction movement's scheme, and forming a new mark in educators' minds that adapts to a new social order. Specifically in the teaching, men who believe in social reconstructionism adhere that the basic orientation of teaching objectives is to cultivate citizens who can solve significant social issues, holding that by such men, new social order can be promoted and various key problems that are encountered in the process of establishing new social order can be solved; thus, social democratic efficiency and influence improved.

The attention to humans is the biggest difference between humanism educational philosophy schools and others. Humanists care about man's value, believing that achieving man's self-fulfillment is the fundamental purpose of education, so teaching should not only provide students with knowledge, but also help individual freedom and liberation realized through knowledge.[54] In the process of teaching, the knowledge that helps in achieving students' self-fulfilling should be selected in order to help students achieve self-realization, making students' cognitive development combined with emotional development. In humanists' view, the process and the results are unified, the results existing in the process. Therefore, in life, human growth and self-realization are achieved, and students' digestion of knowledge in daily life should be helped by teaching, thus achieving self-fulfillment.

### 7.8.2 About the Curriculum Focus

Pragmatism educational philosophy school holds that an organic combination exists between man and society. Men become the abstraction if the social factors are eliminated from children. Accordingly, society will be a rigid and lifeless collective if specific human factors are removed from society.[55] Therefore, not pointing to either personal development or social requirements, education is an activity in nature that coordinates children's personal interests with social needs. Therefore, the curriculum focuses are children's interests and social needs like democracy and morality.

The learning of specific academic contents is emphasized by structuralism educational philosophy school, which takes the new "three arts," namely reading, writing, and counting, as the main course. In all courses, the most basic contents are the basic concepts and principles constituting the disciplinary system. As students can be helped to understand, memorize, and transfer knowledge by mastering this knowledge, so course focuses should be these basic contents or the basic disciplinary structure.

Eternalists believe that children should be provided with some basic courses in education, which are those perpetual and suitable for any historical stages, not those adapted to a particular historical period in present society. Literature, history, philosophy, and natural science are included in these courses. As human eternal virtues are reflected in them, masterpieces are taken as teaching materials. Literature and history, among all courses, which can cultivate students' more noble interests, are the key courses.

Essentialism emphasizes the cultivation of gifted children and educational equality, advocating mental training of the general children. Based on this understanding, they believe that it should establish a unified curriculum. The basic disciplinary cultural knowledge is the disciplinary "curriculum element" in each curriculum, which should be curriculum focus.

Social reconstructionism educational philosophy school claims that the knowledge that is proven by behavioral science is valuable and that the bases to establish the common goals of mankind is the knowledge and value standard generally acknowledged to be correct. It is required to show them the ways to solve social problems firstly in order to persuade the educated to transform the society they live in, which is based on the standard of the general value through education. Therefore, in social reformists' views, the ways of solving social problems should be the focus of the teaching process; it should integrate knowledge learning with the solutions to social problems, both of which should be incorporated into the formal curriculum.

Humanism educational philosophy school believes that meeting other requirements is the basis of the generation of the need for self-realization and that before the individual has the need for self-realization, there exist other needs. The individual can produce the need for self-realization, becoming a self-fulfilling man only by meeting these needs. Therefore, students' physical and emotional needs should be the focus of the curriculum, which should pay attention to their learning experience's development, thus meeting their self-demands.

### 7.8.3 About the Role of Teachers in Teaching

Pragmatism educational philosophers believe that instead of indoctrination by the external force, experiences can be obtained through experiencers' activities and that the process children obtain experience cannot be dominated by teachers. However, as experience emerges in a certain context, the environment experience can be created and controlled by teachers to indirectly affect children's growth. Therefore, creating a situation where children's experience grows, designing and developing curriculum children interested in, and acting as the facilitators for children's learning are teachers' responsibilities.

In structuralism educational philosophers' view, students' intellectual activities in the learning process are essentially the same as that of the scientists in the process of studying scientific problems. As the research process is scientists' work, instead of leading the research process itself, others can only help the scientific research as an assistant. Similarly, learning is the process of students' self-control, so teachers can provide students with various help but cannot master it. However, as the research processes of students and scientists are different in degrees, some work that requires to finish independently for scientists but needs others' help for students must be taken by teachers. Therefore, in structuralists' views, students inspired and guided to carry out research activities and an environment created for students to study independently are teachers' roles.

Eternalists believe that the essence of education is to acquire knowledge, so instead of enabling children to spend large quantities of time to find knowledge by themselves, it would be better to teach students in a short period. Therefore, understanding subject contents and impart on all students is the task of teachers; thus, their virtues like temperance, justice, and fortitude are gradually cultivated.

The role of teachers in the conceptual framework of eternalists and essentialists are similar, considering the teacher as the occupant of knowledge and truth, whose responsibility is to train students' minds to meet social requirements. Therefore, in the teaching process, the teachers take the center position, mainly responsible for providing students with the curriculum of cultural knowledge, which is matched with the basic discipline in schools.

In social reformists' view, teachers themselves must be thoroughly social reformers since a new social order is established through education. Achieving social transformation through education is the essence of teachers' work, which can be realized by transforming students. Therefore, teachers take responsibility on two sides. The responsibility of conceptual transformation is the first, which means persuading students to strive to establish a new social order. The second is to make students' abilities to solve common problems improved, thus providing them with the capabilities, which is required for establishing a new social order.

Humanism educational philosophers hold that in teaching activities, teachers take the non-dominant position, whose main role is to help students understand learning, promote their self-realization and combine the individual with the learning of students. Therefore, it should be advocated that the curriculum adapts to students, communities, countries, and the world.

### 7.8.4 About Students' Role Positioning in Teaching

Pragmatism educational theory lays emphasis on children's value, holding that the interaction between children and the environment is the process of experience acquirement and that teachers being helpers, children, as the subjects of experience, must have a voice in their own learning activities. Therefore, in the teaching activities, students are not only learners but also participants in the curriculum development is believed in pragmatism educational philosophy.

Structuralists believe that "discovery" is not only that scientists explore the unknown human world but also that for men to use their own minds to discover knowledge. Through their discoveries, all true knowledge is learned. So, students' learning should be actively discovered. Students can experience "the joy of discovery" through discovery, forming the intrinsic motivation for learning. Moreover, the knowledge, which is obtained through their discoveries, can be found in long memory.

Perennialism educational philosophy considers that masterpieces contain some eternal knowledge, advocating that by reading various masterpieces, students should obtain knowledge in the reading process, develop their mental abilities and cultivate the eternal virtues, cultivating and applying them in their life decisions. Essentialism educational philosophy regards teaching as the process of mental training. They think that students' learning of outstanding mankind's cultural elements, as well as cultural knowledge's acquisition and application, is merely a purpose of learning. In the learning process, students should develop their mental abilities, that is, learning and using thinking skills.

Social reformists advocate that the main aim of students is to have the ability of social transformation, so in the learning process, students should learn how to examine social problems and solve them by using thinking skills and knowledge. In humanism educational philosophers' view, in order to achieve self-realization, students in the teaching activities should develop a system that is beneficial to self-health and acquire direct learning experience, thus through self-development achieving self-fulfillment.

### 7.8.5 About Teaching Methods

Pragmatism believes that as experience is obtained in action, accordingly, students can be stimulated by effective teaching methods to explore and discuss, gaining experience in action. In addition, people need to cooperate with others for the exploration and acquirement of experience in social life. Similarly, the process of obtaining experience for children should also be the collaborative one. Therefore, children should be provided with cooperative learning opportunities in teaching activities, and children's social instinct also provides the basis for cooperation.

Structuralists argue that in a certain way, any knowledge can be passed on to children at any age. If the relevant cognitive structure has been established in children's minds at an early age, as they grow up, they can use the previously formed cognitive structure to assimilate new knowledge. Meanwhile, the new learning process is not to reestablish cognitive structure but just to add "building blocks" for the existing cognitive structure, so it is easy to learn. Therefore, early learning, as advocated by structuralists, presents the theory that children in earlier childhood will learn in future learning in a way, which adapts to their current recognizing levels, forming a relative cognitive structure. At the same time, the discovery teaching method is advocated by structuralists because they believe that the essence of students' learning is the same as that of scientists' research. The process of scientific research is the process of discovering problems, so the discovery teaching method should be applied by teachers. Problem-solving method and discovery teaching method are closely related. Discovery is just finding problems, after which it is required to solve problems. Therefore, the problem-solving method is also a teaching method, which is very important.

Perennialism understanding of teaching methods is closely related to that of the roles of teachers and students, believing that in the teaching activities, students should be in the passive position, but teachers should be in the center. As they believe that fundamental truth is recorded in the masterpieces, eternalists hold language and characters should be the center of the teaching method and that the main teaching method should become the lecture method. Essentialism is similar to perennialism, advocating receptive learning that both the truth and the knowledge of children's psychology are mastered by teachers, who also have profound understanding of teaching than children. Teaching activities should be teacher-centered instead of children-dominated, while learning content should not focus on children-experience-focused but be subject-centered.

Social reformists believe that it is not simple to establish a new social order, requiring the common efforts of men in society. Meanwhile, as humans mostly live in the community, the educated should be shown in education how to live in such a social environment. Therefore, in the teaching process, the cooperative learning strategy and group problem-solving should be advocated, and students should be encouraged to analyze problems and apply problem-solving abilities in the learning situation; thus, the ability of social transformation formed. Humanism attaches great importance to students' self-development and self-learning, advocating "non-directive teaching" and the teaching method like cooperative group learning, which can build up students' confidence and provide a larger space for students' self-development.

# Research on Effective Teaching: What Methods Have Been Used?

## 1. Introduction

Teaching is and has always been at the center of all education and educational reform.[1] Classroom teaching is a basic way to achieve the aim of education. So the quality of education is influenced directly by the quality of teachers' classroom teaching, and research on teaching has been one way to try to improve the quality of education. Research on effective teaching has been a concern of educational researchers since 1931. The purpose of research on effective teaching is to promote the quality of teachers' teaching so that the quality of learning in the classroom can be improved. As Clark (1995)[2] said:

> "As the teaching goes, so goes the nation. Schooling is organized so that educational policies, curriculum, and instruction are interpreted and enacted by teachers. Teachers are the important point of contact with students. All other influences on the quality of education are mediated by whom the teacher is and what the teacher does. Teachers have the potential to enhance the quality of education by bringing life to the curriculum and inspiring students through curiosity and self-directed learning. And teachers can also degrade the quality of education through error, laziness, cruelty, or incompetence. For better or for worse, teachers determine the quality of education."

Such views give central importance to teachers, so it is not surprising that research on effective teaching has resulted in many debates about education itself.[3] Studying effective teaching is indeed very important to improve the quality of education, and there were many pieces of research on effective teaching during the last six decades.[4] These researchers have used different methods and have produced different findings about what effective teaching is or what the characteristics of effective teachers are, and each of them makes a useful and important contribution to the understanding of effective teaching. At the same time, it was also found from these research that the research method was a very important factor in conducting the research. Hence, it will be very important for educational researchers to choose one or two suitable research methods or approaches when they conduct their research about it.

The purpose of the paper is to examine what methods have been used to study effective teaching in the different periods over the last six decades and what kinds of methods might be the most suitable for conducting further research on teaching issues. This will lead to further exploration of qualitative and quantitative methods or approaches as used in the research on effective teaching.

## 2. Literature Review

What is effective teaching? Common sense would suggest that this should be the first question educators need to answer when they study effective teaching. In China, as I know, most Chinese educational researchers would begin by simply giving a definition or a concept that they want to study in depth. However, it seems there are indeed some differences between British studies and Chinese studies regarding the research style, and research in the West, like that noted above, has often examined people's perceptions in order to try to get a definition. Even if there is a great deal of research about effective teaching in Britain and USA, it is not easy to find several clear definitions of it in books or articles. An examination of the literature research on effective teaching suggests that, although there has been much research in the area, only a few studies have dealt with the actual concept of effective teaching. This is perhaps because effective teaching itself is very complex, so it is difficult to give a clear definition.

Schmid (1961) pointed out that teaching is a complex activity carried on in a complex environment—school. It is directed by complex organisms—human beings. The beneficiaries of the teaching activity are complex individual students whose characteristics are undergoing continuous and complex change. Therefore, it is difficult to define effective teaching because the elements of effective teaching apparently are not only legion but also intricately interwoven.[5]

Similarly, Perrott also said that: some educators claim that good teaching cannot be defined because the criteria differ for every instructional situation and every teacher. They conceive good teaching as being so complex and creative that it defies analysis. There can be no doubt that teaching is a complex task, yet educators usually find it relatively easy to list the characteristics of a good teacher. Although they may differ about the relative importance of these characteristics, rarely do they disagree on the characteristics to be included in such a list.

A review of the research literature shows that most of the researchers do not discuss the nature of effective teaching in the abstract, but there are a lot of papers that study the characteristics of good teachers and the factors underlying effective teaching in practice. However, even if it is very difficult to define the term "effective teaching" exactly, some authors have still tried to analyze it as a concept. Here I would like to give some comments and analysis about the concept of effective teaching, which some authors have provided in the past years.

For example, Kyriacou (1991) related effective teaching to the teacher's intentions by claiming that "effective teaching is primarily concerned with setting up a learning activity, task or experience for each pupil, which is successful in bringing about the type of pupil learning (knowledge, understanding skills, and attitudes) that the teacher intends." Similarly, Kyriacou also said that "effective teaching can be defined as teaching which successfully achieves the learning by pupils intended by the teacher." At the same time, he thought, in essence, this implies that there are two simple elements to effective teaching:

(1) The teacher must have a clear idea of what learning is to be fostered.
(2) The teacher provides a learning experience that achieves this.

In short, it seems that it is not easy to find a uniform explanation of effective teaching from historical research. Similarly, it is hard to find the best method to study the definition of effective teaching, but it should be based on the pupils' success in learning.[6] However, there were indeed some different methods that people used to study the characteristics or elements of effective teaching. In the next part, I will focus on the methods used by some educators to carry out research on effective teaching in the past sixty years. I will try to examine these methods and analyze their advantages and disadvantages in the next section.

## 3. Research on Effective Teaching: What Methods Have Been Used in the Past?

There has been a lot of research on effective teaching since the 1930s in the West, especially in developed countries like USA and UK. By examining the literature about it, we find that these researchers have used different methods and produced different findings about what effective teaching is or what the characteristics of effective teaching are, and each of them makes a useful and important contribution to the understanding of effective teaching.

### 3.1 Open-Ended Questions on Teachers' Qualities

In the earlier period, effective teaching research could have been called "good teacher" research or "teachers' traits" research. Its history can be traced back to the early 1930s, and as long ago as 1931, Cattell asked 254 people, including directors of education, teacher trainers, school teachers, and pupils, to write down the most important qualities of a good teacher. Overall, the five most frequent qualities reported were as follows (in order of frequency):

(1) Personality and will
(2) Intelligence
(3) Sympathy and tact
(4) Open-mindedness
(5) A sense of humor

There also were some researchers who focused on exploring the pupils' views of teachers' teaching. For example, Taylor (1962) reported a study in which 866 primary school pupils and 513 secondary school pupils were asked to write two short essays on "a good teacher" and "a poor teacher." Overall, the picture that emerged was that a good teacher is firm and keeps order in the classroom, explains the work you have to do and helps you with it, and is friendly with children in and out of school.

In these two studies above, both Cattell and Taylor used an open-ended question as the research method to explore a good teacher's traits, with just one open statement provided for teachers or students, and not a set of questions listed for people to check to give their ideas about a "good teacher." This was a very qualitative approach, with participants' essays being analyzed by the researchers. As we know, on the one hand, a big advantage of an open-ended question as a tool for gathering data is that it can leave space for people's thinking. People can express their own ideas according to the question given by the researcher, resulting in very rich data. On the other hand, it is not easy to give a summary or analyze the different results from people who have been asked an open-ended question, and the summary often lacks the richness of the original answers. So this is a big problem if there is just one open-ended question in the research.

Regarding this kind of research, some educators have expressed unsatisfactory views. Kyriacou pointed out that studies that attempted to relate teacher attributes to educational outcomes (such as examination results) have sometimes been referred to as "black-box" research.[7] The point being made was that such research on effective teaching completely ignored what actually went on in the classroom.

Garrison and Macmillan (1994) pointed out that research on teaching throughout the 20th century has focused on effective teaching, often in terms of the effects of teachers' specific behaviors on students' achievement. This research has been conspicuously lacking in consideration of the intentional nature of teaching and the intention of teachers. The past several decades of research on teaching, however, have brought changes away from this behavioral emphasis. As a result of shifts in conceptions of social science research, researchers have begun to recognize that teachers are intentional agents who have beliefs, desires, emotions, intentions, and goals that help make up their aims and actions in teaching.

Actually, since the 1960s, research on effective teaching has focused fairly and squarely on activities in the classroom, and in particular, the interaction between the teacher and pupils.[8] Observation has been used as a main method to study teachers' characteristics and also effective teaching.

## 3.2 Observation Research on Teachers' Teaching in the Classroom

In 1960, Ryan and his colleagues conducted a program of observational studies to identify factors associated with effective teaching. The program used structured observation, and three main factors emerged from this work. The positive and negative poles of these factors are defined by the following:

(1) Warm and understanding versus cold and aloof
(2) Organized and businesslike versus unplanned and slipshod
(3) Stimulating and imaginative versus dull and routine

Teachers rated nearer the positive poles of each factor are considered more "effective" than those rated nearer the negative poles.

Another set of structured observational studies on teacher effectiveness was carried out by Flanders and his associates in 1970, using a series of categories to describe teacher behavior. Flanders's observations found two contrasting styles of teaching: direct and indirect. Direct teaching is characterized by teacher reliance on lectures, criticism, justification of authority, and the giving of directions. Indirect teaching is characterized by teacher reliance on asking questions, accepting pupils' feelings, acknowledging pupils' ideas, and giving praise and encouragement. A substantial number of studies have found that pupils of "indirect" teachers learn more and have better attitudes toward learning than pupils of "direct" teachers.

Other researchers have studied teacher characteristics by employing observation methods other than direct and indirect teaching. The usual design of these studies is to observe various aspects of teachers' classroom behavior and to test the pupils of these teachers at intervals during the school year. The researchers then look for correlations between observed teacher characteristics and pupil achievement. Standardized achievement tests are frequently used for this purpose. Pupils' scores before and after a period of instruction (e.g., the beginning and the end of a school year) are compared to obtain a measure of achievement gain. Finally, the data are analyzed to determine which teacher behavior is associated with pupil achievement gains.[9]

In 1973, Rosenshine and Furst wrote a useful review of some research about effective teaching. They identified five teacher characteristics consistently associated with gains in pupils' achievement. The first two characteristics are teacher enthusiasm and businesslike orientation, characteristics also identified in Ryan's research (1960). The third characteristic is teacher clarity. Researchers have measured clarity—or lack of it—in various ways, for example, the amount of time the teacher uses to answer pupils' questions requesting clarification of what the teacher has said, the frequency with which pupils respond to teacher's questions without the teacher having to intersperse additional information or questions, the avoidance of vague words (e.g., some, many, of course) in the teacher's exposition. The fourth of Rosenshine and Furst's (1973) characteristics is variety in teaching. This characteristic can be estimated by counting the number of different instructional materials, tests, and teaching through which the teacher varies the cognitive level of classroom discourse. The fifth characteristic is the extent to which the teacher provides opportunities for pupils to learn the curriculum content covered in the achievement tests, or the teacher's ability and preference for classroom activities focused on the kinds of cognitive learning usually measured in achievement tests.

**Table A1 Observable Indicators of Effective Classroom Teaching**

| **Ryan's factors** |
|---|
| 1. Teacher is warm and understanding versus cold and aloof. |
| 2. Teacher is organized and businesslike versus unplanned and slipshod. |
| 3. Teacher is stimulating and imaginative versus dull and routine. |
| **Flanders indicators of indirect teaching style** |
| 1. Teacher asks questions. |
| 2. Teacher accepts pupils' feelings. |
| 3. Teacher acknowledges pupils' ideas. |
| 4. Teacher praises and encourages pupils. |
| **Rosenshine and Furst's correlates** |
| 1. Teacher is enthusiastic. |
| 2. Teacher is businesslike and task-oriented. |
| 3. Teacher is clear when presenting instructional content. |
| 4. Teacher uses a variety of instructional materials and procedures. |
| 5. Teacher provides opportunities for pupils to learn the instructional content. |

Source: E. Perrott, *Effective Teaching* (1982), 3.

Moyles (1988) commented that each of these earlier studies, dating from just after the First World War until the late 1960s, was characterized by the researchers' enormous difficulties, particularly in elementary schools, in identifying real objective measures of teacher effectiveness. Many checklists were devised and refined, but the studies have all failed to reach a clear consensus as to what constitutes good, effective teaching. However, these earlier studies, after all, have contributed to the debate about what effective teaching is and what characteristics it has.

In fact, from using the open-ended question to the observation of teachers' teaching behavior in the classroom, it was indeed a good development in using the method to study effective teaching in this period. As it was mentioned above, teaching is a very complex activity, and just using one open-ended question is not enough to explore it. So observation should be used as a tool for gathering data about effective teaching. However, there was another problem—observation just focused on the teachers' behavior. What is the relationship between the teachers' teaching behavior and students' learning? It means students should be observed when researching effective teaching.

### 3.3 Observation of Pupils

From the middle of the 1970s, researchers started to make a concerted effort to identify teaching behavior that facilitates pupils' learning in specific curriculum areas. This multiplicity of studies gradually moved from research into relatively limited domains of teacher effectiveness to the study of teaching and learning situations. Much of this research focused on reading and mathematics instruction at the primary school level. There was a new trend in observing pupils' learning in the classroom.

Perrott (1982) wrote that observation of the teacher's pupils is also a method of perceiving the quality of teaching. He also gave observable indications of effective teaching indicated by pupils' behavior in the classroom.

**Table A2** Observable Indications of Effective Teaching: Pupils' Behavior and Performance

| |
|---|
| 1. Pupils show knowledge and understanding, skills and attitudes; intended by the curriculum as measured by performance on tests |
| 2. Pupils exhibit independent behavior in learning curriculum content |
| 3. Pupils exhibit behavior that indicates a positive attitude towards the teacher and peers |
| 4. Pupils exhibit behavior that indicates a positive attitude towards the curriculum and the school |
| 5. Pupils exhibit behavior that indicates a positive attitude towards themselves as learners |
| 6. Pupils do not exhibit behavior problems in class |
| 7. Pupils seem actively engaged in learning academically relevant material while the class is in session |

Source: E. Perrott, *Effective Teaching* (1982), 4.

Teaching is, in fact, an interactive activity between teachers and students, especially in the classroom. Communication between teacher and students or students and students is the essence of teaching. So when we use observation as a method to explore what happens in the classroom, we should not only pay attention to the teacher's teaching, but also pay attention to the students' learning. However, even if we agree with the statements above, it might be hard to categorize pupil behavior in these terms. For example, if a pupil constantly calls out, is this an example of a confident, positive attitude towards himself as a learner or an example of a behavior problem?

### 3.4 Surveys Using Ratings for Effective Teaching

Apart from the observational research on effective teaching, there have also been a few surveys using ratings about effective teaching since the middle of the 1970s. These researches also try to identify some of the features of good teachers by using quantitative approaches.

In 1976, Bennet asked nearly 800 primary school teachers to rate each of nine teaching aims on a five-point scale of importance, which ranged from "not important" to "essential." The responses, in order of most frequently rated as essential, were as follows:

(1) The acquisition of basic skills in reading and number work
(2) Acceptance of normal standards of behavior
(3) Help pupils to cooperate with each other
(4) An understanding of the world in which pupils live
(5) The enjoyment of school
(6) The encouragement of self-expression
(7) The development of pupils' creative abilities
(8) Preparation for academic attainment
(9) The promotion of a high level of academic attainment

The findings of this study also illustrated a marked difference of opinions between teachers on some of these items. For example, 10 percent of the teachers rated the item "preparation for academic work in the secondary school" as essential, while 7 percent rated this as not important.

Similarly, in 1982, Kyriaco conducted a survey of 142 heads of departments in secondary schools and pointed to diversity amongst teachers in their views about effectiveness. He asked the teachers to rate the importance of each of the five criteria as an indicator of the effectiveness of teaching their subjects, using a four-point scale labeled from "not important" to "very important." The five criteria were as follows:

(1) The grades achieved by pupils in the subject
(2) The development of an increased interest by pupils in the subject

(3) The proportion of pupils who go on to take the subject at an advanced level
(4) The proportion who develop a good understanding of the subject
(5) The proportion of pupils who feel they had enjoyed the course

From the 1970s to 1980s, quantitative approaches like survey by rating were very popular in educational research, as mentioned above by both Bennet (1976) and Kyriacou (1982). Meanwhile, people also wanted to study effective teaching by using objective methods like Berliner and Tichenoff (1976) mentioned above. One of the advantages of quantitative methods is that they can get data from more people. But one of the disadvantages of quantitative methods is that they cannot explore particular issues in depth in some cases, like complicated teaching situations in the classroom or teachers' feelings and humor. However, interviewing could be a good method to finish this kind of task because it allows participants to express their ideas in more depth.

### 3.5 Interviewing Students about Effective Teaching

Brown and McIntyre (1993) reported a study about good teachers.[10] They asked pupils to identify their "best teachers" and describe what they thought made them good teachers. The pupils' comments on what they felt these teachers did well were grouped into ten categories:

(1) Creating a relaxed and enjoyable atmosphere in the classroom
(2) Retaining control in the classroom
(3) Presenting work in a way that interests and motivates pupils
(4) Providing conditions so pupils understand the work
(5) Making clear what pupils are to do and achieve
(6) Judging what can be expected of a pupil
(7) Helping pupils with difficulties
(8) Encouraging pupils to raise their expectations of themselves
(9) Developing personal, mature relationships with pupils
(10) Teacher's personal talents (subject-related or other)

The study then focused on 16 teachers (four primary and twelve secondary school teachers) identified by these pupils and asked them to talk about their teaching. These accounts were used to explore how "good" teachers think about and evaluate their own "good teaching." Brown and McIntyre (1993) found that when they asked these teachers questions about their teaching, they almost talked about what the pupils were doing. In effect, these teachers were very adept at keeping their focus on pupil activity during the lesson, and using a range of skills to maintain pupils' interest, diffuse discipline problems quickly, and generally manage the lesson so that pupils were kept very much engaged in what the teachers wanted them to do.

Interviewing indeed has the advantage of exploring some kinds of issues about teachers' and students' perceptions of teaching, because it is a face-to-face communication between the interviewer and the interviewee. But if the questions used in the interview are not designed well by researchers in advance, or the interviewer has not got good communication skills with others, the results will not be very valid. Similarly, the interviewer should be aware of the feelings of the interviewees. For example, as mentioned above, the teachers preferred to talk about their students, rather than their own teaching, in the research conducted by Brown and McIntyre (1993). So the researcher should keep in mind the purpose of the research during the interview.

### 3.6 Context-Process-Product Research on Effective Teaching

Among the research projects on effective teaching, process-product studies have dominated for many years. This basic framework was mainly developed by Kyriacou. It is a good framework to consider for effective teaching, which can be divided into three main classes of variables.

The first is called context variables, which consists of seven aspects. These include teacher characteristics, pupil characteristics, class characteristics, school characteristics, community characteristics, and characteristics of the occasion. The second is called process variables, which consists of three aspects, including the characteristics of teacher perceptions, strategies, and behavior; the characteristics of pupil perceptions, strategies, and behavior; the characteristics of the learning task and activities. The third is called product variables, which consists of two aspects. It includes short-term/long-term, cognitive/affective educational outcomes.[11]

Reviews of process-product studies have typically identified the following ten characteristics of effective teaching:

(1) Clarity of the teacher's explanations and directions
(2) Establishing a task-oriented classroom climate
(3) Making use of a variety of learning activities
(4) Establishing and maintaining momentum and pace for the lesson
(5) Encouraging pupil participation and getting all pupils involved
(6) Monitoring pupils' progress and attending quickly to pupils' needs
(7) Delivering a well-structured and well-organized lesson
(8) Providing pupils with positive and constructive feedback
(9) Ensuring coverage of the learning objectives
(10) Making good use of questioning techniques

Garrison and Macmillan (1994) pointed out that the process-product research program developed out of a half-century of research on teacher effectiveness. Research on teacher effectiveness has focused on one central theme: the search for specific criteria that indicate effective teaching. While the original search for teacher effectiveness manifested itself in ratings of teacher characteristics, it steadily moved to the examination of teacher behaviors and corresponding student behaviors and achievement (process-product). These different emphases within the study of teachers have followed changes in philosophical thought throughout the century. As the philosophy of social science shifted from a preliminary focus on the scientific method to logical positivism, the conceptions within these philosophies were adopted by researchers' studying to teachers. The development of research following these underlying conceptions culminated in a focus on finding law-like generalizations connecting specific teacher behaviors with student achievement and a lack of consideration of the teacher's beliefs, desires, emotions, and intentions.

Even if this research has had a great influence on later research about effective teaching in more recent years, there still are some shortcomings. Kyriacou (1997) thought that there were two major problems facing such process-product studies. First, they employ a simplistic research design, attempting to focus on small, discrete, observable behaviors that are then associated relatively independently with the product variables. The idea, for example, that such discrete behaviors as "use of praise" or "repeating questions" can be explored independently of each other and everything else going on during the lesson, and that each will contribute in its own separate and identifiable way to effectiveness, is very suspect and has contributed to a mass of contradictory data. The second problem is that such a research design cannot distinguish between those aspects of classroom processes which simply occur when effective teaching is in progress and those aspects which in themselves constitute effective teaching.

In my opinion, this process-product approach tried to make a detailed consideration of effective teaching by three different variables. The researchers have not only considered some of the factors which influence the process of teaching, but also the background factors which influence the teaching and the results of teaching. The advantage of this approach was that it would lead to an all-round consideration of effective teaching. Maybe it could be called "a holistic consideration." However, it is indeed not easy to consider so many factors for teachers in the classroom, and an example of this complex approach will be discussed in more detail next.

### 3.7 OECD's Holistic Study

In the 1990s, research on effective teaching tended to generate lists of different qualities, dispositions, attributes, and behaviors of effective teachers. A typical study conducted by the Organisation for Economic Co-operation and Development (OECD) collected data from 11 countries, including the UK, the United States, France, Japan, and Australia (OECD, 1994). This study was based on the view that teaching quality should be regarded as a holistic concept, made up of competencies across five key dimensions:

(1) Knowledge of substantive curriculum areas and content
(2) Pedagogic skill, including the acquisition of and ability to use a repertoire of teaching strategies
(3) Reflection and the ability to be self-critical are the hallmarks of teacher professionalism
(4) Empathy and the commitment to the acknowledgment of the dignity of others
(5) Managerial competence, as teachers assume a range of managerial responsibilities within and beyond the classroom

Turner-Bisset (2001) thought that this list was interesting because it was the first one to mention subject knowledge as a key quality. At the same time, she pointed out that subject mastery was often overlooked in studies of effective teaching, perhaps because its importance was so obvious, but more importantly, because researchers were looking for generic teaching qualities applicable across all subjects, age phases, and teaching contexts. She saw this as a serious weakness of research into effective teaching. Because of this, Turner-Bisset (2001) has developed a new paradigm of teaching: that of teaching as a knowledge-based profession. In addition, reflection on teaching was thought of as an important aspect of effective teaching. This means that if teachers can re-think their teaching practice often, their teaching will be improved. This also is a very new idea in the list of OECD's studies.

Why can OECD's study be thought of as a very holistic research on effective teaching? It was found by reviewing the OECD's study that one important reason is that there are several different methods that have been employed to conduct the research on effective teaching, including case studies, interviews, and surveys. In addition, the data also come from several different countries, like USA and UK.

In my opinion, OECD's study has shown us that each research method has its strength. If a researcher wants to make more clear understanding to the research topic, he/she had better choose at least two methods, for example, one qualitative method and one quantitative method, to conduct the research for a holistic result.

## 4. Analysis

How did the researchers collect the data while they studied effective teaching in the past years? Who would be the information source? Kyriacou used to give a very good summary of the methods of data collecting below:

(1) Studies based on teachers' opinions regarding effective teaching (usually employing questionnaires or interviews)

(2) Studies based on pupils' opinions regarding effective teaching (usually employing questionnaires or interviews; some studies have sought pupils' opinions about their own teacher's teaching)
(3) Studies based on classroom observation by an outside observer (using their recording Schedules, video and audio tapes, rating scales, or participant observation techniques)
(4) Studies based on descriptions of the behavior of teachers identified as effective by their headteacher, pupils, or others
(5) Studies based on teachers' descriptions of their own teaching
(6) Studies by teachers of their own teaching (which may include keeping detailed notes about their lesson, and getting the reactions of others such as their pupils or colleague)

This is indeed a good summary of data collecting and information sources for research on effective teaching, I think. But there is rather a pity that no examples of authors and research topics are given in this summary. Here I would like to give an outline of which methods have been employed to study effective teaching in the past years according to a literature review of the research on effective teaching which I have carried out. The methods here refer to the 'tools' for conducting the research. The methods can be listed according to the historical development of research on effective teaching (see Table A3).

We can see from Table A3 that different methods have been used to conduct the studies of effective teaching. There are not only some using qualitative methods, but also some using quantitative methods to do this kind of research. However, it is very easy to find that observation and interview are the main methods that have been employed. Meanwhile, we can see that most researchers have focused on qualitative methods, particularly using observation and interviews. But, even if observation was used as the main method, there still are some differences in the actual methods used when researchers were doing the research in the classroom.

Most researchers have employed observation as a main method of research on effective teaching in the past years, from Table A3. Why did they choose observation as the main method? The reason is probably that teaching is an interaction between teachers and students, and observation can give both direct access to social interactions and can give permanent and systematic records of them.

**Table A3** The Methods Used in Research on Effective Teaching

| Researcher | Year | Topic | Methods |
|---|---|---|---|
| Cattell, R. B. | 1931 | Teachers' qualities | Questionnaire: Open-ended question |
| Ryan, D. | 1960 | Effective teaching | Structured observational studies to identify factors |
| Taylor, P. H. | 1962 | Good teacher and poor teacher | Questionnaire: Open-ended questions |
| Flanders, N. A. | 1970 | Teacher effectiveness | Structured observation; two contrasting styles of teaching |
| Rosenshine and Furst | 1973 | Good teaching | participant observation of various aspects of teachers' classroom behavior |
| Berliner and Tichenoff | 1976 | Effective teaching | Structured observation of the teacher's pupils |
| Bennet | 1976 | Good teaching | Survey-rating |
| Kyriacou | 1982 | Teacher effectiveness | Survey-rating |
| Perrott | 1982 | Effective teaching | Structured observation |
| Brown and McIntyre | 1993 | | Interview and structured observation |
| OECD | 1994 | Quality of teaching | Case studies, structured and unstructured observation, interviews, teacher's seminar |
| Cooper, P. | 1996 | Effective teaching | Interview and participant observation |
| Kyriacou | 1997 | Effective teaching | Factor analysis (Context-process-product study) |

## 5. Conclusion

After examining some main research on effective teaching and discussing the methods used, we can get some useful ideas below:

There is still no clear uniform conception of effective teaching. Some feel that the main reason is that researchers have used qualitative methods, which do not tend to give straightforward answers, while others feel the concept itself is subjective. For example, Abercrombie (1988) argues that social science research can never be objective because of the subjective perceptions of those involved, both informant and researcher; because all propositions are limited in their meaning to particular language contexts and particular social groups; because all researchers impose their own value judgment unwittingly and because all observations are theory-laden.[12]

Many kinds of educational research methods have been employed to conduct research on effective teaching in the last six decades, including open questions, observation, interviews, questionnaires, case studies, and surveys by rating. It concludes the qualitative method and the quantitative method. Among these methods, the majority of them have been used in the context of qualitative approaches. It would seem that the qualitative methods are seen as more suitable for conducting research on teaching. The main reason given is that the teaching is all about human behavior. As Burns (2000) points out that only qualitative methods, such as participant observation and unstructured interviewing, permit access to individual meaning in the context of ongoing daily life.

It is also very obvious that observation has been used as the main method to conduct research on effective teaching. In fact, observing teachers at work has long been part of the normal routine in many schools, mainly because staff realizes that timely and effective observation and feedback are of immense value.[13] Observation methods can be qualitative (e.g., participant observation) or structured and more quantitative in practical application, so more and more educators and researchers are therefore paying much more attention to observation in the classroom.

Research methods used to research effective teaching have also followed a trend from a single method to using a variety of them. For example, in the early research, there was often just one method—open-ended questions or observation. Open-ended questions do have a number of advantages. For example, they allow the interviewer to probe so that he or she may go into more depth if they choose or to clear up any misunderstandings. But, after all, it is only one of the many tools for collecting data. So, by the early 1990s, in OECD's study (1994), several methods were being employed to conduct the research, including interviewing, case studies, and surveys. The survey showed that people want to get information from different sources in the hope that the results of the research will be fairer and objective.

Similarly, research methods used to research effective teaching have followed a general trend from qualitative methods to quantitative methods and then to both in combination. Teaching is a very complex activity. It is very hard to use just quantitative methods to conduct research on teaching. The consensus seems to be that qualitative methods should be the main method to conduct the research, but, at the same time, quantitative methods should be combined with them.

# Changes in Research Approaches and Research Methods in Education from 1960 to Now: A Literature Survey

## 1. Introduction

Research in education is a disciplined attempt to address questions or solve problems through the collection and analysis of primary data for the purpose of description, explanation, generalization, and prediction.[1]

Qualitative research and quantitative research are two foundational research approaches in education so far. At the same time, there are also many kinds of methods that can be used in qualitative research or quantitative research.

Quantitative research synthesis is not merely defined by statistical analysis of studies. Jackson (1980) discussed six tasks comprising an integrative review or research synthesis: specifying the questions or hypotheses for investigation; selecting or sampling the studies for synthesis; coding or representing the characteristics of the primary studies, analyzing, "meta-analyzing"; statistically synthesizing the study findings; interpreting the results and reporting them. Explicit methods of quantitative synthesis call for statistics; two are most often employed—the vote count or box score and the effect size.[2]

Qualitative research is empirical research when the data are not in the form of numbers.[3] In fact, qualitative research is traditionally an inductive form of inquiry. Qualitative inquiry in education connotes a subjective process of understanding and assessing educational phenomena, and it can lead to qualitative understanding. Qualitative inquiry plays an important role in educational research by assisting us in raising new questions, leading us to question assumptions, cultivating an appreciation for complexity, and finally, expanding our frames of reference. Qualitative inquiry also expands our understanding of research by making us conscious of our assumptions and by fostering an appreciation for complexity. Qualitative inquiry, by raising questions, challenging assumptions, embracing complexity, and expanding our frames of reference, provides educational researchers with an important lesson: the knowledge that our understanding, both as individuals and as researchers, is limited.

As Fraenkel and Wallen (1990) point out that there are many different types of qualitative methodologies, but there are certain general features that characterize most qualitative research studies. Not all qualitative studies will necessarily display all of these characteristics with equal strength. Nevertheless, taken together, they give a good overall picture of what is involved in this type of research. Robert Bogdan and Sari Knopp Biklen describe five such features:

(1) The natural setting is the direct source of data, and the researcher is the key instrument in qualitative research.
(2) Qualitative data are collected in the form of words or pictures rather than numbers.
(3) Qualitative researchers are concerned with process as well as product.
(4) Qualitative researchers tend to analyze their data inductively.
(5) How people make sense of their lives is a major concern of qualitative research.
(6) Kincheloe gives the characteristics of qualitative research below.
(7) One of the most important aspects of qualitative research is its concern with context.
(8) Qualitative research views experience holistically, as researchers explore all aspects of an experience.
(9) One of the most important characteristics of qualitative inquiry is the belief that methods of inquiry must be appropriate to the aims of inquiry.
(10) Another common aspect of qualitative research involves the idea of making judgments.

However, quantitative researchers have often seen qualitative research as lacking in objectivity, rigor, and scientific controls.[4] Lacking the resources of quantification, qualitative research cannot produce the requisite generalizations to build up a set of laws of human behavior, nor can it apply adequate tests for validity and reliability. Moreover, the positivist fact/value distinction is often employed to discredit the claims of qualitative inquiry to produce knowledge, since knowledge is seen as value-free, whereas qualitative research is irreducibly value-laden and subjective. In short, qualitative research falls short of the high standards of objectivity and the tight criteria for the truth of the quantitative or "scientific" paradigm. Given the prestige of science, and a positivist view of scientific inquiry, it is easy to see why quantitative researchers have sometimes even seen qualitative research as opposed to the sound scientific method.

In reply, many qualitative researchers, invoking the explanation/understanding distinction, claim that the genuinely and distinctively human dimension of education cannot be captured by statistical generalizations and causal laws. Knowledge of human affairs is irreducibly subjective. It must grasp the meanings of actions, the uniqueness of events, and the individuality of a person. From this perspective, it is easy to see the quantitative tradition as an intrusive, even alien and antihuman, approach to the study of education. Similarly, qualitative researchers always emphasize some of the advantages that qualitative research has.

These contrasting approaches raise a number of questions. For example, how do people use different approaches and different methods to conduct educational research in practice? Which approach has been more popular? And which methods are most often chosen as the main methods when people are doing educational research? Have there been any developmental trends over the years in the methods of educational research? Burns argues that research in professional social science areas, like research in other subjects, has generally followed traditional objectives using scientific methods. Since the 1960s, however, there has been a strong move towards a more qualitative, naturalistic, and subjective approach which has left social scientists divided between two competing methods: the scientific empirical tradition and the naturalistic phenomenological mode.[5]

As a researcher, of course, you have to employ the specific method(s) to collect the data for your research purpose when you want to do any kind of research, even if your research approach is qualitative or quantitative. As we know, there are many kinds of research methods that can be used in qualitative research and quantitative research, like questionnaire surveys, interviews, observation, and so on. Sometimes, however, there is just one approach and method to be employed by research for reaching research purposes and gathering data in one research project, and sometimes there will be two approaches and several methods to be combined in one research project. That is to say that there is no one best method or best approach that can be used to do any kind of research and then can get the best result in practice. Different people for different research purposes may employ different approaches and different methods when they conduct their research. However, what are the changes in research approaches and research methods in education from 1960 to now? This should be an available question to be answered for us. That is the purpose of my study.

The purpose of this article is to try to analyze the development and changes in research approaches and research methods in education from around 1960 to now through a literature survey. At the same time, I try to summarise the application of different research methods in the field of education in different periods since 1960, and further explore the developmental trends and some problems of educational research methods. Through the literature survey, I also want to answer the following main questions about educational research approaches and methods since 1960:

(1) Which research approach has been the more popular as the main approach in educational research since 1960, the qualitative approach or the quantitative approach?
(2) Which methods were popular as the main methods when people conducted educational research from the 1960s to 1990s?
(3) What are the main developmental trends of educational research methods since 1990?
(4) Is there the best method that can be used in any situation in educational research?
(5) What can we see about the application of different research methods in education in different periods since 1960?

## 2. Literature Review

In this part of the literature review, I will focus on identifying the methods of qualitative research and methods of quantitative research, and then building a category of different research approaches and research methods.

As was said in the introduction, qualitative research and quantitative research are two fundamental approaches to educational research. In this study, however, it should be clearly recognized which kinds of methods are seen as belonging to qualitative and which to quantitative approaches, so that they can be divided into different areas for the purpose of this study. As we know, even if there are many books about research methods in education, it still seems not easy to identify the families of research methods. Let us, first of all, look at some of the literature about these issues.

Fenstermacher (1986) argued in *The Philosophy of Research on Teaching: Three Aspects*:

> "Educational research currently makes use of a number of different methods, many of them classifiable as either quantitative or qualitative. Depending on how they are applied in specific contexts, quantitative methods are also known as confirmatory, hypothesis testing, or predictive methods. Qualitative methods are also often known as exploratory, hypothesis-generating, descriptive, or interpretive methods. Among the techniques of quantitative methods are the experiment, quasi-experiment, correlational study, and survey research. These methods typically employ both logical design and statistical techniques as controls for the collection, analysis, and interpretation of data."

Linn (1986) pointed out in *Quantitative Methods in Research on Teaching*:

> "Quantitative methods are generally associated with systematic measurement, experimental and quasi-experimental methods, statistical analysis, and mathematical models. Qualitative methods, on the other hand, are associated with naturalistic observation, case studies, ethnography, and narrative reports. It should be recognized, however, that the boundaries between the methods sometimes get blurred."

The person using quantitative methods must make many qualitative decisions regarding the question to pose, the design to implement, the measures to use, the analytical procedures to employ, and the interpretations to stress. The person who relies on quantitative methods often finds certain quantitative summaries, classifications, and analyses a useful part of the research.

Fraenkel and Wallen note that there are three techniques commonly used by qualitative researchers: observation, interviewing, and document analysis.

Denzin and Lincoln (1994), in the *Handbook of Qualitative Research*, identify some of the qualitative methods below:

(1) Interviewing
(2) Observational Techniques
(3) The Interpretation of Documents and Material Culture
(4) Visual Methods
(5) Personal Experience Methods
(6) Narrative, Content, and Semiotic Analysis
(7) Case Studies
(8) Biography
(9) Clinical Research

However, Cohen (2000)'s[6] categories of research methods are different from others. His categories are below:

*Style of education research*

(1) Naturalistic and ethnographic research
(2) Historical research
(3) Survey research, longitudinal, cross-section, and trend studies
(4) Case study
(5) Correlational research
(6) Ex post facto research
(7) Experiment, quasi-experiment, and single-case research
(8) Action research

*Strategies for data collection and research*

(1) Questionnaire
(2) Interview
(3) Accounts
(4) Observation
(5) Tests
(6) Personal constructs
(7) Multi-dimensional measurement
(8) Role-playing

Kincheloe pointed out that "qualitative is distinguished from quantitative research frequency while quantitative research is concerned with abstract characteristics of events.[7] Qualitative researchers maintain that many natural properties cannot be expressed in quantitative terms—indeed, they will lose their realty if expressed simply in terms of frequency." He also said:

> "Qualitative researchers are not attempting to argue that there is no need for quantitative research in education. Quantitative research is very important to serve as a check on qualitative data. Well-executed quantitative research with an understanding of context and a concern with purpose can provide important insight into certain human affairs. Quantitative methods allow us to focus on variables of interest, and the use of mathematical symbols is an economic summary of information."

In short, it is obvious that there are different ideas about which kinds of methods belong to the qualitative approach and which kinds of methods belong to the quantitative approach. But, the research above has given us a basic structure for the category of research approaches and research methods in educational research.

In fact, sometimes, it is not very easy to identify these two different research families strictly with a specific method. But it also can be done by their different main functions in doing research. For the purpose of my study, I here try to give a summary of different research families according to some authors' identification so that I can pick up the different methods from different approaches. However, I know that it is indeed very difficult to give a very detailed summary of research families, including all methods in social science research.

According to the former research obtained by literature review and my understanding, I try to identify the different methods into different research approaches. They are quantitative methods, quantitative methods, and both together (see Table B1). The research methods which people used to conduct their studies can be examined by this category. So, in this study, I will just focus on the educational research area, and the data used will come mainly from the journal: *Educational Research*, which is published by the National Foundation for Educational Research in England and Wales (NFER).

**Table B1** The Category of Research Approaches and Research Methods

| Qualitative methods | Quantitative methods | Mixture |
|---|---|---|
| Observation<br>Interview<br>Action research<br>Ethnography survey<br>Case study<br>Historical research<br>Diary research<br>Life history<br>Document analysis<br>Content analysis | Test<br>Measurement<br>Examination<br>Descriptive statistics<br>Meta-analysis<br>Experiment<br>Rating scale<br>Questionnaire survey<br>National survey | Combine one qualitative method and one quantitative method together, for example, observation and questionnaire |

As well known, in fact, it is indeed not easy to give a very clear structure about research approaches and research methods. For example, if you employ different kinds of methods like unstructured interviews and structured observation in your case studies, you are using a mixture method or mixture approach. But people normally may use unstructured interviews and unstructured observation in their case studies in most cases of research practice. That is because the case study is often seen as a qualitative approach in many books on research methods in education. Of course, I have to try to make a basic category of research approach and research method for the purpose of this research. It has been done in Table B1 above.

## 3. Methodology

### 3.1 Survey

Survey research is one of the most common forms of research engaged in by educational researchers. Survey research in education involves the collection of information from members of groups of students, teachers, or other persons associated with the educational process, and the analysis of this information is used to illuminate important educational issues. Most surveys are based on samples or specified target populations—the group of persons in whom the interest is expressed. The researcher often wishes to generalize the results obtained from the samples to the populations from which the samples were drawn.

Surveys are usually associated as a research approach with the idea of asking a group of people questions. There is, however, a related meaning of survey which is also relevant to the social sciences. This is when the subjects being studied by the researcher are really objects: materials or artifacts rather than people. Thus, most small-scale research projects will involve some kind of literature survey; but in some cases, as when the documentary analysis is extensively used, this may be the basis for the whole project.[8] That is to say that some kinds of data may be collected by doing a literature survey.

### 3.2 Sample

This is a small-scale research project, and literature survey research was employed as a research method in this study. The sample in this study is the journal: *Educational Research*, which is a review for teachers and all concerned with progress in education. It is published for the National Foundation for Educational Research in England and Wales (NFER). The NFER is Britain's leading research institution in the educational field. It is an independent foundation looking at issues of current interest in all sectors of the education system. The journal is published in the Spring, Summer, and Winter. It was first published in 1958. In this study, the author has chosen all of the articles published in this journal from 1960 to 2001 as the data source. At the same time, it was divided into four phases for doing statistics: the first phase is the 1960s; the second phase is the 1970s; the third is the 1980s, and the fourth is the 1990s. The rest is 2000–2001, just two years.

There are three reasons to choose this journal as a sample for collecting the data for the purpose of this study.

Firstly, This is a typical educational research journal in UK, and it can be regarded as a representation of the educational research journals in UK.

Secondly, there is a typical research article's framework in this journal. Most of the articles published in this journal have a very clear research paper structure. It makes up of six parts, namely: introduction, literature review, method/methodology, findings (results), discussion (analysis), and conclusion. With this basic structure, it is easy for the researcher to find which approach and method are used by each author in his / her article. And at the same time, it is also convenient to do the statistics about the research methods.

Thirdly, it is very easy to find all of the issues of *Educational Research* from 1960 to 2001 in the Education Library of the University of Leicester, which I am learning. But it is hard to find other educational journals with all issues from 1960 to 2001 like this journal.

However, because this is small-scale research, the object of analysis is all of the articles published in this journal from 1960 to 1999. By the way, all of the articles published in the journal from 2000–2001 also were counted so that some of the comparisons can be made. The total number of issues is 126, and the total number of articles is 1,099. Among them, the available articles for statistics are 696, or 63.3 percent. Hence the size of the sample for this study should be significant.

This survey focuses on the research approaches and research methods of all of the articles published in the journal of *Educational Research*. Two criteria were used in collecting data below:

(1) All of the articles and short research reports published in the journal of *Educational Research* from 1960–2001 were examined for the purpose of this study.
(2) Only the articles and short research reports that clearly showed the methods used in the study were collected as data to be counted for this study.

### 3.3 Categorizing and Statistics

It is very important to collect the data according to certain standards in the literature survey. This means categorizing the content must be done for the study. In this study, the methods were categorized by some of the keywords, which can represent one kind of method like test or observation and so on. As we know, there are many kinds of research methods that can be used to conduct educational research. The most important thing is to find keywords that can represent different research methods. According to some books on educational research methods like Cohen's (2000), Denzin and Lincoln's (1994) and Burns's (2000), and so on, some of the keywords used in doing research and collecting data are listed in Table B2.

**Table B2** Key Words for Collecting Data from the Journal Articles

| | | |
|---|---|---|
| Method | Questionnaire | Content analysis |
| Methodology | Interview | Diary analysis |
| Instrument | Case study | Historical analysis |
| Study | Survey | Evaluation |
| Test | Investigation | Experiment |
| Examination | Action research | Sample |
| Rating scale | Qualitative | Date |
| Observation | Quantitative | Research design |

In addition, hand-statistics was used to list and identify the research approaches and research methods in this study, and some charts about the findings were made by computer. It has taken a lot of time to complete this task for the purpose of this study.

## 4. Findings and Analysis

### 4.1 General Situations

As Table B3 shows, there were 1,099 articles published in the journal of Educational Research from 1960 to 2001, and 696 used one or two methods to conduct the study, giving 63.3 percent of the total number of articles. That is to say, more than half of the authors and researchers chose to use one research method, like a questionnaire or test (examination), to collect the data when they conducted their study. The statistics also show the numbers using qualitative, quantitative, and a mixture of approaches in the different periods since 1960.

**Table B3** Numbers and Percentages of Three Research Approaches

| Years | Total articles | Used articles | % | Qual methods | % | Quan methods | % | Mixture methods | % |
|---|---|---|---|---|---|---|---|---|---|
| 1960s | 233 | 82 | 35.2 | 6 | 7.3 | 72 | 87.8 | 3 | 3.6 |
| 1970s | 293 | 187 | 63.8 | 23 | 12.3 | 161 | 86.1 | 3 | 1.6 |
| 1980s | 271 | 161 | 59.4 | 35 | 21.7 | 120 | 74.5 | 6 | 3.7 |
| 1990s | 252 | 227 | 90.1 | 63 | 27.8 | 144 | 63.4 | 20 | 8.8 |
| 00-01 | 50 | 39 | 78 | 10 | 25.6 | 25 | 64.1 | 4 | 10 |
| Total | 1099 | 696 | 63.3 | 137 | 19.7 | 522 | 75 | 36 | 5.2 |

Notes: Total articles means all of the articles published in *Educational Research* from 1960 to 2001; Used articles means the articles using research methods among the total articles; Qual methods=qualitative methods; Quan methods=quantitative methods.

### 4.2 Different Methods Used from 1960 to 2001

Tables B4 and B5 show us the numbers of different methods used from 1960 to 2001. It is very clear that there were many kinds of research methods used to conduct educational research during the last four decades. Some of them were typical of qualitative research, some of them were typical of quantitative research in tradition, and a few of them involved a mixture of approaches. It is not easy to do a more large-scale literature survey about how people used the methods. So, in this study, the statistical data just came from one educational journal. Of course, it will be more significant if a large-scale survey can be done in the future by collecting data from more educational journals.

However, some significant results have been found even if this was a small-scale literature survey with a focus on just one journal. As Table B4 shows, quantitative methods, like questionnaires, tests, experiments, and rating scales, have been used as the main methods when educators were doing their research. Since 1960, the interview has been one method which is being used more and more, especially in the 1990s and the early years of this century.

**Table B4** Numbers of Different Methods Used from 1960–2001

| Order | Methods | 1960s | 1970s | 1980s | 1990s | 2000–2001 | Total |
|---|---|---|---|---|---|---|---|
| 1 | Questionnaire | 18 | 40 | 36 | 70 | 17 | 181 |
| 2 | Test (Examination) | 22 | 60 | 35 | 28 | 8 | 153 |
| 3 | Experiment | 16 | 25 | 10 | 15 | 0 | 66 |
| 4 | Rating scale | 5 | 13 | 12 | 14 | 0 | 44 |
| 5 | Interview | 4 | 12 | 14 | 41 | 6 | 77 |
| 6 | Observation | 0 | 8 | 12 | 8 | 2 | 30 |
| 7 | Measurement | 2 | 5 | 1 | 2 | 1 | 11 |
| 8 | Statistics | 2 | 13 | 21 | 3 | 0 | 39 |
| 9 | National survey | 7 | 5 | 5 | 6 | 1 | 24 |
| 10 | Diary analysis | 1 | 1 | 1 | 0 | 0 | 3 |
| 11 | Action research | 0 | 0 | 0 | 2 | 0 | 2 |
| 12 | Case study | 1 | 1 | 0 | 9 | 3 | 14 |
| 13 | Document analysis | 0 | 1 | 0 | 2 | 1 | 4 |
| 14 | Content analysis | 0 | 0 | 0 | 1 | 3 | 4 |
| 15 | Mixed methods | 3 | 3 | 6 | 20 | 4 | 36 |

In Table B5, we can see the numbers of people using three different research approaches, while we also can see the development and changes in the use of three different research approaches since 1960 in Figure B1. It is very obvious from Figure B1 that quantitative methods have been used as a main approach to carry out educational research from 1960 to 2001. The total numbers are 522 articles, and it is 75 percent of the total articles. In particular, the use of qualitative methods has increased since 1960. There were, for example, just six articles using qualitative methods in the 1960s, but it became 63 articles in the 1990s.

**Table B5** Numbers of Different Research Approaches

| Years | Qualitative methods | Quantitative methods | Mixture methods |
|---|---|---|---|
| 1960s | 6 | 72 | 3 |
| 1970s | 23 | 161 | 3 |
| 1980s | 35 | 120 | 6 |
| 1990s | 63 | 144 | 20 |
| 2000–2001 | 10 | 25 | 4 |
| Total | 137 | 522 | 36 |

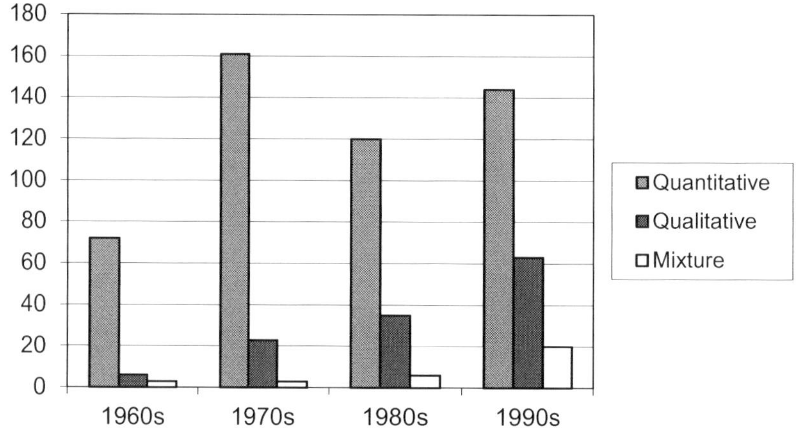


**Figure B1** Numbers' Changing of Different Research Methods

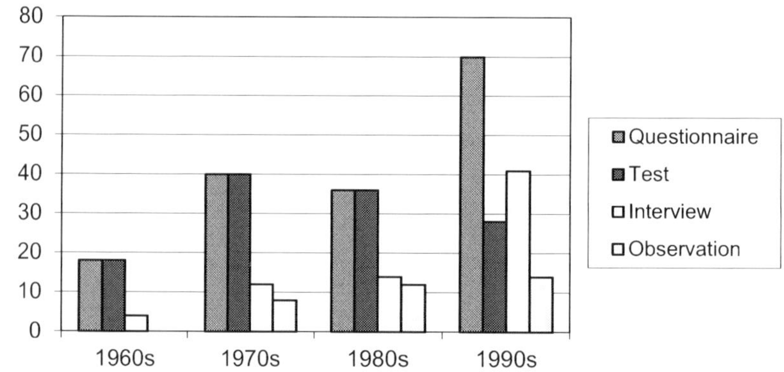


**Figure B2** Development and Changing of Four Kinds of Research Methods

## 4.3 Development and Change of the Different Research Approaches and Methods

These findings have shown us at the same time that there is a developmental trend from using a single method to using a mixture. I believe, according to this finding, there will be more and more mixed approaches and methods to be used in educational research in the future.

In addition, we can see the situation of development and changes in the use of interviews and observation during the last four decades in Figure B3. It shows us an increased trend since the 1970s. Many researchers used interviews and observation as the main tools for collecting data in classroom teaching research. That is to say, more and more educators/teacher researchers have recognized the importance of

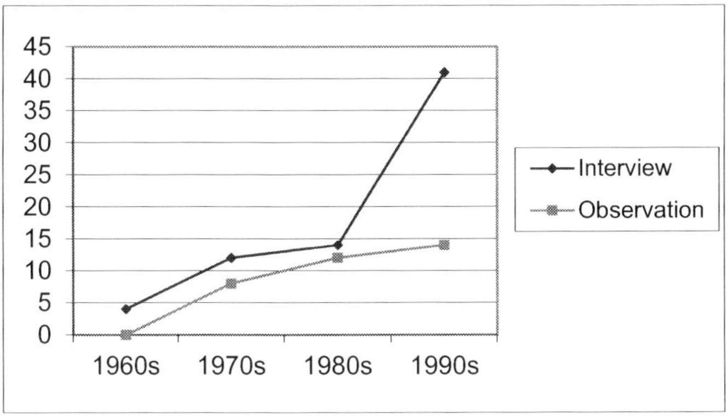


**Figure B3** The Development and Changing of Using Interview and Observation

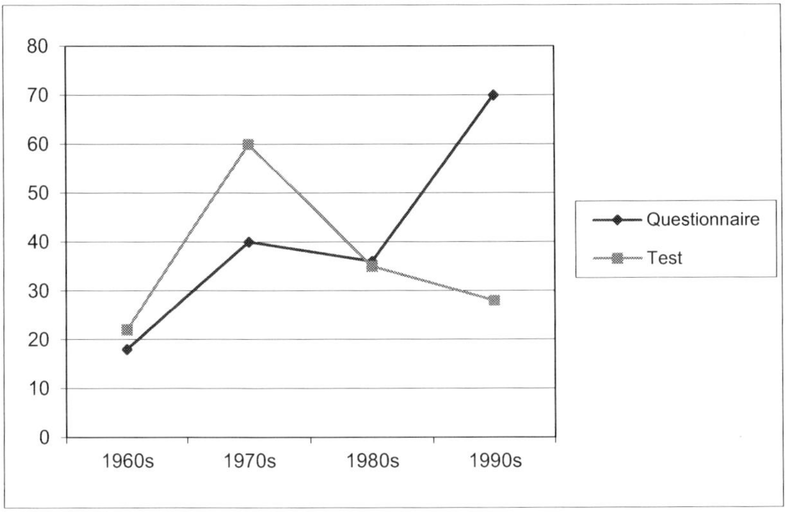


**Figure B4** Development and Changing Use of Questionnaires and Tests

using interviews and observation in doing educational research up to now. As the main methods for qualitative research, interview and observation indeed have their own advantages in collecting the understanding data in depth, making them very suitable for people who want to get data about something in detail to use when doing educational research. One important reason for this change was that more and more people found that teaching was very complicated. It was hard to understand teaching deeply by just employing the quantitative approach and the data of numbers form. So, it should be much better for people to collect qualitative data by using one-to-one interviews or focus group interviews and participant observation in the classroom.

By Figure B4, on the other hand, we also can see the development and changes in using questionnaires and tests in educational research since the 1960s. Due to the influence of the movement of measurement, which began in the late 1960s, many educators chose to use the test as a main method to collect the data. However, the questionnaire as a main quantitative method in tradition became more and more popular in the 1990s. It is very easy to find why people like to employ questionnaires to collect data in some of the books about research methods. A questionnaire is indeed a good way for educators to conduct their research on many kinds of educational topics. But it also has its limitations.

## 5. Discussion

### 5.1 Using Qualitative or Quantitative?

As the findings have shown us, many researchers used the more quantitative method than the qualitative method for their educational research from 1960 to 1990.

But, at the same time, we also found qualitative approach became an increased trend since the mid-1980. Hence, it is very hard to say which approach is the best one for doing educational research so far. It depends on the research topics and the purpose of the research. Before the mid-1980, educators mainly focus on the quantitative approach because of the research topics of experiments in education. However, more and more educators have recognized that both education and teaching is a very complex activity. You have to know what happened in the real classroom setting if you want to know teachers' and students' understanding of education and teaching. Whereas the main advantage of the qualitative approach just is to go deeper and live classroom practice.

Punch said that quantitative research is empirical research where the data are in the form of numbers. Qualitative research is empirical research where the data are not in the form of numbers.[9]

"Qualitative" implies a direct concern with experience as it is "lived" or "left" or "undergone." (In contrast, "quantitative" research, often taken to be the opposite idea, is indirect and abstracts and treats experiences as similar, adding or multiplying them together, or "quantifying" them).

As Punch indicates, quantitative research is, as the term suggests, concerned with the collection and analysis of data in numeric form. It tends to emphasize relatively large-scale and representative sets of date, and is often, falsely in our view, presented or perceived as being about the gathering of "facts." Qualitative research, on the other hand, is concerned with collecting and analyzing information in as many forms, cheifly non-numeric, as possible. It tends to focus on exploring, in as much detail as possible, small numbers of instances or examples which are seen as being interesting or illuminating, and aims to achieve "depth" rather than "breadth."

There has been widespread debate in recent years within many of the social sciences regarding the relative merits of quantitative and qualitative strategies for research. The positions taken by individual researchers vary considerably, from those who see the two strategies as entirely separate and based on alternative views of the world, to those who are happy to mix these strategies within their research projects. Because quantitative strategies have been seen as more scientific or "objective," qualitative researchers have felt the need to argue their case strongly. Qualitative research has become increasingly popular over the past two decades. Because some of the advantages of qualitative research have been recognized by many educational researchers. For example, it can explore the deeper and more complex problems in education. More and more qualitative researchers believe that since humans are conscious of their own behavior, the thoughts, feelings, and perceptions of their informants are vital. How people attach meaning and what meanings they attach are the bases of their behavior. The qualitative researcher is not concerned with objective truth, but rather with the truth as the informant perceives it.

How distinctive are qualitative and quantitative forms of research? On first consideration, the use of questionnaires as a research technique might be seen as a quantitative strategy, whereas interviews and observations might be thought of as qualitative techniques. In practice, however, it is often more complicated than that. Thus, interviews may be structured and analyzed in a quantitative manner, as when numeric data are collected or when non-numeric answers are categorized and coded in numeric form. Similarly, surveys may allow for open-ended responses and lead to the in-depth study of individual cases.

Hence, if we ask the question: which research approach is the best one for doing educational research? The answer might be that there is no best one that can be used to do any kind of research and also can get the best result. It depends on the topic of which the researcher has and the purpose which the researcher wants to reach. With the changes in the research topics in education that people concern about, the approach people use may be changed in different directions, for example, from quantitative to qualitative or a mixture of two approaches together in one research project. Even if different approaches have different functions, a mixture of approaches should be better to get a comprehensive understanding of all-round research on a topic.

## 5.2 Using One Method or More?

It is common, of course, for researchers to use more than one method. This is even more likely if you are carrying out your research project as part of a group, rather than on your own. Your main method might, for example, be a questionnaire survey, a set of interviews, or a series of observations, but this is likely to be complemented, at the very least, by some documentary analysis to enable you to explore relevant literature or policy. Most research projects in the social sciences are, therefore, in a general sense, multi-methods. Through this study, we have also found that there is no one method that can be used in any situation to get the best results. Using more than one method or combining two different approaches in the same research project should be one good way for people to get the best outcome from their research.

## 6. Conclusion and Recommendation

By the literature survey research focusing on the research approaches and research methods in education in this study, some conclusions have been drawn up below.

(1) The quantitative approach has been employed as a main research approach in education since the 1960s, in both small-scale research and large-scale research. The qualitative approach in educational research has begun to increase since the 1980s.
(2) Even if these two different approaches have their own advantages in doing educational research, they all have some limitations in terms of data collection and data analysis. To overcome the disadvantages and limitations of these two research approaches, more and more educational researchers have combined the qualitative and quantitative methods together since the 1990s. At the same time, more and more educational researchers pay much more attention to triangulation. Since the early 1990s, more and more mixed research, which combines the quantitative and qualitative approaches together, has been used to do educational research. The main reason is that people have recognized to combine the qualitative and quantitative together in doing educational research can make use of the advantages of each and also can get much better results.
(3) Questionnaire as a main method of quantitative approach has been used by different kinds of researchers. Interview as a main method of qualitative approach has become more and more popular in today's educational research.
(4) In this study, it was found by literature survey that the function of the traditional single method like questionnaire or observation, or interview has been enlarged. Sometimes, it is not easy to say whether the method really belongs to either a qualitative or quantitative approach, because the qualitative and quantitative aspects have been combined together in one method. As Blaxter et al. (2001) argue:

> How distinctive are qualitative and quantitative forms of research? On first consideration, the use of questionnaires as a research technique might be seen as a quantitative strategy, whereas interviews and observations might be thought of as qualitative techniques. In practice, however, it is often more complicated than that. Thus, interviews may be structured and analyzed in a quantitative manner, as when numeric data are collected or when non-numeric answers are categorized and coded in numeric form. Similarly, surveys may allow for open-ended responses and lead to the in-depth study of individual cases.

In sum, the different methods have different functions. Hence, different research purposes should employ different methods when people conduct research in most cases. However, this literature survey research has shown us that there has been a new trend in educational research in recent years in that mixed-methodology approaches are becoming more and more popular in education. The reason is very clear because a mixed methodology, of course, has a number of advantages within educational research, as well as other social science disciplines, and may be able to enhance the quality of research work.

The purpose of this study is not to suggest that a mixed methodology is the only suitable research design for any educational research topics, but rather that it is indeed often an appropriate, and at times desirable design. In practice, there is no one best method that can be used to do any kind of research and get the most reliable and valid results. The overall choice needs, of course, to be the most suitable one to achieve the objectives of many kinds of educational research. So, by adopting some assumptions, the educational researcher should ensure that the final product maximizes the strengths of a mixed methods approach. For example, by using qualitative methods, like observation, or unstructured interviews, the educational researcher may develop an overall "picture" of the subject under investigation. This may guide the initial phases of the research. Quantitative analysis may be more appropriate to assess students' learning achievement and school effectiveness, and so on.

In addition, quantitative analysis in educational research may confirm or disconfirm any apparently significant data that emerge from the study. Quantitative methods can be used to enable statistical testing of the strength of such a relationship. If such a relationship is determined, then quantitative methods are weaker in providing an explanation. Qualitative methods may assist the researcher in understanding the underlying explanations of significance.

# Understanding Classroom Observation: Theory and Application

## 1. Introduction

### 1.1 Research on Teaching and Learning in Classroom

Teaching and learning are always regarded as the center of the educational activity of school in modern society. At the same time, teaching and learning in the classroom have been concerned with their special position and functions in the implementation of the school curriculum and reaching the educational aim. As Professor Bert Creemers points out on the cover of Daniel Muijs and David Revnolds's (2001) book *Effective Teaching: Evidence and Practice* that research into student learning and achievement shows that classroom teaching is at the heart of the process of schooling. What teachers do in the classroom is the factor which most strongly affects pupils' progress in school. There are many reasons that can be used as evidences for showing this very important position of classroom teaching to improve the quality of education. One of the important reasons is that students spend a vast amount of time in their classroom when they are at school. As well known, the purpose of teaching is to facilitate students' learning by using a variety of instructional strategies in the special classroom setting. Up to now, classroom is still the main instructional setting where the various activities of teaching and learning take place all over the world, even if there have been greatly changed in teaching organization with the learning society comes, like teaching and learning by the Internet.[1]

Jackson's (1968) book *Life in the Classroom* estimates that this is as high as approximately 7,000 hours by the end of primary school, whereas the title of Rutter et al.'s (1979) book *Fifteen Thousand Hours* suggests that this figure rises to 15,000 hours by the completion of secondary.[2] Every day in classrooms around the world, billions of events take place: teachers ask children questions, new concepts are explained, pupils talk to each other, some of those who misbehave are reprimanded, and others are ignored. Jackson (1968) reported a study in which it was found that primary teachers engaged in as many as 1,000 such interpersonal exchanges in a single day. This means if the pattern is repeated, 5,000 in a week, 200,000 in a year, and millions in a professional career. In another study of videotapes by Adams and Biddle (1970), there was a change in activity every 5 to 18 seconds, and there was an average each lesson of 174 changes in who talked and who listened each. The job of teaching can be as busy as that of a telephonist or a sales assistant during peak shopping hours.[3]

As these results above, it, no doubt, is very important for educators and teachers to improve the quality of classroom of teaching and learning by doing research on classroom teaching and learning, or evaluating classroom teaching.

## 1.2 Observation as a Valid Method of Research on Classroom Teaching and Learning

There are many research methods that can be used by researchers or teachers to conduct their research projects on teaching and learning according to the information provided by some relative books and articles, like tests, experiments, questionnaires, interviewings, and so on. Of course, classroom observation is one of research methods on classroom teaching and learning among them. Hopkins points out that "classroom research, in the sense that I refer to it here, is an act undertaken by teachers, to enhance their own or educational theory in practice, or as a means of evaluating and implementing whole school priorities."[4]

There is much research on classroom teaching using observation. One famous study of them is the ORACLE, namely Observational Research and Classroom Learning Evaluation. The original ORACLE study was carried out in 1976, and the second one was conducted in 1996 after 20 years. The findings of ORACLE included different aspects of teaching and learning in the primary classroom in UK. It was seen as a typical study using classroom observation.

Why do some researchers like to use observation as a method of collecting data? The answer is because that "observational data are attractive as they afford the research the opportunity to gather 'live' data from 'live' situations."[5] In addition, the researcher is given the opportunity to look at what is taking place *in situ* rather than secondhand. This enables researchers to understand the context of programs, to be open-ended and inductive, to see things that might otherwise be unconsciously missed, to discover things that participants might not only freely talk about in interview situations, to move beyond perception-based data (e.g., opinions in interviews), and to access personal knowledge.

### 1.3 The Purposes of This Assignment

Since the strong interest in classroom observation, the purposes of this assignment are planned to review the basic functions, principles, and main methods and techniques of classroom observation by related research literature, to examine the strengths and limitations of using classroom observation as a method and data source for studying teaching and learning or improving both of them, and then further to consider the differences of doing classroom observation in different cultural context.

The key questions in this study are below:

(1) Why do people use classroom observation as a method for doing research on teaching and learning? Can the classroom observation be used for qualitative or quantitative?
(2) What are the functions of classroom observation?
(3) What are the basic principles of classroom observation?
(4) What are the main techniques and methods of classroom observation?
(5) What are strengths and limitations of using classroom observation? And why?
(6) Are there some differences in doing classroom observation between English researchers and Chinese researchers?

## 2. The Theory of Classroom Observation

### 2.1 The Functions and Purposes of Classroom Observation

Classroom observation is now becoming far more common than it once was.[6] However, why do people choose classroom observation? What functions and purposes does classroom observation have? Is there some important worth for people to do classroom observation? These questions should be answered before starting to talk about the application of classroom observation in practice. These also are regarded as the basic theory that we should know when we want to do classroom observation.

From some books and articles of research on classroom observation, we know that classroom observation has many functions and also can be used to reach different purposes, broadly speaking, in modern educational research. In this part of my study, I will examine the main functions and purposes of classroom observation by reviewing the relative literature in this area. The purpose of doing this work is to better understand the reason why people choose to use classroom observation as a method to do research, and make more clear about the functions and purposes of classroom observation.

Actually, many researchers have mentioned the functions and purposes of classroom observation in their studies about observation. For example, observation plays a crucial role not only in classroom research, but also more generally in supporting the professional growth of teachers and in the process of school development. Classroom observation should be part of routine monitoring, and observing teachers' work has long been part of the normal routine in many schools, mainly because staff's timely and effective observation and feedback are of immense value. They are helpful in giving them support and encouragement. In relation to school development, the more information a school has on the quality of teaching and learning, that is, on what actually happens in the classrooms, the more effective the planning to raise and maintain standards is likely to be.

Wragg thinks that the classroom observation for the purpose of evaluation can be listed in at least several aspects below. For example, a primary teacher is being appraised by the deputy head who comes for the morning to look at language and number work; a secondary science teacher is watched by the head of the department during a one-and-a-half-hour laboratory session as part of the school's teacher appraisal exercise; a student on teaching practice is seen by a supervising teacher or tutor; a maths lesson is watched by a local authority inspector conducting a review of mathematics teaching in the local authority; a class of seven-year-olds is observed by a teacher who is also a textbook writer preparing a series of gymnastics cards for young children; a researcher studying teachers' questioning techniques watches a secondary history class, noting down the question asked by the teacher and the responses obtained.

In addition, some researchers also agree that classroom observation is more successful as a strategy for improvement than for making personal decisions. If it is used for personnel decisions, the system must be carefully constructed and carried out. Helping teachers develop through the classroom, using observing for reflective teaching, and positive teacher appraisal through classroom observation, and so on, are also the functions and purposes of classroom observation.[7]

Finally, as a classroom teacher, the information you collect as an observer can be used to analyze student learning, the learning environment, and student attitudes toward learning and scho oling. Based on these analyses, you will make certain conclusions about your teaching effectiveness and the progress your students are making academically and socially. These conclusions will then form the basis for the next phase of instructional planning.

In short, classroom observation, by the analysis from above, indeed has many functions and also can be used to serve different purposes, from research or improvement to teaching and learning. Understanding these functions and purposes of classroom observation is very important for those who want to do classroom observation.

### 2.2 The Process and Principles of Classroom Observation

Hopkins (2002), in his book *A Teacher's Guide to Classroom Research*, has developed a "three-phase observation cycle" according to early research in North America. I strongly believe that it is a very useful process model for both researchers and teachers when they plan to do classroom observation. In my opinion, it also can be seen as a good example of doing systematic classroom observation. Herein I would like to give a brief description of his cycle below.

According to Hopkins, the "three-phase observation cycle," originally called "clinical supervision," was initially developed in North America as a method of supervising student teachers, but it is well suited for use in classroom research situations. The three essential phases of this classroom observation process are *a planning meeting, the classroom observation itself,* and *a feedback discussion.* The *planning meeting* provides the observer and teacher with an opportunity to reflect on the proposed lesson, and this leads to a mutual decision to collect observational data on an aspect of the teacher's classroom practice. During the *classroom observation* phase, the observer observes the teaching in the classroom and collects objective data on that aspect of the teaching or learning they agreed upon earlier. It is during the feedback discussion that the observer and the teacher share the information gathered during the observation, decide on appropriate action, agree with a record of the discussion, and often plan another round of observation. He thinks that it is important to realize that all three phases of the process need to be gone through systematically to be effective.

Hopkins points out at the same time that there are a number of principles that are important to consider in this approach to classroom observation. First, the climate of interaction between teacher and observer needs to be non-threatening, helping, and one of mutual trust. Second, the focus of the activity should be on improving classroom practice and reinforcing successful strategies, rather than on criticism of unsuccessful patterns of behavior, or changing the teacher's personality. Third, the process depends on the collection and use of objective observational data, not unsubstantiated value judgments. Fourth, teachers are encouraged to make inferences about their teaching from the data, and to use the data to construct 'hypotheses' that can be tested out in the future. Next, each cycle of observation is part of an ongoing process that builds on the other. Finally, both observer and teacher are encouraged in a mutual process of professional development that can lead to improvement in teaching and observational skills for both. And he believes, in all these ways, classroom observation can support both specific purposes, as well as the more general aspirations of teacher and school development.

It is very obvious that Hopkins' cycle model has shown us that systematic observation would give more benefit for teacher's improvement, as well as for research purposes. However, the next step for doing classroom observation is to choose suitable methods and techniques.

## 3. The Methods and Techniques of Classroom Observation

There are many different methods and techniques that can be used to serve the classroom observation from the literature. As I know it will be very hard to examine all kinds of methods and techniques of classroom observation in detail for a shorter paper. So, in this study, I will focus on examining five main methods of classroom observation with related techniques, namely open classroom observation, focused classroom observation, structured classroom observation, and systematic classroom observation.

### 3.1 Open Observation

Open observation in classroom teaching and learning is a simple kind of method used by different people, especially the teachers' colleagues. In this approach, the observer literally uses a blank sheet of paper to record the lesson. The observer either notes down key points about the lesson or uses a personal form of shorthand for making a verbatim recording of classroom transactions. The aim is usually to enable subsequent reconstruction of the lesson. Variation of this approach is to agree to record only those events that fit into following broad categories or under certain headings:

(1) Presentation
(2) Indirect teaching
(3) Direct teaching
(4) Voice
(5) Questioning strategies
(6) Feedback
(7) Subject matter
(8) Expectations

A problem with this approach is that it is often unfocused and can lead to premature judgments. The best way to handle this approach is to make an open recording as factual as possible and leave interpretation until a discussion after the lesson. Because of its general nature, it is important to stick closely to each component of the three-phase cycle; otherwise, what began as a mutual approach to observation could result in a one-way monologue.

As one of the classroom observations, open observation has its own strengths. For example, for classroom teachers and their colleagues, it is simple way and very easy to do because there are no rigors requirements to use it; There is no usually need to use a tape-recorder or videotape for keeping real classroom circumstances; And there is always no more pressure to the teacher when observed during classroom. But this method also has its limitations. The information obtained by this method will not be enough if a researcher wants to know more information about the classroom activities and to give a detailed analysis or evaluation of teaching and learning. The obvious shortcoming of open observation is its less focus and systematic. So this kind of observation is better to use for improving teaching but not research on teaching.

### 3.2 Focused Observation

There are, in practice, different kinds of focused observations developed for severing different purposes. Hopkins lists five key features of classroom observation, including joint planning, focus, establishing criteria, observation skills, and feedback. Meanwhile, he points out that there are two broad ways of categorizing the focus of classroom observation activities: general and specific. The more specific and negotiated the focus of the classroom observation, the more likely it is that the 'data' so gathered will be useful for developmental purposes. If the focus for classroom observation is related to the development plan, then the observation could contribute both to teacher and school development.

Marriott also divided classroom observation into two broad categories: general and focused. At the same time, he argues that focused observation can be done in three different kinds: whole class, group, and individual.[8] Examples of focused whole-class observation could include questioning techniques, the participation of boys and girls or different ethnic groups, the effectiveness of time management, and group dynamics within the class. The main advantages of this approach are that it enables the researcher to concentrate on a more limited aspect of teaching and learning and not be concerned about what you might be missing. You are in a position to give detailed feedback to the teacher on an aspect of teaching that you have both agreed is important. The main disadvantages is that in certain types of specific focus, for example, time management, it can be difficult to reach conclusions about what pupils are actually learning, and it would not be easy to make judgment on the effectiveness of differentiation. It is easier to record the mechanics of teaching than it is to evaluate its impact.

However, an observation with a group focus would normally involve the observer in working with one group of pupils, observing their response to the lesson and evaluating what they are doing. This is often used to look at the provision for and response of pupils with special educational needs or English as an additional language, but it could be equally well used with a mixed-ability group. This approach also enables you to concentrate on a more limited aspect of teaching and learning.

The main disadvantage of this approach is that too close a focus on a group may distort your view of the effectiveness of the teaching for the class as a whole.

Finally, an individual focus could be to track a pupil for a specific period of time, such as a morning, if time permits, a whole day, to see what sort of experience the pupil has and how well the work is matched to his or her needs. This has the additional advantage of providing a great deal of information about the quality of teaching and the implementation of whole-school policies in different classes and subjects.

### 3.3 Structured Observation

Structured observation, as used to monitor classroom events, requires an observer to assign such events into previously defined categories. The three stages of the process involve (a) the recording of events in a systematic manner as they happen, (b) the coding of these events into prespecified categories, and (c) subsequent analysis of the events to give descriptions of teacher-pupil interaction.[9]

In structured observation, systematic recording can often be used as a technique in which the observer assigns what is observed into previously specified or defined categories, and records it on a prepared schedule according to agreed procedures. These procedures are used to gather data that can be treated quantitatively, summarised in numerical form, and related to other data using simple statistical techniques. Normally, the purpose of studies that use these types of schedules is to quantify the incidence of particular classroom events, to seek a relationship which can be tested by statistical methods and which may be generalized to hold across similar cases.

Even if structured observation can provide both quantitative data and qualitative data for researchers, in China so far many people still think it is a difficult method for using it to do classroom research. Because you have to do much more preparation before doing it in the classroom, as mentioned above.

### 3.4 Systematic Observation

Moore divided classroom observation into two basic types: non-systematic and systematic.[10] With non-systematic observation, the observer or teacher simply watches and takes note of the behaviors, characteristics, and personal interactions that seem significant. With systematic observation, the observer typically measures the frequency, duration, magnitude, or latency of specific behaviors or events.

Interest in systematic observation as a practical technique has been gaining wider use since the 1980s. Systematic observation helps those with posts of responsibility to identify strengths and weaknesses in individuals and in the school as a whole. They are then in a position to spread good practice and help teachers to learn from each other. Likewise, where weaknesses are identified, individuals can be supported, and whole-school needs can be fed into the professional development program.

Systematic observation is often seen as a way of observing behavior in classroom by using a schedule, or list of categories, of probable behavior. Each category is then 'checked off' as the behavior is observed. The technique assumes that the teacher has already carried out sufficient preliminary, exploratory investigations to be able to decide which behaviors are relevant. Nevertheless, having devised the schedule, it can be a very quick and easy-to-administer technique for collecting information.

In addition, using scales also is a tool when doing systematic observation. However, Hopkins thinks that there are some potential problems in the use of coding or interaction scales. The first problem is that most scales were not designed for use by teachers. Their original intent was as research tools for analyzing classroom. It is important to stress that these are tools teachers can use to enhance their practice. The teacher-researcher's orientation is always action. The second difficulty is that each scale represents the author's concept of a situation. One is looking at classroom through someone else's eyes: their purpose and perceptions could be very different from one's own. It is easy, therefore, to get trapped within the intentions of the researcher who designed the scale. Third, there is a heavy emphasis on quantitative methods in systematic observation. This frequently results in a conflict between statistical rigour and analytical richness.

As I know, there are just very few educational researchers now in China who use systematic observation just for the purpose of their teaching reform experiments towards the new national curriculum. Most Chinese educators think that it is very hard to do because of the time spent and difficulty planning. In addition, there are no better techniques for doing systematic observation developed up to now.

## 4. Discussion

Classroom teaching is a complex enterprise, with a very large number of interacting variables at play. Because of this, classroom observation becomes highly challenging. Simpson and Tuson argue that when faced with the variety of research techniques available for the collection of information, it may seem difficult to decide which approach would be best.[11] In coming to a decision, it is important to remember that no data collection procedure is perfect. Each has its own strengths and deficiencies of the most relevant technique for your particular purposes. So when we decide to use classroom observation as a data collection procedure for our special research purposes, we have to consider its advantages and disadvantages in advance. Even if I have talked about some strengths and limitations of different kinds of classroom observations above, in this part, I will focus on discussing the general strengths and limitations of using classroom observation to gather research data and to improve teachers' teaching and students' learning. At the same time, I will make some considerations about classroom observation used in different cultural contexts, for example, in the Chinese classroom settings and British classroom settings.

### 4.1 The Strengthens of Using Classroom Observation

For many experienced researchers, observation is the most satisfying technique to use in investigations since it brings forth the "sweetest of data." As Delamont (1992) said, "Actually observing life in educational institutions is my favorite kind of data collection. A pile of documents, a well-written book, or a cooperative interviewee may excite others, but I would always prefer to sit and watch something. The data gathered by watching and listening over weeks, even months, are for me the sweetest jams and the most aromatic oils and spices." At the same time, classroom observation also is the favorite kind of data collection of some professional researchers and teacher researchers.

How to be more specific, what are the key strengths of using classroom observation as a method of data collection? I think there are at least four aspects of it according to examine the literature above and some of my understanding from my own experiences of doing research:

(1) Real setting

Classroom observation permits access directly to the classroom setting and see what happens in classroom. Compared with other techniques like questionnaire surveys or interviews with teachers and students, classroom observation can give the researcher a good opportunity to watch the teacher's teaching and student's learning in a real situation of teaching practice. The information comes from the researcher's observing and recording of classroom situations.

(2) Multiple angles

As Blaster mentions that "the observation method involves the researcher in watching, recording, and analyzing events of interest." Indeed, classroom observation can combine watching, listening, and recording together to get research information. In China, there is a proverb: if you want to know the taste of a pear, you have to eat it by yourself. There is the same sense for using classroom observation. By observing in classroom, you can see not only the behaviors of the teacher and students, but also can listen to their talking and record the data. As a researcher, you will believe the data are indeed fair and objective.

(3) Multiple techniques

One feature of classroom observations is their flexibility. It can be used through multiple techniques to get different types of data. For example, as mentioned in the third part of this study, open observation, focused observation, structured observation, or systematic observation. And the data will be qualitative or quantitative according to different research purposes.

(4) First-hand evidence

By observing the activities of teachers and students in the classroom, as a researcher, you can get first-hand evidence, whatever your purposes are for studying teaching and learning or trying to improve teachers' teaching, and or for professional development. Classroom observation also can be used as evidence to check the data from other methods.

### 4.2 The Limitations of Using Classroom Observation

Even if there are many strengths to using classroom observation as a method of data collection, it still has some limitations. As we know, there is no perfect method without shortcomings in the world. Simpson and Tuson say that if observation as a technique is so useful, why is it not used more often in research? Generally speaking, it has two main weaknesses: its high demand on time, effort, and resources; and its susceptibility to observer bias. However, in my opinion, there are at least four limitations below.

(1) Time spend

Blaster uses observation as a method of collecting data—whether you also act as a participant in the events you are observing or not—is, like interviewing, which is potentially very time-consuming. The time absorbed occurs not just during the observation, but afterwards as well, when you come to interpret and analyze what you have recorded. Pre-categorizing and structuring your observation can reduce the time commitment dramatically, though at the risk of losing both detail and flexibility.

(2) Small sample

In large survey research by using a questionnaire, you may have a big sample of 500 subjects or much more for investigation. And also, the sample will have a broad representative. However, it is very hard for you to observe several hundred people in a classroom observation research. So, many case studies use observation as a method for collecting data. Normally the sample in a case study is related small. Even if there is a related small sample in observation research, it will last a longe time for the researcher to go to the classroom many times to get the research data.

(3) Setting limited

Setting limited should be an obvious feature of classroom observation. The classroom is a special setting for researchers to do their study. You, as a researcher, must be sitting at the back of the classroom and observing the teaching and learning, not sitting at home waiting for the questionnaires to come back. You could not get any information if you have no opportunity to sit in the classroom. So, as a classroom researcher, classroom is your research setting, not any other places.

(4) Personal perspectives

As we know, observation is a personal activity in most cases. One sits at the back of the classroom and watches the activities which teachers and students are doing with taking some records. In this kind of research, personal perspectives often are involved with the results of observation because of the different angles to observe and different tools to use. In addition, everyone has past experiences and biases that can easily distort what he or she sees. Just for this reason, many researchers would like to do their observation with some other methods together, like interviewing after observation, so that they can get more information from more angles.

### 4.3 Classroom Observation: Qualitative Approach and Quantitative Approach

Classroom observation can be used for collecting quantitative or qualitative data in light of different research purposes. There are many ways of attempting to quantify what happens in the classroom. At the same time, there are also some researchers who would like to explore classroom life by qualitative approach. It largely depends on the sense in which researchers have to see the study. However, quantitative and qualitative approaches need not be seen as polar opposites as they can often complement each other. In other words, classroom observation not only can use quantitative methods, and but also can use qualitative methods. It is perfectly possible to adopt a variety of approaches to classroom observation, as well as favor a single one.

Wragg argues that systematic analysis of lessons has often concentrated on a number of matters in the classroom. They include the following, some of which overlap with each other:

(1) Personality
(2) Verbal interaction
(3) Non-verbal
(4) Activity
(5) Management skills
(6) Affective
(7) Cognition
(8) Sociological

Of course, all of these aspects of classroom life can also be studied by qualitative methods, and indeed have been, especially such matters as relationships, emotional tone, the use or misuse of power, and status.

Rating scales is one of the techniques used during quantitative classroom observation. Many researchers choose this one to conduct their quantitative observation. Especially the rating scales are often best employed by observers who will see many classrooms, as they are more likely to be able to build up experience at assigning the grades in different contexts, whereas those who see only one or two teachers may not be sure how to use a particular scale. Sometimes observers will use a measure of frequency, rather than intensity, and concentrate more on actual behavior instead of personality.

This approach was criticized for a number of reasons, some self-evident, others more technical. The most frequent comment is that one rater's "4" may not mean the same as another rater's, though it is possible to train observers until they show quite high agreement with each other.

To avoid the shortcomings of the rating scale in a quantitative observation, some researchers have developed another technique called the category system. In view of the difficulty of devising homemade categories, many observers prefer to use someone else's schedule. The classroom observation literature is now full of published category systems, some devised for research projects, others for teacher training or appraisal. The Flanders Interaction Analysis Category System (FIAC) is one of the famous category systems used in doing classroom observation. It is a typical example of a simple category system that has been widely used in its original or modified form in teacher training, lesson analysis, and research. The advantage of FIAC is not difficult to learn or apply in practice. But its limitation is more time be used. So it should be a good method and more suitable for professional researchers than teacher researchers.

In practice, classroom observation not only can apply quantitative methods, but also can use qualitative methods. As Wragg says that just as there are many ways of quantifying what happens in the classroom, so there are numerous approaches that try to probe beneath the surface of events, to elicit the meanings sometimes deeply buried, the interpretations and explanations, significance and impact of classroom life. For reaching these kinds of purposes, qualitative methods should be employed as data collection. Observers who use qualitative methods are of many kinds. Most informal and semi-formal observations of lessons, such as teachers sitting in on each other's class, the supervision of student teachers, and visitors to schools who have come to "watch some teaching," tend to adopt qualitative rather than quantitative approaches. In the literature on qualitative research, there are numerous overlapping concepts for qualitative approaches, like phenomenology, symbolic interactionism, naturalism and ethogenics, and so on. These are not the only key terms and concepts, but some of their relevance to classroom observation and the issues they raise. However, in practice, most teachers are not familiar with these concepts. So, it is not easy for teachers to use it. In addition, quantitative methods and qualitative methods often are combined to use by some researchers in one observation project.

## 5. Conclusion

By examining the functions and the methods of classroom observation above, there are some ideas following that can be found as the conclusions of using classroom observation in this study.

First, classroom observation is an important method or tool for collecting research data about what happens in real classroom life. It also can be used for different research purposes and different contexts. There is an increased trend to use classroom observation for researching classroom life or improving teaching and learning. Wragg points out that classroom observation can be used in several different but related contexts. He outlines seven contexts for classroom observation. They are initial teacher training, in-service training, and professional development, studying pupils, curriculum development and evaluation, job analysis, teacher appraisal, and observation by laypeople. Except for these kinds of setting, there are also some classroom observations focusing on researching the teachers' teaching and reflective practice. It should be recognized that the research on teaching and learning by classroom observation is the main context.

Secondly, there are many useful observational methods that can be used to conduct research projects in classroom. But it is very important for researchers to choose the best ones to suit their project. It is also necessary for people to know the advantages and limitations of classroom observation before they do it.

Thirdly, classroom observation not only can be used to collect qualitative data, but also quantitative data. It largely depends on what the research purpose is. Quantitative data is good for giving an assessment level on teachers' teaching or students' learning. And the qualitative data is good for giving some suggestions to teachers to improve their teaching.

Fourthly, there will be some new changes in classroom observation with the development of new teaching techniques like multi-medium used in classroom. More and more interactions will be changed from teachers and students to techniques (computer). This will indeed influence the traditional methods of classroom observation.

Finally, classroom observation as a method for data collecting seems not very popular in China up to now. Most Chinese educational researchers and teachers still think that it is very hard to use because of the time spent and the hard recording of data. But I believe that Chinese researchers and teachers will recognize very soon the importance of using classroom observation to improve teaching and learning over time.

# Notes

## CHAPTER ONE CONTEMPORARY TEACHING AND ITS PARADIGMS

1. T. Husen, "Research Paradigms in Education," in *Issues in Educational Research*, ed. J. P. Keeves and G. Lakomski (Oxford: Pergamon, 1999), 31.
2. Norman K. Denzin and Yvonna S. Lincoln, *Handbook of Qualitative Research* (London: Sage Publications, 1994), 107.
3. J. C. Walker and C. W. Evers, "Research in Education: Epistemological Issues," in *Issues in Educational Research*, ed. J. P. Keeves and G. Lakomski (Oxford: Pergamon, 1999), 31.
4. R. B. Burns, "Paradigms for Research in Teaching," in *The International Encyclopaedia of Teaching and Teacher Education*, ed. L.W. Anderson, 2nd ed. (Oxford: Pergamon, 1995), 96.
5. R. B. Burns, "Paradigms for Research in Teaching," in *The International Encyclopaedia of Teaching and Teacher Education*, ed. L.W. Anderson, 2nd ed. (Oxford: Pergamon, 1995), 91.
6. G. Highet, *The Art of Teaching* (London: Methuen and Co., Ltd., 1951), 17–24.
7. Ibid.
8. E. W. Eisner, *The Educational Imagination: On the Design and Evaluation of School Program* (New York: Macmillan, 1985), 175–76.
9. Rosie Turner-Bisset, *Expert Teaching: Knowledge and Pedagogy to Lead the Profession* (London: David Fulton Publishers, 2001), 2.
10. Ibid.
11. P. Woods, *Researching the Art of Teaching: Ethnography for Educational Use* (London and New York: Routledge, 1996), 15.
12. B. Joyce et al., *Models of Learning: Tools for Teaching* (Buckingham: Open University Press, 1997), 24–34.
13. R. F. Biehler and J. Snowman, *Psychology Applied to Teaching*, 7th ed. (Boston: Houghton Mifflin Company, 1993), 20.
14. R. D. Parsons, *Educational Psychology: A Practitioner-Researcher Model of Teaching* (London: Wadsworth, 2001), 10.
15. Rosie Turner-Bisset, *Expert Teaching: Knowledge and Pedagogy to Lead the Profession* (London: David Fulton Publishers, 2001), 3.
16. L. B. Kezima, *College Teaching Methods* (New York and London: Longman, 1985), 22–23.
17. Rosie Turner-Bisset, *Expert Teaching: Knowledge and Pedagogy to Lead the Profession* (London: David Fulton Publishers, 2001), 5.

18. A. R. Tom, *Teaching as a Moral Craft* (London: Penguim, 1984), 5.
19. D. A. Schon, *The Reflective Practitioner: How Professional Think in Action* (New York: Basic Books).
20. A. Pollard, *Reflective Teaching in the Primary School: A Handbook for the Classroom*, 3rd ed. (London: Cassell, 1983), 66–68.
21. D. G. Armstrong et al., *Teaching Today: An Introduction to Education*, 6th ed. (New Jersery: Merrill prentice Hall, 2001), 11–15.
22. Rosie Turner-Bisset, *Expert Teaching: Knowledge and Pedagogy to Lead the Profession* (London: David Fulton Publishers, 2001), 10.

## CHAPTER TWO DEVELOPMENTAL CHARACTERISTICS OF CONTEMPORARY TEACHING THEORY AND PRACTICE

1. Ministry of Education, *Basic Education Curriculum Reform Outline*, 2001.
2. Shirley R. Steinberg and Joe L. Kincheloe, eds., *Students as Researchers: Creating Meaningful Classrooms*, trans. Zou Jin (China Light Industry Press, 2002), 17.
3. Allen. C. Ornstein and Francis P. Hankins, *Curriculum: Basics, Principles, and Problems* (Jiangsu Education Press, 2002), 163.
4. Shirley R. Steinberg and Joe L. Kincheloe, eds., *Students as Researchers: Creating Meaningful Classrooms*, trans. Zou Jin (China Light Industry Press, 2002), 55.
5. Yaspers, *What Is Education*, trans. Zou Jin (Sanlian Reading Press, March 1991), 70.
6. Shirley R. Steinberg and Joe L. Kincheloe, eds., *Students as Researchers: Creating Meaningful Classrooms*, trans. Zou Jin (China Light Industry Press, 2002), 19.
7. Serena Williams Doerr, *Postmodern Curriculum View*, trans. Wang Hongyu (Education Science Press, 2001), 238.
8. Liu Xilang, *Clinical Guidance in Classroom Teaching—Analysis and Guidance of Teaching Behavior* (People's Education Press, 1998), 87.
9. Allen. C. Ornstein and Francis P. Hankins, *Curriculum: Basics, Principles, and Problems* (Jiangsu Education Press, 2002), 400.
10. Ibid., 342.
11. F. W. Parkay and B. H. Stanford, *Becoming A Teacher* (Boston: Allyn and Bacon, 2001), 465.
12. Li Dingren and Xu Jicun, "Progress and Trend Analysis of Teaching Theory Research in China," *Journal of Northwest Normal University* (2001).
13. Ibid.
14. Qin Bing, "Meta-Analysis of Several Issues in the Study of Teaching Theory: On the Scientific Teaching Theory," *Journal of Luoyang Normal University* (2001).
15. Li Changji, "Scientism Research Methods in Pedagogy: Background, Trajectory, and Characteristics," *Journal of Qiqihar University* (1999).
16. Ibid.
17. Li Changji, "The Humanist Research Paradigm of Pedagogy: Background, Trajectory, and Characteristics," *Journal of Qiqihar University* (2001).
18. Ibid.
19. Xu Jicun, "Conceptual Analysis of Teaching Theory," *Journal of Northwest Normal University* (1999).
20. Sun Yingguang, "What Is It That Guides Teaching," *Education Theory and Practice* (2002).
21. Ibid.
22. Wang Liusheng, "Theoretical Reflections on Pedagogical Research," *Curriculum, Textbooks, and Teaching Methods* (1994): 11.

23. Zhang Chuting, ***Teaching Theses*** (Beijing: Higher Education Press, 1999), 4–5.
24. Tan Xiaolong, "Review of the Development of Chinese Pedagogy in the 20th Century," *Journal of Hubei Institute of Education* (1997): 3.
25. Ibid.
26. Wang Liusheng, "Teaching Theory toward Modernization: Progress and Reflection on China's Teaching Theory in the 90s," *Curriculum, Textbooks and Teaching Methods* (1998): 10.
27. Zhang Xiongfei, Inducing ***Thinking and Exploring-Developing Quality Teaching*** (Liaoning People's Publishing House, 1999), 35.
28. Ibid., 23.
29. Ibid., 23.
30. Ibid., 26.
31. Ibid., 41.
32. Ibid., 35.
33. Yang Qiliang, ***Confusion and Choice—New Teaching Theory in the 20th Century*** (Shandong Education Press, 1996), 259.
34. Zhang Xiongfei, ***Inducing Thinking and Exploring-Developing Quality Teaching*** (Liaoning People's Publishing House, 1999), 184.
35. Xiao Wen'e, ***Primary School Teaching Theory*** (Higher Education Press, 1997), 206.
36. Zhang Xiongfei, ***Inducing Thinking and Exploring-Developing Quality Teaching*** (Liaoning People's Publishing House, 1999), 11.
37. Ibid., 189.
38. Ibid., 54–56.
39. As a member of the research group, the author has observed many experimental courses of inquiry teaching in different disciplines in the experimental school, and analyzed the interaction effect of teachers and students with the experimental teachers at the seminar.
40. Zhang Xiongfei, ***Inducing Thinking and Exploring-Developing Quality Teaching*** (Liaoning People's Publishing House, 1999), 103.

## CHAPTER THREE HOT ISSUES IN CONTEMPORARY INTERNATIONAL TEACHING THEORIES

1. C. T. Fosnot, ***Theory, Perspectives, and Practice*** (New York and London: Teachers College Press, 1996).
2. Ibid.
3. Ibid., 21.
4. Ibid., 35–44.
5. Ibid., 101–118.
6. R. I. Arends et al., *Exploring Teaching: An Introduction to Education*, 2nd ed. (Boston: McGraw-Hill Higher Education, 2001).
7. Harvey F. Silver et al., *So Each May Learn: Integrating Learning Styles and Multiple Intelligence* (ASCD products, 2000), 5, 7, 8–9, 16–17, 109.
8. Ibid.
9. David G. Armstrong et al., *Teaching Today* (Prentice-Hall, Inc., 2001), 23.
10. Ibid., 26.
11. Harvey F. Silver et al., *So Each May Learn: Integrating Learning Styles and Multiple Intelligence* (ASCD products, 2000), 5, 7, 8–9, 16–17, 109.
12. Ibid.

13. Ibid.
14. Allan C. Ornstein and Francis Hunkinsp, ***Curriculum: Foundations, Principles, and Theory*** (Allny and Bacon, 1997), 120.
15. "Multiple Intelligence," https:// www.Thomas Armstrong.com.
16. Ibid.
17. Harvey F. Silver et al., *So Each May learn: Integrating Learning Styles and Multiple Intelligence* (ASCD products, 2000), 5, 7, 8–9, 16–17, 109.
˙8. "Multiple Intelligence," https:// www.Thomas Armstrong.com.
19. Harvey F. Silver et al., *So Each May Learn: Integrating Learning Styles and Multiple Intelligence* (ASCD products, 2000), 5, 7, 8–9, 16–17, 109.
20. Rosie Turner-Bisset, *Expert Teaching: Knowledge and Pedagogy to Lead the Profession* (London: David Fulton Publishers, 2001), 1, 6, 7, 126.
21. A. J. Koppi et al., "Effective Teaching and Learning in a High-tech Environment," *Innovations in Education and Training International* 34, no. 4 (1997): 245.
22. C. Kyriacou, ***Effective Teaching in Schools: Theory and Practice*** (Starley Thornes Publishers, 1997), 5, 5–7, 16–17.
23. B. Geogra and M. Atkins, ***Effective Teaching in Higher Education*** (London: Routledge, 1998), 1.
24. V. Koshy, ***Effective Teaching of Numeracy for The National Mathematics Framework*** (London: Hodder and Stoughton, 1999), 4.
25. A. Harris, ***Teaching and Learning in the Effective School*** (Aldershot: Ashgate, 1999), 31, 33–34.
26. L. A. Braskamp, ***Evaluating Teaching Effectiveness: A Practical Guide*** (Beverly Hills: Sage Publications, 1984), 29.
27. C. Kyriacou, ***Effective Teaching in Schools: Theory and Practice*** (Starley Thornes Publishers, 1997), 5, 5–7, 16–17.
28. Ibid.
29. E. Perrott, ***Effective Teaching: A Practical Guide to Improving Your Teaching*** (New York: Longman, 1986), 1–4.
30. J. R. Moyles, *Self-Evaluation: A Primary Teacher's Guide* (The NFEN-NELSON Publishing Company, 1988), 7.
31. E. Perrott, ***Effective Teaching: A Practical Guide to Improving Your Teaching*** (New York: Longman, 1986), 1–4.
32. Ibid.
33. Ibid.
34. A. Harris, ***Teaching and Learning in the Effective School*** (Aldershot: Ashgate, 1999), 31, 33–34.
35. Rosie Turner-Bisset, *Expert Teaching: Knowledge and Pedagogy to Lead the Profession* (London: David Fulton Publishers, 2001), 1, 6, 7, 126.
36. Ibid.
37. C. M. Clark, ***Thoughtful Teaching*** (Cassell Wellington House, 1995), 13.
38. C. Kyriacou, ***Effective Teaching in Schools: Theory and Practice*** (Starley Thornes Publishers, 1997), 5, 5–7, 16–17.
39. Ibid.
40. Ibid.
41. C. M. Clark, ***Thoughtful Teaching*** (Cassell Wellington House, 1995), 13.
42. Rosie Turner-Bisset, *Expert Teaching: Knowledge and Pedagogy to Lead the Profession* (London: David Fulton Publishers, 2001), 1, 6, 7, 126.

43. Zhong Qiquan, *Interpretation of the Outline of Basic Education Reform* (East China Normal University Press, 2001), 23.
44. Ibid.
45. Xiong Chuanwu, ***Reflective Teaching*** (East China Normal University Press, 1999), 5.
46. A. Pollard, ***Reflective Teaching in the Primary School: A handbook for the Classroom***, 3rd ed. (London: Cassell, 1997), 11, 14.
47. J. Soler et al., *Teacher Development: Exploring Our Own Practice* (Buckingham: The Open University Press, 2001), 74–80.
48. L. S. Shulman, ***Knowledge and Teaching: The Foundations of Neo-Reform*** (Harvard Educational Review 1987), 57.
49. Rosie Turner-Bisset, *Expert Teaching: Knowledge and Pedagogy to Lead the Profession* (London: David Fulton Publishers, 2001).
50. D. D. Ross et al., ***Reflective Teaching for Student Empowerment: Elementary Curriculum and*** *Methods* (New York: Macmillan Publishing Company, 1993), 5–15.
51. G. J. Posner, ***Field Experience: A Guide to Reflective Teaching***, 5th ed. (New York: Longman, 2000), 21.
52. A. Pollard, ***Reflective Teaching in the Primary School: A Handbook for the Classroom***, 3rd ed. (London: Cassell, 1997), 11, 14.

## CHAPTER FOUR BASIC STRATEGIES OF CONTEMPORARY TEACHING

1. Xiao Wen'e, ***Teaching Theory of Primary School*** (Beijing: Higher Education Press, 1997), 170–171.
2. Guan Suxia, *Principles of Pedagogy* (Xi'an: Shaanxi People's Education Press, 1992), 196–197.
3. D. Bligh, ***Teach Thinking by Discussion*** (NFER Publishing Company Ltd., 1986).
4. B. Cockburn and A. Ross, *Patterns and Procedures* (Lancaster: University of Lancaster, 1980).
5. P. A. Daniel, "Assessing Student-Led Seminar through a Process of Negotiation," *Journal of Geography in Higher Education*, no. 1 (1991): 15.
6. C. Evans, "Teaching the Humanities: Seminar as Metalogues," *Studies in Higher Education* 15, no. 3 (1990).
7. G. Gibbs and T. Habeshaw, *253 Ideas for Your Teaching* (Technical and Educational Services Ltd., 1988).
8. A. Heim, *Teaching and Learning in Higher Education* (London: NFER Publishing Company Ltd., 1976).
9. N. K. Henderson, *University Teaching* (Hong Kong: Hong Kong University Press, 1969).
10. H. E. Howard and W. P. Jones, "Effectiveness of a Freshman Seminar in an Urban University: Measurement of Selected Indicators," *College Student Journal* 34, no. 4 (2000).
11. Yuan Huaiyuan, "Using Seminar Techniques to Improve Oral English: Chinese Experience," *System* 16, no. 2 (1988).
12. C. Lamb et al., "Developing a Freshman Seminar: Challenges and Opportunities," *Journal of Management Education* 21, no. 1 (1997).
13. D. Layton, *University Teaching in Transition* (Edinburgh: Oliver and Boyd, 1968).
14. G. Petty, *Teaching Today: A Practical Guide* (Stanley Thornes Publishers Limited, 1993).
15. D. Russell, "More Effective Seminar," *New Academic* 3, no. 2 (1994).
16. I. Watt, "The Seminar," *University Quarterly* (1964): 18.
17. B. Weissberg, "The Graduate Seminar: Anthoer Research-Process Genre," *English For Specific Purposes* 12, no. 1 (1993).

## CHAPTER SIX CONTEMPORARY INTERNATIONAL BASIC EDUCATION CURRICULUM AND TEACHING REFORM

1. J. Sweetman, ***Curriculum Confidential 14: The Complement Guide to the National Curriculum*** (Courseware Publications, 1993), 19.
2. R. Griffith, *National Curriculum: National Disaster?* (London: Routledge Falmer, 2000), 199.
3. C. Noble, J. Brown, and J. Murphy, *How to Raise Boy's Achievement* (London: David Falton Publishers, 2001), 5.
4. R. C. White, *Curriculum Innovation: A Celebration of Classroom Practice* (Open University Press, 1999), 12.
5. R. Griffith, *National Curriculum: National Disaster?* (London: Routledge Falmer, 2000), 31.
6. G. McCulloch, "Teachers and National Curriculum in England and Wales: Socio Historical Frameworks," in *Teachers and the National Curriculum* (London: Cassell, 1997), 31.
7. M. Gallon et al., ***Inside The Primary Classroom: 20 Years On*** (London: Routledge, 1999), 68.
8. S. Acker, ***The Realities of Teachers Work: Never a Dull Momen***t (London: Cassell, 1999), 51.
9. V. Koshy, ***Effective Teaching of Numeracy for the National Mathematics Framework*** (London: Hodder and Stoughton, 1999), 7.
10. DfEE, ***The National Numeracy Strategy: Framework for Teaching Mathematics from Reception to Year*** *6* (London: Department for Education and Employment, 1999), 11.
11. Ibid., 13.
12. M. Gallon et al., ***Inside The Primary Classroom: 20 Years On*** (London: Routledge, 1999), 88.
13. R. C. White, *Curriculum Innovation: A Celebration of Classroom Practice* (Open University Press, 1999), 10.
14. SCAA, *A Guide to the National Curriculum* (School Curriculum and Assessment Authority for Wales, 1996), 10.
15. A. V. Kelly, ***The Curriculum: Theory and Practice*** (London: Paul Chapman Publishing Ltd, 1999), 128.
16. D. Hayes, ***The Handbook for Newly Qualified Teachers: Meeting the Standards in Primary and*** *Middle Schools* (London: David Falton Publishers, 2000), 20.
17. Zhong Qiquan, *A Perspective on Foreign Curriculum Reform* (Xi'an: Shaanxi People's Education Press, 1993), 15.
18. Zhao Changmu and Xu Jicun, "20 Years of Research on Curriculum Reform in China: Review and Prospect," *Curriculum, Textbooks, and Teaching Methods*, no. 1 (2002).
19. Zhong Qiquan, *Interpretation of the Outline of Basic Education Curriculum Reform (Trial)* (Shanghai: East China Normal University Press, 2001), 56, 64, 189, 352.
20. Zhao Changmu and Xu Jicun, "20 Years of Research on Curriculum Reform in China: Review and Prospect," *Curriculum, Textbooks, and Teaching Methods*, no. 1 (2002).
21. Zhong Qiquan, *Interpretation of the Outline of Basic Education Curriculum Reform (Trial)* (Shanghai: East China Normal University Press, 2001), 56, 64, 189, 352.
22. Ibid.
23. Colin Brook and Witold Tulasiewicz, *Education in a Single Europe*, 2nd ed. (London and New York: Routledge, 2002), 337.
24. Zhang Huihua, "Discussion on the National Curriculum Standards of the United States," *Modern Primary and Secondary Education*, no. 2 (1996).
25. Wang Xia, *Evolution of Curriculum in Foreign Primary and Secondary Schools* (Jinan: Shandong Education Press, 1998), 103, 116, 118.

26. Ibid.
27. Ibid.
28. Ibid.
29. Ibid.
30. Li Zhongshan and Chen Xiaoduan, *Research on General Education Curriculum Reform in B.C. Province, Canada, Canadian Education Research* (Xi'an: Shaanxi Normal University Press, 1994), 172–175.
31. Ibid.
32. Wang Kai, "The Development and Implementation of the British 'Curriculum 2000,'" *Foreign Education Research* (September 2002).
33. Zhu Huifang, "2000 National Education Standards and New Curriculum Plan in the United States," *Curriculum (Textbook Teaching Law)* (November 1994).
34. Chen Xia, "Characteristics and Enlightenment of the Current National Curriculum Standards in the UK," *Curriculum (Textbook Teaching Law)* (June 2003).
35. Susan Capel et al., *Learning to Teach in the Secondary School* (London and New York: Routledge Falmer, 2001).
36. Chen Xia, "The Evolution and Enlightenment of the UK National Curriculum Evaluation Policy," *Global Education Outlook* (July 2003).
37. Chen Xiaoduan, "An Analysis of Curriculum and Teaching Reform in Contemporary British Primary and Secondary Schools," *Education Research* (April 2003).
38. Zhou Yong, "Research and Enlightenment on Science Curriculum Evaluation in Canada," *Global Education Outlook* (July 2003).
39. Feng Qinggao, "Reform and Development of Science Curriculum in Canada," *Journal of Guangdong Vocational and Technical College* (February 2002).
40. Ibid.

## CHAPTER SEVEN A COMPARATIVE STUDY ON THE TEACHING THOUGHT OF THE MAIN WESTERN PEDAGOGICAL PHILOSOPHY SCHOOLS

1. Shi Liangfang and Guo Yun, *Teaching Theory: Principles, Strategies and Research of Classroom Teaching* (Shanghai: East China Normal University Press, 1999), 43.
2. Gene D. Shepherd and William B. Ragan, *Modern Elementary Curriculum* (New York: CBS College Publishing, 1982), 434.
3. F. W. Parkary and B. H. Stanford, *Becoming a Teacher* (New York: Simon & Schuster, 1995), 235.
4. George S. Morrison, *Teaching in America* (New York: Viacom Company, 1997), 99–400.
5. Ibid., 398–399.
6. Ibid., 400.
7. Ibid., 400.
8. Ibid., 390.
9. Huang Ji, *Education of Philosophy* (Beijing: Beijing Normal University Press, 1985), 275.
10. Ibid., 274.
11. George S. Morrison, *Teaching in America* (New York: Viacom Company, 1997), 391.
12. Tian Benna, *History of Foreign Teaching Thoughts* (Beijing: People's Education Press, 1994), 351.
13. George S. Morrison, *Teaching in America* (New York: Viacom Company, 1997), 392–393.
14. Ji Peng, *Historical Analysis on Schools of Modern Educational Thoughts of West Countries* (Beijing: Beijing Normal University Press, 1995), 175.

15. A. C. Ornstein, *The Foundation of Educational Pedagogy* (Beijing: People's Education Press, 1984), 102.
16. Yang Qiliang, *Confusion and Choice—New Pedagogy Theory in the Twentieth Century* (Jinan: Shandong Education Press, 1995), 11.
17. Tian Benna, *History of Foreign Teaching Thoughts* (Beijing: People's Education Press, 1994), 352.
18. F. W. Parkary and B. H. Stanford, *Becoming a Teacher* (New York: Simon & Schuster, 1995), 237.
19. Ibid., 238
20. George S. Morrison, *Teaching in America* (New York: Viacom Company, 1997), 238.
21. Ibid.
22. Tian Benna, *History of Foreign Teaching Thoughts* (Beijing: People's Education Press, 1994), 353.
23. Ibid., 354.
24. Ibid., 353–354.
25. Bruner, *Education Process* (Beijing: Culture Education Press, 1982), 2.
26. Tian Benna, *History of Foreign Teaching Thoughts* (Beijing: People's Education Press, 1994), 362.
27. Ibid., 467.
28. Ibid., 467.
29. Ibid., 469.
30. Bruner, "Re-research on Education Process," *Education Research*, no. 1 (1979): 62.
31. Zhong Qiquan, *Modern Curriculum Theory* (Shanghai: Shanghai Education Press, 1989), 110.
32. Bruner, *Education Process* (Beijing: Culture Education Press, 1982), 30.
33. Zhong Qiquan and Huang Zhicheng, *The American Schools of Pedagogy* (Xi'an: Shaanxi People's Education Press, 1998), 3–4.
34. Bruner, *Education Process* (Beijing: Culture Education Press, 1982), 30–31.
35. Ibid., 49.
36. Zhong Qiquan and Huang Zhicheng, *The American Schools of Pedagogy* (Xi'an: Shaanxi People's Education Press, 1998), 32.
37. Ibid., 30–32.
38. Wu Wenkan, *Contemporary Foreign Pedagogy Theory* (Fuzhou: Fujian Education Press, 1990), 37.
39. Ibid., 196.
40. Fang Zhanhua, "The Commentary on Modern Western Humanism Education Theory," *Pedagogy (The Photocopying Material by Renmin University of China)*, no. 5 (1999): 145.
41. Zhong Qiquan, *The Development of Modern Pedagogy* (Beijing: Education & Science Press, 1988), 202–203.
42. Tian Benna, *History of Foreign Teaching Thoughts* (Beijing: People's Education Press, 1994), 361.
43. Ibid.
44. George S. Morrison, *Teaching in America* (New York: Viacom Company, 1997), 400–401.
45. F. W. Parkary and B. H. Stanford, *Becoming a Teacher* (New York: Simon & Schuster, 1995), 244.
46. A. C. Ornstein, *The Foundation of Educational Pedagogy* (Beijing: People's Education Press, 1984), 112.
47. Huang Ji, *Philosophy of Education* (Beijing: Beijing Normal University Press, 1985), 283–284.
48. George S. Morrison, *Teaching in America* (New York: Viacom Company, 1997), 401.
49. Ibid.
50. A. C. Ornstein, *The Foundation of Educational Pedagogy* (Beijing: People's Education Press, 1984), 111–112.
51. F. W. Parkary and B. H. Stanford, *Becoming a Teacher* (New York: Simon & Schuster, 1995), 245.
52. Yang Qiliang, *Confusion and Choice—New Pedagogy Theory in the Twentieth Century* (Jinan: Shandong Education Press, 1995), 130–131.

53. F. W. Parkary and B. H. Stanford, *Becoming a Teacher* (New York: Simon & Schuster, 1995), 246–247.
54. Zhang Hua, Shi Weiping, and Ma Qingfa, ***Researches on the Schools of Curriculum Theories*** (Jinan: Shandong Education Press, 2001), 155.
55. Zhang Hua, ***Curriculum and Instruction Theory*** (Shanghai: Shanghai Education Press, 2000), 201.

## APPENDIX A RESEARCH ON EFFECTIVE TEACHING: WHAT METHODS HAVE BEEN USED?

1. F. K. Oser, Andreas Dick, and Jean-Luc Party, ***Effective and Responsible Teaching: The New Synthesis*** (San Fransisco: Jossey-Bass Publishers, 1992).
2. C. M. Clark, ***Thought of Teaching*** (London: Cassell, 1995).
3. A. Harris, ***Teaching and Learning in the Effective School*** (Ashgate Publisher Company, 1999).
4. D. Ryan, *Characteristics of Teachers* (Washington DC: American Council on Education, 1960).
5. J. R. Moyles, *Self-Evaluation: A Primary Teacher's Guide* (The NFER-NELSON Publishing, 1988).
6. C. Kyriacou, ***Effective Teaching in Schools: Theory and Practice*** (Stanley Thornes, 1997).
7. Ibid.
8. J. W. Garrison and C. J. B. Macmillan, "Process-Product Research on Teaching: Ten Years Later," ***Educational Theory***, no. 4 (Fall, 1994): 44.
9. Perrott and Elizabeth, ***Effective Teaching: A Practical Guide to Improving Your Teaching*** (London and New York: Longman).
10. OECD, *Quality in Teaching* (Paris: OECD, 1994).
11. Rosie Turner-Bisset, *Expert Teaching: Knowledge and Pedagogy to Lead the Profession* (London: David Fulton Publishers, 2001).
12. R. B. Burns, *Introduction to Research Methods* (London: Sage Publications, 2000).
13. L. Cohen et al., *Research Methods in Education*, 5th ed. (London and New York: Routledge Falmer, 2000).

## APPENDIX B CHANGES IN RESEARCH APPROACHES AND RESEARCH METHODS IN EDUCATION FROM 1960 TO NOW: A LITERATURE SURVEY

1. G. Anderson and Nancy Arsenault, *Fundamentals of Educational Research* (London: Falmer Press, 1998).
2. M. C. Wittrock, *Handbook of Research on Teaching* (New York: Mecmillan Publishing, 1986).
3. J. L. Kingheloe, *Teachers as Researchers: Qualitative Inquiry as a Path to Empowerment* (London: The Falmer Press, 1991).
4. J. P. Keeves and G. Lakomski, *Issues in Educational Research* (Oxford: Elsevier Science, Pergamon, 1999).
5. R. B. Burns, *Introduction to Research Methods* (London: Sage, 2000).
6. L. Cohen et al., *Research Methods in Education* (London: Routledge Falmer, 2000).
7. J. L. Kingheloe, *Teachers as Researchers: Qualitative Inquiry as a Path to Empowerment* (London: The Falmer Press, 1991).
8. L. Blaxter, C. Hughes, and M. Tight, *How to Research* (Open University Press, 2001).
9. M. Punch, *Introduction to Social Research: Quantitative and Qualitative Approaches* (London: Sage, 1998).

## APPENDIX C UNDERSTANDING CLASSROOM OBSERVATION: THEORY AND APPLICATION

1. P. Jarvis, *The Theory and Practice of Teaching* (London: Hogan Page, 2002).
2. B. J. Fraser, *Classroom Environment* (London: Croon Helm, 1986).
3. E. C. Wragg, *An Introduction to Classroom Observation* (London: Routledge, 1994).
4. D. Hopkins, *A Teacher's Guide to Classroom Research* (Open University Press, 2002).
5. L. Cohen et al., *Research Methods in Education* (London: Routledge, 2000).
6. Ibid.
7. N. West, *Classroom Observation in the Context of Appraisal* (London: Longman, 1992).
8. G. Marriott, *Observation Teachers at Work* (Oxford: Heinemann Educational Publishers, 2001).
9. M. Galton et al, *Inside the Primary Classroom: 20 Years On* (London: Routledge, 1997).
10. K. D. Moore, *Classroom Teaching Skills* (McGraw-Hill, Inc, 1995).
11. M. Simpson and J. Tuson, "Using Observation in Small-Scale Research: A Beginner's Guide," *The Scottish Council for Research in Education* (1995).

# Index

## R



## S



## T

## ABOUT THE AUTHOR

CHEN XIAODUAN is a professor of education at the School of Education, Shaanxi Normal University (SNNU), Xi'an, China. He graduated with a bachelor's degree in education from the Xi'an Physical Education Institute in 1982. He studied master's course in the Department of Education at the Shaanxi Normal University, and obtained his master's degree in Education from Northwest Normal University in 1989. He spent two semesters (2001–2002) to study doctoral course at the School of Education in the University of Leicester, UK. So far, he has written over 90 journal articles, published more than 30 books, also undertaken more than 15 research projects. His research interests are in three main areas: basic theories of curriculum and teaching, teacher education, and teacher professional development.

## ABOUT THE TRANSLATOR

DAI KUN is an associate professor at the School of International Studies, Shaanxi Normal University. She obtained her Bachelor's degree in English Education from Shaanxi Normal University and her Master's degree in Educational Studies from the University of Warwick. She received her PhD in Psychology from Shaanxi Normal University. She has published twelve papers and is the project leader of one national and four provincial and ministerial projects. Dai Kun's research interests include English education, educational psychology, and intercultural communication.